The UN Security Council and Domestic Actors

This book analyses the exercise of authority by the UN Security Council and its subsidiary organs over individuals. The UN Security Council was created in 1945 as an outcome of World War II under the predominant assumption that it exercises its authority against states. Under this assumption, the UN Security Council and those individuals were 'distanced' by the presence of member states that intermediate between the Security Council's international commands and those individuals that are subject to member states' domestic law. However, in practice, the UN Security Council's exercise of authority has incrementally removed the presence of state intermediaries and reduced the Security Council's distance from individuals.

This book demonstrates that this phenomenon has increased the relevance of domestic law in developing the international normative frameworks governing the UN Security Council and its subsidiary organs in safeguarding the rights, obligations, and interests of those affected individuals. This book presents how the UN Security Council's exercise of authority has been received at the domestic level, and what would be the international implications of the Security Council's extensive encounter with the actors who primarily reside in a domestic legal order.

Machiko Kanetake is Assistant Professor of Public International Law at Utrecht University.

Routledge Research in International Law

For a full list of titles in this series, visit www.routledge.com/Routledge-Research-in-International-Law/book-series/INTNLLAW

Available:

Peacemaking, Religious Belief and the Rule of Law
The Struggle between Dictatorship and Democracy in Syria and Beyond
Paul Zwier

China, Cultural Heritage, and International Law
Hui Zhong

The UN Security Council and Domestic Actors
Distance in International Law
Machiko Kanetake

Human Security Discourse and International Law
A Principled Approach
Shireen Daft

Fighting and Victimhood in International Criminal Law
Joanna Nicholson

Prosecuting Juvenile Piracy Suspects
The International Legal Framework
Milena Sterio

Nationalization, Natural Resources and International Investment Law
Contractual Relationship as a Dynamic Bargaining Process
Junji Nakagawa

Queering International Law
Possibilities, Alliances, Complicities, Risks
Edited by Dianne Otto

The UN Security Council and Domestic Actors

Distance in International Law

Machiko Kanetake

Routledge
Taylor & Francis Group
LONDON AND NEW YORK

First published 2018 by Routledge

2 Park Square, Milton Park, Abingdon, Oxfordshire OX14 4RN
52 Vanderbilt Avenue, New York, NY 10017

Routledge is an imprint of the Taylor & Francis Group, an informa business

First issued in paperback 2019

British Library Cataloguing in Publication Data
A catalogue record for this book is available from the British Library

Library of Congress Cataloging in Publication Data
Names: Kanetake, Machiko, author.
Title: The UN security council and domestic actors : distance in international law / Machiko Kanetake.
Description: New York, NY : Routledge, 2017. | Series: Routledge research in international law | Includes bibliographical references and index.
Identifiers: LCCN 2017030196 | ISBN 9781138858589 (hardback)
Subjects: LCSH: United Nations. Security Council--Powers and duties.
Classification: LCC KZ5038 .K36 2017 | DDC 341.23/23--dc23
LC record available at https://lccn.loc.gov/2017030196

ISBN: 978-1-138-85858-9 (hbk)
ISBN: 978-0-367-87246-5 (pbk)

Typeset in Galliard
by Taylor & Francis Books

Contents

List of cases

International and regional

International Court of Justice

Permanent Court of International Justice

EU courts

European Court of Human Rights (and European Commission of Human Rights)

International criminal tribunals

UN Human Rights Committee

UNMIK Human Rights Advisory Panel

National

Argentina

Austria

Belgium

Canada

Croatia

Israel

Netherlands

Switzerland

United Kingdom

United States

Security Council Resolutions

List of abbreviations

ANF	Al Nusrah Front (or Al-Nusra Front)
CFI	Court of First Instance
CJEU	Court of Justice of the European Union
DFS	United Nations Department of Field Support
DPKO	United Nations Department of Peacekeeping Operations
DRC	Democratic Republic of the Congo
EC	European Community
ECHR	European Convention on Human Rights
ECJ	European Court of Justice (Court of Justice of the European Communities)
ECOSOC	Economic and Social Council
ECtHR	European Court of Human Rights
EU	European Union
EULEX	European Union Rule of Law Mission in Kosovo
FATF	Financial Action Task Force
GATT	General Agreement on Tariffs and Trade
GCEU	General Court of the European Union
ICCPR	International Covenant on Civil and Political Rights
ICISS	International Commission on Intervention and State Sovereignty
ICJ	International Court of Justice
ICRC	International Committee of the Red Cross
ICTR	International Criminal Tribunal for Rwanda
ICTY	International Criminal Tribunal for the former Yugoslavia
ILO	International Labour Organization
INTERFET	International Force for East Timor
IS	Islamic State
ISIL	Islamic State in Iraq and the Levant
ISIS	Islamic State of Iraq and Syria
KFOR	Kosovo Force
NAM	Non-Aligned Movement
NATO	North Atlantic Treaty Organization
OAS	Organization of American States
OFAC	Office of Foreign Assets Control

ONUC	United Nations Operation in the Congo/Opération des Nations Unies au Congo
OSCE	Organization for Security and Co-operation in Europe
PCIJ	Permanent Court of International Justice
RUF	Revolutionary United Front of Sierra Leone
SRSG	Special Representative of the Secretary-General
UN	United Nations
UNDP	United Nations Development Programme
UNITA	National Union for the Total Independence of Angola
UNMIK	United Nations Interim Administration in Kosovo
UNOSOM II	United Nations Operation in Somalia II
UNPROFOR	United Nations Protection Force
UNTAES	United Nations Transitional Authority in Eastern Slavonia, Baranja and Western Sirmium
UNTAET	United Nations Transitional Administration in East Timor
UNTEA	United Nations Temporary Executive Authority

Preface

This book is the result of academic opportunities I have been fortunate to have during my studies, research, and teaching in Japan, the UK, the US, and the Netherlands. One of the initial encounters that encouraged me to work on the topic of this book was the 'United Nations Law' course I took in 2006–2007 during my LLM program at LSE. The course taught by Nico Krisch inspired me in many respects. After completing my LLM, I conducted my doctoral research at Kyoto University with the financial support of the Japan Society for the Promotion of Science, which also allowed me to spend a year at NYU's School of Law as the Global Fellows Program's Hauser Visiting Doctoral Researcher. Many parts of this book are based on my doctoral thesis submitted to Kyoto University in 2011. Others are built on my postdoctoral research conducted in 2011–2014 at the Amsterdam Center for International Law (ACIL). The 'International Security Law' module I taught at Utrecht University in 2016 also helped me put my thoughts into perspective.

A number of people have helped me in the process of drafting various parts of this book. First and foremost, my appreciation goes to Ryuichi Ida, my doctoral thesis supervisor at Kyoto University, who spent so many hours with me discussing the topic of this book and various theories and practices of international law. Without his foresight, encouragement, and patience, I could not have completed my doctoral research, let alone any subsequent professional steps. I also owe much gratitude to André Nollkaemper, my mentor and colleague for my postdoctoral research at the ACIL. I benefited enormously from Shotaro Hamamomto and his Kyoto University graduate seminars. I also thank Masahiko Asada and Hironobu Sakai for their succinct advice. I appreciate José Alvarez for supporting my visit at NYU, and I am grateful to Armin von Bogdandy for his valuable comments on parts of my doctoral thesis at JSD Forum. I wish to thank Ingo Venzke for his encouragement and insight during my postdoctoral project on the interfaces between national and international law at the ACIL. I also owe thanks to Bas Schotel for inspiring me to get this book published in the first place. I would further like to thank participants at seminars and workshops in which I presented the topic of the book, including those at Kyoto University, NYU Law School, the University of Amsterdam, Australian National University, the Australian and New Zealand Society of International Law, the National University of Singapore, and the Hertie School of Governance.

Some parts of the book are based on my previous publications. Insofar as targeted sanctions are concerned, some parts of chapters 3–6 and the annex appeared as: 'Enhancing Community Accountability of the Security Council through Pluralistic Structure: The Case of the 1267 Committee', *Max Planck Yearbook of United Nations Law*, vol. 12 (2008), pp. 113–75; 'The Interfaces between the National and International Rule of Law: The Case of UN Targeted Sanctions', *International Organizations Law Review*, vol. 9, no. 2 (2012), pp. 267–338; and 'Catching up with Society – How, What, and Why: The Case of the Regulatory Development for the UN Security Council's Targeted Sanctions', in Shotaro Hamamoto et al. (eds), *"L'être situé", Effectiveness and Purposes of International Law: Essays in Honour of Professor Ryuichi Ida* (Leiden: Brill 2015), pp. 255–83. Parts of chapter 6 appeared as 'Subsidiarity in the Maintenance of International Peace and Security', *Law and Contemporary Problems*, vol. 79 (2016), pp. 165–87. Parts of chapter 7 appeared as 'The Interfaces between the National and International Rule of Law: A Framework Paper', in Machiko Kanetake and André Nollkaemper (eds), *The Rule of Law at the National and International Levels: Contestations and Deference* (Oxford: Hart Publishing, 2016), pp. 11–41.

Machiko Kanetake
January 2017

1 Introduction

The UN Security Council and individuals are primarily 'distanced' by the presence of member states that intermediate between the international commands and those individuals subject to member states' domestic law. Nevertheless, this 'distance' has been modified from the early stage of the UN and especially since the 1990s. This book analyses how the change in distance over time alters the role of domestic law and ultimately modifies international normative standards regulating the UN Security Council's exercise of authority. This introductory chapter aims at visually presenting three groups of the practices which guide the reminder of the book.

At every moment of its life, law may be placed in non-identical social settings in which facts and values undergo constant alterations in one way or another. Many of those daily vicissitudes do not seriously disturb law or institutions that apply it, as both the legal terms and the discretion accorded to those institutions are often broad enough to allow the law to be adapted to the altered settings. As a result of incremental accommodation of new settings into their own sphere of application, however, law and institutions may be situated in a context in which they claim authority against not only those who were originally envisaged by the drafters, but a variety of new categories of actors which would likely invoke new agendas about how the law ought to be designed and applied against them. Law's encounter with the demands of new constituencies often necessitates legal reforms in order not to lose the law's regulatory relevance within the context in which it resides.[1]

Constituent instruments of international organisations[2] are agreements between states concluded with a view to achieving the purposes with which the states are commonly concerned but for which they themselves are not best qualified to serve. The maintenance of international peace and security is one of such purposes, for the achievement of which states concluded the Charter of the United Nations (UN) and constituted the organisation with its peace and security arm which was expected to exert unique political weight and legal authority. Just as

1 In this book, a 'constituency' is understood as a group of individuals and entities over which law or an institution claims authority.

2 In this book, an 'international organisation' means an intergovernmental organisation established by a treaty concluded between states.

with any other laws and institutions, the facts and values which constitute international peace and security undergo constant alterations. Studying how the UN's peace and security organ has applied the UN Charter and absorbed new settings into its own sphere of work highlights how the laws and institutions which maintain international peace and security sustain themselves in a constantly evolving international society.

With the utmost concern 'to save succeeding generations from the scourge of war',[3] the UN Security Council was created in 1945 by the inter-state treaty of the UN Charter which was drafted and signed by some 50 states called upon to gather in San Francisco from April to June of that year with the predominant assumption that they would this time create a robust international peace and security organ against aggressor governments. The drafters' assumption was shaped by the historical genesis of the UN as an outcome of World War II, which epitomises the bitter past of the first collective security institution established under the Covenant of the League of Nations. The original drafters' historically embedded preoccupation is best captured by the above-quoted first paragraph of the preamble to the Charter, namely, 'to save succeeding generations from the scourge of war'.[4] After many decades since the Charter was created, and in a world in which non-inter-state armed conflicts are commonplace, it is not an easy task for us to imagine the state-centric assumption that shaped the wording of the UN Charter. Yet it is still important to remember that the term 'war' here was predominantly understood to refer to 'inter-state' war (as opposed to intra-state war), which was then considered serious enough to threaten 'international' peace and security and to bestow upon the UN Security Council the unprecedented authority to take measures which collectively coerce aggressor governments with the powers accorded under Chapter VII of the UN Charter.

Under the UN Charter, the UN Security Council's authority is constituted by the organ's 'functions and powers' as laid down in Articles 24–26 of the UN Charter. The Council's 'function' is the maintenance of international peace and security, and its specific 'powers' are provided in Chapters VI, VII, VIII, and XII of the UN Charter. Due to the historical preoccupation of the drafters, it is not surprising that the UN Security Council's functions and powers were designed in relation to the rights and interests of states – and not those of individuals. Nevertheless, from the early stage of its life, the Security Council's exercise of authority for the purpose of maintaining international peace and security has impacted on the rights of individuals not only in an indirect and consequential manner but also in a way that allows member states to have little discretion over individuals under their jurisdiction. Especially since the 1990s, the UN Security Council's exercise of authority has had significant impact on the rights of individuals; illustrative are the practices of targeted sanctions, territorial administrations, and ad hoc international criminal tribunals.

3 Charter of the United Nations, 26 June 1945, 1 UNTS XVI (entered into force 24 October 1945) (the first paragraph of the preamble).

4 Ibid.

This book is guided by these intriguing phenomena – that the UN Security Council and its subsidiary organs have been exercising their authority over individuals by restricting, or effectively removing, the discretion of member states over such individuals. This is intriguing, precisely because, on the one hand, the rights, obligations, and interests of those individuals are primarily safeguarded by *domestic* law, while, on the other hand, the Security Council's exercise of authority is governed by *international* law. This has led me to examine how the UN Security Council's exercise of authority has been received at the *domestic* level, and what would be the *international* implications of the Security Council's extensive encounter for the actors which primarily reside in a *domestic* legal order.

In analysing both domestic and international implications of the Security Council's exercise of authority, this book employs the concept of 'distance' in order to capture the changes in the Security Council's exercise of authority and in the normative frameworks governing it. The distance analysed in this book concerns the one between the UN Security Council's exercise of authority to maintain 'international' peace and security on the one hand, and affected individuals which are primarily governed by domestic law on the other hand.

Traditionally, the UN Security Council and those individuals had been 'distanced' by the presence of member states that 'intermediate' between the Security Council's international commands and those individuals that are subject to their domestic law. If the decisions of the Security Council have implications over domestic actors, the Council's authority and domestic actors were 'intermediated' by member states, which would translate the organ's international commands into their domestic law that should determine the rights and obligations of their subjects. In other words, the presence of member states was to connect the international and domestic legal orders, and thereby the residents in these two different legal orders. (I indicated this traditional model as [1] in Figure 1 regarding the distance between the Council and domestic actors.)

The 'intermediary' presence of member states (as illustrated in [1] in Figure 1) is of crucial importance for member states, affected individuals, and the UN Security Council itself. Member states can implement international institutional decisions in such a way that they fit in with their own domestic law and politics. The affected individuals can contest the decisions of the national government which retains discretion. The intermediary presence of member states also protects the UN Security Council from being challenged by states and affected individuals. In other words, the fact that the UN Security Council and individuals are distanced by member states' intermediary presence provided governments, individuals, and the UN Security Council with a legal and political safeguard or shield.

Nevertheless, the UN Security Council's exercise of authority has incrementally removed the presence of state intermediaries and reduced the Council's 'distance' from individuals. The Security Council has been directly addressing individuals under its resolutions, including those adopted under Chapter VII. (I indicated this scenario as [2] in Figure 1.) The Security Council has also instigated a number of economic sanctions under Article 41 of the UN Charter against specific individuals and entities, either as the overall strategic target of sanctions regimes, or more

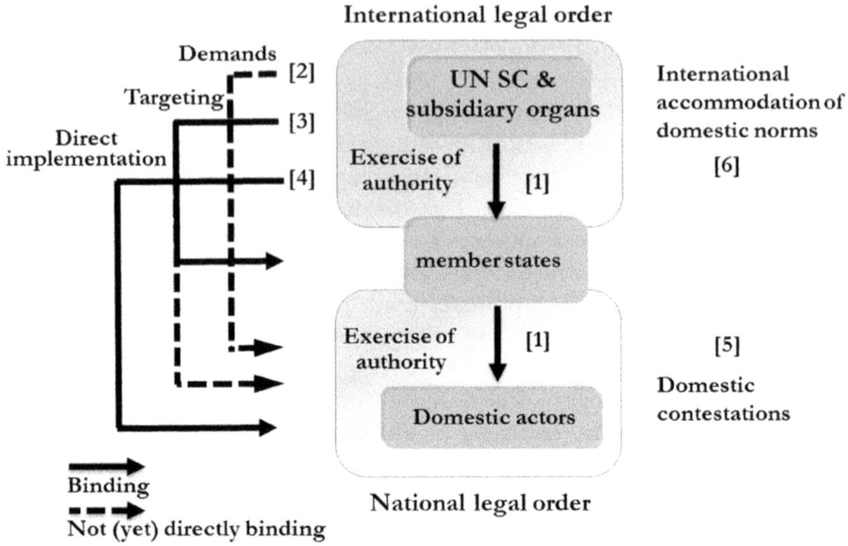

Figure 1 Distance between the UN Security Council and domestic actors

often as the specific targets of restrictive measures. (This scenario is indicated as [3] in Figure 1.) Finally, the Security Council, through its subsidiary organs, has directly executed its decisions vis-à-vis individuals and entities. UN transitional territorial administrations and ad hoc international criminal tribunals are cases in point. (This scenario is shown as [4] in Figure 1.)

The central argument of the book is that the Security Council's exercise of authority against individuals, who are primarily the subjects of domestic law, has situated the Security Council's decision making in a new normative context, in which its exercise of authority would have to be justified according to new normative standards. The exercise of authority against individuals has not only tested the Council's exercise of authority against legality yardsticks, but also exposed it to wider normative standards developed through interactions with domestic law. Traditionally, the presence of such 'state intermediaries' served the legitimacy of the UN Security Council's exercise of authority. Yet the incremental removal of state intermediaries situated the Security Council's exercise of authority in the context in which *individuals* and *domestic law* concerning them play a greater role in developing normative standards for the UN Security Council's exercise of authority.

The Security Council's exercise of authority over individuals has encouraged the affected individuals and entities to contest, directly or indirectly, the UN's international institutional decisions in the domestic legal order. (This scenario is indicated as [5] in Figure 1.) Domestic contestations, accompanied by other contestations raised by member states and the wider international community, incrementally urged the Security Council and its subsidiary organs to accommodate some of the norms accepted at the national level which have been developed for the regulation of *governmental* authority. The Security Council and its subsidiary organs increasingly justify their exercise of authority not only in terms of state consent and member states' interests but also in terms of the interests and rights of domestic actors affected by international institutional decisions. (This aspect is indicated as [6] in Figure 1.)

While there are a number of actors subject to domestic law, this book's main focus is on *individuals*. To focus on individuals as the primary subjects of domestic law allows us to identify the tension between the national and international legal orders with respect to the Security Council's exercise of authority. While individuals still enjoy various international rights, especially those under human rights treaties, this does not alter the fact that the legal order which regulates the individuals' acts in an immediate sense is domestic law, and not international law.

It is not within the primary focus of this book to analyse, for instance, the UN Security Council's exercise of authority against terrorist groups and other non-state armed groups which, almost by definition, refuse to subject themselves to their state's domestic law.[5] The acts of these groups often justify the Security Council's exercise of authority against specific individuals, but separate analysis is required in order to analyse the relationships between the UN's collective security and non-state armed groups.[6] Nor does the book analyse the impact of the UN Security Council's decision making on other UN organs and other international organisations. While international organisations have domestic legal personality and are subject to certain domestic laws of the territorial states in which they conduct their activities,[7] the legal order which generally governs their acts is international law, notably their constituent instruments, their decisions,[8] and the rules of international law commonly applicable to international organisations.[9]

5 This is one of the reasons why the development of international legal frameworks governing the conduct of non-state armed groups is important. One of the main fields of international law regulating the conduct of such groups has been international humanitarian law: see, e.g., Liesbeth Zegveld, *Accountability of Armed Opposition Groups in International Law* (Cambridge; New York, Cambridge University Press, 2002). International human rights law may also be binding upon non-state armed groups, although its basis and the scope of such obligations are by no means settled: compare, e.g., Andrew Clapham, *Human Rights Obligations of Non-State Actors* (Oxford, Oxford University Press, 2006) 279–85; Zegveld, *Accountability of Armed Opposition Groups in International Law* 51–5; Katharine Fortin, *The Accountability of Armed Groups under Human Rights Law* (Oxford, Oxford University Press, 2017).

6 Machiko Kanetake, 'The UN Security Council's Encounter with Non-State Armed Groups: Testing the Soft Inclusiveness' *Young Scholars Workshop 2010, AsianSIL Working Paper 2010/11, Asian Society of International Law (2010)*.

7 Niels M. Blokker and Henry G. Schermers, *International Institutional Law: Unity within Diversity* (5th revised edn, Boston, Martinus Nijhoff Publishers, 2011) 1021–40.

8 The term 'decision' in this book does not automatically signify 'binding' decisions in accordance with Article 25 of the UN Charter. For the purpose of this book, the 'decisions' can include recommendations, and they take a number of different forms (e.g., resolution, regulations, orders, bulletins).

9 For the legal order pertaining to international organisations, see generally Blokker and Schermers, *International Institutional Law: Unity within Diversity* (n 7) 723–839.

Extensive studies have already been conducted on *Kadi* and other judicial contestations at the national and EU levels against the UN's targeted sanctions.[10] This book nevertheless contextualises the case of targeted sanctions in the broader trend of the Security Council's exercise of authority over individuals. It does so by comparing the practice of targeting sanctions (illustrated as [3] in Figure 1) with two other groups of practices: namely, the Security Council's practices to issue demands to individuals (indicated as [2] in Figure 1) and the practices to directly execute institutional decisions against domestic actors (indicated as [4] in Figure 1). This book analyses how differences in distance among these three scenarios (indicated as [2]–[4] in Figure 1) affect the ways in which domestic actors contest the UN Security Council's decisions and ultimately develop international normative standards governing the Security Council's exercise of authority.

The rest of the book is structured in seven chapters. It starts by overviewing the historical path leading to the UN Security Council's practice by assessing the distance between the League of Nations' authority and domestic actors in the area of international peace and security (chapter 2). It then elaborates on the notion of 'threats to the peace' as a conceptual vehicle to connect the UN Security Council's Chapter VII authority with domestic actors (chapter 3), and analyses how such conceptual proximity has been translated into the concrete measures of the Security Council and its subsidiary organs under Chapter VII of the UN Charter (chapter 4). It moves on to examine *international* legal frameworks regulating the Security Council's exercise of authority vis-à-vis domestic actors through the interpretation of treaties and the analysis of practices relating to it (chapters 5–6). The analysis of international legal frameworks leads me to consider the *domestic* reception of the decisions of the UN Security Council and its subsidiary organs (chapter 7). The study of the domestic reception brings me to consider its *international* implications by highlighting the roles of *domestic actors* and *domestic law* in the process of developing legitimacy standards for the UN Security Council's exercise of authority (chapter 8 and conclusion).

10 See section 7.3 of this book.

2 The League of Nations and domestic actors

2.1 Introduction

In order to understand the location of the UN Security Council, it is necessary to revise its predecessor's experiences in the maintenance of international peace and security. As the first collective endeavour to establish a collective security mechanism, the League of Nations was created in 1919 by the Covenant of the League of Nations which restricted member states' entitlement to go to war and simultaneously envisaged economic sanctions against member states.[1] Given that the League of Nations is a product of World War I at the beginning of the twentieth century, it may seem, on the face of it, far-fetched to compare the practice of the League of Nations with that of the UN Security Council and to see if the League of Nations has also exercised its authority over individuals and any other actors who primarily reside in a domestic legal order.

There is no denying that the historical contexts which defined the mandate of these two bodies significantly differ. The notion of international peace and security, which guides the direction of the collective security mechanisms, was understood differently in the League of Nations' era from that of the UN Security Council. Not surprisingly, the concept of 'international peace and security' or 'international peace' was almost equated to the absence of war and comparable armed confrontations between sovereign states (as discussed in section 2.2 below). Given this conceptual background, it might appear unrealistic to envisage situations where the Council of the League of Nations exercised its authority over individuals or the 'groups' of individuals for the sake of the maintenance of peace and security. Ostensibly, individuals and their groups appear to have little relevance to the practices of the League of Nations in the spheres of peace and security.

Nevertheless, as highlighted in this chapter, there are two situations in which the Council of the League of Nations exercised its authority in the fields of peace and security in a manner which directly concerns the rights and interests of individuals or groups of individuals. The initial occasion was when the League Council

1 For the historical development of the ideas of collective security and the institutionalisation of such ideas before the League of Nations, see Elizabeth York, *Leagues of Nations: Ancient, Medieval, and Modern* (London, The Swarthmore Press, 1919).

engaged with the treatment of minorities as part of the question of peace and security (section 2.3). The League Council was reluctant to treat minorities questions as a matter of international peace, which helps us understand the meaning given to it during the era of the League of Nations. The second opportunity arrived as the administration of certain territories by the League of Nations (section 2.4). The League's involvement in territorial administration met resistance from local populations for whom the League did not provide sufficient safeguards. Some inhabitants utilised local courts as a venue for contestation. To overview these experiences of the League Council thus allows us to fully appreciate both continuation and discontinuation between the two mechanisms of collective security.

2.2 'International peace and security' under the League Covenant

Having brought the idea of collective security into reality, the League of Nations should be credited for its role in altering the decentralised approaches to international peace and security. For the first time in history, as many as 63 states agreed to restrict war and decided to regard it as a matter of concern to the whole League of Nations. Under Article 10 of the Covenant of the League of Nations, member states agreed to 'respect and preserve as against external aggression the territorial integrity and existing political independence of all Members of the League'.[2] This is followed by Article 11, which transformed 'any war or threat of war' into a common concern for the League.[3] A more specific obligation was provided in Article 12 of the Covenant, under which member states were prohibited from resorting to war for three months after a judicial decision or the League Council's report was issued.[4] Unlike its successor, the UN Security Council, whose function is restricted to the maintenance of international peace and security, the Council of the League of Nations was authorised to deal with not only matters 'affecting the peace of the world', but also 'any matter within the sphere of action of the League'.[5]

For the purpose of this book, it is important to note that the maintenance of international peace and security – which is the mandate of the UN Security Council – was also one of the general aims of the League of Nations. The fact that these two institutions pursue the same mandate is not surprising, given that both regimes were conceived 'in the midst of war and in the fear of war'.[6] According to the preamble of the Covenant of the League of Nations:[7]

2 Covenant of the League of Nations, 28 June 1919, AJIL Supp. 128 (1919) (entered into force 10 January 1920) (1919) Article 10.
3 Ibid., Article 11(1).
4 Ibid., Article 12.
5 Ibid., Article 4(4).
6 Clyde Eagleton, *International Government* (Revised, New York, Ronald Press, 1948) 302 (in relation to the description that the UN was the product of the victors of war).
7 Covenant of the League of Nations (n 2) preamble (emphasis added).

THE HIGH CONTRACTING PARTIES,

In order to promote international co-operation and *to achieve international peace and security*

by the acceptance of obligations not to resort to war,

by the prescription of open, just and honourable relations between nations,

by the firm establishment of the understandings of international law as the actual rule of conduct among Governments, and

by the maintenance of justice and a scrupulous respect for all treaty obligations in the dealings of organised peoples with one another,

Agree to this Covenant of the League of Nations.

As encapsulated at the beginning of the preamble, one of the purposes of the League of Nations was 'to achieve international peace and security'.[8] The preamble of the Covenant contains the League's objectives and several means to achieve them, and some of these promises reappear in Article 1 of the UN Charter as the overall purposes of the UN.[9] Both regimes aspire to the achievement or maintenance of 'international peace and security'. Both the preamble of the League Covenant and Article 1 of the UN Charter refer to the promotion of international co-operation, justice, and the respect for international obligations. One notable difference still is that the preamble of the League Covenant does not refer to the protection of respect for human rights and fundamental freedoms.

While the Covenant of the League of Nations and the UN Charter share the same terms, the concept of 'international peace and security' has been given different meanings depending on the political contexts in which the notion has been employed. Under the League Covenant, the achievement of 'international peace and security' has been understood as the restriction of 'war', or, more precisely, inter-state war.[10] The League of Nations' emphasis on war was understandably far more evident and stronger than that of the UN Charter. This is already suggested by the fact that 'the acceptance of obligations not to resort to war' is listed first as a means 'to achieve international peace and security' in the preamble to the Covenant of the League of Nations.[11] Many provisions of the Covenant employ

8 Ibid., preamble.

9 Charter of the United Nations, 26 June 1945, 1 UNTS XVI (entered into force 24 October 1945) Article 1. See Hans Kelsen, 'The Old and the New League: The Covenant and the Dumbarton Oaks Proposals' (1945) 39 *American Journal of International Law* 45, 45–6 (regarding the similarities and differences between the purposes of the League and those of the UN).

10 It must be noted that the legal significance of 'war' differs between the pre-1945 period and the post-1945 era. In the pre-1945 period, the term 'war' automatically produced certain legal consequences, although there were disagreements over the definition of 'war' between the subjective school, based on a state's declaration of war, and the objective approach based on certain objective criteria. On the other hand, in the post-1945 period, in general, the term 'war' no longer has direct legal consequences. For details see Christopher Greenwood, 'The Concept of War in Modern International Law' (1987) 36 *International and Comparative Law Quarterly* 283.

11 Covenant of the League of Nations (n 2) preamble.

the term 'war'. For instance, Article 11(1) of the Covenant provides that '[a]ny *war* or threat of *war* … is hereby declared a matter of concern to the whole League'[12] while Article 16 says that '[s]hould any Member of the League resort to *war* in disregard of its covenants under Articles 12, 13 or 15, it shall ipso facto be deemed to have committed an act of *war* against all other Members of the League'.[13]

An exception was Article 11(2) of the Covenant, which enabled the League to exercise its authority over a wide range of peace and security issues beyond inter-state war scenarios. According to Article 11(2) of the Covenant:[14]

> It is … declared to be the friendly right of each Member of the League to bring to the attention of the Assembly or of the Council *any circumstance whatever affecting international relations which threatens to disturb international peace or the good understanding between nations upon which peace depends …*

On the face of it, the terms of Article 11(2) of the Covenant of the League of Nations are broadly formulated so as to allow the League of Nations to deal with a wide range of circumstances that threaten to disturb international peace. This turned out to be true in the practice of the League of Nations, in which Article 11 of the Covenant worked as a catalyst in enabling the League Council to respond to inter-state disputes at an earlier stage and prevent them from developing into a war.[15]

The frequent reliance on Article 11 did not, however, go so far as to alter the inter-state understanding about the scope of the provision. The phrase 'international peace' under Article 11(2) of the Covenant was assumed to signify, at least within the practice of the League Council, the restriction of inter-state war or analogous inter-state confrontations. Member states assessed the League's capacity as to whether it was capable of 'preventing war'.[16] The phrase 'international peace' under Article 11(2) was indeed combined immediately with 'the good understanding between nations' upon which peace depends and the League Council also employed these terms as if they were one set of notions. For instance,

12 Ibid., Article 11(1) (emphasis added).
13 Ibid., Article 16(1), and (2) (emphasis added).
14 Ibid., Article 11(2) (emphasis added).
15 Thomas P. Conwell-Evans, *The League Council in Action: A Study of the Methods Employed by the Council of the League of Nations to Prevent War and to Settle International Disputes* (London, Oxford University Press, Humphrey Milfordat, 1929); Hitoshi Nasu, *International Law on Peacekeeping: A Study of Article 40 of the UN Charter* (Leiden; Boston, Martinus Nijhoff Publishers, 2009) 42–69. See also Conwell-Evans, *The League Council in Action* 278–81 (Appendix II, list of disputes submitted to the Council).
16 E.g., 'Statement Made in the Dail by the Minister for External Affairs of the Irish Free State on Wednesday May 13th, 1925' (1925) 6 *League of Nations Official Journal* 1214 ('The Covenant of the League of Nations, while it marked a notable advance in the direction of international peace, cannot be regarded as an instrument capable in all circumstances of preventing war') (in relation to the Protocol for the Pacific Settlement of International Disputes).

when the question of Upper Silesia, involving the settling of the boundary between Germany and Poland, was brought to the attention of the Council of the League of Nations in 1921, the League Council took up the question under Article 11(2) of the Covenant by referring to the disturbances that occurred in Upper Silesia as well as some disagreements relating to the settlement of the territorial problem.[17] These two facts, according to the League Council, proved 'the urgent necessity of a settlement in the interest of peace and good understanding between the nations'.[18]

2.3 Minorities questions and the concept of 'international peace'

In order to understand further how the Council of the League of Nations interpreted Article 11(2) of the Covenant, it would be useful to consult the League Council's treatment of the question of minorities. The protection of minorities was one of the limited spheres in which the League of Nations became fully operational.[19] In theory, two different mechanisms were available for the League Council in order to discuss the protection of minorities. The first option was under Article 11(2) of the League Covenant, under which a wide range of circumstances relating to international peace could be brought to the attention of the League Council.[20] The second mechanism was according to minority treaties,[21] under which the League of Nations received and examined petitions

17 'Report by Viscount Ishii on the Request Addressed by the Supreme Council of the Principal Allied Powers to the Council of the League of Nations to Find a Solution of the Question of Upper Silesia, Adopted by the Council on August 29th, 1921' (1921) 2 *League of Nations Official Journal* 1220, 1221. As for the League Council's handling of the Upper Silesia question, see Conwell-Evans, *The League Council in Action* (n 15) 201–10.

18 'Report by Viscount Ishii on the Request Addressed by the Supreme Council of the Principal Allied Powers to the Council of the League of Nations to Find a Solution of the Question of Upper Silesia, Adopted by the Council on August 29th, 1921' (n 17) 1221.

19 See Athanasia Spiliopoulou Åkermark, *Justifications of Minority Protection in International Law* (London, Kluwer Law International, 1997) 101–18.

20 Covenant of the League of Nations (n 2) Article 11(2). For the text of the provision, see (n 14) above and the corresponding text.

21 For instance, Article 12 of the Polish Minority Treaty, which served as a model for the subsequent treaties, provides: 'Poland agrees that any member of the Council of the League of Nations shall have the right to bring to the attention of the Council any infraction, or any danger of infraction, of any of these obligations [under the foregoing articles regarding the minorities protection], and that *the Council may thereupon take such action and give such direction as it may deem proper and effective in the circumstances*': Treaty of Peace Between the United States of America, the British Empire, France, Italy, and Japan and Poland, 28 June 1919, AJIL Supp. 423 (1919) Article 12. For the list of minorities treaties and the overview of pertinent provisions, see Helmer Rosting, 'Protection of Minorities by the League of Nations' (1923) 17 *American Journal of International Law* 641, 646–9; Richard Veatch, 'Minorities and the League of Nations', *The League of Nations in Retrospect: Proceedings of the Symposium Organized by the United Nations Library and the Graduate Institute of*

regarding the infraction or danger of infraction of treaty obligations and thereby observed the implementation of such treaty obligations.[22]

Despite the availability of both mechanisms (i.e., Article 11 of the League Covenant and minority treaties), the questions regarding the protection of minorities were often brought under the second mechanism, namely, minority treaties.[23] This means that the League Council preferred not to regard a minority issue itself as a circumstance relating to international peace under Article 11(2) of the Covenant. The preference of minority treaties over Article 11(2) of the Covenant was a deliberate choice of the League Council which was well aware of the differences between these two procedures.

The practice of the League of Nations drew a clear demarcation line between the minority questions *per se* and international disputes which may have fallen under Article 11(2) of the Covenant. As Stone observed, 'once it has become clear that no threat to peace arises from the alleged infraction of the minorities treaty, the consideration from the minorities question is *scrupulously separated* from the general dispute'.[24] As Stone's observation suggests, a 'threat to peace' might have arisen from the alleged infraction of minority treaties; yet the League Council still tried its best to confine minorities questions within the treaty-based protection procedure.

The following two specific episodes involving the questions of minorities illustrate how the League Council construed Article 11(2) of the Covenant.[25] The first episode concerns the Polish–Lithuanian dispute over the treatment of Lithuanians in Vilna (Vilnius). After Lithuania declared its independence in February 1918, Lithuania and Poland had disputes over the city of Vilna involving military confrontations.[26] In October 1920, Polish troops took control of the city of Vilna

International Studies, Geneva, 6–9 November 1980 (Berlin, Walter de Gruyter, 1983) 369, 369–72.

22 Petitions are received by the Secretariat, who examines their admissibility; they are then sent to the Council (whose three or five members form the Minorities Committees). The League of Nations received petitions not only from Council members but also from the minorities themselves: see 'The Guarantee of the League of Nations in Respect of the Minorities Clauses of Certain Treaties, Procès-Verbal of the Tenth Session of the Council, 20th to 28th October, 1920' (1920) 1 *League of Nations Official Journal* 8, 9. It is noted, however, that the latter's 'right' was the merely informatory submission without any legal effect of seizing the Council: Julius Stone, *International Guarantees of Minority Rights* (London, Humphrey Milford, Oxford University Press, 1932) 38–40. For details of the procedure before the League, see Stone, ibid., 35–123; Rosting, 'Protection of Minorities by the League of Nations' (n 21) 655; Veatch, 'The League of Nations in retrospect' (n 21) 372–3.

23 As Christian Raitz von Frentz observes, 'Article 11 was considered a means of last resort' in dealing with minority questions: see Christian Raitz von Frentz, *A Lesson Forgotten: Minority Protection Under the League of Nations: The Case of the German Minority in Poland, 1920–1934* (Münster, LIT Verlag, 1999) 90–1.

24 Stone, *International Guarantees of Minority Right* (n 22) 146 (emphasis added).

25 See Conwell-Evans, *The League Council in Action* (n 15) 225–6; Veatch, 'The League of Nations in Retrospect' (n 21) 373–4.

26 For the background to the disputes and the League Council's response, see W.J. Brockelbank, 'The Vilna Dispute' (1926) 20 *The American Journal of International Law* 483.

while the League of Nations had barely begun functioning without a strong will to respond to Lithuania's appeal to the League Council.[27] As Polish troops continued to occupy the city, the Lithuanian government drew the League's attention to the treatment of Lithuanians in Vilna by the Polish authorities.[28] In response, Poland lodged a similar complaint regarding the treatment of the Polish population in Lithuania.[29] In 1922, the League Council managed to discuss these minority questions 'under Article 11 in the face of a threat to international peace' on the basis that '[o]ne of the causes of that threat was the alleged oppression of minorities in violation of international obligations'.[30] Nevertheless, the League Council's attempt to examine the questions of minorities under Article 11 of the Covenant was short-lived. In 1923, the League Council separated the questions of minorities from the coverage of Article 11 of the Covenant by deciding to utilise the treaty-based procedure for 'all questions relating to the protection of the non-Polish elements in the region of Vilna'.[31] A similar response was given in 1927 when the question of the Polish–Lithuanian minorities was brought again under Article 11 of the Covenant.[32]

The second episode was the Albania–Greece dispute over the treatment of the Albanian minority in Greece. As it was in the case of the Polish–Lithuanian dispute, the Council of the League of Nations was reluctant to conceptualise the question of minorities as a circumstance threatening to disturb international peace or the good understanding between nations upon which peace depends. In 1924, the Albanian Government appealed to the League Council under Article 11(2) of the Covenant in order to prevent the deportation of Albanians from Greece to Turkey.[33] The Greek representative, in response, disputed the applicability of Article 11 to the question presented before the League. He denied the existence of inter-state controversy between Greece and Albania, and argued that the treatment

27 Ibid., 487–8; Conwell-Evans, *The League Council in Action* (n 15) 89–100.
28 Stone, *International Guarantees of Minority Rights* (n 22) 138–9.
29 Ibid., 139.
30 Ibid. See also ibid., 140 ('the extraordinary nature of the measures proposed suggests that [the League] was acting rather under Article 11 for the preservation of peace').
31 'Protection of the Non-Polish Elements in the Region of Vilna, Ninth Meeting (Public), Twenty-Third Session of the Council, 1 February 1923' (1923) 4 *League of Nations Official Journal* 227, 229 (resolution). See Stone, *International Guarantees of Minority Rights* (n 22) 140–1.
32 Stone, *International Guarantees of Minority Rights* (n 22) 144–146; 'Request of the Lithuanian Government dated October 15th, 1927 under Article 11 of the Covenant: Request dated October 26th, 1927 with respect to the Expulsion of Eleven Polish Nationals on Lithuanian Territory, Fourth Meeting (Public), Forty-Eighth Session of the Council, 7 December 1927' (1928) 9 *League of Nations Official Journal* 144; 'Request of the Lithuanian Government, dated October 15th, 1927 under Article 11 of the Covenant: Request dated October 26th, 1927 with regard to the Expulsion of Eleven Polish Nationals on Lithuanian Territory (continuation), Seventh Meeting (Public), Forty-Eighth Session of the Council, 10 December 1927' (1928) 9 *League of Nations Official Journal* 176, 177 (resolution).
33 Stone, *International Guarantees of Minority Rights* (n 22) 141.

of minorities could be discussed 'only between the Council of the League and the Greek Government in accordance with the ordinary procedure adopted by the Council for minority questions'.[34] The Greek representative thereby claimed that Article 11 of the Covenant would not apply to the treatment of minorities *per se*.

Having accepted the argument of the Greek representative, the League Council decided to treat the matter 'as a question of the application of the Greek Treaty for the Protection of Minorities'[35] rather than as an issue to be discussed under Article 11 of the Covenant. A similar classification was used in 1928 when Albania invoked Article 11 of the Covenant on the treatment of the Albanian minority, which Albania claimed was deprived of civil, cultural, and political rights in Greece.[36] Greece disputed the applicability of Article 11 of the League Covenant to the question of the treatment of minorities *within* its own country.[37] While the representative of Greece acknowledged that he was 'not asking that Article 11 should never be used in connection with minorities', he claimed that Article 11(2) of the Covenant should be reserved for 'a sudden catastrophe' and 'exceptional circumstances'.[38]

The League Council endorsed Greece's objection and declined to consider the situation of the Albanian minority. The approach of the League Council was well captured by the rapporteur who observed that:[39]

> Article 11 of the Covenant should only be invoked in *grave cases* which produce a feeling that facts exist which might effectively menace the maintenance of peace *between the nations*. In normal cases, on the other hand, an appeal to Article 11 would create the very dangers which the Minorities Treaties were intended to avert.

34 'Moslems of Albanian Origin in Greece, Sixteenth Meeting (Public and then Private), 29 September 1924' (1924) 5 *League of Nations Official Journal* 1353, 1355 (M. Politis of Greece).

35 'Moslems of Albanian Origin in Greece, Eighteenth Meeting (Public), 30 September 1924' (1924) 5 *League of Nations Official Journal* 1367, 1368.

36 See 'Question of the Properties of Albanians in Greece and the Albanian Minority in Greece: Request by the Albanian Government under Article 11 of the Covenant, Second Meeting (Public), Fiftieth Session of the Council, 5 June 1928' (1928) 9 *League of Nations Official Journal* 868, 871–3 (M. Mehdi Frasheri of Albania).

37 The representative of Greece argued that the complaints against the Greek Government were of such minor importance in regard to the level of danger posed to the relations of the two countries that to treat the Albanian minority issue under Article 11(2) would frustrate one of the essential reasons of minority treaties to avoid external intervention: 'Question of the Properties of Albanians in Greece and the Albanian Minority in Greece', ibid., 873–7 (M. Politis of Greece).

38 Ibid., 876 (M. Politis of Greece).

39 'Question of the Properties of Albanians in Greece and the Albanian Minority in Greece: Request of the Albanian Government under Article 11 of the Covenant (Continuation), Eighth Meeting (Public), Fiftieth Session of the Council, 9 June 1928' (1928) 9 *League of Nations Official Journal* 942, 942 (M. Zaleski, rapporteur) (emphasis added).

The rapporteur's observation is illuminating as it makes it clear that the circumstances under Article 11 of the League Covenant were restricted to the inter-state conflicts of certain gravity.

Overall, the League Council's treatment of the questions of minorities guides our understanding about what constituted a threat to 'international peace or the good understanding between nations upon which peace depends' during the era of the League of Nations.[40] The League Council was evidently reluctant to include minority questions within the coverage of Article 11 of the Covenant. This reluctance was intertwined with the fact that minorities treaties during the League of Nations' era were designed primarily to protect states (as opposed to their minorities) from 'the danger of interference by other Powers in their internal affairs'.[41] While the League Council still took up a situation involving minority issues under Article 11(2) as well, the aspect of minority questions was often treated as secondary to other issues.[42]

What counts for the purpose of this book is that during the era of the League of Nations there was a fundamental conceptual distance between the League Council's exercise of authority (in the sphere of international peace and security) on the one hand, and the rights and interests of individuals as well as the 'groups' of individuals, on the other hand. The protection of minorities, as an issue which mattered for the groups of individuals, was not considered a threat to international peace unless the questions would be a 'menace [to] the maintenance of peace *between nations*'.[43]

2.4 Administration of territories by the League Council

At the same time, there was an occasion where the League Council and its subsidiary organs exercised their authority in such a manner that their decisions had immediate effect on individuals without the intermediation of national government. The case in point is the administration of territories undertaken by the League of Nations, in which the decisions of the administering organs under the League's authority were directly applied to local populations.

The League of Nations engaged in the temporary administration of territories outside the Mandate system in several instances.[44] While the League's

40 Covenant of the League of Nations (n 2) Article 11(2).

41 'Question of the Properties of Albanians in Greece and the Albanian Minority in Greece: Request of the Albanian Government under Article 11 of the Covenant (Continuation), Eighth Meeting (Public), Fiftieth Session of the Council, 9 June 1928' (n 39) 942 (M. Zaleski, rapporteur).

42 Malcolm D. Evans, *Religious Liberty and International Law in Europe* (Cambridge, Cambridge University Press, 2008) 156–7.

43 'Question of the Properties of Albanians in Greece and the Albanian Minority in Greece: Request of the Albanian Government under Article 11 of the Covenant (Continuation), Eighth Meeting (Public), Fiftieth Session of the Council, 9 June 1928' (n 39) 942 (M. Zaleski, rapporteur) (emphasis added).

44 Méir Ydit, *Internationalised Territories, From the "Free City of Cracow" to the "Free City of Berlin": A Study in the Historical Development of a Modern Notion in International Law and International Relations (1815–1960)* (Leyden, A.W. Sythoff, 1961)

administration of the Saar Basin (1920–1935),[45] the Free City of Danzig (1920–1939),[46] and the Memel Harbour (1924–1939)[47] was in part already envisaged in the Treaty of Versailles,[48] the temporary administration of Leticia (1933–1934)[49] was an initiative of the Council of the League of Nations which should be further explained here.

Leticia is a district which Colombia acquired from Peru in accordance with the treaty of 24 March 1922 which fixed the frontiers between the two countries and gave Colombia access to the Amazon River.[50] In September 1932, some Peruvian soldiers attacked the town of Leticia, which was later endorsed by the Peruvian government as well and resulted in armed confrontations between the two countries.[51] On 25 February 1933, the Committee of Three, appointed by the League Council in accordance with Article 15(4) of the Covenant, communicated to Peru and Colombia its proposals involving the establishment of 'international forces'.[52]

41–4; Carsten Stahn, *The Law and Practice of International Territorial Administration: Versailles to Iraq and Beyond* (Cambridge, Cambridge University Press, 2008) 73–91. The Mandate system of the League was created in order to administer the colonies controlled by Germany and the Ottoman Empire before the WWI, as a result of the compromise between some of the victorious powers' original plan to annex the defeated states' colonies, and US President Wilson's counter-plan to create a trust for such territories and subject them to the supervision and ultimate control of the League. The indirect form of administration by the League was adopted, which reflects the Allies' reluctance to empower the League to directly administer the territories, and the League's managerial capacity to do so.

45 Ydit, *Internationalised Territories* (n 44) 44–5; Ralph Wilde, *International Territorial Administration: How Trusteeship and the Civilizing Mission Never Went Away* (Oxford, Oxford University Press, 2008) 49, 111–4; Stahn, *The Law and Practice of International Territorial Administration* (n 44) 163–73.

46 See further Ydit, *Internationalised Territories* (n 44) 50–1, 185–230; Wilde, *International Territorial Administration* (n 45) 49, 114–27; Stahn, *The Law and Practice of International Territorial Administration* (n 44) 173–85.

47 See Ydit, *Internationalised Territories* (n 44) 48–50; Wilde, *International Territorial Administration* (n 45) 49–50, 127–8; Stahn, *The Law and Practice of International Territorial Administration* (n 44) 185–7.

48 On the Saar: Treaty of Peace between the Allied and Associated Powers and Germany, 28 June 1919, 112 BFSP 1, reprinted in (1919) 13 AJIL Supp. 51 Part III, Section IV, Articles 45–50, and Annex, Articles 1–40. On the City of Danzig: ibid., Section XI, Articles 100–108. With respect to the Memel Territory: ibid., Section X, Article 99; Convention Concerning the Territory of Memel, 8 May 1924, 29 LNTS 87 Articles 2, 5.

49 See Ydit, *Internationalised Territories* (n 44) 59–62; F.P. Walters, *A History of the League of Nations*, vol. II (London, Oxford University Press, 1952) 525–6, 536–40; Wilde, *International Territorial Administration* (n 45) 49, 128–9; Stahn, *The Law and Practice of International Territorial Administration* (n 44) 233–6; Nasu, *International Law on Peacekeeping: A Study of Article 40 of the UN Charter* (n 15) 61–3.

50 L.H. Woolsey, 'The Leticia Dispute between Colombia and Peru' (1933) 27 *American Journal of International Law* 317, 317.

51 Ibid., 317–19.

52 'Report of the Council, Provided for in Article 15, Paragraph 4, of the Covenant (Submitted by the Committee of the Council, in Accordance with the Decision Taken by the Council on March 8th, 1933)' (1933) 14 *League of Nations Official Journal* 598, 605–6 (the Committee's proposals on 25 February 1933, and the Committee's

The Committee of Three recommended that a Commission of the League of Nations would take charge of the territory in which the 'international forces', placed 'under the sole authority and control of the Commission' of the League, would be responsible for the maintenance of the order in the territory during the negotiations.[53] On 25 May 1933, Colombia and Peru signed the agreement to give effect to the proposals, although under the provision that the League's Commission would take charge of the administration of the territory 'in the name of the Government of Colombia'.[54] While Leticia remained Colombian territory during the League of Nations' administration,[55] the League's Commission set up three administrative branches in charge of security, public health, and the claims for damages suffered during the attack of the Peruvian forces.[56] Albeit for a short period of time, the League Commission exercised its authority until after the conclusion of the Protocol of Friendship and Cooperation between the two countries in 1934.[57]

According to Ydit, the administration of Leticia marked 'a turning point in international relations' in that the steps to restore the peace were taken not by a consortium of powerful states but by the 'organised international community' acting as the League of Nations and based on its rules, procedures, and competence.[58] While the successor of the League of Nations rather integrated powerful states into the structure of the organised community, the idea of international territorial administration found continuation during the UN's era in which the UN Security Council established transitional administrations under Chapter VII of the UN Charter without the need for separate international treaties.[59] In those instances of the UN-led territorial administration, it has often been difficult to

interpretation on 3 March 1933). The draft report of the Committee was approved by the League Council on 18 March 1933: 'Dispute Between Colombia and Peru, Appeal of the Colombian Government under Article 15 of the Covenant: Draft Report of the Council, Provided for in Article 15, Paragraph 4, of the Covenant, Submitted by the Committee of the Council' (1933) 14 *League of Nations Official Journal* 516, 525.

53 'Report of the Council, Provided for in Article 15, Paragraph 4, of the Covenant (Submitted by the Committee of the Council, in Accordance with the Decision Taken by the Council on March 8th, 1933)' (n 52) 605–6 (the Committee's proposals on 25 February 1933, and the Committee's interpretation on 3 March 1933). While Colombia immediately accepted the proposals, Peru expressed its concerns over the content of the proposals: ibid., 606–7.

54 Agreement Between Colombia and Peru Relating to the Procedure for Putting into Effect the Recommendations Proposed by the Council of the League of Nations in the Report Which It Adopted on March I8th, I933, in Order to Avoid Any Incident That Might Aggravate the Relations Between the Two Countries, with Annexes (signed on 25 May 1933), 138 LNTS 251. The text is produced in: (1933) 14 *League of Nations Official Journal* 944–5.

55 Ydit, *Internationalised Territories* (n 44) 62; Wilde, *International Territorial Administration* (n 45) 129.

56 Ydit, *Internationalised Territories* (n 44) 61–2.

57 Ibid., 61–2; Protocol of Friendship and Co-Operation Between the Republic of Colombia and the Republic of Peru, 164 LNTS 21 (24 May 1934).

58 Ydit, *Internationalised Territories* (n 44) 62 (original emphasis omitted).

59 See section 4.4 of this book.

avoid political and judicial challenges from local populations, as will be discussed in chapter 7 of this book.[60]

Noteworthy is that contestations from local populations also existed during the League of Nations' experience of administering territories. During the administration of the Saar Basin for 15 years from 1920 to 1935, the League's exercise of authority met resistance from local residents and their political parties, which is not surprising, given the length of the League of Nations' governing authority in the territory and the political context in which the international administration was situated. The administration of the Saar Basin was based on the Treaty of Versailles which entrusted the government of the territory of the Saar Basin to a 'Commission representing the League of Nations'.[61] Under the Treaty of Versailles, the Governing Commission was entrusted to possess 'all the powers of government' previously belonging to Germany.[62] This meant that the Commission's authority was not limited to the executive power to appoint officials, create administrative bodies, administer public services, levy taxes, and use German property other than mines.[63] The Commission also had the legislative power to modify the local laws and regulations after 'consultation' – and thus not approval – with the locally elected representatives,[64] and the judicial authority to establish and operate civil and criminal courts to hear appeals from the local courts.[65]

Having been entrusted with authority virtually comparable with that of the government, the League's Governing Commission issued a whole range of decrees and orders which had immediate legal effect on local inhabitants. To give a few examples, the Governing Commission issued orders concerning working hours[66] and the employment of women and young persons,[67] and took measures to deal with the housing shortage in the Saar territory.[68] In order to maintain public order and security, the Governing Commission prohibited certain newspapers, tightened regulations on political meetings and demonstrations, and introduced administrative detention for armed forces.[69] The Governing Commission also promulgated decrees concerning the plebiscite in the Saar territory.[70]

60 See section 7.4 of this book.
61 Treaty of Versailles (1919) (n 48) Part III, Section IV, Annex, Article 16.
62 Ibid., Part III, Section IV, Annex, Article 19.
63 Ibid., Part III, Section IV, Annex, Articles 19, 22, 26. The Governing Commission was also given broad power to 'ensure … the protection abroad of the interests of the inhabitants': ibid., Part III, Section IV, Annex, Article 21.
64 Treaty of Versailles (1919) (n 48) Part III, Section IV, Annex, Article 23.
65 Ibid., Part III, Section IV, Annex, Article 25.
66 'League of Nations: Saar Territory, Order: Hours of Work' (1924) *Legislative Series* 2.
67 'League of Nations: Saar Territory, Orders: Employment of Women and Young Persons' (1923) *Legislative Series* 2.
68 'Special Report by the Governing Commission of the Saar Territory on the Steps Taken from 1920 to 1930 to Deal with the Housing Shortage' (1930) 11 *League of Nations Official Journal* 833.
69 'Saar Territory, Fifty-Fourth Periodical Report of the Governing Commission (April 1st–June 30th, 1933)' (1933) 14 *League of Nations Official Journal* 1124, 1126–7.
70 'Saar Territory, Sixtieth Periodical Report of the Governing Commission (October 1st to December 31st, 1934)' (504) 16 *League of Nations Official Journal* 505–7.

Despite the impact that the decisions of the League's Governing Commission had on the inhabitants of the Saar territory, the Treaty of Versailles provided only limited safeguards for individuals who would be subject to the authority of the international administration. The Versailles Treaty gave assurance to the inhabitants' local assemblies, and granted them their religious liberties, schools of their language, and the right to vote.[71] Yet other provisions were designed to empower the Governing Commission without envisaging the limits vis-à-vis the inhabitants. For instance, under the Versailles Treaty, it was 'the duty of the Governing Commission to provide in all cases for the protection of persons and property in the Saar Basin',[72] which was to affirm the authority of the Governing Commission in security and military services.[73] While the Governing Commission was required to consult with the elected representative of the inhabitants in modifying laws and regulations, the consultation was conducted 'in such a manner as the Commission may determine'.[74]

Understandably, some of the Governing Commission's decisions met resistance from local inhabitants and their political factions. Some local residents in the Saar Basin engaged in protests and the local Advisory Council did not fully cooperate with the Governing Commission.[75] Local inhabitants, as well as their political groups, also tried to obtain redress by bringing petitions and memorials to the League Council.[76] Furthermore, some of the local inhabitants sought to utilise local courts in order to challenge the ordinance issued by the League's Governing Commission that prohibited the German Imperial flag. The local court seems to have joined in the contestation, and held that the ordinance of the Governing Commission was indeed *ultra vires*. The local court in the Saar territory took the view that the prohibition of the German flag was issued 'without consulting the elected representatives of the people' and that the flying of the flag was contrary neither to the laws of the Saar nor to the Treaty of Versailles.[77]

71 Treaty of Versailles (1919) (n 48) Part III, Section IV, Annex, Article 28.
72 Ibid., Part III, Section IV, Annex, Article 30.
73 At the same time, the same provision of the Versailles Treaty provided that '[o]nly a local gendarmerie for the maintenance of order may be established': ibid. This provision, which referred to both the sole authority of the local gendarmerie and the duty of the Governing Commission, led to the controversy as to whether the Commission was able to deploy an 'international' gendarmerie: see, e.g., 'Supplementary Petitions from the "Deutsche Front" Section of the Advisory Council of the Saar' (1934) 15 *League of Nations Official Journal* 1217, 1223; 'Maintenance of Order in the Territory' (1934) 15 *League of Nations Official Journal* 1140, 1141–2.
74 Treaty of Versailles (1919) (n 48) Part III, Section IV, Annex, Article 23(2). The insufficiency of consultation was in part remedied by the establishment of an Advisory Council (*Landesrat*) by the Governing Commission in 1922.
75 Stahn, *The Law and Practice of International Territorial Administration* (n 44) 168.
76 Ibid., 168–9; Frank Marion Russell, *The International Government of the Saar* (Berkeley, University of California Press, 1926) 200.
77 'German Flag in the Saar: Dispute with the Governing Commission' *The Times* (25 June 1925) page 13. See Stahn, *The Law and Practice of International Territorial Administration* (n 44) 168–9, fn. 49.

2.5 Conclusion

Overall, the experience of the League of Nations gives us many seeds for understanding the 'distance' between the League Council's exercise of authority (in the sphere of peace and security) on the one hand, and individuals and their immediate groups on the other hand. First of all, during the League era, there was indeed an apparent conceptual distance between the plight of individuals and the scope of 'any circumstance whatever affecting international relations which threatens to disturb international peace' under Article 11(2) of the Covenant of the League of Nations. The League Council's attempt to separate the questions of minorities from the ambit of Article 11 of the Covenant well illustrates the fundamental conceptual distance. At the same time, it is noteworthy that when the League Council discussed in 1922 the treatment of Lithuanians in Poland, the League Council, at least initially, conceptualised the oppression of minorities as one of the cases of the threat to international peace. The phrase 'any circumstance ... which threatens to disturb international peace ...' under Article 11(2) of the League Covenant reminds us of Article 39 of the UN Charter, under which the UN Security Council determines the existence of a 'threat to the peace'. Clearly, during the League era, a paradigm change did not occur at the conceptual level with respect to the interpretation of 'international peace' and circumstances that threaten to disturb it.

Second, through the administration of several territories, the League of Nations indeed rendered a number of decisions addressed directly to local residents. It is true that the international territorial administrations were devised as part of interstate dispute settlement and neutralisation;[78] the territorial administrations in Saar, Danzig, and Memel were established as part of post-conflict settlements, and the case of Leticia was aimed at the cessation of conflict and the facilitation of a negotiated solution.[79] Nevertheless, the fact remains that the territorial administrations rendered a wide range of decisions which directly concerned the rights and interests of local individuals, some of whom ended up challenging the manner in which the decisions were rendered by the international administrations.

Finally, the inadequate consideration given to local residents' interests invited contestations in the Saar Basin, including those before local courts. These non-judicial and judicial challenges made by local residents in the Saar Basin bear resemblance to those initiated by inhabitants under UN territorial administrations, and even to those raised by individuals targeted by the UN's sanctions committees, as will be discussed in chapter 7 of this book. Unfortunately, history did not allow the League Council to systematically respond to contestations raised by affected individuals.

Despite its historical significance and some records of successful conflict resolution, the reach of the League of Nations' efforts to maintain peace and security was limited mainly by a number of factors. To begin with, the operative body of

78 Stahn, *The Law and Practice of International Territorial Administration* (n 44) 162–3.
79 Ibid., 23, 63.

the League Covenant provided only the partial restriction of 'war' rather than the 'use of force'.[80] During the process of drafting the Covenant, there were in fact several proposals to include the broader prohibition of the use of force; US President Wilson's drafts and the British–US Miller–Hurst draft had attempted to include more comprehensive restriction covering the use of military force 'short of war'.[81] Nevertheless, after the ten meetings held between 3 and 13 February 1919, the drafting commission eventually replaced the proposed broader restriction with the narrower term of 'war'. The Covenant of the League of Nations thus employed the term 'war' for the restraint of the use of military force by member states, as contrasted with Article 2(4) of the UN Charter, which laid down the broad prohibition of the use of force in international relations.

Furthermore, the prohibition of war itself was limited in scope. Article 12(1) of the League Covenant imposed the prohibition of war, but it was limited to 'three months' after the arbitrators' award or judicial decision. Articles 13(4) and 15(6) of the Covenant could be construed as not prohibiting the resort to war against those member states which fail to comply with the arbitral award, judicial decision, or the League Council's recommendations. The most significant gap was Article 15(7) of the Covenant, which seems to have reserved for members the right to resort to self-help if the League Council failed to reach a report.[82] The Covenant's restriction upon war was even less stringent than the conditions established under customary international law.[83] The unanimity rule generally applied in the decision making of the Assembly and the Council of the League of Nations in part slowed down their decision making.[84] Finally, perhaps most significantly, the failure to include the US in its formal membership weakened the internal unity of the League of Nations.[85] The history thus led to the creation of the UN and its peace and security arm as a renewed imperative to collectively maintain international peace and security.

80 This has led to the discussion as to whether, and to what extent, Articles 12–15 of the Covenant of the League of Nations restricted states' use of force short of war. See Quincy Wright, 'Opinion of Commission of Jurists on Janina-Corfu Affair' (1924) 18 *American Journal of International Law* 536.

81 See David Hunter Miller, *The Drafting of the Covenant*, vol. 2 (New York, G.P. Putnam's Sons, 1928) 4 (Wilson's First Draft, Article VII), 74 (Wilson's Second Draft or First Paris Draft, Article V), 100–1 (Wilson's Third Draft or Second Paris Draft, Articles V, VII), 231, 234 a Draft Covenant or British–US Draft, preamble, Article 10 (later Article 12 under the Covenant).

82 Covenant of the League of Nations (n 2) Articles 10, 13(4), 15(6), and 15(7).

83 Ian Brownlie, *International Law and the Use of Force by States* (Oxford, Clarendon Press, 1963) 56.

84 Covenant of the League of Nations (n 2) Article 5(1). See Julius Stone, 'The Rule of Unanimity: The Practice of the Council and Assembly of the League of Nations' (1933) 14 *British Year Book of International Law* 18; Robert Kolb, *Introduction au droit des Nations Unies* (Bâle; Bruxelles, Helbing Lichtenhahn; Bruylant, 2008) 27.

85 For the reasons for the failure of the League of Nations, see Kolb, *Introduction au droit des Nations Unies* (n 84) 26–31.

3 Conceptual distance

3.1 Introduction

The League of Nations' attempt 'to achieve international peace and security'[1] encountered a critical setback with the occurrence of yet another World War, which reawakened the gravity of human and social costs associated with modern inter-state war. A bitter lesson from the League era created the political environment wherefrom materialised what has been described as the 'legalised hegemony'[2] of a post-war collective security mechanism. The UN Charter internalised major powers as 'policemen', gave them permanent seats at the Security Council, and accorded the organ primary responsibility for the maintenance of international peace and security.[3] Reflecting the very fact of war that became the genesis of the Organisation, the maintenance of international peace and security was primarily understood as the prevention and removal of inter-state armed confrontations.[4] As the Chairman of the US delegation reported, '[i]t was to prevent a third recurrence of [the] great disaster' that the San Francisco Conference was called in 1945.[5] In order to prevent inter-state wars and analogous scenarios, states

1 Covenant of the League of Nations, 28 June 1919, AJIL Supp. 128 (1919) (entered into force 10 January 1920) (1919) preamble.

2 Gerry Simpson, *Great Powers and Outlaw States: Unequal Sovereigns in the International Legal Order* (Cambridge, Cambridge University Press, 2004) 165–93.

3 For the details of a series of conferences leading to the San Francisco Conference (namely, Moscow (1943), Tehran (1943), Dumbarton Oaks (1944) and Yalta conferences (1945)), see Ruth B. Russell, *A History of the United Nations Charter: The Role of the United States 1940–1945* (Washington, DC, The Brookings Institution, 1958).

4 Inger Österdahl, *Threat to the Peace: The Interpretation by the Security Council of Article 39 of the UN Charter* (Uppsala, Iustus, 1998) 18; Daniel W. Abbott, 'The United Nations and Intrastate Conflict: A Legislative History of Article 39 of the United Nations Charter' (2002) 8 *U.C. Davis Journal of International Law & Policy* 275; Jochen A. Frowein and Nico Krisch, 'Article 39' in B. Simma (ed.), *The Charter of the United Nations: A Commentary* (2nd edn, Oxford, Oxford University Press, 2002) 717, 720; Nico Krisch, 'Article 39' in B. Simma and others (eds), *The Charter of the United Nations: A Commentary* (3rd edn, Oxford, Oxford University Press, 2012) 1272, 1282.

5 Hearings before the Committee on Foreign Relations, US Senate, Seventy-Ninth Congress, First Session on the Charter of the United Nations for the Maintenance of

managed to agree on the principle of non-use of force by states 'in their international relations'[6] as a foundation for the UN's collective security.

This chapter attempts to understand the *conceptual* distance between the UN Security Council and domestic actors. The chapter overviews the points of conceptual connection between, on the one hand, the mandate of the UN Security Council to maintain international peace and security and, on the other hand, the interests of individuals or groups of individuals. If the mandate of the Security Council is understood as the prevention of inter-state armed confrontations, individuals would merely be some remote and *de facto* beneficiaries of the Security Council's exercise of authority to maintain international peace and security. While the absence of inter-state armed confrontations would consequentially benefit individuals who reside in conflict-prone areas, the plight of the individuals does not constitute a justification for the UN Security Council's exercise of authority.

From the drafting process of the UN Charter, it is evident that the drafters situated the prevention of inter-state wars as the primary rationale for establishing the UN's collective security mechanism. At the same time, the drafters were aware of the need for flexibility in the scope of Article 39 of the UN Charter, and some of them also envisaged the linkage between the maintenance of international peace and security and the protection of fundamental rights (section 3.2 below). From the early phase, the UN Security Council has utilised this flexibility and started to apply Article 39 to a wide range of situations other than the inter-state armed confrontations (section 3.3). In the practice of the Council, the concept of the threats to international peace accommodates civil wars, the deliberate targeting of civilians, the serious violations of human rights and humanitarian law, terrorism, and the proliferation of weapons of mass destruction. What matters for the purpose of this book is that individuals are no longer constituted as consequential *de facto* beneficiaries. The greater visibility of individuals' rights and interests in the concepts of the threats to the peace necessitates and justifies the UN Security Council and its subsidiary organs in exercising their authority in a manner much more proximate to individuals.

3.2 At the drafting stage

3.2.1 Preserving the conceptual flexibility

In order to maintain international peace and security, the drafters of the UN Charter entrusted the Security Council with the authority to apply provisional and enforcement measures under Chapter VII of the UN Charter. The gateway to Chapter VII is Article 39 of the UN Charter, which reads in full:

International Peace and Security, Submitted by the President of the United States on July 2, 1945: Report to the President on the Charter of the United Nations (Washington: US Government Printing Office, 1945) 2.

6 Charter of the United Nations, 26 June 1945, 1 UNTS XVI (entered into force 24 October 1945) Article 2(4).

> Article 39
> The Security Council shall determine the existence of any threat to the peace, breach of the peace, or act of aggression and shall make recommendations, or decide what measures shall be taken in accordance with Articles 41 and 42, to maintain or restore international peace and security.[7]

Under the provision, the Security Council shall determine the existence of one (or more) of three triggers: any threat to the peace, breach of the peace, or act of aggression.[8] Among these three triggers listed in Article 39 of the UN Charter, it was the definition of an act of aggression that provoked one of the most heated debates among the delegates at the San Francisco Conference in 1945.[9]

Several amendments have been proposed in view of defining the notion of aggression and thereby circumscribing the discretion of the UN Security Council;[10] for instance, Bolivia's proposal attempted to ensure the Council's 'automatic' actions in certain listed circumstances. Yet the Bolivian proposal met rejection by the majority of delegates at the San Francisco Conference.[11] Other proposals that had aimed at restricting the Security Council's exercise of authority were likewise rejected. As the Rapporteur, Paul-Boncour, noted, many delegations were aware that it would be difficult to provide an exhaustive list of acts of aggression.[12] The drafters were thus aware of the fact that whatever the definitions of aggression were, the changes in political contexts, such as the progress in the techniques of modern warfare, would have rendered the list 'necessarily incomplete'.[13] After the extensive debates on the concept of an act of aggression, the drafters thus chose not to define even this relatively familiar term of aggression.[14]

7 Ibid., Article 39.
8 Ibid. It is noted that the term 'breach of the peace or act of aggression' was inserted upon request of the Soviet delegation at Dumbarton Oaks. Initially, the proposal included only one trigger of 'any threat to the peace': see Russell, *A History of the United Nations Charter* (n 3) 464–5.
9 See the proposals relating to the definition of aggression: Documents of the United Nations Conference on International Organization, San Francisco, 1945 (London; New York, United Nations Information Organizations, 1945) vol. 3, at 584–5 (Bolivia), 538 (Philippines), 459 (Egypt), 469 (Czechoslovakia).
10 Ibid., vol. 3, at 584–5 (Bolivia, Doc 2, G/14(r), 5 May 1945, at 8–9), 538 (Philippines, Doc 2, G/14(k), 5 May 1945), 459 (Egypt, Doc 2, G/7(p)(1), 5 May 1945, at 7), 469 ('Observations of the Czechoslovak Government on the Dumbarton Oaks Proposals', Doc 2, G/14(b), 1 May 1945).
11 The Bolivian amendment was rejected by 22 votes to 12: ibid., vol. 12, at 348–9 ('Summary Report of Tenth Meeting of Committee III/2', Doc 502, III/3/22, 23 May 1945, at 1–2).
12 Ibid., vol. 12, at 505 ('Report of Mr. Paul-Boncour, Rapporteur, on Chapter VIII, Section B', Doc 881, III/3/46, 10 June 1945, at 4).
13 Ibid., vol. 12, at 505 ('Report of Mr. Paul-Boncour, Rapporteur, on Chapter VIII, Section B', Doc 881, III/3/46, 10 June 1945, at 4).
14 The concept of aggression had also been subject to debate during the era of the League of Nations. For the debate in the League of Nations era, see Quincy Wright, 'The Concept of Aggression in International Law' (1935) 29 *American Journal of International Law* 373. The concept of aggression continued to stir debate at the UN

Article 39 of the UN Charter envisages two further triggers: namely, any 'threat to the peace' and 'breach of the peace'. Little discussion was dedicated to the elaboration of these two concepts themselves at the San Francisco Conference in 1945. While the Iranian proposal attempted to ensure that '[a]ny threat to the territorial integrity or independence of a Member State' should constitute a 'threat to the maintenance of peace and international security',[15] this passage in the Iranian proposal did not lead the drafters to discuss a general definition of the threats to the peace.

The fact that little time was devoted to the concepts of any 'threat to the peace' and 'breach of the peace' contrasts with lengthy debates on an act of aggression during the San Francisco Conference. This contrast first indicates that the drafters' priority was directed at ensuring the Security Council's response to inter-state wars and analogous inter-state armed confrontations which could constitute an act of aggression. The shortage of debate also suggests that the drafters chose to leave the Security Council to define what constitutes threats to the peace on a case-by-case basis.[16] As the US delegation reported on the San Francisco Conference, there was indeed 'some sentiment' among states for laying down more precise duties of the Security Council with respect to Article 39 determination. Nevertheless, an overwhelming majority took the view that the provision 'should be left as broad and as flexible as possible', since 'the circumstances in which threats to the peace or aggression might occur are so varied'.[17] Overall, the drafters were aware of the possibility that the triggers under Article 39 would be invoked in the future for certain circumstances which they did not, and indeed could not, specify at the drafting stage.

3.2.2 The meaning of 'any threat to the peace'

Although the drafters did not provide concrete definition of any of the three triggers under Article 39 of the UN Charter, the drafting process still provides

General Assembly. With respect to the debate leading to the adoption of the General Assembly's resolution on the Definition of Aggression in 1974 (UN Doc A/RES/3314 (XXIX) (14 December 1974)), see Benjamin B. Ferencz, *Defining International Aggression, the Search for World Peace: A Documentary History and Analysis*, vols. 1, 2 (Dobbs Ferry, NY, Oceana Publications, 1975); Ahmed M. Rifaat, *International Aggression: A Study of the Legal Concept: Its Development and Definition in International Law* (Stockholm, Almqvist & Wiksell International, 1979) 242–62.

15 UNCIO Documents (n 9) vol. 3, at 556 (Iran, Doc 2, G/14(m), 5 May 1945, at 3).

16 It is by no means an exaggeration to say that at the San Francisco Conference the Committee III/3 left to the Council 'the entire decision' as to what constitutes a threat to peace, a breach of the peace, or an act of aggression: UNCIO Documents, ibid., vol. 12, at 505 ('Report of Mr. Paul-Boncour, Rapporteur, on Chapter VIII, Section B', Doc 881, III/3/46, 10 June 1945, at 4).

17 Hearings before the Committee on Foreign Relations (1945) (n 5) 57. Abbott also observes that the US State Department's approach to Article 39, like that of the majority of the Conference, was 'one of flexibility': Abbott, 'United Nations and Intrastate Conflict' (n 4) 278.

several clues about the original assumption of the drafters regarding the term 'any threat to the peace' which, in the practice of the UN, became the almost exclusively used trigger for Chapter VII measures. The drafting process informs us of the following facets of the concept of 'any threat to the peace'.

First, the drafting phase seems to confirm that the term 'the peace' simply signifies 'international' peace. This is relatively self-evident already from the structural interpretation of the Charter; while Article 39 of the UN Charter itself does not use the prefix 'international', other relevant Charter provisions employ the term 'international' peace.[18] The structural reading thus provides a cogent basis for the understanding that 'the peace' signifies 'international' peace. In particular, Article 24(1) of the UN Charter, which prescribes the overall job description of the Security Council, entrusts it to engage in the maintenance of 'international' peace and security, and not any other forms of peace 'beyond' the international one.

This interpretation finds support from the drafting documents. Article 39 of the UN Charter corresponds to Section B(2) of Chapter VIII of the Dumbarton Oaks Proposals. Section B(2) of the Proposals provides as follows, along with paragraph 1, which was ultimately deleted:[19]

> Section B. DETERMINATION OF THREATS TO THE PEACE OR ACTS OF AGGRESSION AND ACTION WITH RESPECT THERETO.
>
> 1. Should the Security Council deem that a failure to settle a dispute in accordance with procedures indicated in paragraph 3 of Section A [now Article 33], or in accordance with its recommendations made under paragraph 5 of Section A [now Article 36(1)], constitutes a threat to the maintenance of international peace and security, it should take any measures necessary for the maintenance of *international* peace and security in accordance with the purposes and principles of the Organization.
>
> 2. In general the Security Council should determine the existence of any threat to *the peace*, breach of the peace or act of aggression and should make recommendations or decide upon the measures to be taken to maintain or restore *peace* and security.[20]

Under Section B(1), which was designed to bridge Chapter VI and Chapter VII, the Security Council is instructed to take necessary measures if the failure to reach a peaceful settlement constitutes 'a threat to the maintenance of *international* peace and security'.[21] This provision is followed by Section B(2) which referred to

18 See other relevant provisions in the Charter that employ the term 'international' peace: UN Charter (n 6) Articles 1(1), 24(1), 33(1), 34, 37(2), 39, 42, 43(1), 48(1).

19 This first paragraph was deleted because the second paragraph (i.e., Article 39) alone would be sufficient for the Security Council to make necessary determinations: Hearings before the Committee on Foreign Relations (1945) (n 5) 56–7.

20 Dumbarton Oaks Proposals, UNCIO Documents (n 9) vol. 3, at 14–15 (Doc 1, G/1, at 13–14), Chapter VIII, Section B(2) (emphasis added).

21 UNCIO Documents (n 9) vol. 3, at 14–15 (Doc 1, G/1, at 13–14), Chapter VIII, Section B(2) (emphasis added).

'the peace'. It thus appears that 'the peace' under Section B(2) is meant to refer to 'international peace' contained in Section B(1). Also, other provisions in Section B regarding military enforcement measures likewise employed the terms 'international' peace.[22] While the phrase '*peace* and security' under Section B(2) is without any prefix,[23] the final text of the UN Charter added the adjective 'international' to the phrase 'peace and security'. In short, the structural reading of the Dumbarton Oaks Proposals confirms the international character of 'the peace' under Article 39 of the UN Charter.

The second and more important dimension is the meaning of 'international' peace and threats to it as envisaged by the drafters. At the San Francisco Conference convened at the end of World War II, the drafters have, not surprisingly, understood the term 'international' to mean an inter-state scenario.[24] At the same time, some of the delegates at the San Francisco Conference had already contemplated the possibility that the UN Security Council's mandate could encompass circumstances other than inter-state military confrontations. For instance, during the debate on Article 2(7) of the UN Charter concerning domestic jurisdiction, the Norwegian representative commented that the UN Security Council 'may have to act in a situation *not* involving a dispute of two states' such as a case akin to the Spanish Civil War.[25] Namely, the Norwegian delegate anticipated the Security Council's exercise of authority over intra-state wars.

Other delegations further suggested a possible connection between the denial of fundamental rights and 'peace' to be guarded by the UN Security Council. Noteworthy is the French proposal tabled with regard to the domestic jurisdiction clause which was meant to exclude the matters within states' domestic jurisdiction from the Security Council's dispute settlement authority. The French delegation suggested – albeit unsuccessfully – to add the following sentence as an exception to the domestic jurisdiction clause: 'unless the clear violation of essential liberties and of human rights constitutes in itself a threat capable of compromising peace'.[26] The Australian representative also referred to the scenario that the Security Council 'deal[s] with grave infringements of basic rights within a state'.[27] Furthermore, in the debate concerning Article 1(3) of the UN Charter, the Subcommittee I/1/A:

> held that assuring or protecting such fundamental rights is primarily the concern of each state. If, however, *such rights and freedoms were grievously outraged so as to create the conditions which threaten peace* or to obstruct the

22 UN Charter (n 6) Articles 42, 43(1), 48(1).
23 See (n 20) above and accompanying text.
24 See (n 4) above.
25 UNCIO Documents (n 9) vol. 6, at 432 ('Statement by the Norwegian Delegation (Dr. Arnold Raestad) on Paragraph 8, Charter II', Doc 929, I/1/37, 12 June 1945, at 3) (emphasis added).
26 Ibid., vol. 6, at 498 (regarding domestic jurisdiction clause).
27 Ibid., vol. 6, at 439 (Australia, Doc 969, I/1/39, 14 June 1945, at 4).

application of provisions of the Charter, then they cease to be the sole concern of each state.[28]

The Subcommittee I/1/A here envisaged the possibility that the flagrant abuse of fundamental rights and freedoms could 'create conditions which threaten peace'.[29] While these remarks by France, Australia, and the Subcommittee I/1/A were made outside the deliberation of Article 39 itself, the fact remains that some delegates apparently contemplated the possibility that civil wars and the appalling abuse of fundamental rights could threaten peace.

Overall, what can be observed from the drafting process of the UN Charter is a certain degree of flexibility with respect to the circumstances threatening peace – and, by extension, the Security Council's exercise of authority as a guardian of international peace and security. At the same time, the significance of the observations made by France, Australia, and the report of the Subcommittee I/1/A should be understood in a nuanced manner. Using the term 'peace' without a prefix may still indicate conceptual dissonance between 'international' peace on the one hand, and the severe infringement of fundamental rights on the other hand. Also, at the San Francisco Conference, the delegates associated the protection of human rights with peace and security by taking into account the protection of minorities.[30] As overviewed in section 2.3 of this book, already during the era of the League of Nations, the protection of minorities had been discussed as part of the issue of international peace and security. Therefore, while some drafters of the UN Charter conceptually embraced the flagrant abuse of fundamental rights as a possible circumstance threatening peace, the content of fundamental rights was tailored by the drafters' longstanding concern over the protection of minorities.

3.3 The concept of 'any threat to the peace' in the practice of the Security Council

3.3.1 'Inter-state' peace

Despite certain reference to the flagrant abuse of fundamental rights, the drafters of the UN Charter primarily contemplated the occurrence of 'any threat to the peace' in the contexts of inter-state military confrontations.[31] This historically

28 Ibid., vol. 6, at 705 ('Report of Rapporteur, Subcommittee I/1/A', Doc 723, I/1/A/19, 1 June 1945, at 10) (emphasis added). See Hans Kelsen, *The Law of the United Nations: A Critical Analysis of Its Fundamental Problems: With Supplement* (London, Stevens & Sons, 1950) 29.

29 UNCIO Documents, ibid.

30 See UNCIO Documents (n 9) vol. 6, at 439 (Australia, Doc 969, I/1/39, 14 June 1945, at 4). See also Christian Tomuschat, 'L'adaptation institutionnelle des Nations Unies au nouvel ordre mondial' in R.B. Achour and S. Laghmani (eds), *Les Nouveaux aspects du droit international* (Paris, Pedone, 1994) 159, 164 (drawing attention to the French delegation's remark on minorities).

31 See (n 4) above.

embedded assumption is in part illustrated by the intriguing discussion which took place in the earliest stage of the UN as to whether the 'threats' to the peace should be limited to those of an inter-state character. Such a discussion took place in 1948 in relation to the Palestinian question. The US delegation contended that the term 'any' (threat) under Article 39 of the UN Charter was deliberately chosen to include not only international but also 'all other kinds of threats to the peace'.[32] Yet other members of the Security Council did not fully agree with the US' understanding of Article 39. The UK, Belgium, and China instead preferred a more restrictive reading of it, and they hesitated, at least initially, to extend the scope of 'any threat to the peace' to non-international affairs.[33] At the same time, the point of contention was the interpretation of the term 'any' threat, as opposed to the concept of 'the peace'. All the delegates, despite their disagreements about the scope of threats, seem to have commonly constructed the concept of 'the peace' as *inter-state* peace during the debate in 1948 regarding the Palestinian question.

The the UK, Belgium, and China soon overcame their hesitation amid the escalating conflict in Palestine; yet they did so, not necessarily because they altered their general understanding of 'any threat to the peace' but rather because it became clear that the Palestinian conflict had been an inter-state conflict by the proclamation of independence by the Provisional Government of Israel on 14 May 1948. The fact that some members of the UN Security Council still preserved an inter-state understanding of threats to the peace is reflected in the wording of Resolution 54 adopted on 15 July 1948, in which the Security Council:

> Taking into consideration that the *Provisional Government of Israel* has indicated its acceptance in principle of a prolongation of the truce in Palestine; that the *States members of the Arab League* have rejected successive appeals of the United Nations Mediator, and of the Security Council in its resolution 53 (1948) of 7 July 1948, for the prolongation of the truce in Palestine; and that there has *consequently* developed a renewal of hostilities in Palestine,
>
> 1. Determines that *the situation in Palestine constitutes a threat to the peace* within the meaning of Article 39 of the Charter of the United Nations ...[34]

32 UN Doc S/PV.296 (19 May 1948) 7 (Mr. Austin of the US).

33 Ibid., 2 (Sir Alexander Cadogan of the UK), 11 (Mr. van Langenhove of Belgium), 22 (Mr. Tsiang of China). The UK government's view was expressed based on the recognition that the juridical status of Palestine was still uncertain: see ibid., 2–4 (Sir Alexander Cadogan of the UK). Nevertheless, it must be noted that the conflict was already inter-state by the time the Security Council's debate took place on 18 May 1948, which was after the proclamation of independence of the State of Israel by the Provisional Government of Israel on 15 May.

34 UN Doc S/RES/54 (15 July 1948) the preamble and para 1 (original emphasis omitted, current emphasis added). Paragraph 1 was adopted by 8 votes to 1 (Syria) with 2 abstentions (Argentina, China). See also the earlier Resolution 50 in which the Security Council threatened to invoke Chapter VII: see UN Doc S/RES/50 (29 May 1948) para 11.

In determining the existence of the threat to the peace with regard to the situation in Palestine, the Security Council made sure to refer to the acts of relevant governments, including the refusal of the UN's appeals by states members of the Arab League. In the preamble, a renewal of hostilities in Palestine was constructed as a 'consequence' of the differences in view between the Provisional Government of Israel and the Arab League's member states – as opposed to, for instance, the human dimensions of the hostilities in Palestine.

3.3.2 Non-inter-state crises as 'extrinsic' factors

The reserved approach taken in 1948 by some members of the UN Security Council is somewhat contrasted with the observation of the UN's Commission of Human Rights in 1946. Only a year after the adoption of the Charter, the Commission, appointed by the Economic and Social Council (ECOSOC), took the view that it would be within the Commission's competence to 'aid the Security Council in the task entrusted to it by Article 39 of the Charter, by pointing to cases where violation of human rights may constitute a threat to the peace'.[35] Within the UN Security Council itself, however, it took some time before its resolutions started to conceptualise such a connection between human rights violations and a threat to the peace.

It was in the 1960s and 1970s that the Security Council removed the hesitation to determine the threats beyond the contexts of inter-state armed confrontations. During the Congo crisis in the early 1960s, the Security Council heavily engaged itself with the situation of civil wars; the Security Council also encountered racist national policies in Rhodesia and South Africa in the 1960s and 1970s. At the same time, the manner in which the Security Council applied Article 39 of the UN Charter to the Congo's civil war and the policies of apartheid illuminates the conceptual dissonance between the Council's mandate and non-inter-state crises. As will be seen below, the Security Council still conceptually treated civil wars and apartheid systems as *external*, and not intrinsic, elements to the threats to international peace and security.

The Congo crisis in the early 1960s was literally the UN's largest engagement in civil wars during the Cold War. Civil unrest followed immediately the independence of the Democratic Republic of the Congo (then the Republic of Congo) from Belgium on 30 June 1960. On 10 July, Belgium sent troops to Elisabethville, Luluabourg, Boma, and Matadi in the Congo[36] in order, allegedly, to protect Belgian nationals as well as other members of the population[37] at the request of Moise Tshombe, the head of the provisional Katanga government.[38] The UN Security Council responded to the crisis by not only calling upon Belgium to withdraw its troops from the Congo; the Council also decided to authorise the

35 UN Doc E/38/Rev.1 (21 May 1946) 5.
36 *Keesing's Contemporary Archives*, vol. 12 (1959–1960) 17640.
37 UN Doc S/PV.873 (13–14 July 1960) 34, para 183; UN Doc S/PV.877 (20–21 July 1960) 30, para 142.
38 UN Doc S/PV.873 (13–14 July 1960), ibid., 34–5, paras 186–8.

UN Secretary-General – Dag Hammarskjöld – to take the necessary steps to provide the Congolese government with military assistance.[39] Already on 15 July, the first UN forces arrived in the Congo.[40] In mid-1961, the UN maintained a 20,000-strong force for the purpose of assisting the central government of the Congo to restore and maintain law and order and of preventing the occurrence of civil war in the Congo.[41]

Despite the UN Security Council's unprecedented commitment in civil wars, its resolutions relevant to the Congo crisis still accommodated conceptual distance between the restoration of the Congo's internal order and international peace and security. For instance, Security Council Resolution 145 adopted in July 1960 states that 'the complete restoration of law and order in the Republic of the Congo *would effectively contribute* to the maintenance of international peace and security'.[42] In this resolution, the Security Council still regarded the restoration of the Congo's law and order as one of the 'contributing factors'. Likewise, the manner in which Resolution 161 constituted the threats is noteworthy. Under the resolution, the Security Council was:

> Having considered the situation in the Congo,
>
> Having learnt with deep regret of the announcement of the killing of the Congolese leaders …
>
> Deeply concerned at the grave repercussions of these crimes and the danger of widespread civil war and bloodshed in the Congo *and* the threat to international peace and security …[43]

In this resolution, adopted in February 1961, the grave repercussions of the crimes in the Congo and the danger of widespread civil war therein did not unequivocally constitute the threat to international peace and security. Instead, the Security Council inserted the term 'and' between, on the one hand, 'the danger of widespread civil war and bloodshed in the Congo' and, on the other hand, 'the threat to international peace and security'. This indicates that, in the early 1960s, civil war may not have been regarded as *intrinsic* to the threat to international peace and security.

The conceptual distance can still be identified with regard to the UN Security Council's response to the apartheid in South Africa. Noteworthy in this regard is Resolution 418, in which the Security Council:

39 UN Doc S/RES/143 (14 July 1960) paras 1–2.
40 Alan P. Merriam, *Congo, Background of Conflict* (Northwestern University Press, 1961) 216.
41 UN Doc S/RES/169 (24 November 1961) para 3 of the preamble.
42 UN Doc S/RES/145 (22 July 1960) para 5 of the preamble (emphasis added).
43 UN Doc S/RES/161 (21 February 1961) A, para 3 of the preamble (original emphasis omitted, current emphasis added). A similar disconnection can be seen in the first preamble of the Part B: see ibid., B, para 1 of the preamble.

> Strongly condemning the South African Government for its acts of repression, its defiant continuance of the system of *apartheid* and its attacks against neighbouring independent States,
>
> Considering that the policies and acts of the South African Government are fraught with danger to international peace and security,
>
> ...
>
> 1. Determines, having regard to the policies and acts of the South African Government, that the acquisition by South Africa of arms and related matériel constitutes a threat to the maintenance of international peace and security ...[44]

In the preamble, the Security Council directed its strong condemnation against the South African government's apartheid system,[45] and indicated that 'the policies' (which presumably included apartheid policies) could endanger international peace and security.[46] However, when it comes to the determination of threats in the first operative paragraph, it was rather 'the acquisition by South Africa of arms and related matériel' that the Security Council considered a threat to international peace and security.[47] By referring to the acquisition of weapons by South Africa, the UN Security Council conceptually detached the threat to international peace and security from the domestic policy of apartheid itself.

Even in the early 1990s, the UN Security Council still hesitated to fully treat a humanitarian crisis as intrinsic to the threats to the peace. In Resolutions 713 and 721 on Yugoslavia, for instance, the Security Council referred not only to 'a heavy loss of human life' but also to 'the consequences for the countries of the region' (namely, an inter-state variable) as some of the factors that would lead to a threat to international peace and security.[48] The similar distance between human suffering and international peace and security is illustrated by Resolution 688 regarding the treatment of Kurdish people in northern Iraq.[49] Likewise, Resolution 733 concerning Somalia captures the conceptual gap, in which the Security Council was:

> Gravely alarmed at the rapid deterioration of the situation in Somalia and the heavy loss of human life and widespread material damage resulting from the conflict in the country and aware of *its consequences on stability and peace in the region*,

44 UN Doc S/RES/418 (4 November 1977) paras 6–7 of the preamble, and para 1 (original emphasis omitted (apart from 'apartheid'), current emphasis added).
45 Ibid., para 6 of the preamble.
46 Ibid., para 7 of the preamble.
47 Ibid., para 1 (original italics omitted).
48 UN Doc S/RES/713 (25 September 1991) paras 3–4 of the preamble; UN Doc S/RES/721 (1991) paras 3–4 of the preamble. Noteworthy still, however, is that the Security Council recognised that 'the provision of humanitarian assistance in Bosnia and Herzegovina is an important element in the Council's effort to restore international peace and security in the area': UN Doc S/RES/770 (13 August 1992) preamble; UN Doc S/RES/787 (16 November 1992) preamble.
49 UN Doc S/RES/688 (5 April 1991) para 3 of the preamble.

> Concerned that *the continuation of this situation* constitutes, as stated in the report of the Secretary-General, a threat to international peace and security ...[50]

In Resolution 733, the preamble embraces both the conflict's internal implication ('the heavy loss of life') and its regional impact ('its consequences on stability and peace in the region').[51] Having referred to these variables, the Security Council determined that, in a general term, the 'continuation of this situation' constituted a threat to international peace and security.[52] In sum, what is suggested by a series of Security Council resolutions from the 1960s to the beginning of the 1990s is the extrinsic character of civil wars, racist national policies, the heavy loss of human rights, and other humanitarian aspects of conflicts in the Security Council's determination of the threats to international peace and security. The Council, while referring to these intra-state crises, referred also to cross-border elements and thereby preserved the conceptual distance between certain human dimensions of the conflicts or policies on the one hand, and the threats to international peace and security on the other hand.

3.3.3 Non-inter-state crises as 'intrinsic' factors

A symbolic turning point came with Resolution 794 on Somalia which was adopted in December 1992.[53] In Resolution 794, the Security Council fully eliminated conceptual distance between the human suffering of Somali people and the threats to the peace. Under Resolution 794, the Council was:

> Recognizing the *unique* character of the present situation in Somalia and mindful of its deteriorating, complex and *extraordinary* nature, requiring an immediate and *exceptional* response,
>
> Determining that *the magnitude of the human tragedy caused by the conflict in Somalia*, further exacerbated by the obstacles being created to the distribution of humanitarian assistance, *constitutes a threat to international peace and security* ...[54]

In this preamble, the Security Council regarded, in a single paragraph, 'the magnitude of the human tragedy caused by the conflict in Somalia' as constituting a threat to international peace and security.[55] Under Resolution 794, the Security Council apparently tried to keep Somalia as an isolated instance of 'unique ... and extraordinary nature, requiring an ... exceptional response'.[56] Such an attempt was

50 UN Doc S/RES/733 (23 January 1992) paras 3–4 of the preamble (original emphasis omitted, current emphasis added).
51 Ibid., para 3 of the preamble.
52 Ibid., para 4 of the preamble.
53 UN Doc S/RES/794 (3 December 1992).
54 Ibid., paras 2–3 of the preamble (original emphasis omitted, current emphasis added).
55 Ibid., para 3 of the preamble.
56 Ibid., para 2 of the preamble.

short-lived, however;[57] under Resolution 841 on Haiti adopted in June 1993, the Security Council noted with concern 'the incidence of humanitarian crises, including mass displacements of population, becoming or aggravating threats to international peace and security'.[58] This resolution was followed in June 1994 by Resolution 929 on Rwanda, in which the Security Council considered 'the magnitude of the humanitarian crisis in Rwanda' as constituting a threat to peace and security in the region.[59] These examples were followed by other instances in which the Security Council found the deterioration of humanitarian situations as constituting the primary, if not exclusive, element that threatens international peace and security.[60]

The conceptual turn in the practice of the Security Council was combined with its general statement on the changing nature of threats to the peace. This came in the form of the Presidential Statement in January 1992 following the meeting of the heads of states and the highest-level officials after the end of the Cold War. In the Presidential statement, the Security Council expressed the view that:

> The absence of war and military conflicts amongst States does not in itself ensure international peace and security. The non-military sources of instability in the economic, social, humanitarian and ecological fields have become threats to peace and security. The United Nations membership as a whole, working through the appropriate bodies, needs to give the highest priority to the solution of these matters.[61]

In this statement, the Council recognised 'non-military' sources of instability as threats to peace and security. While the January 1992 statement pertained to a broad shift, what was represented by Resolution 794 on Somalia was a conceptual transformation that sought to focus on the human dimensions of conflicts. Such a change in perspective is formulated in a general manner by paragraph 5 of Resolution 1296 in April 2000 on the protection of civilians in armed conflict, in which the Security Council:

57 Some Security Council members stressed the unique character of Somalia: UN Doc S/PV.3145 (3 December 1992) 7 (Zimbabwe), 12–14 (Ecuador), 17 (China), 49 and 51 (India).

58 UN Doc S/RES/841 (16 June 1993) para 9 of the preamble; UN Doc S/25344 (26 February 1993).

59 UN Doc S/RES/929 (22 June 1994) para 10 of the preamble. Similarly, UN Doc S/RES/1203 (24 October 1998) para 11 of the preamble; UN Doc S/RES/1244 (10 June 1999) para 6 of the preamble (Kosovo).

60 See, e.g., UN Doc S/RES/1529 (29 February 2004) paras 2, 3, 9 of the preamble (Haiti). The threats to peace determination was presumably based on: the deterioration of the political, security, and humanitarian situation in Haiti, the continuing violence in Haiti, the potential for a rapid deterioration of the humanitarian situation in Haiti, and its destabilising effect on the region.

61 'Note by the President of the Security Council' (1992) UN Doc S/23500 (31 January 1992) 3.

> 5. Notes that the deliberate targeting of civilian populations or other protected persons and the committing of systematic, flagrant and widespread violations of international humanitarian and human rights law in situations of armed conflict may constitute a threat to international peace and security, and, in this regard, reaffirms its readiness to consider such situations and, where necessary, to adopt appropriate steps ...[62]

The Security Council here made an assertion that international peace and security might be threatened by the deliberate targeting of civilians and the systematic (and flagrant and widespread) violations of international humanitarian and human rights law in armed conflicts. Lloyd Axworthy, the Canadian delegate and Minister of Foreign Affairs who presided over the Security Council meeting, was particularly eager to stress the link between 'the security and basic rights of people' and world stability and peace.[63] The Canadian delegate observed that Resolution 1296 'entrenches the principle that, in the pursuit of peace, the security of people is at least as worthy a subject as the security of States'.[64] Although '[t]his does not mean that the State is obsolete',[65] there is a shift, according to the Canadian representative, in the perspective of the Security Council, where the security of people is not a by-product but a 'central tenet' of the Council's work.[66] In the earlier meeting of the Security Council, the French delegate also took the view that 'large-scale violations of human rights and international humanitarian law ... *in themselves*' would threaten international peace and security.[67]

The conceptual transformation of the threats has not been without resistance. This is precisely because the recognition of additional threats would mean the

62 UN Doc S/RES/1296 (19 April 2000) para 5 (on protection of civilians in armed conflicts) (original emphasis omitted). Reiterated in, e.g., UN Doc S/RES/1674 (28 April 2006) para 26; UN Doc S/RES/1738 (23 December 2006) para 9; UN Doc S/RES/1894 (11 November 2009) para 3. Similarly, UN Doc S/RES/1314 (11 August 2000) para 9 (on children in armed conflicts). In specific contexts, see UN Doc S/RES/808 (22 February 1993) para 6 of the preamble (ICTY); UN Doc S/RES/827 (25 May 1993) para 3 of the preamble (ICTY); UN Doc S/RES/955 (8 November 1994) para 4 of the preamble (ICTR).

63 UN Doc S/PV.4130 (19 April 2000) 27 (Mr. Axworthy of Canada).

64 Ibid., 26 (Mr. Axworthy of Canada).

65 Ibid.

66 Ibid. Similarly, UN Doc S/PV.3977 (12 February 1999) 31 (Mr. Axworthy of Canada) ('[p]romoting the protection of civilians in armed conflict is no sideshow to the Council's mandate for ensuring international peace and security; it is central to it. The ultimate aim of the Council's work is to safeguard the security of the world's people, not just the States in which they live').

67 UN Doc S/PV.4109 (9 March 2000) 7 (Mr. Dejammet of France) (a remark made in connection to the Kosovo intervention in 1999, arguing the case for military intervention) (emphasis added). Compare with the French proposal at the San Francisco Conference; see UNCIO Documents (n 9) vol. 6, at 498 (regarding domestic jurisdiction clause).

expansion of the scope of the Security Council's exercise of authority.[68] For instance, in relation to the January 1992 Presidential statement, Zimbabwe, while recognising that the Council would be increasingly called upon to deal with conflicts and humanitarian situations of a domestic nature, still expressed caution against the use of domestic conflicts 'as a pretext for the intervention of big Powers in the legitimate domestic affairs of small States'.[69] Also, in March 2000, Pakistan warned that a clear distinction must be made between, on the one hand, humanitarian crises 'as a result of wars, conflicts or disputes which by their very nature constitute threats to international peace and security', and, on the other hand, other human rights issues which are not within the purview of the Security Council.[70] In this statement, Pakistan appears to have conceptually narrowed down the threat to 'wars, conflicts or disputes' without treating humanitarian crises themselves as a threat to the peace.

Despite certain member states' caution, paragraph 5 of Resolution 1296 has been echoed by subsequent resolutions on the protection of civilians in armed conflict.[71] This is accompanied by conflict-specific resolutions which instigated Chapter VII measures with reference to the deliberate targeting of civilians and the systematic violations of international humanitarian and human rights law in armed conflicts. Examples include Resolution 1973 on Libya adopted in March 2011, in which the determination of a threat to international peace and security was guided by, among other things, heavy civilian casualties, the gross and systematic violation of human rights, and the widespread and systematic attacks against the civilian population.[72] A series of resolutions concerning the Democratic Republic of Congo were also led by the lengthy preamble containing the Security Council's concern over attacks on civilian populations and the violations of human rights and international humanitarian law.[73] Overall, paragraph 5 of

68 For the divergence of opinions among member states about the inclusion of human rights issues in the Security Council's agenda, see Michael J. Glennon, *Limits of Law, Prerogatives of Power: Interventionism After Kosovo* (New York, Palgrave, 2001) 133.

69 UN Doc S/PV.3046 (31 January 1992) 131 (Mr. Shamuyarira of Zimbabwe).

70 UN Doc S/PV.4109 (Resumption 1) (9 March 2000) 9 (Mr. Ahmad of Pakistan).

71 See (n 62) above. Resolution 1296 is part of the thematic resolutions on the protection of civilians in armed conflict. For an empirical study of thematic resolutions, see Rossana Deplano, *The Strategic Use of International Law by the United Nations Security Council: An Empirical Study* (Springer, 2015) 33–50.

72 UN Doc S/RES/1973 (17 March 2011) paras 3, 5, 7 of the preamble. In a similar vein, e.g., UN Doc S/RES/1468 (20 March 2003) para 2 (condemning the massacres and other systematic violations of international humanitarian law and human rights in the Democratic Republic of the Congo).

73 E.g., UN Doc S/RES/2053 (27 June 2012) para 10 of the preamble (referring to the persistent high levels of violence and human rights abuses and violations against civilians); UN Doc S/RES/2147 (28 March 2014) para 18 of the preamble (referring to the high levels of violence and violations and abuses of human rights, and the targeted attacks against civilians). Likewise, regarding the situation in Sudan, e.g., UN Doc S/RES/2003 (29 July 2011) para 15 of the preamble (condemning all violations of international human rights and humanitarian law in Darfur).

Resolution 1296, accompanied by subsequent resolutions that reiterated or applied its content, represents a fundamental shift in the concept of a threat to the peace as a trigger for Chapter VII measures. As symbolically represented by Resolution 794 on Somalia, the threat to the peace is conceptualised not at the level of cross-border crises but at the level of the magnitude of the human tragedy caused by conflicts.

3.3.4 Background to the conceptual transformation

As illustrated by a series of resolutions adopted since the early 1990s, the UN Security Council has incrementally regarded humanitarian crises, the violations of human rights and humanitarian law, and the attacks on civilian populations as intrinsic, as opposed to extrinsic, variables for a threat to international peace and security. This shift – from inter-state crises to the human dimensions of conflicts – also allows us to understand the Security Council's recognition of terrorism[74] and the proliferation of weapons of mass destruction[75] as a trigger for Chapter VII measures. The greater attention to the human dimensions of conflicts inevitably reveals the role of individuals not only as civilians or the victims of violence but also as perpetrators whose conduct may eventually threaten international peace and security. In this regard, one must remember that, under Security Council resolutions, 'terrorism' in general – and not only 'international' terrorism[76] – is regarded as a threat to international peace and security.[77]

74 In the aftermath of the 9/11 attacks in New York, the Security Council adopted Resolution 1368, in which it regarded such attacks, 'like any act of international terrorism', as a threat to international peace and security: UN Doc S/RES/1368 (12 September 2001) para 1. Reaffirmed, for instance, by: UN Doc S/RES/1373 (28 September 2001) para 3 of the preamble. In a number of other resolutions, the Council reaffirmed that terrorism constituted a threat to international peace and security: e.g., UN Doc S/RES/1636 (31 October 2005) paras 3, 19 of the preamble (terrorist bombing in Beirut).

75 The Presidential Statement in January 1992 recognised that '[t]he proliferation of all weapons of mass destruction constitutes a threat to international peace and security': 'Note by the President of the Security Council' (n 61) 4. Resolution 1540 also added the proliferation of the 'means of delivery' to the threat: UN Doc S/RES/1540 (28 April 2004) para 1 of the preamble. Many states have expressed support for such a conceptual enlargement, including, albeit with some reservations, the Non-Aligned Movement (NAM): e.g., UN Doc S/PV.4950 (Resumption 1) (22 April 2004) 3–4 (Mr. Rastam of Malaysia, on behalf on NAM). Cf. UN Doc S/PV.4950 (22 April 2004) 15 (Pakistan).

76 E.g., UN Doc S/RES/1368 (12 September 2001) para 1 ('any act of *international* terrorism, as a threat to international peace and security') (emphasis added).

77 E.g., UN Docs S/RES/1617 (2005) para 4 of the preamble ('threats to *international* peace and security caused by terrorist acts') (emphasis added); S/RES/1735 (22 December 2006) para 4 of the preamble ('threats to *international* peace and security caused by terrorist acts') (emphasis added); S/RES/2253 (17 December 2015) para 3 of the preamble ('terrorism poses a threat to *international* peace and security') (emphasis added). Cf. UN Docs S/RES/1456 (20 January 2003) annex ('terrorism … threats to peace and security'); S/RES/1535 (26 March 2004) para 2 of the

The conceptual enlargement or transformation can be ascribed to a number of political, sociological, and normative factors. While this book does not intend to provide detailed accounts on the background of the conceptual shift, a commonly held idea that the end of the Cold War led to the outbreak of civil wars does not hold water. According to one survey, while the number of internal conflicts has steadily increased from 1950 onward, the number decreased in the 1990s, contrary to the popular belief.[78] Thus, the treatment of non-inter-state elements as intrinsic elements of the threats cannot be accounted for by the occurrence of civil wars.

Instead, political, sociological, and normative factors provide us with better explanations for the transformation of what constitutes a threat to the peace. First, on the political front, one of the crucial inputs was provided through the political campaign in the 1960s and 1970s of Asian and African states that advocated the inclusion of human rights agendas into the matter of international peace and security. Confronted with the Rhodesian and South African questions, newly independent Asian and African states demanded that human rights agendas be treated as matters of international peace and security.[79] These states' political campaigns to uphold self-determination and fundamental rights led the UN General Assembly to predetermine the 'threats' even before the Security Council did. In November 1965, the General Assembly's resolution drew the Council's attention to the situation in Southern Rhodesia which, according to the General Assembly, 'threatens international peace and security'.[80] Likewise, in December 1965, the General Assembly, following its Special Committee's determination,[81] drew the Security Council's attention to the situation in South Africa which 'constitutes a threat to international peace and security'.[82]

preamble ('terrorism ... threats to peace and security'); S/RES/1787 (10 December 2007) para 2 of the preamble ('terrorism ... threats to peace and security').

78 Lotta Harbom and Peter Wallensteen, 'Armed Conflict, 1989–2006' (2007) 44 *Journal of Peace Research* 623, 624 (Table II).

79 See Nigel D. White, *Keeping the Peace: The United Nations and the Maintenance of International Peace and Security* (2nd edn, Manchester; New York, Manchester University Press, 1997) 164–9; Sydney D. Bailey, *The UN Security Council and Human Rights* (New York, St. Martin's Press, 1994) 3–15.

80 UN Doc A/RES/2022 (XX) (5 November 1965) para 13. Subsequently, the Security Council determined the existence of the threats: UN Doc S/RES/217 (20 November 1965) para 1; UN Doc S/RES/232 (16 December 1966) (16 December 1966) para 1. See White, *Keeping the Peace* (n 79) 164–9.

81 E.g., 'Second Interim Report of the Special Committee on the Politics of Apartheid of the Government of the Republic of South Africa' (1963) UN Doc S/5353 (17 July 1963) paras 4, 22; 'Report of the Special Committee on the Policies of Apartheid of the Government of the Republic of South Africa' (1963) UN Doc S/5426-A/5497 (16 September 1963) para 459.

82 UN Doc A/RES/2054 (XX)(A) (15 December 1965) (1965) para 6. Cf. UN Doc A/RES/1761(XVII) (6 November 1962) para 3 ('seriously endangers international peace and security'). See also the request of 13 Asian-African states for the inclusion of the South African question on the General Assembly's agenda: UN Doc A/2183 (12 September 1952) (12 September 1952) ('The race conflict in the Union of South

Second, the conceptual shift we can observe from the resolutions of the UN Security Council is apparently part of a wide range of sociological transitions that occurred since the creation of the UN. A comparison between international attention given to the genocide in Rwanda in the 1960s and that of 1994 may summarise some of the changes that the world has experienced. In the 1960s, despite the scale of violence described as 'the most horrible and systematic massacre' since the Holocaust,[83] international attention was scarce given that little information became available about the massacre of Tutsis in Rwanda. By contrast, the Rwandan genocide in 1994 provoked an outcry from the media and humanitarian communities around the globe, in the course of which the UN and particularly its peace and security arm encountered a storm of criticism for its failure to prevent and stop the human tragedy. Globalisation, in which people, goods, money, and information quickly move across international borders, inevitably helped increase people's awareness of the magnitude of human tragedies occurring even on the other side of the planet, despite the selectivity of information in the mass media. People's greater awareness mobilises money, expertise, and advocacy campaigns, which may put their governments in a position to be in favour of Chapter VII measures in response to some of the reported human tragedies in the world.

Finally, the UN Security Council's interpretation of a threat to the peace should be understood as part of wider norms and ideas which construct how UN organs exercise their authority. Human rights are apparently embedded in the discourse of the UN which has been a vital player in international human rights law ever since the General Assembly's adoption of the Universal Declaration of Human Rights.[84] In addition to their engagement in the development of international human rights law, UN organs have played an active role in developing and disseminating new, normative perspectives which have, in turn, brought changes to the way in which the UN itself performs its mandates.[85] The concepts of 'human security' and 'responsibility to protect' may be two prominent examples in this regard.

Several years after the concept of human security was put forward by the United Nations Development Programme's (UNDP) report in 1994,[86] the UN established the Commission on Human Security which rephrased human security as the

Africa resulting from the policies of apartheid of the South African Government is creating a dangerous and explosive situation, which constitutes both a threat to international peace and a flagrant violation of the basic principles of human rights and fundamental freedoms').

83 An account by Bertrand Russell, *Le Monde* (6 February 1964).

84 Louis B. Sohn, 'The Human Rights Law of the Charter' (1977) 12 *Texas International Law Journal* 129; 'Universal Declaration of Human Rights' UN GA Res. 217A (III) (10 December 1948).

85 See Michael Barnett and Martha Finnemore, 'Political Approaches' in T.G. Weiss and S. Daws (eds), *The Oxford Handbook on the United Nations* (Oxford, Oxford University Press, 2007) 41, 48–50; Richard Jolly, Louis Emmerij and Thomas George Weiss, *UN Ideas That Changed the World* (Bloomington, Indiana University Press, 2009) 163–85.

86 UNDP, *Human Development Report 1994* (New York, Oxford University Press for UNDP, 1994) chap. 2.

protection of 'the vital core of all human lives' in ways that enhance human freedoms and human fulfilment including freedom from want and freedom from fear.[87] The concept of human security was included in the General Assembly's World Summit Outcome in 2005.[88] While the Security Council has not explicitly adopted the concept in its resolutions, the combination of the concept of 'security' with human freedoms has had an impact on the deliberation of security, including international security within the UN.

After the UN and member states' unwillingness to swiftly act on humanitarian crises was painstakingly revealed by the genocide in Rwanda in 1993, the massacre in Srebrenica in 1995, and the unilateral intervention in Kosovo by the North Atlantic Treaty Organization (NATO) in 1999, the International Commission on Intervention and State Sovereignty (ICISS) put forward a more proactive concept of the responsibility to protect, also known as 'R2P'.[89] The concept quickly garnered support within the UN, in part because the concept provided the UN organs with a much-needed and coherent framework for their exercise of authority to protect people's lives and maintain order within a particular state.[90] The concept was included in the General Assembly's World Summit Outcome in 2005 as follows:

> Responsibility to protect populations from genocide, war crimes, ethnic cleansing and crimes against humanity
>
> 138. Each individual State has the responsibility to protect its populations from genocide, war crimes, ethnic cleansing and crimes against humanity …
>
> 139. The international community, through the United Nations, also has the responsibility to use appropriate diplomatic, humanitarian and other peaceful means, in accordance with Chapters VI and VIII of the Charter, to help to protect populations from genocide, war crimes, ethnic cleansing and crimes against humanity. In this context, we are prepared to take *collective action*, in a timely and decisive manner, *through the Security Council*, in

87 Commission on Human Security, *Human Security Now* (New York, Commission on Human Security, 2003) 4, 10. See also Fen O. Hampson and Christopher K. Penny, 'Human Security' in T.G. Weiss and S. Daws (eds), *The Oxford Handbook on the United Nations* (Oxford, Oxford University Press, 2007) 539 (explaining the UN's involvement in these three elements of human security).

88 '2005 World Summit Outcome' UN Doc A/RES/60/1 (24 October 2005) para 143.

89 International Commission on Intervention and State Sovereignty, *The Responsibility to Protect: Report of the International Commission on Intervention and State Sovereignty* (Ottawa, International Development Research Centre, 2001).

90 Anne Orford, *International Authority and the Responsibility to Protect* (Cambridge, Cambridge University Press, 2011) especially 1–10, 25–6, 165, 205–7. The concept was invoked, albeit not in a uniform manner, in the Report of the High-Level Panel in 2004 as well as in the Secretary-General's report in 2005: Report of the High-Level Panel on Threats, Challenges and Change, 'A More Secure World: Our Shared Responsibility' (2004) UN Doc A/59/565 (2 December 2004); Report of the Secretary-General, 'In Larger Freedom: Towards Development, Security and Human Rights for All' (2005) UN Doc A/59/2005 (21 March 2005).

> accordance with the Charter, including Chapter VII, on a case-by-case basis and in cooperation with relevant regional organizations as appropriate, ***should peaceful means be inadequate and national authorities are manifestly failing to protect their populations from genocide, war crimes, ethnic cleansing and crimes against humanity.***[91]

As contrasted with the ICISS's report in 2001,[92] the World Summit Outcome narrowed down the application of the concept to four international crimes. Paragraph 139 of the World Summit Outcome has, however, particular bearing on the UN Security Council, which is characterised as the focal point through which the international community takes peaceful and coercive measures to protect populations from genocide, war crimes, ethnic cleansing, and crimes against humanity. While the Security Council itself reaffirmed paragraphs 138 and 139 of the World Summit Outcome,[93] the Council has subsequently invoked the 'responsibility to protect' in a cautious manner. Under Council resolutions, the concept of the 'responsibility to protect' is directed not at the Council itself but rather at ***national authorities*** which bear the primary responsibility to protect civilians.[94] This does not mean that the idea of the responsibility to protect has little effect on the Security Council's exercise of authority. On the contrary, the concept of the 'responsibility to protect' has empowered member states, the UN Secretariat, the media, human rights organisations, and individuals in scrutinising and commenting on the exercise of authority by the Security Council in the protection of civilian population.

On balance, these political, sociological, and normative factors sustained the legitimacy of the fundamental shift in perspective in determining the existence of the threats to the peace and thus opening the possibility for enforcement measures under Chapter VII. The UN's vital role in the promotion of international human rights law, and the concepts of human security and the responsibility to protect, have incrementally helped to shape the interests, mind-set, and languages of those

91 '2005 World Summit Outcome' (n 88) paras 138–9 (emphasis added).

92 International Commission on Intervention and State Sovereignty, ***Responsibility to Protect*** (n 89).

93 UN Doc S/RES/1674 (28 April 2006) (n 62) para 4. The resolution provides: '*Reaffirms* the provisions of paragraphs 138 and 139 of the 2005 World Summit Outcome Document regarding the responsibility to protect populations from genocide, war crimes, ethnic cleansing and crimes against humanity': ibid.

94 E.g., on Libya, UN Doc S/RES/1973 (17 March 2011) (n 72) para 4 of the preamble (reiterating the responsibility of the Libyan authorities to protect the Libyan population and the primary responsibility of parties to armed conflicts to ensure the protection of civilians); Nigel D. White, 'Libya and Lessons from Iraq: International Law and the Use of Force by the United Kingdom' in I.F. Dekker and E. Hey (eds), *Netherlands Yearbook of International Law 2011* (T. M. C. Asser Press, 2012) 215, 220–1. Similarly, e.g., UN Doc S/RES/2093 (6 March 2013) para 12 of the preamble (recognising the responsibility of the Federal Government of Somalia); UN Doc S/RES/2139 (22 February 2014) para 9 (stressing the primary responsibility of the Syrian authorities).

diplomats and staff working within the UN in such a way that the UN Security Council can, and indeed should, be guided by the protection of the rights and interest of individuals in exercising its authority to maintain international peace and security.

3.4 Conclusion: Conceptual distance between the Security Council's exercise of authority and domestic actors

The conceptual transformation of 'international peace and security' and 'threats to the peace' has significantly reduced the conceptual distance between individuals and the Security Council's exercise of authority. The Security Council's greater emphasis on the protection of individuals and their rights has also enabled it to exercise its authority in such a way that its international institutional decisions have immediate relevance to individuals. In essence, individuals and other non-state actors have a dual role in relation to the Security Council's mandate. On the one hand, individuals are foremost part of civilian population in armed conflict and possibly the victims of the systematic violations of international humanitarian and human rights law. According to Resolution 1296, the deliberate targeting of civilian populations may threaten international peace and security and trigger Chapter VII measures. Under Resolution 794 on Somalia, individuals were at the centre of the 'human tragedy' which constituted the threat to the peace. As the World Summit Outcome enunciated, populations are the very objects for whom the UN Security Council is expected to take action. The trend is that the Security Council has been placing a greater emphasis on the 'protection of *individuals* and their rights'.[95]

At the same time, individuals could likewise be those who, in the eyes of the Security Council, threaten international peace and security. In a remote sense, individuals can be part of non-state armed groups or terrorist networks whose conduct, as a group, constitutes a threat to the peace.[96] It is, however, not only armed groups as a whole but also *individuals* – or even an individual – who may pose a threat to international peace and security. One extraordinary instance was Resolution 1638 on Liberia adopted in November 2005; under the resolution, the Security Council determined that former President Charles Taylor's return to Liberia – thus, the conduct of one individual who was supposedly no longer in office – would constitute a threat to the peace of Liberia and to international peace and security in the region.[97] Similarly, in Security Council Resolution 1688,

95 Krisch, 'Article 39' (n 4) 1279 (emphasis original).

96 For example, in Resolution 1521 on Liberia, the Security Council determined that 'the situation in Liberia and the proliferation of arms and armed non-State actors, including mercenaries, in the subregion continue to constitute a threat to international peace and security in West Africa': UN Doc S/RES/1521 (22 December 2003) para 8 of the preamble.

97 UN Doc S/RES/1638 (11 November 2005) para 4 of the preamble. The Security Council used the term '*would* constitute' as the former President's return had yet to take place at the time of adoption.

regarding the Special Court for Sierra Leone, the Council determined that 'the continued presence of former President Taylor' in the subregion constituted a threat to international peace and security in the region.[98]

While this was a historical anomaly involving a former head of state, some other categories of individuals appear as an element of threats to international peace and security. Within the context of counter-terrorism resolution, the Security Council regarded not only terrorist organisations or other non-state armed groups but also *individuals* as threats to international peace and security. For instance, Security Council Resolution 1735, one of the resolutions adopted for the 1267 sanctions regime, stressed the importance of meeting the threat that '*individuals*, groups, undertakings and entities' associated with Al-Qaida, Usama bin Laden and the Taliban represent to 'international peace and security'.[99] Resolution 2170 also noted the 'continued threat posed to international peace and security by ISIL [Islamic State in Iraq and the Levant] ... and all other *individuals*, groups, undertakings and entities associated with Al-Qaida'.[100] In these resolutions, individuals are understood not merely as the specific targets of asset freeze measures but also as part of the overall elements which justify the strategic decision of the UN Security Council to adopt enforcement measures under Chapter VII.

All in all, individuals are no longer the abstract and consequential recipients of some of the benefits of the maintenance of international peace and security. The political and normative environment in which the UN Security Council exercises its authority necessitated and justified the fundamental shift in the concept of international peace and security. Within the concepts of threats to the peace, individuals occupy much more visible presence as those suffering from human tragedy, civilian populations, and the victims of systematic violations of human rights. Individuals are also situated as terrorists and those who partake in the proliferation of the weapons of mass destruction under Security Council resolutions. Individuals are thus deeply internalised in the Security Council's Chapter VII resolutions whose level of success, in turn, depends on the acts of those individuals.

98 UN Doc S/RES/1688 (16 June 2006) para 14 of the preamble. ('*Noting* that former President Taylor has been brought before the Special Court at its seat in Freetown and determining that the continued presence of former President Taylor in the subregion is an impediment to stability and a threat to the peace of Liberia and of Sierra Leone and to international peace and security in the region').

99 UN Doc S/RES/1735 (22 December 2006) para 15 of the preamble (emphasis added). On the sanctions regime based initially on Resolution 1267, see section 4.3 of this book.

100 UN Doc S/RES/2170 (15 August 2014) para 18 of the preamble (emphasis added). Likewise, UN Doc S/RES/2199 (12 February 2015) para 22 of the preamble; UN Doc S/RES/2214 (27 March 2015) para 16 of the preamble.

4 Distance in the Security Council's Chapter VII measures

4.1 Introduction

By accommodating a number of non-inter-state situations in the concept of a threat to international peace and security, the UN Security Council has incrementally reduced the conceptual distance between its mandate and those individuals whose plight could trigger Chapter VII measures.[1] The determination of the existence of threats under Article 39 of the UN Charter then paves the way for more substantial measures under Chapter VII, including non-military and military enforcement measures in accordance with Articles 41 and 42 of the UN Charter.

In determining what measures shall be taken under Chapter VII of the UN Charter, the Security Council engages in essentially three levels of decision making. In the first place, the Security Council chooses any steps *short of* enforcement measures it wishes to take. One typical example is a ceasefire call or demand. For example, under Resolution 1973 on Libya adopted in March 2011, the Security Council, having determined a threat to international peace and security, 'demand[ed]' a ceasefire and a complete end to all attacks against civilians.[2] On top of the ceasefire calls and demands, second, the Security Council determines whether enforcement measures ought to be taken, what types of enforcement measures should be applied, and precisely against whom those measures should be applied. For instance, Resolution 1973 on Libya authorised member states to take military action in order to protect civilians under threat of attack in Libya and to enforce compliance with a no-fly zone in Libya.[3] Finally, the Security Council sets out the modality through which enforcement measures are implemented. In the case of Resolution 1973 on Libya, the Security Council allowed member states to use force virtually without any institutionalised control at the UN level apart from member states' reporting requirements.[4]

1 See chapter 3 of this book.
2 UN Doc S/RES/1973 (17 March 2011) paras 21–2 of the preamble and para 1.
3 Ibid., paras 4, 8.
4 Ibid; Nigel D. White, 'Libya and Lessons from Iraq: International Law and the Use of Force by the United Kingdom' in I.F. Dekker and E. Hey (eds), *Netherlands Yearbook of International Law 2011* (T. M. C. Asser Press, 2012) 215, 220 (observing that the absence of any control at the UN level is both alarming and unsurprising).

What matters for the purpose of this book is that the Security Council and its subsidiary organs became involved, over the years, in these three levels of decision making in such a manner that restricts member states' discretion over individuals. This may be counterintuitive when one considers the example of Resolution 1973 on Libya, under which NATO and its coalition members were given almost a free hand in operationalising all necessary measures to protect civilians. Yet in many other areas of the Security Council's action under Chapter VII, the Security Council and its subsidiary organs have been exercising their authority *over individuals* by *restricting the intermediary presence of member states* over individuals.

Such a trend is illustrated by the following three groups of practices – which also correspond to the aforementioned three levels of decision making – which are examined in this chapter and the rest of this book.[5] To begin with, the Security Council has issued 'orders' and 'demands' under Chapter VII of the UN Charter not only against member states and non-state armed groups but also against *individuals* (section 4.2). Second, the UN Security Council and its sanctions committees have directly designated specific individuals and entities as the targets of sanctions regimes themselves and the targets of asset freezes and travel bans (section 4.3). In addition, the Security Council, through its subsidiary organs, directly executes their decisions vis-à-vis individuals and entities (section 4.4). In these practices, the *distance* between the UN Security Council's exercise of authority and individuals is significantly reduced not only in conceptual terms, as discussed earlier in chapter 3 of this book, but also within substantial measures taken under Chapter VII by the guardian of international peace and security.

4.2 Addressing individuals

In its increasingly lengthy and complex resolutions, the Security Council addresses a wide variety of actors beyond the circle of UN member states. The obligatory term 'decide' is basically reserved for addressing states as well as the Security Council and its subsidiary organs.[6] Yet other verbs – such as 'demand', 'order', 'call upon', 'require', 'call for', 'direct', 'request', 'encourage', 'urge', and 'invite' – have been convenient vehicles for conveying the Security Council's messages to various sectors of the international community. While the terms of a resolution ought to be interpreted on a case-by-case basis by taking into account all circumstances,[7] to combine the term 'demand' with reference to Chapter VII signals the Security Council's intention to *oblige* an addressee.[8] The noteworthy

5 These three groups of practice are indicated in Figure 1 of this book.

6 Except for certain occasions: see (n 34) and accompanying text.

7 *Legal Consequences for States of the Continued Presence of South Africa in Namibia (South West Africa) notwithstanding Security Council Resolution 276 (1970)* [1971] ICJ Reports 16 (Advisory Opinion of 21 June 1971) 53, para 114.

8 See Nico Krisch, 'Introduction to Chapter VII: The General Framework' in B. Simma and others (eds), *The Charter of the United Nations: A Commentary* (3rd edn, 2012) 1237, 1265.

aspect of the Council's practice is that the Security Council's obligatory messages have been directly addressed to *individuals*.

4.2.1 Non-state actors other than individuals

Individuals can be seen as part of a broader category of actors *other than* UN member states. In this sense, it is perhaps not surprising that individuals joined the addresses of Security Council resolutions. The Security Council regularly issues its calls, requests, etc., toward: the Secretary-General, the Secretary-General's envoys, the Secretariat, other principal organs of the UN, the UN's funds and programmes, regional organisations, inter-governmental forums, international courts, and, in an inclusive manner, the 'international community' as a whole.[9] Apart from the actors of essentially international nature, the UN Security Council has also been directly addressing non-state armed groups. While the primary focus of this book is on the Security Council's exercise of authority over individuals, it is necessary to discuss the Security Council's reference to non-state armed groups as a background for the organ's connection to individuals.

4.2.1.1 The calls for ceasefire and compliance

One of the earliest precedents in which the Security Council referred to non-state armed groups was in April 1948 in the context of the Palestinian conflict.[10] Confronted with the escalating violence in Palestine, the Security Council called upon 'Arab and Jewish armed groups in Palestine' to cease acts of violence immediately under Resolution 43.[11] The Security Council also called upon 'all persons and organizations in Palestine, and especially upon the Arab Higher Committee and the Jewish Agency' to cease acts of violence under Resolution 46[12] before making the determination of threats to the peace under Resolution 54.[13] Formally

9 There are a number of examples. For illustration, (i) under Resolution 2253 on the Islamic State, the Security Council requested that the Secretary-General and the Secretariat provide additional resources and publish information, encouraged relevant UN missions to provide assistance, and also encouraged the Financial Action Task Force to continue its efforts to prioritise counter-terrorism financing: UN Doc S/RES/2253 (17 December 2015) paras 18, 48, 52, 92. (ii) Resolution 1593 on the referral of the situation in Darfur to the International Criminal Court invited the Court and the African Union to discuss arrangements to facilitate the work of the Court: UN Doc S/RES/1593 (31 March 2005) para 3. (iii) Resolution 1674 on the protection of civilians urged the 'international community' to provide support and assistance to states: UN Doc S/RES/1674 (28 April 2006) para 13.

10 Pieter H. Kooijmans, 'The Security Council and Non-State Entities as Parties to Conflicts' in K. Wellens (ed.), *International Law: Theory and Practice, Essays in Honour of Eric Suy* (The Hague, Martinus Nijhoff Publishers, 1998) 333, 334.

11 UN Doc S/RES/43 (1 April 1948) para 3.

12 UN Doc S/RES/46 (17 April 1948) para 1. After Israel proclaimed independence on 14 May 1948, Security Council resolutions refer to 'all Governments and authorities': UN Doc S/RES/49 (22 May 1948) para 1.

13 UN Doc S/RES/54 (15 July 1948) para 1.

speaking, the addressees of these 'calls' involved non-state groups, given that these resolutions were adopted before the Provisional Government of Israel proclaimed independence on 14 May 1948.

During the 1990s, as the response to civil wars started to predominate the UN's activities in the field of peace and security, it became commonplace for the Security Council to issue ceasefire calls toward all warring factions, including non-state groups, before invoking Chapter VII. For instance, in relation to the Somali civil war, the Security Council called on 'all parties, movements and factions in Somalia' to cease hostilities.[14] Similar ceasefire calls were addressed to 'all factions in Liberia',[15] the 'RUF [Revolutionary United Front of Sierra Leone] and all other armed groups in Sierra Leone',[16] and 'rebel movements' in the Democratic Republic of the Congo.[17] The Council also 'demanded' ceasefire to all parties and factions in, to name a few, Angola, Rwanda, Burundi, and Afghanistan during the 1990s.[18]

These ceasefire calls and demands are combined with the Security Council's call and demand for the observance of not only international humanitarian law[19] but also 'applicable' human rights law. In Resolution 1265 in September 1999, the first thematic resolution on the protection of civilians, the Security Council urged all parties to armed conflicts to comply strictly with their obligations under international humanitarian, human rights, and refugee law.[20] The Security Council

14 UN Doc S/RES/751 (24 April 1992) para 9; UN Doc S/RES/767 (1992) para 4; UN Doc S/RES/775 (1992) para 5 ('all parties, movements and factions in Somalia'). Similarly, UN Doc S/RES/733 (23 January 1992) para 4 ('all parties to the conflict'); UN Doc S/RES/746 (1992) para 2 ('the Somali factions').

15 UN Doc S/RES/950 (21 October 1994) para 4 (calling on 'all factions in Liberia to cease hostilities').

16 UN Doc S/RES/1260 (20 August 1999) para 8 (calling upon 'the RUF and all other armed groups in Sierra Leone to begin immediately to disband and give up their arms'). Similarly, UN Doc S/RES/1270 (22 October 1999) para 4 (calling upon 'the RUF, the Civil Defence Forces, former Sierra Leone Armed Forces/Armed Forces Revolutionary Council (AFRC) and all other armed groups in Sierra Leone to begin immediately to disband and give up their arms').

17 UN Doc S/RES/1258 (6 August 1999) para 4 (calling upon 'all parties to the conflict, in particular the rebel movements, to cease hostilities').

18 (i) Angola: e.g., UN Doc S/RES/851 (15 July 1993) para 5 (demanding that 'UNITA immediately cease military actions)'. (ii) Rwanda: e.g., UN Doc S/RES/918 (17 May 1994) para 1 (demanding that 'all parties to the conflict immediately cease hostilities'). (iii) Burundi: e.g., UN Doc S/RES/1072 (30 August 1996) para 4 (demanding that 'all sides in Burundi declare a unilateral cessation of hostilities'). (iv) Afghanistan: e.g., UN Doc S/RES/1193 (28 August 1998) para 2 (demanding that 'all Afghan factions stop fighting'); UN Doc S/RES/1214 (8 December 1998) para 1 (demanding that 'the Taliban, as well as other Afghan factions, stop fighting').

19 E.g., UN Doc S/RES/950 (21 October 1994) (n 15) para 7 (demanding that 'all the factions strictly abide by applicable rules of international humanitarian law').

20 UN Doc S/RES/1265 (17 September 1999) para 4. This resolution followed the Council's open debate and the UN Secretary-General's report, which highlighted the importance of the adherence by non-state actors to these bodies of law. In February 1999, during the Council's open debate on the protection of civilians, delegates and

repeatedly requested that all parties comply with these fields of law,[21] particularly international humanitarian law.[22]

4.2.1.2 Chapter VII demands

On top of these calls and demands, the Security Council frequently directs demand towards non-state armed groups when it is acting under Chapter VII. During the Cold War, the Security Council still hesitated to directly address actors if their statehood was uncertain under international law. This hesitation can be seen in a series of resolutions adopted in the 1960s and 1970s on Southern Rhodesia. The Security Council, while condemning the minority regime in Southern Rhodesia and denying the legal validity of its declaration of independence,[23] did not direct its calls and requests toward the minority regime itself,[24] presumably out of deference to the UK, which had still asserted sovereignty over the territory.

Such hesitation yet incrementally disappeared in the practice of the Security Council. Since the 1990s, the Council has regularly generated demand under Chapter VII toward parties including non-state armed groups. For instance, Resolution 942 in September 1994 on the Bosnian war demanded under Chapter VII that 'the Bosnian Serb party' – whose statehood was contested[25] – accept a

participants have referred to the growing impact of non-state actors on conflicts, and the need to ensure the compliance of international humanitarian and human rights law by such actors: UN Doc S/PV.3977 (12 February 1999) (on the protection of civilians in armed conflict). In September 1999, the Secretary-General's report recommended that the Security Council call on 'Member States and *non-state actors*' to adhere to international humanitarian, human rights, and refugee law: 'Report of the Secretary-General to the Security Council on the Protection of Civilians in Armed Conflict' (1999) UN Doc S/1999/957 (8 September 1999) para 36 (recommendation 2) (emphasis added).

21 E.g., UN Doc S/RES/1894 (11 November 2009) para 1 (demanding that 'parties to armed conflict comply strictly with the obligations applicable to them under international humanitarian, human rights, and refugee law').

22 E.g., UN Doc S/RES/2175 (29 August 2014) para 1.

23 UN Doc S/RES/217 (20 November 1965) para 3.

24 UN Doc S/RES/232 (16 December 1966) (16 December 1966); UN Doc S/RES/277 (18 March 1970); UN Doc S/RES/409 (27 May 1977). It was only after the Lancaster House agreement was concluded in 1979 that the Council called upon 'all parties' to comply with the agreement: see Kooijmans, 'The Security Council and Non-State Entities as Parties to Conflicts' (n 10) 334.

25 The Republic of the Serb People of Bosnia and Herzegovina, later to be called the Republika Srpska, declared independence in January 1992. While the regime did not receive international recognition as a sovereign state, the regime enjoyed '*de facto* control of substantial territory, and the loyalty of large numbers of Bosnian Serbs', as the ICJ noted in the *Bosnian Genocide* case (2007): *Application of the Convention on the Prevention and Punishment of the Crime of Genocide (Bosnia and Herzegovina v Serbia and Montenegro)* [2007] ICJ Reports 43 (Merits, Judgment of 26 February 2007), para 235. Yet the fact that the Republika Srpska effectively controlled the defined territory would be insufficient to establish statehood under international law. In the case of the Republika Srpska, the regime was not entitled to secede from Bosnia and Herzegovina, as it was not considered to enjoy a right to external self-

proposed territorial settlement.[26] Other examples include Resolution 814 on the Somali civil strife, in which the Council demanded under Chapter VII that all Somali parties and factions comply with their ceasefire agreements.[27] A similar Chapter VII demand was made, for instance, under Resolution 1545 in the context of the Burundi civil war,[28] and Resolution 2206 on South Sudan demanding the parties to respect the ceasefire agreements.[29]

Not only 'all parties' but also specific non-state armed groups were addressed by the Security Council's resolutions under Chapter VII. For instance, Resolution 1199 on Kosovo in September 1998 demanded under Chapter VII that 'the Kosovo Albanian leadership' take immediate steps to improve the humanitarian situation and to avert the impending humanitarian catastrophe.[30] Likewise, under paragraph 15 of Resolution 1244 adopted in June 1999, the Security Council demanded under Chapter VII that 'the KLA [Kosovo Liberation Army] and other armed Kosovo Albanian groups' end immediately all offensive actions and comply with the requirements for demilitarisation.[31] The specification of non-state addressees was also seen, for instance, in a series of resolutions concerning the Democratic Republic of Congo[32] or Resolution 2216 on Yemen which directed demand toward the Houthis under Chapter VII.[33]

To summarise, on a number of occasions, the Security Council situated non-state armed groups as addressees of Chapter VII demands, presumably with the intention to oblige them to act in a certain manner, such as in the cessation of hostilities and the compliance with applicable rules of international law. In a rare instance, the Security Council may have also invoked the term 'decide' when addressing parties involving non-state armed groups. Under Resolution 771 adopted in August 1992 in the middle of Bosnian wars, the Security Council decided, under Chapter VII, that 'all parties and others concerned in the former

determination. The Arbitration Commission created by the EU (then EC) denied external self-determination of the Serbian population in Croatia and Bosnia-Herzegovina: James R. Crawford, *The Creation of States in International Law* (2nd edn, Oxford, Oxford University Press, 2007) 406–7.

26 UN Doc S/RES/942 (23 September 1994) para 3.

27 UN Doc S/RES/814 (26 March 1993) para 8.

28 UN Doc S/RES/1545 (21 May 2004) para 15 (demanding, under Chapter VII, all parties to fulfil their obligations under the Arusha Agreement).

29 UN Doc S/RES/2206 (3 March 2015) para 3 (demanding, under Article 41 of Chapter VII, the parties to respect all aspects of the Cessation of Hostilities Agreement).

30 UN Doc S/RES/1199 (23 September 1998) para 2.

31 UN Doc S/RES/1244 (10 June 1999) para 15.

32 For instance, Resolution 1355 demanded, under Chapter VII, that armed groups act according to a ceasefire agreement, and made explicit reference to Front de Libération du Congo (FLC) and Rassemblement Congolais pour la Démocratie (RCD): UN Doc S/RES/1355 (15 June 2001) paras 2, 5, 6. Likewise, Resolution 2277 demanded the Democratic Forces for the Liberation of Rwanda (FDLR), the Allied Democratic Forces (ADF), and the Lord's Resistance Army (LRA) cease all forms of violence: UN Doc S/RES/2277 (30 March 2016) para 17.

33 UN Doc S/RES/2216 (14 April 2015) (n 29) para 1.

Yugoslavia' must comply with the resolution.[34] Given that the armed conflicts in the former Yugoslavia were exceptionally complex and had both non-international and international aspects,[35] the Security Council effectively attempted to oblige those parties whose conduct was not attributable to any state.

4.2.2 Individuals

While the aforementioned Chapter VII demands were addressed to non-state armed groups, it was Resolution 2170 adopted in August 2014 that further extended the scope of the addressees of Chapter VII demand to ***individuals***. In order to strengthen the sanctions regime built by Resolution 1267 and subsequent resolutions, Resolution 2170 extended asset freeze measures to six additional individuals in ISIL and Al-Nusra Front.[36] Resolution 2170 differs from previous resolutions adopted under the 1267 sanctions regime in that the Security Council directly demanded 'individuals' act in a certain manner for the sake of the maintenance of international peace and security. Under Resolution 2170, the Security Council:

> Noting with concern the continued threat posed to international peace and security by ISIL, ANF [Al-Nusra Front] and all other individuals, groups, undertakings and entities associated with Al-Qaida, and reaffirming its resolve to address all aspects of that threat,
>
> Acting under Chapter VII of the Charter of the United Nations, …
>
> 4. *Demands* that ISIL, ANF, and ***all other individuals***, groups, undertakings and entities associated with Al-Qaida cease all violence and terrorist acts, and disarm and disband with immediate effect; …
>
> Foreign Terrorist Fighters
>
> 7. … *demands* that all foreign terrorist fighters associated with ISIL and other terrorist groups withdraw immediately …[37]

34 UN Doc S/RES/771 (13 August 1992) para 7. (i) While Resolution 771 did not contain the determination of threats to the peace, the resolution referred to Resolution 770 which had recognised the situation in Bosnia and Herzegovina as a threat to international peace and security: UN Doc S/RES/770 (13 August 1992) para 5 of the preamble. (ii) In adopting Resolution 771, however, the Chinese delegate still expressed his reservation that it was 'inappropriate to invoke Chapter VII of the Charter in this resolution': UN Doc S/PV.3106 (13 August 1992) 52 (Mr. Li Daoyu of China).

35 Case No IT-94-1-AR72 *Prosecutor v Duško Tadić, Appeals Chamber, Decision on Jurisdiction* (1996) 35 ILM 32 (ICTY, Decision of 2 October 1995), para 77; Rein Mullerson, 'International Humanitarian Law in Internal Conflicts' (1997) 2 *Journal of Armed Conflict Law* 109, 111.

36 UN Doc S/RES/2170 (15 August 2014) para 19. The six individuals were still described as those individuals associated with Al-Qaida, as it was still before the adoption of Resolution 2253 which expanded the strategic target of the sanctions regime to ISIL. On the 1267 sanctions regime, see section 4.3 of this book.

37 Ibid., paras 4, 7 (original emphasis omitted in the preamble; the second emphasis added).

In paragraph 4, the Security Council directed the Chapter VII demand toward 'all other individuals' associated with Al-Qaida. Those individuals were instructed to cease all violence and disarm 'with immediate effect'.[38] The demand was apparently the attempt of the Security Council to directly address those individuals under Chapter VII without any intermediaries of member states. Paragraph 7 of Resolution 2170 further placed the demand directly on 'all foreign terrorist fighters' as opposed to the terrorist groups to which such fighters belong.[39] If one assumes that the Chapter VII 'demand' could be meant to impose obligations, Resolution 2170 was intended to create an international obligation not on member states but on ***individual terrorist fighters themselves.***

A similar demand was made by Resolution 2178 on foreign terrorist fighters, which was adopted at the meeting of 24 September 2014 at the level of Heads of State and Government. The primary aim of Resolution 2178 was to reduce the divergence in rules across different domestic legal systems as part of the Security Council's counter-terrorism efforts.[40] One of the noteworthy features that differentiates Resolution 2178 from previously adopted terrorist-related resolutions is its operative paragraph 1 in which the Security Council:

> Acting under Chapter VII of the Charter of the United Nations,
>
> 1. Condemns the violent extremism, which can be conducive to terrorism, sectarian violence, and the commission of terrorist acts by foreign terrorist fighters, and *demands* that *all foreign terrorist fighters* disarm and cease all terrorist acts and participation in armed conflict ...[41]

What counts in this paragraph is the fact that the Security Council directly demanded under Chapter VII 'all foreign terrorist fighters' to disarm and cease all terrorist acts.[42]

Before Resolutions 2170 and 2178, there were many instances in which certain individuals (apart from the Secretary-General or other persons appointed by the UN) were referred to by Security Council resolutions under Chapter VII. Usama bin Laden, for instance, was mentioned in several resolutions. Resolution 1267 demanded that the Taliban turn over Usama bin Laden to appropriate authorities,[43] and Resolution 1333 obliged member states to freeze the funds and assets of Usama bin Laden.[44] The conduct of particular individuals also constituted an

38 Ibid., para 4.
39 Ibid., para 7.
40 Cian C. Murphy, 'Transnational Counter-Terrorism Law: Law, Power and Legitimacy in the "Wars on Terror"' (2015) 6 *Transnational Legal Theory* 31, 43–7.
41 UN Doc S/RES/2178 (24 September 2014) para 1 (original emphasis omitted except for 'demands'; the second emphasis added).
42 Anne Peters, 'Security Council Resolution 2178 (2014): The "Foreign Terrorist Fighter" as an International Legal Person, Part I' *EJIL: Talk!* (20 November 2014) <https://perma.cc/PM4P-GTGQ>.
43 UN Doc S/RES/1267 (15 October 1999) para 2.
44 UN Doc S/RES/1333 (19 December 2000) para 8(c).

impediment to stability and a threat to international peace and security, as illustrated by Security Council Resolution 1638 on President Charles Taylor's return to Liberia.[45] Furthermore, Resolution 1737 on the Iranian sanctions listed a number of individuals and entities as specific targets of the asset freeze measures.[46]

Yet Resolutions 2170 and 2178 should be distinguished from these previous resolutions in that the Security Council did not merely regard individuals as the elements leading to the adoption of Chapter VII measures or the specific targets of asset freeze. Instead, individuals were constituted as direct addressees of Chapter VII demands. According to the statement of the US President on the adoption of Resolution 2178, to prevent 'those individuals' from moving across the borders was critical to the strategy against ISIL.[47] Still, the primary addressees of Resolution 2178 remained member states which were, among others, obligated to establish serious criminal offences for the purpose of prosecuting or penalising individuals who engaged in terrorist acts abroad.[48] Yet at the same time, under Resolutions 2170 and 2178, the Security Council has chosen to directly speak to 'all foreign terrorist fighters' and those 'individuals' associated with Al-Qaida.

Overall, the Security Council's practice has developed so as to constitute certain categories of individuals as the addressees of the Chapter VII demand. At least within the operative paragraphs of Resolutions 2170 and 2178, the distance between the UN's peace and security arm and individual terrorist fighters is eliminated as part of the UN's concrete response to threats to international peace and security. Such enclosure of individuals in the mandate of the UN Security Council is much more substantive than the mere conceptual proximity (overviewed in chapter 3 of this book) between the Security Council's exercise of authority and individuals.

4.3 Target specification

The second dimension that illustrates the altered distance between the Security Council and individuals is the practice of economic sanctions. The Security Council and its sanctions committees have directly designated individuals and entities as the targets of asset freezes and travel bans instigated under Article 41 of the UN Charter. The designation of targeted individuals became a common practice within the Security Council as an alternative to comprehensive economic sanctions which had devastating humanitarian side effects. The active use of targeted sanctions, in which individuals are listed as the 'specific' targets of restrictive measures, must be understood together with the expansion of the 'overall' targets of sanctions regimes to non-state actors.

45 UN Doc S/RES/1638 (11 November 2005) para 4 of the preamble. See section 3.4 of this book.
46 UN Doc S/RES/1737 (27 December 2006) Annex.
47 UN Doc S/PV.7272 (24 September 2014) 4.
48 UN Doc S/RES/2178 (24 September 2014) (n 41) para 6.

4.3.1 Non-state actors as overall targets

During the Cold War, the UN Security Council utilised economic sanctions only twice: one against South Rhodesia and another against South Africa. The first mandatory sanctions were introduced against Southern Rhodesia in December 1966.[49] Interestingly, if we assume that Rhodesia remained formally subject to the UK's sovereignty at that time, the first instance of economic sanctions was already against the conduct of 'non-state' regimes.[50] As economic sanctions became an integral part of the Security Council's work in the 1990s,[51] the Council established several sanctions against non-state armed groups. For instance, Resolution 820 adopted in April 1993 was one of such occasions in which the Security Council imposed sanctions against the Bosnian Serb party and forces which had not gained statehood.[52]

A more straightforward example was Resolution 864 in September 1993 on Angola, according to which an arms embargo was imposed with a view to prohibiting all sale or supply of arms to the National Union for the Total Independence of Angola (UNITA).[53] In a similar vein, the strategic target of the arms embargo under Resolution 1171 in June 1998 was 'non-governmental forces in Sierra Leone'.[54] Resolution 1343 against Liberia in 2001 was also considered a measure against the conduct of rebel groups.[55] The strategic targets of the Yemen sanctions under Resolution 2140 apparently included the Houthis;[56] and the South Sudan sanctions regime based on Resolution 2206 also aimed at directing the conduct of parties including opposition forces;[57] finally, a series of so-called

49 UN Doc S/RES/232 (16 December 1966) (n 24).

50 See Jean Combacau, *Le pouvoir de sanction de l'O.N.U.: Étude théorique de la coercition non militaire* (Paris, A. Pedone, 1974) 136–8.

51 David Cortright and George A. Lopez, *The Sanctions Decade: Assessing UN Strategies in the 1990s* (Boulder; London, Lynne Rienner Publishers, 2000).

52 With regard to the political status of Bosnian Serbs, see (n 25) above. The Security Council obligated member states to prohibit the import to, export from, and transhipment through areas 'under the control of Bosnian Serb forces': UN Doc S/RES/820 (17 April 1993) para 12. The Security Council strengthened the sanctions under Resolution 942 and tied the sanctions with the acceptance by the Bosnian Serb party of the proposed territorial settlement: UN Doc S/RES/942 (23 September 1994) (n 26) paras 3, 21.

53 UN Doc S/RES/864 (15 September 1993) para 19.

54 UN Doc S/RES/1171 (5 June 1998) para 2. The sanctions regime was initially established under Council Resolution 1132 against Sierra Leone: UN Doc S/RES/1132 (8 October 1997). The sanctions regime initially targeted the military junta in Sierra Leone: ibid., para, 5. After the restoration of the democratically elected government, the sanctions regime altered its strategic targets to the former military junta and the Revolutionary United Front (RUF) under Council Resolution 1171.

55 UN Doc S/RES/1343 (7 March 2001). The sanctions' primary strategic target was the Liberian government whose conduct led to a threat to international peace in the region: ibid., para, 9 of the preamble. However, one of the purposes of the sanctions was to force the Liberian government not to support rebel groups, including the RUF in Sierra Leone: ibid., para 7(a).

56 UN Doc 2140 (26 February 2014); UN Doc S/RES/2216 (14 April 2015) (n 29).

57 UN Doc S/RES/2206 (3 March 2015).

'legislative' resolutions – such as Resolutions 1373, 1540, and 2178 – have been primarily designed to alter the conduct of non-state actors, including individuals.[58]

The most noteworthy precedent, however, which significantly altered the legal and political narrative on the use of targeted sanctions, is the sanctions mechanism built on Resolution 1267 and subsequent resolutions. The overall strategic targets of the sanctions regime have undergone changes during 1999 and 2015. Initially, the 1267 sanctions regime aimed at altering the conduct of the *de facto* government. Triggered by the bombings of the US embassies in Kenya and Tanzania and the US' executive orders against specifically designated terrorists,[59] the UN Security Council adopted Resolution 1267 in October 1999 and imposed a travel ban and asset freeze against the Taliban for its failure to stop providing sanctuary to Usama bin Laden and his associates.[60] At this stage, the sanctions regime was devised against the Taliban authorities who arguably constituted the *de facto* government of Afghanistan.[61] While Resolution 1333, adopted in December 2000, extended the reach of the asset freeze to members of Al-Qaida,[62] the sanctions mechanism remained focused on the Taliban as an overall strategic target. According to Resolution 1333, it was 'the failure of the Taliban authorities', and not the acts of Al-Qaida, that constituted a threat to international peace and security.[63]

Nevertheless, the September 11 terrorist attack in New York in 2001 changed the overall targets of the sanctions regime in two ways. First, the subsequent US-led military invasion in Afghanistan effectively reconstituted the status of the Taliban from the *de facto* government of Afghanistan to one of a non-state armed group without effective control over the territory. Second, Resolution 1390,

58 UN Doc S/RES/1373 (28 September 2001); UN Doc S/RES/1540 (28 April 2004) paras 1, 2; UN Doc S/RES/2178 (24 September 2014) (n 41). In particular, Resolution 1540 on the non-proliferation of weapons of mass destruction expressly focuses on 'non-state actors' which are defined as an 'individual or entity, not acting under the lawful authority of any State in conducting activities which come within the scope of this resolution'. On the analysis of Resolution 1540, see Masahiko Asada, 'Security Council Resolution 1540 to Combat WMD Terrorism: Effectiveness and Legitimacy in International Legislation' (2008) 13 *Journal of Conflict & Security Law* 303.

59 After the bombings, the US listed Usama bin Laden and Al-Qaida as the targets of the prohibition of transactions: US Presidential Executive Order 13099 of 20 August 1998, 3 C.F.R. 208 (1998). In July 1999, the US prohibited transactions with the Taliban which the US claimed was allowing the territory of Afghanistan to be used for bin Laden and Al-Qaida: 'Blocking Property and Prohibiting Transactions with the Taliban', US Presidential Executive Order 13129 of 4 July 1999, 3 C.F.R. 200 (1999).

60 UN Doc S/RES/1267 (15 October 1999) (n 43) para 4.

61 See Christiane E. Philipp, 'Taliban' in R. Wolfrum (ed.), *The Max Planck Encyclopedia of Public International Law* (Oxford, Oxford University Press, online edition, January 2007) paras 4–11, especially para 7 (the analysis of the status of the Taliban as a non-recognised *de facto* 'regime').

62 UN Doc S/RES/1333 (19 December 2000) (n 44) para 8(c). In addition, the Security Council introduced an arms embargo with respect to the territory of Afghanistan: ibid.

63 UN Doc S/RES/1267 (15 October 1999) (n 43) para 14 of the preamble.

adopted in January 2002, rephrased and widened the threats themselves that prompted the economic sanctions. Under the resolution, it was no longer 'the failure of the Taliban authorities' but 'acts of international terrorism' in general that constituted a threat to international peace and security.[64] The resolution thus widened the overall targets to both the (non-state) Taliban and the Al-Qaida terrorist group.[65] In June 2011, the Security Council created a separate sanctions regime for the Taliban and confined the 1267 sanctions regime to Al-Qaida.[66] In December 2015, the Security Council formally expanded the overall targets of the 1267 sanctions regime to ISIL, also known as the Islamic State of Iraq and Syria (ISIS) or the Islamic State (IS).[67]

In brief, the Security Council has established a number of economic sanctions against non-state groups and networks and, in this regard, the 1267 sanctions regime was a mere continuation of the Council's previous practice. At the same time, a striking feature of the 1267 sanctions regime against Al-Qaida and ISIL was the *geographical extent to which the terrorist groups proliferated* across the world. The overall targets of the 1267 sanctions regime were different, in the geographical sense, from rebel groups in a particular state or region. The territorial flexibility of the sanctions' overall targets – together with the designation of individuals as the specific targets of restrictive measures, as will be discussed below – thus multiplied the international visibility of the effects that the UN's economic sanctions had on individuals.

4.3.2 Individuals as specific targets

The institutional direction to constitute non-state armed groups as an overall target of the UN's sanctions has been combined with the Security Council's practice to utilise targeted sanctions. Since 1994, the UN Security Council and its sanctions committees have directly designated a number of individuals as specific targets of asset freezes and travel bans. Before the introduction of targeted sanctions, the Security Council, having determined the overall strategic targets of economic sanctions, still left it for each state to specify the targets of restrictive measures. For instance, in the sanctions regime imposed against Southern Rhodesia during the 1960s and 1970s, the Security Council required member states to prevent, except for medical, educational, and humanitarian purposes: the import of all commodities from Southern Rhodesia, the sale of commodities to any person therein, the transfer of funds, and the entry of Southern Rhodesian citizens and those residents who 'furthered or encouraged' the unlawful actions of the illegal regime in Southern Rhodesia.[68] While the frameworks of comprehensive sanctions were designed at the UN's level, it was still left for member states to specify the scope of

64 UN Doc S/RES/1390 (28 January 2002) para 9 of the preamble.
65 Ibid., para 2.
66 UN Doc S/RES/1989 (17 June 2011). The Security Council established a separate regime for the Taliban: UN Doc S/RES/1988 (17 June 2011).
67 UN Doc S/RES/2253 (17 December 2015) (n 9).
68 UN Doc S/RES/253 (29 May 1968) paras 3(a), 3(d), 4, 5(a), 5(b).

permissible humanitarian exceptions or a resident who 'furthered or encouraged' the unlawful actions.[69] While, at that time, there was also a sanctions committee called Watchdog Committee, it only had a passive mandate to gather and report information about national implementation.[70]

Security Council Resolution 917 against Haiti, adopted in May 1994, was the first resolution which empowered the UN itself to designate specific individuals and entities.[71] Resolution 917 was meant to strengthen the sanctions regime established in June 1993 under Resolution 841.[72] The sanctions had a strategic purpose of reinstating the democratically elected government which had been ousted by the military coup d'état in September 1991. Initially, the UN Security Council had refrained from actively engaging in the aftermath of the coup d'état.[73] Instead, the US and the Organization of American States (OAS) took the lead in issuing the condemnation[74] and imposing economic sanctions against Haiti in October 1991.[75] The growing pressure from the OAS and the worsening of human rights and humanitarian situations in Haiti led the Security Council to adopt Resolution 841 in June 1993 to internationalise a petroleum embargo, an

69 Vera Gowlland-Debbas, 'Implementing Sanctions Resolutions in Domestic Law' in V. Gowlland-Debbas (ed.), *National Implementation of United Nations Sanctions: A Comparative Study* (Leiden, M. Nijhoff Publishers; Brill, 2004) 33, 51.

70 UN Doc S/RES/253 (29 May 1968) (n 68) para 20; 'Establishment of a Committee of the Security Council in Pursuance of Paragraph 20 of Security Council Resolution 253 (1968)' UN Doc S/8697 (29 July 1968); P.J. Kuyper, 'The Limits of Supervision: The Security Council Watchdog Committee on Rhodesian Sanctions' (1978) 25 *Netherlands International Law Review* 159.

71 UN Doc S/RES/917 (6 May 1994).

72 UN Doc S/RES/841 (16 June 1993).

73 David Malone, *Decision-Making in the UN Security Council: The Case of Haiti, 1990–1997* (Oxford, Clarendon Press, 1998) 63–82. A majority of Security Council members were still not convinced that the crisis represented a threat to international peace and security: ibid., 73 (on the Council's view around mid-1992).

74 OAS, Resolution of the Permanent Council, 'Support to the Democratic Government of Haiti' (1991) OEA/Ser.G, CP/RES. 567 (870/91) (30 September 1991); OAS, Resolution of Ad Hoc Meeting of Ministers, 'Support to the Democratic Government of Haiti' (1991) OAS-MRE/RES 1/91 (3 October 1991); Malone, *Decision Making in the UN Security Council* (n 73) 61–2.

75 On 4 October 1991, the US imposed restrictive measures against Haiti: 'Prohibiting Certain Transactions with Respect to Haiti' US Presidential Executive Order 12775 (4 October 1991). On 8 October, the OAS resolution urged its member states to impose an asset freeze and travel ban on Haiti: OAS-MRE/RES 2/91 (8 October 1991); Malone, *Decision Making in the UN Security Council* (n 73) 65. On 28 October 1991, the US Presidential Executive Order was issued to implement the OAS resolution, which blocked all property and interests in property of the Government of Haiti located within the US, prohibited payments to the *de facto* regime in Haiti, and prohibited import and export with certain exceptions: 'Prohibiting Certain Transactions with Respect to Haiti' US Presidential Executive Order 12779 (28 October 1991). For the summary of US' sanctions against Haiti, see Michael P. Malloy, *United States Economic Sanctions: Theory and Practice* (The Hague, Kluwer Law International, 2001) 118–22.

arms embargo, and financial sanctions against Haiti.[76] Under Resolution 841, the asset freeze measures were applied not only to the governmental funds but also to the funds controlled 'directly or indirectly' by entities 'owned or controlled' by the Haiti government or the *de facto* authorities.[77] Despite the vagueness of its terms, Resolution 841 did not purport to specify the targets of financial sanctions.

The US government drew up the original list of individuals for the purpose of imposing sanctions against Haiti. On 3 June 1993, 13 days before the adoption of Resolution 841, the US President directed the Treasury Department to designate individuals who would be subject to asset-freeze measures under previously adopted executive orders.[78] Those specially designated nationals included those Haitians (a) who had seized power illegally from the Aristide government, (b) who were substantially owned or controlled by the *de facto* regime, and (c) who acted or purported to act directly or indirectly on behalf of the *de facto* regime (or under the asserted authority thereof).[79] Thirty-five institutions and 83 individuals were listed by the US government.[80] The US subsequently extended the list to encompass not only the persons within the *de facto* regime but also those who had 'contributed to the violence in Haiti' and those who had 'materially and financially supported' such persons.[81]

In May 1994, almost a year after the US drew up the list of designated individuals, the UN Security Council adopted Resolution 917. Under Resolution 917, all states were mandated to impose travel bans and asset freezes against a potentially wide range of individuals, including: (a) Haitian military/police officers (and their immediate families), (b) participants in the coup and the subsequent governments (and their immediate families), and (c) those employed by or acting on behalf of the Haitian military (and their immediate families).[82] The designation of these individuals was left in the hands of the Security Council's Sanctions

76 UN Doc S/RES/841 (16 June 1993) (n 72) paras 5, 6, 8. For the events leading to the adoption of resolution, see Malone, *Decision Making in the UN Security Council* (n 73) 82–5.

77 UN Doc S/RES/841 (16 June 1993) (n 72) para 8.

78 Executive Order 12775 (n 75); Executive Order 12779 (n 75).

79 US President, 'Statement on Sanctions Against Haiti (4 June 1993)', *Public Papers of the Presidents of the United States, William J. Clinton, 1993, Book I* (Washington, United States Government Printing Office, 1994) 810, 811; US President, 'Letter to Congressional Leaders on Haiti (13 November 1993)', *Public Papers of the Presidents of the United States, William J. Clinton, 1993, Book II* (Washington, United States Government Printing Office, 1994) 1991, 1994. The Treasury Department amended 'Haitian Transactions Regulations' 31 C.F.R. part 580.

80 Steven A. Holmes, 'Haitian Rulers Are Target of New Sanctions by U.S.' *New York Times* (5 June 1993) <https://perma.cc/ZEW4-7NK9>; *Les Nations Unies et Haïti: 1990–1996, Série Livres bleus des Nations Unies*, vol. XI (New York, Département de l'information des Nations Unies, 1996) 38, para 180.

81 'Blocking Property of Persons Obstructing Democratization in Haiti' (1993) US Presidential Executive Order 12872 (18 October 1993). See also 'Blocking Property of Certain Haitian Nationals' US Presidential Executive Order 12922 (21 June 1994).

82 UN Doc S/RES/917 (6 May 1994) (n 71) paras 3, 4. See also the Executive Order of the US government to implement Council Resolution 917 one day later:

Committee which was mandated to maintain an updated list of targeted persons, based on information provided by states and regional organisations, and to approve exceptions to the travel bans.[83] The targeted sanctions regime against Haiti continued until the democratically elected President Aristide returned to the country in October 1994.[84]

Since Resolution 917 on the Haiti sanctions, it has been a common practice of the UN Security Council to designate individuals and entities as specific targets of asset freezes and travel bans. Between 1994 and March 2015, the Security Council instigated as many as 21 targeted sanctions.[85] For instance, Resolutions 1127 and 1173 on Angola instructed the Angola Sanctions Committee to designate senior officials of UNITA and adult members of their immediate families so that their funds and financial resources would be frozen by member states.[86] Based on the reports of the Monitoring Mechanism established for the Angola

'Prohibiting Certain Transactions With Respect to Haiti' (1994) US Presidential Executive Order 12914 (7 May 1994).

83 UN Doc S/RES/917 (6 May 1994) (n 71) para 3.

84 UN Doc S/RES/944 (29 September 1994) para 4; UN Doc S/RES/948 (15 October 1994) (1994) para 10.

85 (i) Haiti: UN Doc S/RES/917, paras 3–4. (ii) Bosnian Serbs: UN Doc S/RES/942 (23 September 1994) (1994), para 14. The list was not drawn: see Final Report of the Security Council Committee Established Pursuant to Resolution 724 (1991) Concerning Yugoslavia, S/1996/946 (15 November 1996), para 63. (iii) Angola: UN Doc S/RES/1127 (28 August 1997), para 4(a), para 4(b); UN Doc S/RES/1173 (12 June 1998), para 11. (iv) Sierra Leone: UN Doc S/RES/1132 (8 October 1997), para 5; UN Doc S/RES/1171 (5 June 1998), para 5. (v) Al Qaida and Taliban: UN Doc S/RES/1267 (15 October 1999), para 4; UN Doc S/RES/1333 (19 December 2000), para 8, para 10, para 11; UN Doc S/RES/1390 (28 January 2002), para 2. In June 2011, the sanctions regime was split into two: for Al Qaida, UN Doc S/RES/1989 (17 June 2011). For Taliban, UN Doc S/RES/1988 (17 June 2011). In December 2015, the Al-Qaida Sanctions Committee was expanded to the Islamic State in Iraq and the Levant (ISIL) and Al-Qaida Sanctions Committee: UN Doc S/RES/2253 (17 December 2015). (vi) Liberia; UN Doc S/RES/1343 (7 March 2001), para 7(a). (vii) Iraq: UN Doc S/RES/1483 (22 May 2003), para 23(b). (viii) Liberia, UN Doc S/RES/1521 (22 December 2003), para 4(a); UN Doc S/RES/1532 (12 March 2004) para 1. (ix) DRC: UN Doc S/RES/1533 (12 March 2004), paras 13, 15; UN Doc S/RES/1596 (18 April 2005); UN Doc S/RES/1807 (31 March 2008). (x) Côte d'Ivoire: UN Doc S/RES/1572 (15 November 2004), para 9, para 11. (xi) Sudan: UN Doc S/RES/1591 (29 March 2005), para 3. Cf. UN Doc S/RES/1054 (26 April 1996), para 3(b). (xii) Lebanon/Syria, UN Doc S/RES/1636 (31 October 2005), para 3. (xiii) North Korea: UN Doc S/RES/1718 (14 October 2006), para 8. (xiv) Iran: UN Doc S/RES/1737 (27 December 2006), para 10, para 12. (xv) Eritrea/Somalia: UN Doc S/RES/1844 (20 November 2008); UN Doc S/RES/1907 (23 December 2009). (xvi) Libya: UN Doc S/RES/1970 (26 February 2011). (xvii) Taliban: UN Doc S/RES/1988 (2011). (xviii) Guinea-Bissau: UN Doc S/RES/2048 (18 May 2012). (xix) Central African Republic: UN Doc S/RES/2127 (5 December 2013); UN Doc S/RES/2134 (28 January 2014). (xx) Yemen: UN Doc S/RES/2140 (26 February 2014). (xxi) South Sudan: UN Doc S/RES/2206 (3 March 2015).

86 UN Doc S/RES/1127 (28 August 1997) para 11(a); UN Doc S/RES/1173 (12 June 1998) para 11.

sanctions regime,[87] the Sanctions Committee issued in October 2001 a consolidated version of the list of designated persons subject to asset freeze and travel bans.[88]

While the practice of targeted sanctions started in 1994, it was the post-September 11 development of the 1267 sanctions regime that attracted international attention to the impact of targeted sanctions on individuals. Primarily at the initiative of the US, the list of targeted individuals dramatically grew in size within several weeks after the September 11 terrorist attacks in 2001.[89] This was followed by Resolution 1390 in January 2002 which expanded the scope of targets to those 'associated with' members of Al-Qaida.[90] This has led to the further growth of the list of targets. More than 50 individuals were listed in 2001 and approximately 70 individuals were listed in 2003.[91] When the 1267 Sanctions Committee first published the consolidated list of targets in November 2001, the list contained 90 Al-Qaida related individuals.[92] The number of designated individuals associated with Al-Qaida has grown: 182 individuals as of September 2005,[93] 205 by the end of 2005,[94]

87 E.g., 'Final Report of the Monitoring Mechanism on Angola Sanctions' (2000) UN Doc S/2000/1225 (21 December 2000); 'Addendum to the Final Report of the Monitoring Mechanism on Sanctions against UNITA' UN Doc S/2001/363 (18 April 2001).

88 See the EU (then EC)'s regulation updated accordingly: Commission Regulation (EC) No 2231/2001 of 16 November 2001 amending, for the second time, Council Regulation (EC) No 1705/98 concerning the interruption of certain economic relations with Angola in order to induce the 'União Nacional para a Independência Total de Angola' (UNITA) to fulfil its obligations in the peace process, and repealing Regulation (EC) No 2229/97 [2001] OJ L301/17.

Commission Regulation (EC) No 2231/2001 of 16 November 2001 amending, for the second time, Council Regulation (EC) No 1705/98 concerning the interruption of certain economic relations with Angola in order to induce the 'União Nacional para a Independência Total de Angola' (UNITA) to fulfil its obligations in the peace process, and repealing Regulation (EC) No 2229/97 [2001] OJ L301/17.

89 Eric Rosand, 'The Security Council's Efforts to Monitor the Implementation of Al Qaeda/Taliban Sanctions' (2004) 98 *American Journal of International Law* 745, 749. For instance, the Security Council announced the addition of 20 individuals on 19 October and 16 individuals on 9 November: UN Press Release, SC/7180 (19 October 2001); UN Press Release, AFG/163-SC/7206 (9 November 2001).

90 UN Doc S/RES/1390 (28 January 2002) (n 64) para 2.

91 'Sixteenth Report of the Analytical Support and Sanctions Monitoring Team Submitted Pursuant to Resolution 2161 (2014) concerning Al-Qaida and Associated Individuals and Entities' UN Doc S/2014/770 (29 October 2014) para 45 (Figure I: Listings and delistings of individuals).

92 'Second Report of the Monitoring Group Established Pursuant to Security Council Resolution 1363 (2001) and Extended by Resolution 1390 (2002) and 1455 (2003)' UN Doc S/2003/1070 (2 December 2003) para 15.

93 'Third Report of the Analytical Support and Sanctions Monitoring Team Appointed Pursuant to Resolution 1526 (2004) Concerning Al-Qaida and the Taliban and Associated Individuals and Entities' (2005) UN Doc S/2005/572 (9 September 2005) para 20.

94 'Fourth Report of the Analytical Support and Sanctions Monitoring Team Appointed Pursuant to Security Council Resolutions 1526 (2004) and 1617 (2005) Concerning

223 in September 2007,[95] 254 in February 2009,[96] 256 in February 2011,[97] and 234 in March 2015.[98] After the 1267 sanctions regime formally extended its overall target to ISIL in December 2015, several names were added to the list. As of 3 August 2016, the list contained 258 individuals.

Kadi, whose judicial action altered the human rights narrative on the UN Security Council's exercise of authority, was among the many individuals designated shortly after the September 11 terrorist attacks.[99] On 12 October 2001, Kadi was first designated by the Office of Foreign Assets Control (OFAC) of the US Department of the Treasury as a 'specifically designated global terrorist' or 'SDGT' in accordance with the International Emergency Economic Powers Act and the Executive Order No. 13224.[100] On 15 October 2001, the US government mailed Kadi a 'Notice of Blocking' advising him of the administrative procedures available to challenge the designation.[101] Two days later, on 17 October 2001, Kadi was designated by the UN Security Council's sanctions committee[102] – and remained subject to the UN's sanctions until 5 October 2012, upon which Kadi was delisted after a series of judicial proceedings and the review by the Office of Ombudsperson.[103]

On the whole, what matters for the purpose of this book is the normalisation of the undertaking by the UN to designate specific individuals as the targets of restrictive measures imposed under Article 41 of the UN Charter. With a vast number of decisions to designate individuals within the UN's sanctions regimes,

Al-Qaida and the Taliban and Associated Individuals and Entities' (2006) UN Doc S/2006/154 (10 March 2006) para 23.

95 'Seventh Report of the Analytical Support and Sanctions Monitoring Team Appointed Pursuant to Security Council Resolutions 1617 (2005) and 1735 (2006) Concerning Al-Qaida and the Taliban and Associated Individuals and Entities' (2007) UN Doc S/2007/677 (29 November 2007) para 24 (the number as of 30 September 2007).

96 'Ninth Report of the Analytical Support and Sanctions Monitoring Team, Submitted Pursuant to Resolution 1822 (2008) Concerning Al-Qaida and the Taliban and Associated Individuals and Entities' (2009) UN Doc S/2009/245 (13 May 2009) para 36 (the number as of 28 February 2009).

97 'Eleventh Report of the Analytical Support and Sanctions Implementation Monitoring Team Established Pursuant to Security Council Resolution 1526 (2004) and Extended by Resolution 1904 (2009) Concerning Al-Qaida and the Taliban and Associated Individuals and entities' (2011) UN Doc S/2011/245 (13 April 2011) para 10 (the number as of 22 February 2011).

98 'Seventeenth Report of the Analytical Support and Sanctions Monitoring Team Submitted Pursuant to Resolution 2161 (2014) Concerning Al-Qaida and Associated Individuals and Entities' UN Doc S/2015/441 (16 June 2015) para 72 (the number as of 31 March 2015).

99 For the procedural history, see *Yassin Abdullah Kadi v Timothy Geithner, et al* Civil Action No. 09–108(JDB), 2012 WL 898778 (D.D.C.) (19 March 2012).

100 International Emergency Economic Powers Act, 50 U.S.C. § 1701; US Presidential Executive Order 13224 (23 September 2001).

101 *Kadi (US District Court of Columbia)* (n 99).

102 The listing was announced on 19 October 2001: UN Press Release, SC/7180 (19 October 2001) (n 89).

103 UN Press Release, SC/10785 (5 October 2012). See further section 7.3 of this book.

the UN Security Council created a number of direct connections between its exercise of authority and individuals. The lists of targets, containing the names and details of hundreds of individuals, cannot but be regarded as the epitome of proximity that international law constructed between the international organisation's exercise of authority and individuals.

4.4 Direct implementation

The third dimension of the UN Security Council's exercise of authority concerns the modality through which Chapter VII measures are implemented. The Security Council may, through its subsidiary organs, directly execute its decisions vis-à-vis individuals. Territorial administration and ad hoc international criminal tribunals are two main domains of practice in this regard. These two categories of practice are contrasted with the case of targeted sanctions discussed in section 4.3 above; in the context of sanctions, the Security Council obliges the national government to implement international decisions. By contrast, the UN's transitional administrations and ad hoc tribunals prescribe and execute decisions under international law which are directly applicable to certain restricted groups of individuals. Such 'direct implementation' is usually carried out through the UN Security Council's subsidiary organs to which member states provide resources. However, shortly after the inception of the UN, an attempt was made to empower the Security Council *itself* – as opposed to its subsidiary organs – to be as a decision maker over individuals.

4.4.1 By the Security Council itself: The planned administration of the Free Territory of Trieste

Such an attempt was made in 1947 with respect to the administration of the Free Territory of Trieste, which was a strategically important seaport situated between Italy and former Yugoslavia.[104] Within the context of the post-World War II settlement, the plan to internationally administer the territory of Trieste emerged as a provisional solution to the territorial dispute between Italy and Yugoslavia and to ease the East–West tension surrounding the status of Trieste.[105] A striking feature of the planned administration was to place the Free Territory of Trieste not only under the authority of a Council-appointed governor but also 'under the *direct* authority of the Security Council', as Ydit explained.[106] While the UN-led administration did not in practice take shape due to political disagreements,[107] the

104 See generally Méir Ydit, *Internationalised Territories, From the "Free City of Cracow" to the "Free City of Berlin": A Study in the Historical Development of a Modern Notion in International Law and International Relations (1815–1960)* (Leyden, A.W. Sythoff, 1961) 231–72.

105 Josef L. Kunz, 'The Free Territory of Trieste' (1948) 1 *Western Political Quarterly* 99, 99–101, 103.

106 Ydit, *Internationalised Territories* (n 104) 71 (emphasis original).

107 Ibid., 256–61.

case of Trieste still provides useful insights into the Security Council's exercise of authority over individuals.

The framework of the UN's administration of the Free Territory was spelled out in the Permanent Statute of the Free Territory of Trieste.[108] The Permanent Statute was annexed to the Treaty of Peace with Italy in 1947, in which Italy agreed to terminate sovereignty over the area of the Free Territory.[109] The Permanent Statute envisaged a newly formed government in the Free Territory to be composed of a Governor, a Council of Government, a popular Assembly and a Judiciary.[110] Among these organs, the Governor was supposed to be internationally appointed by the UN Security Council after consultation with Yugoslavia and Italy, while the Council of Government was responsible to the locally elected Assembly.[111]

The powers granted to the Governor were much wider than, for instance, those of the High Commissioner of Danzig during the era of the League of Nations.[112] The Permanent Statute accorded the Governor executive powers to prevent the entry into force of treaties,[113] to suspend administrative measures promulgated by the Council of Government,[114] and to appoint key public officials,[115] including the members of the Judiciary.[116] In the case of emergency, the Governor was able to 'directly order and require the execution of appropriate measures' and to control the security services.[117] The Governor was also endowed with the authority to initiate legislation[118] and to block the Assembly's legislation if he found it contradictory to the Statute.[119]

Despite the extent of powers envisaged in the Permanent Statute, the Security Council could not, in the end, appoint a Governor for the Free Territory of Trieste due to political disagreements among member states.[120] If a Governor had

108 Treaty of Peace with Italy, 10 February 1947, 49 UNTS 126 Annex VI (Permanent Statute of the Free Territory of Trieste); UN Doc S/RES/191 (18 June 1964) (approving the Statute).
109 Treaty of Peace with Italy (n 108) Article 21(2) and (3).
110 Ibid., Annex VI (Permanent Statute), Article 9.
111 Ibid., Annex VI (Permanent Statute), Articles 9, 11(1), 13(1). With respect to the Judiciary, while it is established in accordance with the Constitution and laws of the Free Territory, its members were to be appointed by the Governor: ibid., Articles 14, 16(1).
112 On the comparison between the Governor of Trieste and the High Commissioner of Danzig, see Ydit, *Internationalised Territories* (n 104) 253–4.
113 Treaty of Peace with Italy (n 108) Annex VI (Permanent Statute), Article 24(1).
114 Ibid., Annex VI (Permanent Statute), Article 20(1).
115 Ibid., Annex VI (Permanent Statute), Article 27(1) (the Director of Public Security); ibid., Annex VIII (Instrument for the Free Port of Trieste), Article 18(1) (the Director of the Free Port).
116 Treaty of Peace with Italy (n 108) Annex VI (Permanent Statute), Article 16(1).
117 See ibid., Annex VI (Permanent Statute), Article 22(1).
118 See ibid., Annex VI (Permanent Statute), Article 19(1).
119 See ibid., Annex VI (Permanent Statute), Article 19(4).
120 This is illustrated by the exchange of letters between Italy and Yugoslavia: 'Letter from the Italian Observer to the United Nations Addressed to the Secretary-General Dated

been appointed, however, his authority would have been in effect equivalent to that of a subsidiary organ of the UN Security Council. Formally, the Governor was a treaty-based organ under the Treaty of Peace with Italy. Yet, according to the Permanent Statute of the Free Territory of Trieste, the Governor was expected to act as 'the representative of the Security Council' which had appointing authority.[121]

The most noteworthy facet of the Permanent Statute was the element of direct administration of Trieste by the Security Council *itself*, which was envisaged on top of its involvement in the authority exercised by the Governor. The general mandate of the Security Council was provided in Article 2 of the Permanent Statute:

> Article 2. *Integrity and Independence*
>
> The integrity and independence of the Free Territory shall be assured by the Security Council of the United Nations Organization. This responsibility implies that the Council shall:
>
> (a) ensure the observance of the present Statute and in particular the protection of the basic human rights of the inhabitants.
> (b) ensure the maintenance of public order and security in the Free Territory.[122]

Under Article 2, the UN Security Council had a broad mandate to assure the Territory's integrity and independence. In addition to this, the Permanent Statute envisaged the broader legislative and executive authority of the Security Council in the administration of the Free Territory of Trieste. With respect to the legislative aspect, Article 10 of the Permanent Statute provided the UN Security Council's limited involvement in the enactment of the Trieste's Constitution as follows:

> Article 10. *Constitution*
>
> 1. The Constitution of the Free Territory shall be established in accordance with democratic principles and adopted by a Constituent Assembly with a two-thirds majority of the votes cast. The Constitution shall be made to conform to the provisions of the present Statute and shall not enter into force prior to the coming into force of the Statute.
>
> 2. If in the opinion of the Governor any provisions of the Constitution proposed by the Constituent Assembly or any subsequent amendments

12 January 1948 Concerning Candidates for Governor of the Free Territory of Trieste' UN Doc S/644 (13 January 1948); 'Letter from the Italian Observer to the United Nations Addressed to the Secretary-General Dated 15 January 1948, Concerning Candidates for Governor of the Free Territory of Trieste' UN Doc S/647 (15 January 1948); 'Letter from the Representative of Yugoslavia Addressed to the Secretary-General Dated 15 January 1948 and Enclosed Note Concerning the Candidates for Governor of the Free Territory of Trieste' UN Doc S/648 (16 January 1948).

121 Treaty of Peace with Italy (n 108) Annex VI (Permanent Statute), Articles 11, 17(1).

122 Ibid., Annex VI (Permanent Statute), Article 2.

> thereto are in contradiction to the Statute he may prevent their entry into force, *subject to reference to the Security Council if the Assembly does not accept his views and recommendations.*[123]

Under this article, the Permanent Statute enabled 'reference' to the Security Council in the course of promulgating and amending the Constitution if the Assembly of Trieste did not accept the Governor's views and recommendations. While Article 10 did not specify any legal effect of the Security Council's views after referral, the Council's positions might have likewise prevented the entry into force of Constitutional provisions. In a similar vein, Article 19(5) and (6) of the Permanent Statute provided the Security Council's legislative involvement as follows:

> Article 19. *Enactment of Legislation*
>
> ...
>
> 5. If the Assembly makes manifest its refusal to withdraw legislation returned to the Assembly by the Governor or to amend it in conformity with his comments or recommendations, the Governor shall ... immediately *report the matter to the Security Council.* The Governor shall likewise transmit without delay to the Security Council any communication which the Assembly may wish to make to the Council on the matter.
>
> 6. Legislation which forms the subject of a report to the Security Council under the provisions of the preceding paragraph *shall only be promulgated by the direction of the Security Council.*[124]

These provisions anticipated the UN Security Council's direction in the process of promulgating legislation over which disagreement arose between the popular Assembly and the Governor. Although the Security Council's role was not to enact legislation but to provide direction for it, the fact remains that the Statute empowered the Security Council to exercise its authority over specific pieces of legislation in the Free Territory of Trieste.

Finally, the Permanent Statute also accorded the UN Security Council with the executive authority in administering the territory. According to Article 20 of the Permanent Statute:

> Article 20. *Rights of the Governor with Respect to Administrative Measures*
>
> 1. The Governor may require the Council of Government to suspend administrative measures which in his view conflict with his responsibilities as defined in the present Statute (observance of the Statute; maintenance of public order and security; respect for human rights). Should the Council of Government object, the Governor may suspend these administrative measures

123 Ibid., Annex VI (Permanent Statute), Article 10 (emphasis added).
124 Ibid., Annex VI (Permanent Statute), Article 19(5), (6) (emphasis added).

> and the Governor or the Council of Government *may refer the whole question to the Security Council for decision.*
>
> 2. In matters affecting his responsibilities as defined in the Statute the Governor may propose to the Council of Government the adoption of any administrative measures. Should the Council of Government not accept such proposals the Governor may, without prejudice to Article 22 of the present Statute, *refer the matter to the Security Council for decision.*[125]

Under this article, a question or matter could be referred to the Security Council 'for decision' if any administrative measures prompt a disagreement between the Governor and the local Council of Government. Some other provisions of the Permanent Statute also provided for the involvement of the Security Council with respect to the amendment of the Permanent Statute[126] or the emergency power exercised by the Governor and petitioned by the popular Assembly.[127]

Altogether, the Permanent Statute of the Free Territory of Trieste, despite many uncertainties, vested the UN Security Council with authority to provide directions and decisions on the specific legislative and administrative questions. In other words, the Permanent Statute situated the Security Council not merely as an ultimate guardian of security but also as an integral part of local decision making to resolve disagreements between the Governor and locally appointed Assembly or the Council of Government. If the UN-led administration had materialised, the Security Council would have acted as if it were part of the governmental bodies of this particular territory and the populations therein.

4.4.2 Through subsidiary organs

While the Permanent Statute of the Free Territory of Trieste translated the intriguing idea of a territory being administered by the Security Council itself, this

125 Ibid., Annex VI (Permanent Statute), Article 20(1), (2) (emphasis added). The referral to the Security Council seems discretionary, as the term 'may' is employed in Article 20 (as opposed to 'shall' under Article 19(5)).

126 Ibid., Annex VI (Permanent Statute), Article 37. Article 37 (Amendment of Statute) reads in full: 'This Statute shall constitute the permanent Statute of the Free Territory, subject to any amendment which may hereafter be made by the Security Council. *Petitions for the amendment of the Statute may be presented to the Security Council by the popular Assembly* upon a vote taken by a two-thirds majority of the votes cast' (emphasis added).

127 Ibid., Annex VI (Permanent Statute), Article 22(2). Article 22 (Special powers of the Governor) reads in full: '1. In order that he may carry out his responsibilities to the Security Council under the present Statute, the Governor may, in cases which in his opinion permit of no delay, threatening the independence or integrity of the Free Territory, public order or respect of human rights, directly order and require the execution of appropriate measures subject to an immediate report thereon being made by him to the Security Council. In such circumstances the Governor may himself assume, if he deems it necessary, control of the security services. 2. *The popular Assembly may petition the Security Council concerning any exercise by the Governor of his powers under paragraph 1 of this Article*' (emphasis added).

planned administration is apparently an isolated instance. The Council-led administration of war-torn territories such as Kosovo and East Timor has been carried out not by the Security Council itself but by its subsidiary organs. The UN's territorial administration in Kosovo and East Timor also differs from the administration in Trieste which was autonomously created by a separate international treaty.

In Kosovo and East Timor, the UN Interim Administration in Kosovo (UNMIK) and the UN Transitional Administration in East Timor (UNTAET) administered the territories, acting as the Security Council's subsidiary organs established under Chapter VII of the UN Charter. In Kosovo, UNMIK was established in June 1999 by Security Council Resolution 1244 as an international civil presence[128] and exercised nearly comprehensive governing powers until 2008 during which the Assembly of Kosovo adopted a declaration of independence in February, the Constitution of the Republic of Kosovo came into force in June, and the EU deployed the EU Rule of Law Mission in Kosovo (EULEX) which formally operates under the overall authority of UNMIK.[129] In East Timor, UNTAET was established in October 1999 under Security Council Resolution 1272, and UNTAET exercised all legislative and executive authority and had also a military component until May 2002 during which the Constitution of the Democratic Republic of Timor-Leste came into force.[130]

Within the UN's categories, UNMIK and UNTAET are part of UN peacekeeping operations led by the UN's Department of Peacekeeping Operations (DPKO) and the Department of Field Support (DFS). Functionally, UN peacekeeping operations undertake a wide range of not only military but also non-military tasks. Notably, in the early 1960s, the UN Operation in the Congo (Opération des Nations Unies au Congo, ONUC) engaged in civil administration tasks.[131] Having mobilised some 2,000 experts and technicians, ONUC helped the Congolese authorities carry out essential public services, including monetary, foreign exchange, and foreign trade controls.[132]

The UN-led administration of territories became much more comprehensive in the 1990s and the operations have become more structured alongside the accumulation of practices.[133] With respect to UNMIK and UNTAET established in

128 UN Doc S/RES/1244 (10 June 1999) (n 31) para 10.

129 'Report of the Secretary-General on the United Nations Interim Administration Mission in Kosovo' UN Doc S/2008/692 (24 November 2008) paras 21–5, 48–50. On the establishment of EULEX, see, e.g., Erika de Wet, 'The Governance of Kosovo: Security Council Resolution 1244 and the Establishment and Functioning of Eulex' (2009) 103 *American Journal of International Law* 83; Hylke Dijkstra, 'The Planning and Implementation of the Rule of Law Mission of the European Union in Kosovo' (2011) 5 *Journal of Intervention and Statebuilding* 193.

130 UN Doc S/RES/1272 (25 October 1999); 'Report of the Secretary-General on the United Nations Transitional Administration in East Timor' UN Doc S/2002/432 (17 April 2002).

131 Sally Morphet, 'Organizing Civil Administration in Peace-Maintenance' (1998) 4 *Global Governance* 41, 43.

132 Ibid., 44.

133 Apart from UNMIK and UNTAET, the experience was built through the UN Transition Group in Namibia (UNTAG) and the UN Mission for the Referendum in

1999, they prescribed and enforced a wide range of decisions that had immediate effect on local inhabitants. As contrasted with other UN operations which assisted the territorial government in carrying out civil administration, UNMIK and UNTAET themselves exercised powers which are normally assumed by a territorial government. As encapsulated by a Deputy Secretary-General's following words, 'the United Nations *is* the administration' in these territories.[134] Namely, the role of the UN was not to *assist* states which fulfil their governmental functions, but to be 'responsible for fulfilling all the functions of a State'.[135]

In Kosovo and East Timor, the UN's subsidiary organs were vested with all legislative and executive authority, including the administration of the judiciary.[136] Based on this, UNMIK has engaged in determining tax rates,[137] administering social welfare,[138] issuing licences,[139] resolving property claims,[140] privatising

Western Sahara (MINURSO), the UN Transitional Authority in Cambodia (UNTAG), the UN Operation in Somalia II (UNOSOM II), and the UN Transitional Administration for Eastern Slavonia (UNTAES). The objectives of these operations range from state-building to the resolution of territorial disputes and the facilitation of decolonisation process: see Carsten Stahn, *The Law and Practice of International Territorial Administration: Versailles to Iraq and Beyond* (Cambridge, Cambridge University Press, 2008) 12–15.

134 UN Press Release, DSG/SM/91 (3 April 2000) (statement by Deputy Secretary-General Louise Frechétte) (emphasis added). The statement reads: 'It is in Kosovo and East Timor that the tasks entrusted to the United Nations are truly all-encompassing. These two missions are *qualitatively different* from almost any other the Organization has ever undertaken. In each place, *the United Nations is the administration, responsible for fulfilling all the functions of a State* – from fiscal management and judicial affairs to everyday municipal services, such as cleaning the streets and conducting customs formalities at the borders. This is a new order of magnitude for an organization that more customarily *provides States with technical assistance* in such areas, *rather than assuming complete responsibility for them.* And it is a new order of magnitude for peacekeeping operations, as well, making them extraordinarily complex and almost as dependent on civilian experts as on military personnel' (emphasis added). See also Ralph Wilde, *International Territorial Administration: How Trusteeship and the Civilizing Mission Never Went Away* (Oxford, Oxford University Press, 2008) 32–3 (articulating the qualitative difference).

135 UN Press Release, DSG/SM/91 (n 134) (statement by Deputy Secretary-General Louise Frechétte). See also Wilde, *International Territorial Administration* (n 134) 32–3 (articulating the qualitative difference).

136 UNMIK, 'On the Authority of the Interim Administration in Kosovo' UNMIK/REG/1999/1 (25 July 1999) Section 1.1; UNTAET, 'On the Authority of the Transitional Administration in East Timor' UNTAET/REG/1991/1 (27 November 1999) Section 1.1.

137 E.g., UNMIK, 'On Excise Taxes in Kosovo' UNMIK/REG/2000/2 (22 January 2000).

138 E.g., UNMIK, 'On the Establishment of the Administrative Department of Health and Social Welfare' UNMIK/REG/2000/10 (3 March 2000).

139 E.g., UNMIK, 'On the Licensing and Regulation of the Broadcast Media in Kosovo' UNMIK/REG/2000/36 (17 June 2000).

140 E.g., UNMIK, 'On the Establishment of the Housing and Property Directive and the Housing and Property Claims Commission' UNMIK/REG/1999/23 (15 November 1999).

public enterprises,[141] ordering the detention of individuals,[142] and so on and so forth, just as a government would, and exercised its authority directly over local populations in Kosovo. Likewise, in East Timor, UNTAET exercised its authority in determining the rules and procedures for bank licensing,[143] setting the rules on public procurement of goods and services,[144] establishing a taxation regime,[145] promulgating the transitional rules of criminal procedure,[146] and providing the rules for setting minimum wages,[147] just to name a few examples.

The establishment of two ad hoc international criminal tribunals in the 1990s is another instance in which the UN Security Council's subsidiarity organs directly executed their decisions vis-à-vis the restricted categories of individuals. The Security Council established the International Criminal Tribunal for the former Yugoslavia (ICTY) in 1993 according to Resolutions 808 and 827, and the International Criminal Tribunal for Rwanda (ICTR) in 2004 with Resolution 955.[148] These ad hoc international criminal tribunals were accorded with authority to issue orders not only against the states concerned (namely, former Yugoslavian states and Rwanda) or other UN member states but also against the accused and other individuals such as witnesses.[149]

141 E.g., UNMIK, 'On the Establishment of the Kosovo Trust Agency' UNMIK/REG/2002/12 (13 June 2002).

142 See, e.g., Ombudsperson Institution in Kosovo, 'Special Report No. 3: The Conformity of Deprivations of Liberty under "Executive Orders" with Recognised International Standards' (2001) (29 June 2001).

143 UNTAET, 'On Bank Licensing and Supervision' UNTAET/REG/2000/8 (25 February 2000).

144 UNTAET, 'On Public Procurement for Civil Administration in East Timor' UNTAET/REG/2000/10 (6 March 2000).

145 E.g., UNTAET, 'On a Taxation System for East Timor' UNTAET/REG/2000/18 (30 June 2000).

146 UNTAET, 'On Transitional Rules of Criminal Procedure' UNTAET/REG/2000/30 (25 September 2000).

147 'On the Establishment of a Labour Code for East Timor' UNTAET/REG/2002/5 (1 May 2002).

148 UN Doc S/RES/808 (22 February 1993); UN Doc S/RES/827 (25 May 1993); UN Doc S/RES/955 (8 November 1994).

149 Updated Statute of the International Criminal Tribunal for the Former Yugoslavia, adopted 25 May 1993 by Security Council Resolution 827 (last amended 7 July 2009 by Resolution 1877) Article 19(2). Rule 54 of the Rules of Procedure and Evidence further provides: 'At the request of either party or *proprio motu*, a Judge or a Trial Chamber may issue such orders, summonses, subpoenas, warrants and transfer orders as may be necessary for the purposes of an investigation or for the preparation or conduct of the trial': ICTY Rules of Procedure and Evidence (adopted 11 February 1994, last amended 22 May 2013), IT/32/Rev.49 Rule 54. For the details of the ICTY's decisions and orders concerning individuals' rights and obligations, see Shuichi Furuya, 'Legal Effect of Rules of the International Criminal Tribunals and Court upon Individuals: Emerging International Law of Direct Effect' (2000) 47 *Netherlands International Law Review* 111.

4.4.3 Claiming supremacy over domestic law

As described above, in the contexts of territorial administration and ad hoc criminal tribunals, individuals have been directly subject to regulations, orders, and other kinds of decisions of the UN Security Council's subsidiary organs created under Chapter VII of the UN Charter. For the purpose of this book, a critical feature of UNMIK, UNTAET, ICTY, and ICTR is their claim of supremacy *over* domestic law. In the case of territorial administration in Kosovo, UNMIK's regulation promulgated by the Special Representative of the Secretary-General and subsidiary instruments issued thereunder '[took] precedence' over the pre-existing *domestic* law in Kosovo if the latter conflicted with the former.[150] With respect to East Timor, according to UNTAET Regulation No. 1/1999, the laws applied in East Timor prior to 25 October 1999 shall continue to apply 'insofar as they do not conflict' with regulations and directives issued by the Special Representative of the UN Secretary-General or internationally recognised human rights standards.[151]

Likewise, the UN Security Council extended its claim of supremacy with regard to the ICTY and ICTR. Under the tribunals' statutes, the ICTY and ICTR had primacy over national courts.[152] Under the tribunals' rules of procedure, the obligations of states to cooperate with the tribunals[153] 'prevail over any legal impediment' to the surrender or transfer of the accused or of a witness to the tribunals.[154] Such normative primacy is claimed not only over extradition treaties but also over *national* law.[155] The claim of supremacy over domestic law in the contexts of territorial administration and ad hoc international criminal tribunals is not derived from Article 103 of the UN Charter, which pertains to the claim of primacy over other international agreements. Instead, the privileging of international decisions over domestic law is claimed based on the UN Security Council's authority under Chapter VII to maintain international peace and security.

150 UNMIK/REG/1999/24 (12 December 1999) Section 1.1.

151 UNTAET 'On the Authority' (n 136) Section 3.1. The 'laws applied in East Timor prior to 25 October 1999' were eventually interpreted as Indonesian law, and not Portuguese law: Stahn, *The Law and Practice of International Territorial Administration* (n 133) 668–71; Patrícia Jerónimo, 'Analysis: da Costa v Timor-Leste, Appeal judgment, Case No 03/02, 18th July 2003, Timor-Leste' ILDC 1971 (TL 2003) (March 2013) para A8.

152 ICTY Statute (last amended 7 July 2009) (n 149) Article 9(2); Statute of the International Criminal Tribunal for Rwanda, adopted 8 November 1994 by Security Council Resolution 955 (last amended 16 December 2009 by Resolution 1901) Article 8(2).

153 ICTY Statute (last amended 7 July 2009) (n 149) Article 29; ICTR Statute (last amended 16 December 2009) (n 152) Article 28.

154 ICTY Rules of Procedure and Evidence (adopted 11 February 1994, last amended 22 May 2013), IT/32/Rev.49 (n 149) Rule 58; ICTR Rules of Procedure and Evidence (adopted 29 June 1995, last amended 13 May 2015) Rule 58.

155 ICTY Rules of Procedure and Evidence (adopted 11 February 1994, last amended 22 May 2013), IT/32/Rev.49 (n 149) Rule 58; ICTR Rules of Procedure and Evidence (adopted 29 June 1995, last amended 13 May 2015) (n 154) Rule 58.

4.5 Conclusion: Reduced distance in Chapter VII measures

On multiple fronts, the UN Security Council and its subsidiary organs have been exercising their authority over individuals as part of the UN's response to a threat to international peace and security. This chapter shed light on the three groups of practice. First of all, the Security Council, under its Chapter VII resolutions, has directly demanded that individuals alter their course of action. This first category of practice is demonstrated by paragraph 4 of Resolution 2170 in which the Council directly addressed individuals, and not only their groups and networks. Where the words alone are not sufficient, second, the Security Council's sanctions regimes have designated individuals and entities as the specific targets of asset freezes and travel bans. The 1267 sanctions regime epitomises the development of the Council's listing practice in this regard. Finally, the Security Council's subsidiary organs have directly applied a range of regulations, administrative directives, and orders to individuals. The cases in point are the UN's transitional administrations in Kosovo and East Timor and the ad hoc international tribunals for former Yugoslavia and Rwanda.

By exercising authority over certain categories of individuals, the UN Security Council and its subsidiary organs have limited the 'intermediary' presence of member states over those individuals. By directly addressing individuals under Chapter VII, the Security Council may intend to create an international obligation on such individuals without negotiating with member states' authorities. The intermediation of member states remains critical with respect to targeted sanctions inasmuch as asset freezes and travel bans could only be materialised by member states which, for instance, order their banks to freeze relevant bank accounts. At the same time, the UN's targeted sanctions allow virtually no discretion at least with respect to the prescription of targeted individuals and entities.[156] The intermediary presence of member states is effectively oblivious when the Security Council's subsidiary organs execute regulations, directives, or orders in such a way that they are immediately applicable to local populations, the accused, or witnesses.

On the whole, the distance between the Security Council's exercise of authority and individuals has narrowed down not only at the conceptual sphere of determining what constitutes threats to the peace but also within more substantial measures under Chapter VII of the UN Charter. The three sets of practices highlighted in this chapter – namely, to address individuals under Chapter VII (as examined in section 4.2), to designate individuals as specific targets of restrictive measures (section 4.3), and to apply regulations etc. to individuals (section 4.4) – should be understood together with the conceptual transformation of threats to the peace discussed in chapter 3 of this book. For example, Resolution 2170 was based on the reaffirmation that terrorism in all forms threatens international peace

156 It is, however, noted that the European Court of Human Rights in *Nada* (2012) considered that a state enjoyed certain 'latitude' in implementing the UN's listing decisions: see App No 10593/08 *Nada v Switzerland* (ECtHR Grand Chamber, Judgment of 12 September 2012), para 180.

and security.[157] The same reaffirmation is carried over to Resolution 2253, which extended the strategic targets of the 1267 sanctions regime to ISIL.[158] Under Resolution 1244 on UNMIK, the grave humanitarian situation in Kosovo and the acts of violence against the Kosovo population led to the threats that justified the creation of the UN's territorial administration.[159] Likewise, under Resolution 827 on the ICTY, the threats that sustained the creation of the ad hoc international criminal tribunal included widespread and flagrant violations of international humanitarian law.[160] By accommodating non-inter-state crises and acts of violence into the concept of threats to international peace and security, the UN Security Council laid the ground for the exercise of authority over individuals within the specific measures under Chapter VII.

157 UN Doc S/RES/2170 (15 August 2014) (n 36) para 3 of the preamble.
158 UN Doc S/RES/2253 (17 December 2015) (n 9) para 2 of the preamble.
159 UN Doc S/RES/1244 (10 June 1999) (n 31) paras 4–5 of the preamble.
160 UN Doc S/RES/827 (25 May 1993) (n 148) para 3 of the preamble. Similarly for the ICTR, see UN Doc S/RES/955 (8 November 1994) (n 148) para 4 of the preamble.

5 Reception in international law

A general framework

5.1 Introduction

The practices of the Security Council and its subsidiary organs accommodate a number of connecting points with individuals as part of the UN's undertaking to maintain international peace and security. The Security Council directly demands individuals to change their course of action; its sanctions committees designate particular individuals as the global targets of asset freezes; and the regulations promulgated by the Security Council's subsidiary organs apply directly to individuals.[1] The other side of the coin is that these international institutional practices have limited space for autonomous decision making at the level of member states which have jurisdiction over those individuals.

As the exercise of authority by the Security Council has significant impact on a number of individuals, a critical question arises as to how international law regulates such exercise of authority, or, more precisely, to what extent international law safeguards not only the rights and interests of member states but also those of the affected individuals. This question forms part of the broader inquiry of the rule of law at the international level.[2] Since the World Summit Outcome in 2005, the UN General Assembly has given recognition to the need for universal adherence to the rule of law at 'both the national and *international* levels'.[3] The UN organs are not exempt from this normative development. In the 'Declaration of the High-level Meeting of the General Assembly on the Rule of Law and the National and International Levels' adopted in September 2012, the General Assembly recognised that 'the rule of law applies to all States equally, *and to international organizations, including the United Nations and its principal organs*'.[4] This broad formula by no means signifies that there is a common understanding about what is

1 See chapter 4 of this book.
2 For this inquiry, see Machiko Kanetake, 'The Interfaces between the National and International Rule of Law: A Framework Paper' in M. Kanetake and A. Nollkaemper (eds), *The Rule of Law at the National and International Levels: Contestations and Deference* (Oxford, Hart Publishing, 2016) 11.
3 '2005 World Summit Outcome' UN Doc A/RES/60/1 (24 October 2005) para 134 (emphasis added).
4 Resolution adopted by the General Assembly on 24 September 2012, 'Declaration of the High-level Meeting of the General Assembly on the Rule of Law at the National

actually contained in the catalogue of the rule of law applicable to the UN. To understand legal frameworks regarding the Security Council is therefore a process to induce the meaning of the rule of law at the international level.

This chapter presents a general legal framework regulating the UN Security Council's exercise of authority as a basis for a more specific analysis provided in chapter 6. As a starting point for the elaboration of the legal framework, it may be worth reiterating that the UN Security Council is no doubt bound by law and that the organ's exercise of authority ought to be based on applicable law. Just as any other organs of international organisations, the UN Security Council is established by, and operates under, a constituent instrument. Neither the text nor the spirit of the Charter conceives of the Security Council as *legibus solutus* (unbound by law), as pronounced by the Appeals Chamber of the ICTY in *Tadić*.[5]

The crux, however, lies in the content of *legibus* – which cannot be separated from the kind of *actors* that interpret the laws. As enunciated by the International Court of Justice (ICJ) in 1948, the 'political character' of an organ does not release it from the observance of the treaty provisions.[6] The significance of this tenet depends, however, on how international law constitutes and limits the Security Council's powers.[7] The ICJ's jurisprudence in the early stage of the UN favoured the extension, as opposed to restraint, of the powers of the newly created Organisation (section 5.2 below). Charter provisions also do not seem to constrain the exercise of Chapter VII authority by the Security Council to the same degree in Chapter VI (section 5.3). These doctrinal features are accompanied by the virtual absence of judicial review by international courts (section 5.4). The catalogue of *legibus* therefore seems very limited and thin, with the consequence that those affected would have to avail themselves of diplomatic channels without a set of clear-cut legal principles.

5.2 The powers accorded to the Security Council

5.2.1 The principle of speciality

One of the basic legal principles governing international organisations is the principle of speciality or the principle of attributed powers. International organisations do not exist without an agreement between states, and the principle of speciality

and International Levels' UN Doc A/RES/67/1 (30 November 2012) para 2 (emphasis added).

5 Case No IT-94-1-AR72 *Prosecutor v Duško Tadić, Appeals Chamber, Decision on Jurisdiction* (1996) 35 ILM 32 (ICTY, Decision of 2 October 1995), para 28 (in relation to the Council's power under Article 39 of the UN Charter).

6 *Admission of a State to the United Nations (Charter, Art 4)* [1948] ICJ Reports 57 (Advisory Opinion of 28 May 1948) 64.

7 A sceptical view was notably expressed by Oosthuizen, who argues that the Security Council's enforcement powers are unfettered by international law: see Gabriël H. Oosthuizen, 'Playing the Devil's Advocate: The United Nations Security Council is Unbound by Law' (1999) 12 *Leiden Journal of International Law* 549.

reflects the idea that the authority of international organisations must emanate from the agreement as an embodiment of state consent. In the *Nuclear Weapons (WHO Request)* advisory opinion in 1996, the ICJ summarised the cardinal principle in the following passage:

> international organizations are subjects of international law which do not, unlike States, possess a general competence. International organizations are governed by the 'principle of speciality', that is to say, *they are invested by the States which create them with powers*, the limits of which are a function of the common interests whose promotion those States entrust to them. The Permanent Court of International Justice referred to this basic principle in the following terms:
>
> 'As the European Commission is not a State, but an international institution with a special purpose, it *only has the functions bestowed upon it* by the Definitive Statute with a view to the fulfilment of that purpose, but it has power to exercise these functions to their full extent, in so far as the Statute does not impose restrictions upon it.' (*Jurisdiction of the European Commission of the Danube, Advisory Opinion, P.C.I.J., Series B, No. 14*, p. 64.)[8]

As an organ of an international organisation, the principle of speciality applies to the UN Security Council which 'only has the functions bestowed upon it'[9] by the constituent instrument. The idea of loyalty to a constituent instrument embodies the classic paradigm of international law based on the consent of sovereign states.[10] This paradigm was most evidently expressed in 1927 by the Permanent Court of International Justice (PCIJ) in *Lotus*; its most well-known passage on the 'free will' of states was meant to release them from any rules of international law which they have not agreed upon.[11] The loyalty to states' agreement was also expressed by the PCIJ in its earlier advisory opinion No. 13 in 1926 on the competence of the International Labour Organization (ILO) to regulate the working conditions of (not only employees but also) employers. In endorsing the ILO's competence, the PCIJ carefully confined its judicial role in ascertaining 'what it was the Contracting Parties agreed to' and what they had 'clearly intended'.[12] The loyalty to the member states' agreement and their intention thus guided the

8 *Legality of the Use by a State of Nuclear Weapons in Armed Conflict (WHO Request)* [1996] ICJ Reports 66 (Advisory Opinion of 8 July 1996) 78–9, para 25 (emphasis added).

9 *Jurisdiction of the European Commission of the Danube between Galatz and Braila* PCIJ Publications, Series B, no. 14 (PICJ, Advisory Opinion of 8 December 1927) 64.

10 Jan Klabbers, *An Introduction to International Organizations Law* (3rd edn, Cambridge, Cambridge University Press, 2015) 5, 53.

11 *The Case of the SS 'Lotus'* PCIJ Publications, Series A, no. 10 (PCIJ, Judgment of 7 September 1927) 19.

12 *Competence of the International Labour Organization to Regulate, Incidentally, the Personal Work of the Employer* PCIJ Publications, Series B, no. 13 (PCIJ, Advisory Opinion of 23 July 1926) 18, 23.

PCIJ's formal reasoning which refrained from depicting an international organisation as a dynamic entity.

At the same time, the PCIJ's narrative also preserved the flexibility of the exercise of authority by international organisations. This is illustrated by the passage quoted by the ICJ in *Nuclear Weapons (WHO Request)* from the PCIJ's advisory opinion No. 14 in 1927 on the jurisdiction of the European Commission of the Danube.[13] While the PCIJ limited the functions of the international organisation to those bestowed on it by the constituent instrument, the Court suggested that the organisation could fulfil its functions 'to their full extent' unless the constituent instrument imposes restrictions.[14] In essence, therefore, while the principle of speciality requires the UN organs to exercise their powers within the functions bestowed on them by the Charter, the principle of speciality itself seems to accommodate a great deal of flexibility by allowing international organisations to fulfil their functions to their full extent.

5.2.2 Implied powers

While the principle of speciality is not as rigid as it may seem, international law furnishes additional doctrines which ensure the flexibility of the exercise of authority by international organisations. One of such apparatuses is the well-established doctrine of implied powers. Having articulated the principle of speciality,[15] the ICJ in the *Nuclear Weapons (WHO Request)* advisory opinion continued to describe the doctrine of implied powers:

> The powers conferred on international organizations are normally the subject of an express statement in their constituent instruments. Nevertheless, the necessities of international life may point to the need for organizations, in order to achieve their objectives, to possess *subsidiary powers which are not expressly provided for in the basic instruments* which govern their activities. It is generally accepted that international organizations can exercise such powers, known as *"implied" powers.*[16]

The concept of implied powers was formulated notably by the ICJ's advisory opinions in *Reparation for Injuries* and *Effect of Awards* in 1949 and 1954, respectively. In the *Reparation for Injuries* advisory opinion, in explaining the UN's capacity to claim damages on behalf of its agents, the ICJ invoked the presence of the powers conferred on the Organisation 'by necessary implication as being essential to the performance of its duties'.[17] Such implied powers were

13 See (n 8) and accompanying text; *Jurisdiction of the European Commission of the Danube (PCIJ, 1927)* (n 9) 64.
14 *Jurisdiction of the European Commission of the Danube*, ibid.
15 See (n 8) and accompanying text.
16 *Nuclear Weapons (WHO Request) (ICJ, 1996)* (n 8) 78–9, para 25 (emphasis added).
17 *Reparation for Injuries Suffered in the Service of the United Nations* [1949] ICJ Reports 174 (Advisory Opinion of 11 April 1949) 182.

described as 'necessary intendment out of the Charter'.[18] Likewise, the ICJ in the *Effect of Awards* advisory opinion justified the UN General Assembly's competence to establish the UN's Administrative Tribunal by 'necessary intendment out of the Charter'.[19]

Member states seem to have accepted the concept of implied powers developed by the early jurisprudence of the ICJ. As Quincy Wright remarked in 1960, '[m]ost of the members have accepted the opinion that if existing procedures prove inadequate to realize the purposes and principles, other methods within the spirit of the Charter and not forbidden by its letter, should be devised'.[20] The powers of the UN organs, including those of the Security Council, can thus be implied under international law to the extent that they are necessary for the performance of the Council's (and thus the UN's) duties.

The doctrine of implied powers apparently has merit in securing the adaptability of international organisations to changing political circumstances. At the same time, it readily feeds the extension of the powers of organisations potentially in a manner that is detrimental to member states and the wider constituencies. The doctrine of implied powers is supposed to have a built-in limitation in a sense that the powers 'cannot freely be implied' as observed by the ICJ in *Reparation for Injuries.*[21] Nevertheless, in the early stage of the UN, the ICJ formulated the doctrine in a way that favours the extension of powers rather than constraining them. In *Reparation for Injuries* in 1949, the ICJ justified the UN's competence as being necessary for the '*efficient* and independent performance of [the] missions'.[22] Likewise, in the *Effect of Awards* case in 1954, the General Assembly's power to establish the Administrative Tribunal was considered as being 'essential to ensure the *efficient* working of the Secretariat'.[23] The ICJ's narratives suggest the Court's inclination to support and boost the activities of the newly created UN. According to the ICJ's formulation of the implied powers, the UN Security

18 Ibid., 184.

19 *Effect of Awards of Compensation Made by the United Nations Administrative Tribunal* [1954] ICJ Reports 47 (Advisory Opinion of 13 July 1954) 57.

20 Quincy Wright, *International Law and the United Nations* (Westport, Connecticut, Greenwood Press, 1960) 31.

21 *Reparation for Injuries (ICJ, 1949)* (n 17) 198 (dissenting opinion of Judge Hackworth); Jan Klabbers, 'Constitutionalism Lite' (2004) 1 *International Organizations Law Review* 31, 38–9.

22 *Reparation for Injuries (ICJ, 1949)* (n 17) 183 (emphasis added). To ensure 'efficient' performance is more extensive than simply to ensure the 'performance' of the UN's duties: see ibid., 182. It must be noted that the use of such an expansive concept itself was not the main point of dissent by Judge Hackworth; the disagreement was rather factual as to whether the efficient performance of UN mandates necessitated functional protection. According to Judge Hackworth, '[t]he exercise of an additional extraordinary power … has not been shown to be necessary to the *efficient performance of duty* by either the Organization or its agents' (emphasis added): ibid., 198 (dissenting opinion of Judge Hackworth).

23 *Effect of Awards (ICJ, 1954)* (n 19) 57 (emphasis added). Also, in this case, the Court invoked the efficient working of the individual organs, as opposed to the organisation at large: see Klabbers, *An Introduction to International Organizations Law* (n 10) 59.

Council can extend its powers to those that are necessary not only for the mandate but also for the efficient working of the Security Council.

5.2.3 Subsequent interpretive development

The rule of treaty interpretation is another facet of international law that accommodates the flexibility in the scope of the powers of the UN and other international organisations. The established general rule on the interpretation of treaties, including constituent instruments of international organisations, is laid down in Articles 31 and 32 of the Vienna Convention on the Law of Treaties. According to the Vienna Convention, the basic formula of treaty interpretation is simple: namely, one must follow the 'ordinary meaning' given to treaty terms.[24] Yet the 'ordinary' meaning is a highly relative notion which varies depending on the context of treaty terms, the object and purpose of the treaty, subsequent agreement, subsequent practice, and any relevant rules of international law.[25] Reference to preparatory works can also be licensed by Article 32 of the Vienna convention as supplementary means.[26]

The Vienna Convention on the Law of Treaties does not provide guidance on how one should weigh one interpretive element (e.g., object and purpose) against another (e.g., subsequent practice). While texts circumscribe available options, they are apparently not determinative.[27] The history of the UN demonstrates that apparently precise terms have been given various meanings.[28] In the *Certain Expenses* case, for instance, the term 'expenses' under Article 17(2) of the UN Charter did not offer a determinative answer to the question under dispute.[29]

24 Vienna Convention on the Law of Treaties, 23 May 1969, 1155 UNTS 311 (entered into force 27 January 1980) Article 31(1). An exception is when the parties have given a 'special meaning' to a term: Article 31(4). Articles 31–32 is the marriage of three schools of thought: textual (ordinary meaning), teleological (object and purpose), and historical (recourse to preparatory works) approaches: see Gerald G. Fitzmaurice, 'Law and Procedure of the International Court of Justice: Treaty Interpretation and Certain Other Treaty Points' (1951) 28 *British Year Book of International Law* 1, 1–2.

25 Vienna Convention on the Law of Treaties (n 24) Article 31(1), (2), (3).

26 See Robert Kolb, *Interprétation et création du droit international: Esquisses d'une herméneutique juridique moderne pour le droit international public* (Bruxelles, Bruylant, 2006) 644–5 ('il faut se rendre compte que l'existence même de termes «non clairs» ou non «parfaitement clairs» est une notion malléable …'). On the reliance on the preparatory work, see Hersch Lauterpacht, 'De L'Interpretation des Traités: Rapport' (1950) (1950-II) 43 *Annuaire de l'Institute de Droit International* 366, 390–1. For the details of debates regarding the *travaux préparatoires*, see Jan Klabbers, 'International Legal Histories: The Declining Importance of Travaux Préparatoires in Treaty Interpretation?' (2003) 50 *Netherlands International Law Review* 267.

27 Kolb, *Interprétation et création du droit international* (n 26) 407.

28 Oscar Schachter, 'Interpretation of the Charter in the Political Organs of the United Nations' in S. Engel (ed.), *Law, State and International Legal Order: Essays in Honor of Hans Kelsen* (University of Tennessee Press, 1964) 269, 274–5 (classifying Charter terms into specific rules, general principles, and standards, which are interpreted in different manners).

29 Kolb, *Interprétation et création du droit international* (n 26) 404.

Although the principle of effectiveness is still extant as a general rule to be applied when more than one reading is possible,[30] which construction 'enable[s] the treaty to have appropriate effects'[31] may likewise be open to more than one construction.[32]

The ICJ's advisory opinion in *Namibia* in 1971 exposes the fact that the terms of a treaty can be given very different meanings depending on a context.[33] In 1970, the UN Security Council adopted Resolution 284 in order to seek the ICJ's advisory opinion on the continued presence of South Africa in Namibia.[34] In response, South Africa considered Resolution 284 invalid on the basis that two permanent members of the UN Security Council abstained from voting in adopting the resolution. South Africa's claim probably had merit according to the literal reading of Article 27 of the UN Charter, in which the Security Council's decisions on non-procedural matters 'shall be made by an *affirmative* vote of nine members including the *concurring* votes of the permanent members'.[35] Nevertheless, in the 1971 advisory opinion, the ICJ confirmed that the abstention of a permanent member constituted an 'affirmative … [and] concurring' vote, on the basis that Council members' consistent and uniform practice and member states' general acceptance have led to a 'general practice of that Organization [i.e., the UN]'.[36]

The reasoning of the ICJ in *Namibia* suggests the relative weight given to 'subsequent practice' under Article 31(3)(b) of the Vienna Convention among a range of interpretive elements.[37] The relative importance given to subsequent practice can be justified by the UN Charter's 'special characteristics'[38] that it has not only conventional but also institutional dimensions.[39] The UN Charter is one of many living instruments[40] in the sense that it constitutes an organisation of a highly public nature, which is expected to respond to the changing needs of member states and the wider international community, and which is administered on a daily basis by a range of organs and personnel therein. The interpretation of such an instrument requires relative weight to be placed on operational

30 'Draft Articles on the Law of Treaties' (1966) II *Yearbook of the International Law Commission* 177, 219, para 6 (commentary to Article 28 (now Article 32)).
31 Ibid.
32 See generally Elihu Lauterpacht, 'The Development of the Law of International Organization by the Decision of International Tribunals' (1976-IV) 152 *Recueil des Cours* 377, 420–65.
33 *Legal Consequences for States of the Continued Presence of South Africa in Namibia (South West Africa) notwithstanding Security Council Resolution 276 (1970)* [1971] ICJ Reports 16 (Advisory Opinion of 21 June 1971).
34 UN Doc S/RES/284 (29 July 1970).
35 Charter of the United Nations, 26 June 1945, 1 UNTS XVI (entered into force 24 October 1945) Article 27(3) (emphasis added).
36 *Namibia (ICJ, 1971)* (n 33) para 22.
37 Vienna Convention on the Law of Treaties (n 24) Article 31(3)(b).
38 *Certain Expenses of the United Nations (Article 17, Paragraph 2, of the Charter)* [1962] ICJ Reports 151 (Advisory Opinion of 20 July 1962) 157.
39 *Nuclear Weapons (WHO Request) (ICJ, 1996)* (n 8) 75, para 19.
40 Pollux, 'The Interpretation of the Charter' (1946) 23 *British Year Book of International Law* 54, 54.

effectiveness rather than contractual stability. This interpretive ethos leads to a greater emphasis on the subsequent practices as well as purposes, as opposed to the literal reading of the text or a reliance on the drafting process.[41]

In theory, the preference of subsequent practice does not mean that the Security Council's institutional practice 'establishes the agreement of the parties regarding its interpretation'.[42] Judge Spender's warning, expressed in the *Certain Expenses* case, not to equate the practice of the organ with that of member states is perfectly valid.[43] The ICJ has been cautious about sanctioning institutional practices which reflect the will of only parts of states, and they often make sure to refer to the existence of other states' implicit approval. However, the need for other states' implicit approval does not change the fact that the Security Council, like any other UN organ, is in the primary position to give interpretation through its institutional life,[44] which is presumed to be valid[45] and is often unchallenged by member states which may not see any political advantage in contesting the decisions of the UN Security Council. Therefore, in practice, subsequent practice would likely feed the extension of the Security Council's power at the expense of the participation of member states outside the Council.[46]

5.3 Legal limits to the Security Council's powers: Article 1(1) of the UN Charter

Despite the presence of the doctrine of implied powers and the interpretive development, an international organisation does not have the power to exercise

41 See, e.g., *Namibia (ICJ, 1971)* (n 33) 22, para 22; *Legal Consequences of the Construction of a Wall in the Occupied Palestinian Territory, Advisory Opinion* (2004) [2004] ICJ Reports 136 (Advisory Opinion of 9 July 2004), 149, para 27. The emphasis on subsequent practice does not mean that such practice could constitute an autonomous element for the purpose of interpreting the Charter. On this issue, compare, Dapo Akande, 'International Organizations' in M.D. Evans (ed.), *International Law* (Oxford, Oxford University Press, 2014) 248, 259–60; G. Ress, 'The Interpretation of the Charter' in B. Simma (ed.), *The Charter of the United Nations: A Commentary* (2nd edn, Oxford, Oxford University Press, 2002) 13, 27–30; Stefan Kadelbach, 'Interpretation' in B. Simma and others (eds), *The Charter of the United Nations: A Commentary* (3rd edn, 2012) 71, 86–7.

42 Vienna Convention on the Law of Treaties (n 24) Article 31(3)(b).

43 *Certain Expenses (ICJ, 1962)* (n 38) 182–97 (Separate Opinion of Judge Sir Percy Spender).

44 The UN organs' primary authority to interpret their own competence was already recognised by the delegates during the San Francisco Conference in 1945: Documents of the United Nations Conference on International Organization, San Francisco, 1945 (London; New York, United Nations Information Organizations, 1945) vol. 13 at 831–2.

45 *Certain Expenses (ICJ, 1962)* (n 38) 168. The ICJ observed that 'when the Organization takes action which warrants the assertion that it was appropriate for the fulfilment of one of the stated purposes of the United Nations, the presumption is that such action is not *ultra vires* the Organization' (ibid.). Likewise, *Namibia (ICJ, 1971)* (n 33) 21–2, para 20.

46 José E. Alvarez, *International Organizations as Law-Makers* (Oxford, Oxford University Press, 2005) 91–2.

authority if the constituent instrument 'impose[s] restrictions upon it', as the PCIJ noted in its advisory opinion in 1927 on the jurisdiction of the European Commission of the Danube.[47] To what extent the Charter ought to impose general restrictions on the Security Council's exercise of authority was one of the central debates among states at the San Francisco Conference in 1945. The record of the Conference reveals that there was a clear division between small and medium-sized states on the one hand, and the Four Powers on the other hand. The small and medium-sized states did not dispute the need for effectiveness and flexibility in the Security Council's decision making. Also, having been called upon at the final stage of the drafting process, they were aware that a number of key provisions agreed upon by the Four Powers could not be fundamentally changed. Yet the delegations still made a number of attempts to make changes to the Dumbarton Oaks proposals,[48] seeking to reduce 'somewhat the unlimited breadth of the powers' of the Security Council.[49]

One key point of debates at the San Francisco Conference concerned whether to insert the principles of 'justice' or international law after the first line of Article 1(1) of the UN Charter, which lays down the purposes of the UN.[50] The purposes laid down in Article 1 are relevant for the Security Council as its exercise of authority has to conform to them.[51] Under the Dumbarton Oaks Proposals, the provision originally read:

> To maintain international peace and security; and to that end to take effective collective measures for the prevention and removal of threats to the peace and

47 See (n 8) and accompanying text; *Jurisdiction of the European Commission of the Danube (PCIJ, 1927)* (n 9) 64.

48 In addition to the insertion of international law and justice, an attempt was made by small and medium-sized states to institutionally counterbalance the power of the Security Council with that of the General Assembly. New Zealand put forward a proposal with which to prevent the Security Council from taking enforcement measures without the concurring vote of the General Assembly except for cases of extreme urgency: UNCIO Documents (n 44) vol. 3, at 488 ('Amendments to the Dumbarton Oaks Proposals (Document 1 G/1) Submitted by the Delegation of New Zealand', Doc 2, G/14(f), 2 May 1945, at 3). Likewise, Mexico proposed to vest the General Assembly with the authority analogous to the Council, enabling the former to make a preliminary determination, and subjecting non-military enforcement measures with the prior decision of the Assembly: ibid., vol. 3, at 186–7 (Mexico, Doc 2, G/7(c)(1), 5 May 1945, at 12–13).

49 UNCIO Documents, ibid., vol. 3, at 256 (Guatemala, Doc 2, G/7(f), 23 April 1945, at 3).

50 On Article 1(1) of the UN Charter, see further Clyde Eagleton, 'International Law and the Charter of the United Nations' (1945) 39 *American Journal of International Law* 751 (overviewing a 'secondary position' given to international law under the UN Charter, including the issue of Article 1(1)); Leland M. Goodrich, Edvard Isak Hambro and Anne Patricia Simons, *Charter of the United Nations: Commentary and Documents* (3rd and revised edn, New York, Columbia University Press, 1969) 27–8; Terry D. Gill, 'Legal Aspects of the Transfer of Authority in UN Peace Operations' (2011) 42 *Netherlands Yearbook of International Law* 37, 65–7.

51 UN Charter (n 35) Article 24(2).

> the suppression of acts of aggression or other breaches of the peace, and to bring about by peaceful means adjustment or settlement of international disputes which may lead to a breach of the peace.[52]

Small and medium-sized states submitted a range of analogous proposals to revise this provision, particularly in order to subject the Security Council's exercise of authority to 'justice'. For instance, Egypt proposed the addition of 'in accordance with law and justice';[53] Turkey suggested inserting the phrase 'in conformity with right and justice';[54] the Mexican equivalent was the phrase 'within a system of Law, Justice, and Equity';[55] and Bolivia proposed the addition of the phase 'under the rule of justice' in the first line.[56] There were also some other proposals referring to 'international law'. Iran suggested inserting the line 'on the basis of right, justice and the principles of international law';[57] and Panama's proposal was to supplement the provision with the phrase 'in conformity with the fundamental principles of international law'.[58] The Greek and Dutch versions were longer and more comprehensive: Greece submitted the addition of the sentence 'with due respect for contractual obligations and the generally accepted principles of international law, justice and morality';[59] and the Netherlands suggested either inserting the phrase 'in conformity with the elementary principles of morality and justice and on the basis of due regard for international law' or adding a statement setting forth the fundamental rights and duties of states.[60]

These proposals were apparently intended to circumscribe the discretion of the Security Council according to the principles of justice and international law. In proposing to add the term 'justice' to the first paragraph of Article 1(1) of the UN Charter,[61] Uruguay expressed its desire that the ideas of liberty, justice, and law 'may prevail in the system, the program and the work of the international organization'.[62] The 'prevailing opinion of the Conference' was that the chief purpose

52 Dumbarton Oaks Proposals, UNCIO Documents (n 44) vol. 3, at 2 (Doc 1, G/1), Chapter I(1).
53 UNCIO Documents, ibid., vol. 3, at 453 (Egypt, Doc 2, G/7(p)(1), 5 May 1945, at 1) (emphasis omitted).
54 Ibid., vol. 3, at 484 (Turkey, Doc 2, G/14(e)(1), 5 May 1945, at 1).
55 Ibid., vol. 3, at 178 (Mexico, Doc 2, G/7(c)(1), 5 May 1945, at 4).
56 Ibid., vol. 3, at 582 (Bolivia, Doc 2, G/14(r), 5 May 1945, at 6) (emphasis omitted).
57 Ibid., vol. 3, at 554 (Iran, Doc 2, G/14(m), 5 May 1945, at 1).
58 Ibid., vol. 3, at 265 (Panama, Doc 2, G/7(g)(2), 5 May 1945, at 1).
59 Ibid., vol. 3, at 531 (Greece, Doc 2, G/14(i), 4 May 1945, at 1).
60 Ibid., vol. 3, at 323 (The Netherlands, Doc 2, G/7(j)(1), 1 May 1945). Furthermore, in relation to Article 1(2), Australia proposed adding the words 'promote justice and the rule of law in international affairs' after 'universal peace': ibid., vol. 3, at 543 (Doc 2, G/14(l), 5 May 1945, at 1). Uruguay envisaged 'universal peace' to be ensured 'by the rule of morality and law': ibid., vol. 3, at 34 (Uruguay, Doc 2, G/7(a)(1), 5 May 1945, at 1) (emphasis omitted).
61 Ibid., vol. 3, at 34 (Uruguay, Doc 2, G/7(a)(1), 5 May 1945, at 1) (emphasis omitted).
62 Ibid., vol. 3, at 27 (Uruguay, Doc 2, G/7(a), 5 May 1945, at 2).

of the UN must be accomplished 'in accordance with some rules'.[63] The omission of 'justice' or 'international law' would infer, several delegations feared, that the Organisation intended to impose 'a peace of expediency rather than a peace founded on justice' without following 'the rule of justice'.[64] Several member states advocated the explicit reference to justice since the 'clear inference' of the omission would have suggested that 'we do not have to consider the principles of international law and justice' with respect to the maintenance of peace and security.[65] As the Egyptian delegation warned, the Security Council will 'play the part of the political court of law'. It was considered 'indispensable that the principles of justice and law should always be present in its deliberations'.[66]

The efforts made by these small and medium-sized states to fetter the discretion of the Security Council through the rule of law encountered opposition from the sponsoring Powers. Although the major powers upheld that justice and law should be included in Article 1(1) of the UN Charter, they 'differed as to the place in that paragraph'.[67] The delegate of the US famously articulated two different functions that the Security Council was entrusted to assume: one of a policeman, and the other of a jury. The policeman's role is to stop fighting or the beginning of a fight, which must be short and abrupt.[68] The US delegate indicated that it is in the case of a jury phase that the conformity with justice and international law would come into play.[69] The sponsoring Powers therefore proposed to insert the principles of justice and international law into the latter part of Article 1(1) regarding dispute settlement (i.e., 'to bring about by peaceful means ... settlement of international disputes'),[70] and not the former (i.e., 'to take effective collective measures for the prevention and removal of threats to the peace'). The rationale presented by the Four Powers was to secure the effectiveness of the role of policeman, by deferring the assessment into the rights or wrongs of a situation until the phase of peaceful settlement.[71]

63 Ibid., vol. 6, at 318 ('Summary Report of Ninth Meeting of Committee I/1', Doc 742, I/1/23, 1 June 1945, at 2).
64 Ibid., vol. 6, at 318 ('Summary Report of Ninth Meeting of Committee I/1', Doc 742, I/1/23, 1 June 1945, at 2).
65 Ibid., vol. 6, at 28 (statement by Mr. Alfaro of Panama) ('Verbatim Minutes of First Meeting of Commission I', Doc 1006, I/6, 15 June 1945, at 17).
66 Ibid., vol. 6, at 24 (statement by Mandouh Bey Riaz of Egypt) ('Verbatim Minutes of First Meeting of Commission I', Doc 1006, I/6, 15 June 1945, at 13).
67 Ibid., vol. 6, at 23 (statement by Mandouh Bey Riaz of Egypt) ('Verbatim Minutes of First Meeting of Commission I', Doc 1006, I/6, 15 June 1945, at 12).
68 Ibid., vol. 6, at 29 (statement by Mr. Stassen of USA) ('Verbatim Minutes of First Meeting of Commission I', Doc 1006, I/6, 15 June 1945, at 18).
69 Ibid., vol. 6, at 29–30 (statement by Mr. Stassen of USA) ('Verbatim Minutes of First Meeting of Commission I', Doc 1006, I/6, 15 June 1945, at 18–19).
70 The Chinese proposal supported by the Powers: ibid., vol. 3, at 25 (China, Doc 1, G/1(a), 1 May 1945).
71 Ruth B. Russell, *A History of the United Nations Charter: The Role of the United States 1940–1945* (Washington, DC, The Brookings Institution, 1958) 656. See UNCIO Documents (n 44) vol. 6, at 453 ('Report of Rapporteur of Committee 1 to

The Four Powers' contention, however, did not convince a majority of delegations, who still feared that the policeman would be free from the constraints of justice and international law. The voting record evidences their dissatisfaction. The proposal to insert the words 'in conformity with the principles of justice and international law' in the first line was put to vote twice, once at the Committee I/1 and the other at the Commission I. On both occasions, the proposed amendment fell short of winning the two-thirds majority necessary for the adoption of the amendment. Nevertheless, it was still supported by a majority of 19 votes against 15 at the Committee I/1,[72] and by 21 votes against 21 at the Commission I.[73] The report of the Rapporteur of Committee I/1 best captures the common denominator of the delegates at the San Francisco Conference. According to the Rapporteur, despite the rejection of the reference to justice and international law, '[t]here was no intention to let this notion lose any of its weight or strength, as an over-ruling norm of the whole Charter'.[74]

Overall, the drafting history of Article 1 (1) of the UN Charter demonstrates that the drafters did not intend to free the Security Council from justice and international law when acting under Chapter VII, but they fell short of constraining the exercise of Chapter VII authority to the same degree as it is in Chapter VI. While, subsequently, the General Assembly invoked the principles provided in Article 1(1) in various resolutions,[75] they have not led to the formulation of alternative reading of Article 1(1) with regard to the role of international law as a general constraint on the Security Council's exercise of authority under Chapter VII.

5.4 Limited judicial review by international courts

The adaptability of the UN Security Council's authority to changing political requisites is preserved not only by the broadly formulated terms of the UN Charter but also the doctrine of implied powers and the rule of treaty interpretation which often works in favour of endorsing the practices of the UN organ itself. Having said that, the exercise of authority by the UN Security Council can still be

Commission I', Doc. 944, I/1/34, 13 June 1945, at 8), 318 ('Summary Report of Ninth Meeting of Committee I/1', Doc. 742, I/1/23, 1 June 1945, at 2).

72 UNCIO Documents (n 44) vol. 6, at 318 ('Summary Report of Ninth Meeting of Committee I/1', Doc. 742, I/1/23, 1 June 1945, at 2).

73 Ibid., vol. 6, at 34 ('Verbatim Minutes of First Meeting of Commission I', Doc 1006, I/6, 15 June 1945, at 23).

74 Ibid., vol. 6, at 453–4 ('Report of Rapporteur of Committee 1 to Commission I', Doc 944, I/1/34, 13 June 1945, at 8–9). Also, the subcommittee gave an assurance that none of its members wished to contend that 'real and durable peace can be based on anything other than justice': ibid., vol. 11, at 12, 18–19. The concept of justice and international law was considered as finding a 'more appropriate' place in the latter part of Article 1(1) concerning dispute settlements: ibid., vol. 6, at 453 ('Report of Rapporteur of Committee 1 to Commission I', Doc 944, I/1/34, 13 June 1945, at 8).

75 See Rüdiger Wolfrum, 'Article 1' in B. Simma and others (eds), *The Charter of the United Nations: A Commentary* (3rd edn, 2012) 107, 118.

effectively restricted if it is subject to judicial review at the international level. International courts could potentially elucidate a set of principles through the creative interpretation of Charter provisions and any relevant rules of international law. However, the instances of judicial review are almost non-existent, not necessarily because of the limited availability of judicial procedures but owing to the unwillingness of member states and, possibly, of international courts, to put the Security Council's exercise of authority under judicial scrutiny.

5.4.1 Request for advisory opinions

Despite being the principal judicial organ of the UN, the Charter does not expressly situate the ICJ as a site for ensuring legal coherence within the activities of the UN's political organs. As indicated by the ICJ in *Namibia* and *Certain Expenses*, the Charter does not constitute the ICJ as some kind of a higher authority to review the decisions of UN organs.[76] Nor does the Charter expressly prohibit the Court from doing so.[77] In the absence of clear instructions from the UN Charter, the ICJ has maintained the position that it will consider the validity of resolutions of the General Assembly and the Security Council when exercising its judicial function under the UN Charter and the ICJ Statute,[78] even if such questions on validity do not form the subject of the request for an advisory opinion.[79] In theory, the General Assembly is competent under Article 96(1) of the UN Charter to request the ICJ to give an advisory opinion with respect to the Security Council's exercise of authority insofar as the UN General Assembly secures a majority to support such a request. The question does not have to be of a specific case; it can be of an abstract nature insofar as it is a legal one.[80] The absence of universal political approval does not always dissuade the organ from making such requests, as demonstrated by the request for the advisory opinion on nuclear weapons adopted with as many as 43 states against and 38 abstaining.[81]

76 *Namibia (ICJ, 1971)* (n 33) para 89 (observing that the Court does not possess powers of judicial review); *Certain Expenses (ICJ, 1962)* (n 38) 168 (noting that the ICJ does not have the ultimate authority to interpret the Charter).

77 Dapo Akande, 'The International Court of Justice and the Security Council: Is there Room for Judicial Control of Decisions of the Political Organs of the United Nations?' (1997) 46 *International and Comparative Law Quarterly* 309, 326.

78 *Certain Expenses (ICJ, 1962)* (n 38) 157; *Namibia (ICJ, 1971)* (n 33) 45 (para 89), 53 (para 115). Compare *Namibia*, ibid., 143–4 (separate opinion of Judge Onyeama), 151–2 (separate opinion of Judge Dillard), 180–2 (separate opinion of Judge De Castro); with ibid., 105 (separate opinion of Judge Padilla Nervo).

79 *Namibia (ICJ, 1971)* (n 33) 45, para 89. Although the ICJ retains discretion whether to give an advisory opinion under Article 65 of the ICJ Statute, the Court takes the position that only 'compelling reasons' would justify a refusal: *Legality of the Threat or Use of Nuclear Weapons* [1996] ICJ Reports 226 (Advisory Opinion of 8 July 1996) 235, para 14 and cases cited therein.

80 *Admission of a State to the United Nations (Charter, Art. 4)* (n 6) 61.

81 UN Doc A/RES/49/75K (1995) (voted on 15 December 1994).

The history of the UN, in fact, records some general proposals to utilise the General Assembly's power to request an advisory opinion from the ICJ in an effort to control the Security Council. In 1993, Colombia envisaged the use of the ICJ's advisory opinion as one possible way through with which a 'constitutional monitoring body ... would determine the legality of actions taken by United Nations organs'.[82] Likewise, in 1995, Algeria pointed out that 'constitutional control' by the ICJ of the acts of the Council was an 'untapped and unexplored' resource, encouraging the Assembly to leverage it.[83] In 2008, Austria presented before the General Assembly an outcome report of a four-year project on 'the UN Security Council and the Rule of Law',[84] and the report drew attention to the General Assembly's request for ICJ opinions as one way to check the Council's powers.[85]

Nevertheless, these general and sporadic suggestions have not been developed into a tangible momentum at the General Assembly to utilise the ICJ's advisory opinions for the purpose of verifying the compatibility with international law of the Security Council's exercise of power. An exception may be *Certain Expenses*; the question referred to by the General Assembly, on the legal status of UN peacekeeping expenditures, effectively required the ICJ to assess the validity of ONUC established by a Security Council resolution. At the same time, the General Assembly sought the ICJ's opinion in *Certain Expenses*, not to test the Security Council's decisions but to assess the UN Secretary-General's role that was heavily contested by the former Soviet-bloc states.[86]

The apparent lack of incentive for the General Assembly to utilise the ICJ can be explained by the following two interrelated reasons. One factor may be that the General Assembly can directly recommend the Security Council to adjust its practice without relying in the ICJ's apparatus. For instance, the General Assembly in its World Summit Outcome in 2005 called upon the Security Council to ensure 'fair and clear procedures' for the Council's targeted sanctions.[87] Likewise, the General Assembly in its resolution on the rule of law in 2012 encouraged the Security Council to ensure that 'fair and clear procedures' are maintained and further developed.[88] The General Assembly, as it is not as circumscribed as a

82 Report of the Secretary-General, 'Question of Equitable Representation on and Increase in the Membership of the Security Council' UN Doc A/48/264 (20 July 1993) 23, para 19 (reply from Colombia).

83 UN Doc A/50/PV.30 (12 October 1995) 10 (Mr. Lamamra of Algeria).

84 'The UN Security Council and the Rule of Law' UN Doc A/63/69–S/2008/270 (7 May 2008). For details, see Konrad G. Bühler, 'The Austrian Rule of Law Initiative 2004–2008: The Panel Series, the Advisory Group and the Final Report on the UN Security Council and the Rule of Law' (2008) 12 *Max Planck Yearbook of United Nations Law* 410.

85 'The UN Security Council and the Rule of Law' (n 84) para 29.

86 See Certain Expenses of the United Nations (Article 17, Paragraph 2, of the Charter), Pleadings, Oral Arguments, Documents (1962) 271–2 (Memorandum of the USSR Government).

87 '2005 World Summit Outcome' (n 3) para 109. See further chapter 8 of this book.

88 Resolution adopted by the General Assembly on 24 September 2012, High-level Meeting Declaration on the Rule of Law (2012) (n 4) para 29.

judicial organ, can readily engage in developing a new norm for fettering the Security Council's discretion.

Another and related point is that the request for the ICJ's advisory opinion may result in the Court giving official endorsement to the Security Council's practice. In the first two decades of the UN, the ICJ gave its opinions on the competence of the UN organs in a series of cases including *First Admissions*, *Reparation for Injuries*, *Effect of Awards*, and *Certain Expenses*. In these cases, the ICJ attached more weight to the functions and autonomy of UN organs than to the terms of the Charter or the intention of drafters.[89] Although, since the 1990s, some international decisions have started to engage in finding limits to the authority of international organisations,[90] the judicial trend may not be so straightforward as to remove the anxiety that the ICJ might authoritatively approve and legitimise the Security Council's activities.

If the General Assembly does not utilise the ICJ, then there is no good prospect of building international jurisprudence to regulate the exercise of the Security Council's authority through the ICJ's advisory opinions. Although Article 96(1) of the UN Charter paves the way for the Security Council itself to request an opinion from the ICJ, the Council has hardly utilised the ICJ even for dispute settlement, much less for fettering its own powers.[91] Obviously, the permanent members hardly find any incentives for seeking judicial advice to verify the constitutionality of the Security Council's practice. Symbolic in this regard was a response to Belgium's draft resolution in 1947. Belgium proposed to request an advisory opinion of the ICJ after the Netherlands, relying on Article 2(7) of the UN Charter, objected to the Security Council's competence to deal with the Indonesian question.[92] Belgium's proposal was disapproved by the majority of Security Council members. The Chinese delegate stated that the legal opinion 'might turn out to be a very tight straitjacket' and 'very inconvenient' for addressing a problem in a rapidly changing world.[93]

Interestingly, despite the unlikelihood that the Security Council would submit its decisions to the ICJ's review, the Non-Aligned Movement (NAM) still urged in 2006 the Security Council 'to consider its decisions be reviewed by the ICJ', bearing in mind the need to 'ensure their adherence to the UN Charter, and international law'.[94] Such inducement was reiterated by the NAM in its summit

89 Kolb, *Interprétation et création du droit international* (n 26) 189–202.

90 Jan Klabbers, 'The *Bustani* Case before the ILOAT: Constitutionalism in Disguise?' (2004) 53 *International and Comparative Law Quarterly* 455.

91 Otto Spijkers, 'What's Wrong with the Relationship between the International Court of Justice and the Security Council?' in C. Ryngaert and others (eds), *What's Wrong with International Law? Liber Amicorum A.H.A. Soons* (Leiden, Nijhoff, 2015) 347.

92 Repertory of Practice of the United Nations Organs (1945–1954) vol. 1, at 118, paras 287–9; ibid., vol. 5, at 51, paras 67–9.

93 UN Doc S/PV.195 (26 August 1947) UN SCOR, 2nd year, at 2217 (Mr. Tsiang of China); Mohammed Bedjaoui, *The New World Order and the Security Council: Testing the Legality of its Acts* (Dordrecht; Boston, Martinus Nijhoff Publishers, 1994) 162. See also UN Doc S/894 (13 July 1948) (a Syrian draft on the Palestinian question).

94 'Final Document of the Fourteenth Summit Conference of Heads of State or Government of the Non-Aligned Movement (11–16 September 2006)' UN Doc A/61/

document in 2012.[95] Given the highly implausible prospect of the Council's voluntary submission, one cannot help wondering if the NAM's statement rather reflects the reluctance of many members to utilise the ICJ for controlling the Security Council's decision making. Even if some states advocate greater use of the ICJ, an individual state is not competent to request an advisory opinion from the ICJ. A famous episode in this regard is Belgium's unsuccessful proposal at the San Francisco Conference to allow a state which considers that its essential rights are infringed upon by the Security Council to request an ICJ opinion. Austria and Belgium made similar attempts in 1947, which likewise failed to receive endorsement from the core Security Council members.[96] While there are still possibilities that the decisions of the Security Council would be subject to judicial scrutiny in contentious cases, this would only be in rare instances in which the legality of a Security Council resolution and the subject matter of the dispute are inextricably linked, as will be examined below.

5.4.2 Incidental review

Apart from advisory opinions, the ICJ could in principle review the Security Council's exercise of authority in the course of deciding on contentious cases. Opportunities for the ICJ to exercise its incidental jurisdiction are limited, however, in that the validity of the Security Council's exercise of authority has to be intertwined with the subject matter of the dispute. Such a rare occasion occurred in the *Lockerbie* case in which Libya's inter-state claims against the UK and the US gave rise to the validity of relevant Security Council resolutions. The *Lockerbie* case, while being a contentious case between Libya and the UK/US over the extradition of the Lockerbie suspects,[97] raised questions over the validity of Security Council Resolutions 731 and 748 which respectively urged and obligated Libya to respond to the extradition request.[98]

472–S/2006/780 (29 September 2006) Annex I, para 16.8. This is identical to 'Final Document of Fifteenth Ministerial Conference of the Non-Aligned Movement (27–30 July 2008)' UN Doc A/62/929 (11 August 2008) para 16.9.

95 'Final Document of the 16th Summit of Heads of State or Government of the Non-Aligned Movement (Tehran Document)' NAM 2012/Doc.1/Rev.2 (31 August 2012) para 24.9.

96 See Bedjaoui, *The New World Order and the Security Council* (n 93) 164–82.

97 The US and the UK have requested that Libya extradite the suspects: UN Doc A/46/827-S/23308 (31 December 1991) Annex.

98 UN Doc S/RES/731 (21 January 1992) para 3; UN Doc S/RES/748 (1992) para 1. It is noted that paragraph 3 of Resolution 731 urges Libya 'to provide a full and effective response' to extradition requests, and not to adhere to them. Thus, Libya contended that Council resolutions merely imposed an obligation to negotiate: 'Questions d'interprétation et d'application de la convention de Montréal de 1971 résultant de l'incident aérien de Lockerbie (Jamahiriya arabe libyenne c. Royaume-Uni)' (1993) Mémoire de la Libye (20 December 1993) 153–9, 165–6. On this point, see Nigel D. White, 'Case Analysis: To Review or Not to Review? The Lockerbie Cases Before the World Court' (1999) 12 *Leiden Journal of International Law* 401, 415–7.

International courts and tribunals other than the ICJ may also encounter occasion for incidentally reviewing the UN Security Council. In the *Tadić* case in 1995, the Appeals Chamber of the ICTY was placed in a unique position to address the validity of the Security Council's resolution from which the Tribunal itself was established. The Appeals Chamber, having not approved the Trial Chamber's suggestion that the UN Security Council had no intention to empower the ICTY to question the legality of its parent resolution,[99] held that the principle of *la compétence de la compétence* was inherent in any judicial tribunal without being expressly provided for in the constituent documents.[100] The Appeals Chamber of the ICTY thereby upheld its incidental jurisdiction to review the actions of the Council for the purpose of determining its own jurisdiction.[101]

5.4.3 Justiciability of questions

Even in the limited instances where the ICJ and ad hoc criminal tribunals could exercise jurisdiction to review the UN Security Council's exercise of authority, the justiciability (and thus admissibility) of questions could still create an obstacle to subjecting the Council to judicial scrutiny. Justiciability may be contested, first, by the *political question doctrine*, which highlights the nature of the question involved, and, second, by the *doctrine of litispendence*, which concerns the primacy relation between two organs.

The first doctrine of political questions is premised on the dichotomy of legal and political disputes. The doctrine renders a case non-justiciable on the basis that a dispute is of a political nature and thereby does not fall within the task of the judiciary. The political question doctrine is particularly relevant with regard to the determination of threats to the peace under Article 39 of the UN Charter. The determination apparently requires political judgment, and the margin of discretion is so wide that some argue that the Article 39 finding is unsuited for judicial scrutiny.[102] The Trial Chamber of the ICTY in the case of *Tadić* indeed took such a view that the UN Security Council's judgment of threats to the peace was not

99 Case No IT-94-1-T *Prosecutor v Duško Tadić, Trial Chamber, Decision on Jurisdiction* (1995) (ICTY, Decision of 10 August 1995), para 8.

100 *Tadić (Appeals Chamber on Jurisdiction, 1995)* (n 5) paras 14–18.

101 Ibid., paras 20–1.

102 *Questions of Interpretation and Application of the 1971 Montreal Convention Arising from the Aerial Incident at Lockerbie (Libyan Arab Jamahiriya v United Kingdom; Libyan Arab Jamahiriya v United States of America), Provisional Measures* [1992] ICJ Reports 3, 114 (Order of 14 April 1992), 66, 176 (dissenting opinion of Judge Weeramantry); Akande, 'The International Court of Justice and the Security Council' (n 77) 336–41. Cf. B. Martenczuk, 'The Security Council, the International Court and Judicial Review: What Lessons from Lockerbie?' (1999) 10 *European Journal of International Law* 517, 539–44; Hitoshi Nasu, 'Chapter VII Powers and the Rule of Law: The Jurisdictional Limits' (2007) 26 *Australian Year Book of International Law* 87, 108–9.

justiciable.[103] The same position was held by the Trial Chamber of the ICTR in *Kanyabashi* and *Karemera*, which likewise observed that such discretionary assessments were non-justiciable.[104] The position of the ICTY's Trial Chamber in *Tadić* was, however, disapproved by the Appeals Chamber which reviewed the Security Council's determination of a threat to the peace.[105]

In principle, the ICJ has consistently rejected the plea of political question and refused to regard the political implications of a question before the Court as an obstacle to its judicial task.[106] The invocation of the political question doctrine *per se* may be destined to failure, in part because judges may not wish to engage in unresolved controversy on the distinction between political and legal disputes.[107] At the same time, the shadow of the political question doctrine still persists in the record of the ICJ. On occasion, the Court has avoided pronouncing on the issues of highly political nature, relying on a range of judicial techniques other than the doctrine of political question.[108] Such avoidance may thus be used if the ICJ

103 *Tadić (Trial Chamber on Jurisdiction, 1995)* (n 99) paras 23–4. The Trial Chamber held that '[t]he making of a judgement as to whether there was such an emergency in the former Yugoslavia as would justify the setting up of the International Tribunal under Chapter VII is eminently one for the Security Council and only for it; *it is certainly not a justiciable issue* but one involving considerations of high policy and of a political nature. As to whether the particular measure of establishing the International Tribunal is, in fact, likely to be conducive to the restoration of peace and security is, again, pre-eminently a matter for the Security Council and for it alone and *no judicial body, certainly not this Trial Chamber, can or should review that step*': ibid., para 23 (emphasis added).

104 Case No ICTR-96-15-T *Prosecutor v Joseph Kanyabashi, Trial Chamber, Decision on Jurisdiction* (1997) (ICTY, Decision of 18 June 1997), para 20; Case No ICTR-98-44-T *Prosecutor v Édouard Karemera, Trial Chamber, Decision on Jurisdiction* (2001) (ICTR, Decision of 25 April 2001), para 25.

105 *Tadić (Appeals Chamber on Jurisdiction, 1995)* (n 5) para 30.

106 E.g., *Certain Expenses (ICJ, 1962)* (n 38) 155–6; *Aegean Sea Continental Shelf (Greece v Turkey), Jurisdiction* [1978] ICJ Reports 3 (Judgment of 19 December 1978), 13, para 31; *United States Diplomatic and Consular Staff in Tehran (United States of America v Iran), Merits* [1980] ICJ Reports 3 (Judgment of 24 May 1980), 19–20, paras 36–7; *Military and Paramilitary Activities in and against Nicaragua (Nicaragua v United States of America), Jurisdiction and Admissibility* [1984] ICJ Reports 392 (Judgment of 26 November 1984), 435, para 96; *Border and Transborder Armed Actions (Nicaragua v Honduras), Jurisdiction and Admissibility* [1988] ICJ Reports 69 (Judgment of 20 December 1988), 91, para 52.

107 For critical comments on the dichotomy of political/legal disputes, see Rosalyn Higgins, 'Policy Considerations and the International Judicial Process' (1968) 17 *International and Comparative Law Quarterly* 58, 63–74. Cf. Takane Sugihara, 'The Judicial Function of the International Court of Justice with Respect to Disputes Involving Highly Political Issues' in S. Muller, D. Raic and J.M. Thuránszky (eds), *The International Court of Justice: Its Future Role After Fifty Years* (The Hague, Martinus Nijhoff Publishers, 1997) 117, 127–38 (suggesting that the court's 'judicial' function entails certain limitations with respect to highly political issues and that the demarcation line could be drawn objectively).

108 E.g., *Nuclear Tests (Australia v France)* [1974] ICJ Reports 253 (Judgment of 20 December 1974) (on the ostensible ground of mootness); *Northern Cameroons (Cameroon v United Kingdom), Preliminary Objections* [1963] ICJ Reports 15

judges are confronted with politically sensitive questions on the UN Security Council's exercise of authority.

Furthermore, the rejection of the political question doctrine does not mean that the rigorousness of judicial scrutiny is unaffected by the political character of the issue. While the ICTY's Appeals Chamber in *Tadić* rejected the plea of non-justiciability, the Chamber's assessment was formalistic with regard to the Security Council's determination of threats to the peace. The Chamber simply endorsed the Security Council's settled practice, other members' common understanding, and the appellant's withdrawal of objection on this point. While the Chamber noted that the determination of threats was circumscribed by the purposes and principles of the UN Charter,[109] the judicial scrutiny was apparently lax, owing both to the flexibility of the purposes of the UN and the broadness of the concept of threats to the peace.

The second issue of justiciability is the *doctrine of litispendence* which evolved within the domestic legal systems in order to avoid identical matters from being decided on by multiple organs possessing similar jurisdiction.[110] While it is uncertain as to what extent international law has incorporated such a doctrine,[111] it would lead to the contention that, if invoked in the context of the ICJ and the Security Council, the ICJ should give way as far as the Security Council has addressed the identical matter in the first place. Just as the doctrine of political questions, the plea to this effect has been rejected by the ICJ. The Court has consistently adopted the position of functional parallelism that the need to avoid conflicts does not arise in the first place; according to this view, the ICJ and the Security Council respectively perform judicial and political – and thus different – functions with respect to the same event,[112] even when the Security Council is acting under Chapter VII.[113]

(Judgment of 2 December 1963) (mootness); *South West Africa Cases (Ethiopia v South Africa; Liberia v South Africa) (Second Phase)* [1966] ICJ Reports 6 (Judgment of 18 July 1966) (lack of standing).

109 *Tadić (Appeals Chamber on Jurisdiction, 1995)* (n 5) para 29.

110 See David Schweigman, *The Authority of the Security Council Under Chapter VII of the UN Charter: Legal Limits and the Role of the International Court of Justice* (The Hague, Kluwer Law International, 2001) 217.

111 For details, see Dan Ciobanu, 'Litispendence Between the International Court of Justice and the Political Organs of the United Nations' in L. Gross (ed.), *The Future of the International Court of Justice* (Dobbs Ferry, NY, Oceana Publications, 1976) 209.

112 *Tehran, Merits (ICJ, 1980)* (n 106) 21–2, para 40; *Nicaragua, Jurisdiction and Admissibility (1984)* (n 106) 434–5, para 95; *Application of the Convention on the Prevention and Punishment of the Crime of Genocide (Bosnia and Herzegovina v Yugoslavia (Serbia and Montenegro)) (First Provisional Measures)* [1993] ICJ Reports 3 (Order of 8 April 1993), 18–9, para 33. See Schweigman, *The Authority of the Security Council* (n 110) 231–61; Vera Gowlland-Debbas, 'Article 7 UN Charter' in A. Zimmermann, C. Tomuschat and K. Oellers-Frahm (eds), *The Statute of the International Court of Justice: A Commentary* (Oxford, Oxford University Press, 2006) 79, 94–7.

113 *Armed Activities on the Territory of the Congo (Democratic Republic of the Congo v Uganda), Provisional Measures* [2000] ICJ Reports 111 (Order of 1 July 2000), 123–7, paras 35–7.

As a matter of principle, this account given by the ICJ is persuasive. The UN Charter's silence about the hierarchy between the ICJ and the Security Council, save for the preference given to the ICJ when the Security Council is acting under Chapter VI with respect to legal disputes,[114] is best translated into the functional division of labour between the two entities. Given that the doctrine of litispendence is premised on organs having a similar competence, it would not be applicable to the relations between the ICJ and the Security Council, which, to reiterate, possess different functions.

The *Lockerbie* case, however, revealed a limitation to this functional parallelism. In this case, Libya requested the ICJ to endorse the country's right to prosecute alleged offenders under Article 7 of the 1971 Montreal Convention which provided the obligation to extradite or prosecute an alleged offender.[115] This meant that the ICJ was asked to make a legal statement which would contradict the extradition obligation imposed by Security Council Resolution 748. In this case, the idea of functional parallelism did not provide a plausible solution, since the parties to the dispute would have faced conflicting obligations – one from the ICJ's judgment, and the other from the decision of the Security Council, as a result of two organs performing separate functions. Also, while the ICJ's verdict does not bind the Security Council,[116] the Council might have ended up forcing Libya and other member states to act contrary to the ICJ's ruling. In such a situation, the functions played by the guardians of justice and peace cannot be described as parallel or 'complementary'.[117]

Expectations of how the ICJ would overcome this dilemma were not realised in *Lockerbie*. At the stage of provisional measures issued in 1992, the Court paid certain deference to the Security Council without simultaneously excluding the possibility of reviewing Council resolutions. According to the Court, the 'decision' in Security Council Resolution 748 *prima facie* bound parties according to Article 25 of the UN Charter, and, according to Article 103, such obligation prevailed over their obligations under any other international agreement. Based on this finding of *prima facie* obligations, the ICJ declined to indicate provisional measures, holding that 'whatever the situation previous to the adoption of that resolution, the rights claimed by Libya under the Montreal Convention cannot now be regarded as appropriate for protection by the indication of provisional measures'.[118] While the ICJ simultaneously signalled the potentiality of judicial review by adding that it was '*not at this stage* called upon to determine *definitively* the

114 See UN Charter (n 35) Article 36(3).

115 Convention for the Suppression of Unlawful Acts against the Safety of Civil Aviation, 23 September 1971, 974 UNTS 177 Article 7.

116 Statute of the International Court of Justice, 26 June 1945, 39 AJIL Supp. 215 (1945) (entered into force on 24 October 1945) Article 59.

117 *Nicaragua, Jurisdiction and Admissibility (1984)* (n 106) para 95.

118 *Lockerbie, Provisional Measures (ICJ, 1992)* (n 102) 15 (paras 39–40), 126–7 (paras 42–3). Dissenting opinions pointed out that the Court should have indicated provisional measures *proprio motu*: ibid., 41, 48–9, 151, 158–9 (dissenting opinion of Judge Bedjaoui), 67, 70–1, 177, 180–1 (dissenting opinion of Judge Weeramantry), 88–93, 193–7 (dissenting opinion of Judge Ajibola), 110–2, 215–7 (dissenting opinion of Judge El-Kosheri).

legal effect of Security Council resolution 748',[119] such a final finding was not delivered at the end. At the stage of preliminary objections issued in 1998,[120] the ICJ developed no further account on this point. The Court also carried over to the merits the assessment of the UK and the US's objection that Security Council resolutions have rendered the Libyan claims without object, on the ground that the analysis of the objection did not have an exclusively preliminary character.[121] The case was eventually dropped in 2003 after political arrangements were made between the parties regarding the trial of the suspects.[122]

On the whole, at least at the international level, the chance of judicially reviewing the Security Council's exercise of authority is extremely slim, not only because the availability of procedures is formally limited but also because many member states see no particular merit in utilising the ICJ as a venue for scrutinising the Council's practice. This is intertwined with the fact that international law itself leaves broad discretion to the Security Council, through the wording of the UN Charter and a range of doctrines, such as the concept of implied powers. In the absence of international judicial venues, international law essentially empowers the Security Council as an entity which primarily applies the UN Charter and powers endowed by it.

5.5 Conclusion

As overviewed in this chapter, international law imposes only the formalistic limits to the guardian of international peace and security. In principle, the UN Security Council's powers are confined to those conferred upon it by the constitutive instrument. The political character of the organ also does not exonerate it from observing applicable international law. In theory, the act of the UN Security Council may well be *ultra vires* or constitute a breach of separate international obligations, and, should it happen, such an illegal act 'ought not to give rise to valid and permanently effective consequences in law'.[123] Such an illegal act, if it is not automatically void or voidable, gives rise to the question of whether member states' non-compliance can be justified as a form of countermeasure.[124]

Nevertheless, the point is that international law is often too lenient to diagnose *ultra vires* acts or a breach of separate obligations when it comes to the Security

119 *Lockerbie, Provisional Measures (ICJ, 1992)* (n 102) 15 (para 40), 126 (para 43) (emphasis added).

120 *Questions of Interpretation and Application of the 1971 Montreal Convention arising from the Aerial Incident at Lockerbie (Libyan Arab Jamahiriya v United Kingdom; Libyan Arab Jamahiriya v United States of America), Preliminary Objections* [1998] ICJ Reports 9, 115 (Judgment of 27 February 1998).

121 Ibid., 26–9 (paras 46–51), 131–4 (paras 45–50).

122 UN Doc S/1998/795 (24 August 1998); UN Doc S/RES/1192 (27 August 1998); UN Doc S/2003/818 (15 August 2003); ICJ Press Release 2003/29 (10 September 2003).

123 Elihu Lauterpacht, 'The Legal Effect of Illegal Acts of International Organisations', *Cambridge Essays in International Law: Essays in Honour of Lord McNair* (London, Stevens & Sons, 1965) 88, 115.

124 Antonios Tzanakopoulos, *Disobeying the Security Council: Countermeasures Against Wrongful Sanctions* (Oxford, Oxford University Press, 2011).

Council's exercise of authority for the maintenance of international peace and security. The doctrine of implied powers, the inherent ambiguity in treaty provisions, and their interpretive development have enabled the Security Council and its permanent members to readily accommodate changing political priorities. The flexibility of the rule of treaty interpretation allows the practices of the Security Council themselves to lead the changes in treaty interpretation if such practices are accompanied by member states' acquiescence. While there are certain limits under international law on the Security Council's exercise of authority, the significance of such limits has been negated by the extremely limited availability of international judicial venues to assess the compatibility of the Security Council's decision making within the legal limits.

The limited prospect for judicial review does not mean that there is no demand for it. The judicial venue remains an important apparatus for relatively small or politically marginalised states to garner international attention to their claims. While member states could resort to diplomatic measures to contest the Security Council's exercise of authority,[125] such diplomatic challenges are by no means robust, especially for small or politically isolated states which would have to yield to the political predominance of some of the permanent members of the Security Council both inside and outside the UN.[126] Libya's recourse to the ICJ in *Lockerbie* precisely illustrates the political impact of the proceedings before the ICJ. When the Security Council requested extradition of the suspects of the Lockerbie bombing in 1991, Libya's appeal against such a request was clearly an isolated one. The country then employed a liberalistic strategy to resort to judicial process as a champion of the rule of law to garner international attention.[127]

Demand for judicial control has also started to emerge among those individuals whose rights and interests are significantly affected by the decisions of the UN Security Council and its subsidiary organs. Despite the impact that the Security Council's exercise of authority has on individuals, there are no standing judicial venues at the international level accessible to those individuals in legally contesting the UN. As will be further confirmed in chapter 6 of this book, international law provides only formalistic limits to the UN's exercise of authority over individuals. This would eventually trigger a series of court decisions at the *domestic* level, as will be analysed in chapter 7, launched by some of the affected individuals.

125 For member states' available recourses to protest Council decisions, see Nicolas Angelet, 'Protest Against Security Council Decisions' in K. Wellens (ed.), *International Law: Theory and Practice, Essays in Honour of Eric Suy* (The Hague, Martinus Nijhoff Publishers, 1998) 277.

126 The expanded role of the World Court can be much more appealing to developing countries, partly because of the unavailability of other effective means to control the Council. Geoffrey R. Watson, 'Constitutionalism, Judicial Review, and the World Court' (1993) 34 *Harvard International Law Journal* 1, 44.

127 Ian Hurd, 'The Strategic Use of Liberal Internationalism: Libya and the UN Sanctions, 1992–2003' (2005) 59 *International Organization* 495, 509–24. At the Security Council meetings, Libya contended that the issue was 'a purely legal question' and thus should be referred to the ICJ and not to the Council, invoking Article 36(3) of the Charter which provides that legal disputes should, as a general rule, be referred to the Court: UN Doc S/PV.3033 (21 January 1992) 14–5.

6 Reception in international law

Specific Chapter VII measures

6.1 Introduction

Since the 1990s, the UN Security Council and its subsidiary organs have been actively exercising their authority in such a manner that it brings significant impact on individuals and private entities. As illustrated in chapter 4 of this book, the UN Security Council has been addressing 'demands' under Chapter VII of the UN Charter not only to states and non-state armed groups but also to individuals. The comprehensive sanctions were replaced by more targeted sanctions in which the UN Security Council's sanctions committees designate particular individuals as the targets of asset freezes and travel bans. The Security Council's subsidiary organs have been directly executing their legislative, administrative, and judicial decisions against certain restricted categories of individuals. In these sets of practices, the Security Council and its subsidiary organs have narrowed the authority of the territorial government over individuals who effectively bear the consequence of international decisions.

Due to the reduced distance between the UN Security Council and individuals, the regulation of the exercise of authority by the UN acquired greater importance not only for member state authorities but also for affected individuals, which simultaneously created internal tension between the traditional constituencies which generally favour flexibility and the new constituencies which envisage more stringent constraints to safeguard individuals' rights. As overviewed in chapter 5 of this book, the political conditions that led to the establishment of the UN in 1945 accorded the Security Council broad discretion for the maintenance of international peace and security. A set of advisory opinions of the ICJ during the first decades of the UN helped expand the powers exercised by the UN and its organs presumably to facilitate the efficient performance of their mandates under the UN Charter. The general limits imposed by international law appear to be formalistic, especially with respect to the UN's peace and security arm.

Building on the general legal framework of the UN Security Council's exercise of authority, this chapter moves on to analyse the specific framework with respect to the three groups of practices highlighted in chapter 4 of this book. With respect first to the Security Council's Chapter VII demands addressed to individuals, the literal reading of the UN Charter invites me to consider whether the Security

Council has authority to lay down any obligation incumbent on individuals (section 6.2 below). The Security Council has further engaged in designating individuals as specific targets of restrictive measures (section 6.3) and creating its subsidiary organs which directly apply international regulations to local populations (section 6.4). On these two fronts, one of the main questions addressed in this chapter is whether and to what extent international law takes into account the rights and interests of affected individuals in the context of the maintenance of international peace and security.

6.2 Addressing individuals

One of the phenomena that characterise the contemporary relations between the UN Security Council and individuals is that the Security Council has constituted individuals as the addressees of its Chapter VII resolutions.[1] Particularly noteworthy is that the Security Council has been issuing 'demands' under Chapter VII of the UN Charter not only to states and non-state armed groups but also to certain categories of individuals. Although the meaning of the verbs other than 'decide' is one of many uncertainties concerning the interpretation of Security Council resolutions, the use of the term 'demand' under Chapter VII may indicate the Security Council's intention to oblige an addressee.[2] If we assume that the Security Council intends to oblige an addressee, a separate question arises as to whether the UN Security Council has such authority at all to prescribe an obligation incumbent on individuals or, for that matter, on any actors other than member states.

6.2.1 Analogy from the UN's authority over non-member states

In addressing the question, one may argue that an analogy can be drawn from the classic debates on the UN's authority over *non*-member states. After all, non-member states may share a common feature with individuals, in the sense that all these (state and non-state) actors are not parties to the UN Charter and thus have not, at least directly, given their consent to the UN's authority to impose any obligations. With respect to the UN's authority over non-member states, Falk presented in 1965 the careful analysis of the background and validity of Article 2 (6) of the UN Charter which claimed the UN's exercise of authority over non-member states for the maintenance of international peace and security.[3] According

1 See chapter 4.2 of this book.
2 See Nico Krisch, 'Introduction to Chapter VII: The General Framework' in B. Simma and others (eds), *The Charter of the United Nations: A Commentary* (3rd edn, 2012) 1237, 1265.
3 Richard A. Falk, *The Authority of the United Nations over Non-Members* (Princeton, NJ, Princeton University, 1965). On the authority over non-member states of international organisations in general, see, e.g., Finn Seyersted, *Common Law of International Organizations* (Leiden; Boston, Martinus Nijhoff Publishers, 2008) 380–90 (regarding the objective personality).

to Falk, Article 2(6) of the UN Charter is an assertion of a 'quasi-legislative competence' in the international community, which does not fit in with the idea that all obligations must be based on state consent.[4] As Falk observed, the UN's authority over non-member states could only be explained by the *sui generis* nature of the UN Charter, the importance of the maintenance of the peace, the absence of challenge on the part of non-member states, and, ultimately, the will of the international community.[5]

Despite the common feature, it is apparently difficult to use the analogy of non-member 'states' to suggest that the UN claims its authority over 'non-state' actors. This is merely because international law does not formally require consent from private groups and individuals who are subject to a state's jurisdiction in creating obligations incumbent on the private actors. For instance, the consent of rebel groups is traditionally considered unnecessary in order for states to prescribe the rules of international humanitarian law incumbent on rebel groups, even though this leads to the separate question of the effectiveness of such rules in regulating the conduct of rebel groups. The UN, as an international organisation created by a treaty, could prescribe obligations incumbent on non-state actors without seeking their consent provided that, first, the actors are subject to UN member states' jurisdiction and, second, the constituent instrument entrusted the UN with such powers expressly or by necessary implication. When it comes to the UN's authority over individuals, the central question thus remains to be the second condition, namely, the scope of the UN's authority under the UN Charter.

6.2.2 The Kosovo advisory opinion

Whether or not the UN Security Council could impose an obligation on actors *other than* member states and UN organs was one of the questions involved in the *Kosovo Independence* opinion delivered by the ICJ in July 2010.[6] In this case, the ICJ was asked by the UN General Assembly to give advice on the compatibility with international law of the unilateral declaration of Kosovo's independence made in February 2008. The ICJ assessed the lawfulness of the declaration under both general international law and Security Council Resolution 1244 on Kosovo.[7] Having concluded that general international law contains no prohibition of declarations of independence,[8] the ICJ moved on to assess the compatibility of the declaration with Security Council Resolution 1244 and the measures thereafter. In order to examine compatibility, the ICJ first determined precisely which actors had issued the declaration of independence of Kosovo on 17 February 2008.[9] The ICJ came to the conclusion that the declaration of independence was made by the

4 Falk, *The Authority of the United Nations over Non-Members* (n 3) 56, 69.
5 Ibid., 76, 100–1.
6 *Accordance with International Law of the Unilateral Declaration of Independence in Respect of Kosovo* [2010] ICJ Reports 403 (Advisory Opinion of 22 July 2010).
7 Ibid., para 78.
8 *Kosovo Independence Opinion* (n 6) para 84.
9 Ibid., paras 101–9.

authors who 'acted together in their capacity as representatives of the people of Kosovo outside the framework of the interim administration' of the UN.[10]

Having clarified the authors of the declaration, the ICJ needed to decide whether Security Council Resolution 1244 created obligations for the actors which were neither UN member states nor UN organs. According to the Court, 'Resolution 1244 (1999) was expressly adopted by the Security Council on the basis of Chapter VII of the United Nations Charter, and *therefore* clearly imposes international legal obligations'.[11] For the purpose of the present analysis, the key passage is contained in paragraph 115 of the advisory opinion. The ICJ therein referred to paragraph 15 of Security Council Resolution 1244, in which the Security Council, acting under Chapter VII, '[d]emand[ed] that the KLA [Kosovo Liberation Army] and other armed Kosovo Albanian groups' end offensive actions and comply with the requirements for demilitarisation.[12] Having referred to paragraph 15, the ICJ held that '[t]here is no indication, in the text of Security Council resolution 1244 (1999), that the Security Council intended to impose, *beyond that*, a specific obligation to act or a prohibition from acting, addressed to such other actors'.[13]

In the quoted paragraph of the advisory opinion, the ICJ seems to have assumed that it was at least *the Security Council's intention* to impose, under paragraph 15 of Resolution 1244, an obligation on the KLA and other armed Kosovo Albanian groups. Despite the fact these groups were not part of any governmental organs, the Court assumed the Security Council's intention to impose obligations on these non-state actors. At the same time, paragraph 115 of the ICJ's advisory opinion is too brief to be used for the general diagnosis of the UN Security Council's exercise of authority over non-state actors. In particular, the ICJ did not touch on the separate inquiry of whether the Security Council has the authority to oblige non-state actors in the first place, but merely ascertained the intention of the Security Council to impose an obligation on the KLA and other groups.

6.2.3 Legal basis for the Security Council to impose obligations on individuals

Broadly, there are three possible legal arguments for the authority of the UN Security Council to impose an obligation on individuals. The first candidate is the dynamic interpretation of Article 25 of the UN Charter which provides that '[t]he Members of the United Nations agree to accept and carry out the decisions of the Security Council in accordance with the present Charter'.[14] From the literal reading of the provision, one has to observe that the Security Council is not

10 Ibid., 447–8, para 109.

11 Ibid., para 85 (emphasis added).

12 Ibid., 449–50, para 115. The Court also referred to paragraph 14 as a paragraph addressing actors other than member states and UN organs: ibid.

13 *Kosovo Independence Opinion* (n 6) para 115 (emphasis added).

14 Charter of the United Nations, 26 June 1945, 1 UNTS XVI (entered into force 24 October 1945) Article 25.

endowed with the power to adopt decisions binding on actors other than UN member states. Under Article 25 of the UN Charter, it is apparently the 'Members of the United Nations' that have agreed to accept and carry out the decisions of the Security Council in accordance with the present Charter.[15] Of course, first impressions are not always trustworthy when it comes to the interpretation of treaty terms. The dynamic reading of treaty texts may hold true especially for the constitutive instruments of international organisations. While the text of the provision clearly imposes obligations on UN member states, it is theoretically possible for subsequent practice of UN member states to give different meaning to the terms of Article 25 of the UN Charter. Nevertheless, at least the Repertoire of the Practice of the Security Council between 1946 and 2011 contains no significant statement regarding the effect of Security Council resolutions on actors other than member states.[16]

Second, an argument has been put forward to the effect that the restricted international personality of non-state actors provides the legal basis for the UN Security Council's authority to impose obligations on non-state actors. Kooijmans has argued that non-state entities may acquire restricted international legal personality by becoming parties to peace agreements which, despite being concluded between rebels and governments, nevertheless retain the character of international obligation with close relationships with the UN.[17] Yet the argument based on the international legal personality does not seem to hold water; the fact that non-state actors retain international personality does not by itself resolve the question of whether the Security Council is competent to impose an obligation in the first place, inasmuch as the UN organ's competence depends on what the UN Charter instructs, and not whether an addressee retains international personality.

Finally, the remaining option is to rely on Chapter VII of the UN Charter, and, more specifically, the authority of the Security Council to impose non-military enforcement measures under Article 41 of the UN Charter. This almost all-encompassing solution should in theory be able to provide the Security Council with the authority to impose obligations on non-state actors, including individuals. Yet it is still worth critically assessing whether member states are fully aware of the implication of allowing the Security Council to generate a new set of obligations, under international law, incumbent not only on rebel groups but also on *individuals*. The deliberation at the UN Security Council does not readily allow an inclusive discussion among member states on such a crucial legal question which should also affect member states' domestic law and the rights and interests of individuals therein.

15 Ibid.

16 Repertoire of the Practice of the Security Council from 1946 to 2011, available at www.un.org/en/sc/repertoire/functions_and_powers.shtml (last accessed 1 May 2016).

17 Pieter H. Kooijmans, 'The Security Council and Non-State Entities as Parties to Conflicts' in K. Wellens (ed.), *International Law: Theory and Practice, Essays in Honour of Eric Suy* (The Hague, Martinus Nijhoff Publishers, 1998) 333, 337–40.

Overall, these three theories do not seem to furnish a cogent basis for the UN Security Council's authority to prescribe international obligations on individuals. Although the Security Council has broad discretion under Chapter VII, caution has to be exercised in encompassing within this discretion the authority to prescribe obligations on individuals. Deliberation is called for among member states in order to see if they are willing to further narrow down their intermediary presence between the UN Security Council and individuals. Having said that, the analysis here concerns the authority of the UN Security Council *itself* to impose an obligation on individuals. Even if the Security Council itself does not have authority to impose obligations on individuals under its resolutions, no difficulties arise concerning the authority of the subsidiary organs of the UN Security Council to prescribe obligations on individuals, as will be discussed in section 6.4 below.

6.3 Target specification

Individuals are not only the addressees of the UN Security Council's resolutions. Since 1994, the Security Council and its sanctions committees have directly designated specific individuals and entities as the targets of asset freezes and travel bans.[18] Just like many other provisions of the UN Charter or international treaties in general, the absence of explicit reference in the UN Charter does not prevent the UN Security Council from designating individuals and entities as the targets of restrictive measures.[19] The authority of the UN Security Council under Article 41 of the UN Charter is apparently broad enough to accommodate the practice of targeted sanctions. The extensive controversy has instead arisen with regard to the manner in which the Security Council and its sanctions committees specify the names of individuals and entities. The controversy focused on the fact that the UN Security Council, which is supposed to be the promoter of human rights protection, seems to have largely disregarded the rights of targeted individuals, including their right to a fair hearing.

The human rights critique of targeted sanctions is a perfectly legitimate one if one assesses the Security Council's disturbing practices in light of some of the standards used in the *domestic* legal order. This is why the practices of targeted sanctions have invited a series of well-known judicial contestations at the *domestic* levels, as will be discussed later in chapter 7 of this book. However, under *international* law, there remains a surprising degree of uncertainty as to whether the UN is bound by international human rights law which the UN itself has promoted.[20] The uncertainty with regard to the UN's own human rights obligations leaves a gap between, on the one hand, the extent to which the UN Security

18 See section 4.3 of this book.

19 See chapter 5 on the flexibility of international law in justifying the extension of the powers of international organisations.

20 Simon Chesterman, 'An International Rule of Law?' (2008) 56 *American Journal of Comparative Law* 331, 352.

Council's decisions impinge on individuals and, on the other hand, the status of international law in safeguarding the rights of affected individuals.

6.3.1 Legal basis for targeted sanctions

As a product of inter-state wars, it is safe to assume that Article 41 of the UN Charter was designed initially as one of the ultimate mechanisms to coerce *states* to change their policies which undermine international peace and security. According to Article 41 of the UN Charter:

> The Security Council may decide what measures not involving the use of armed force are to be employed to give effect to its decisions, and it may call upon the Members of the United Nations to apply such measures. These may include complete or partial interruption of economic relations and of rail, sea, air, postal, telegraphic, radio, and other means of communication, and the severance of diplomatic relations.[21]

The wording of Article 41, such as 'diplomatic' relations, is already indicative of the fact that the provision was devised primarily to coerce governmental decision making. In fact, during the Parliamentary debate on the United Nations Bill in the UK in 1946, a member of the House of Lords described the Bill as making provision for the eventuality that coercive measures might become necessary 'against some *State* which is indulging, or is apparently about to indulge in acts of *aggression*'.[22] This phrase reflects the predominant assumption at that time that economic sanctions were meant to change the behaviour of states, especially those that had committed an act of aggression.

On the other side of the same coin, it is probably accurate to observe that 'no one at the time [of drafting the UN Charter] thought that Article 41 would be used against individuals'.[23] Yet the initial assumption by no means constitutes a bar to the future utility of Charter provisions. Article 41 has been interpreted flexibly in order to accommodate various political circumstances and transitions. Article 41 thus no doubt allows the UN Security Council to instigate non-military sanctions for the purpose of coercing the conduct of non-state groups, such as

21 UN Charter (n 14) Article 41.

22 HL Deb, 12 February 1946, vol 139 (1946) col 378 (statement by Viscount Samuel) (emphasis added). This remark is cited in *A, K, M, Q & G v HM Treasury* [2008] EWHC 869 (Admin) (UK, High Court of Justice, 24 April 2008), para 15 (Lord Hope), 152 (Lord Phillips). The Lord Chancellor did not suggest that this was an incorrect summary of the purpose of the Bill: HL Deb, 12 February 1946, vol 139 col 379 (Lord Chancellor); *A, K, M, Q & G v HM Treasury* para 15 (Lord Hope).

23 An applicant's submission in relation to the intention of UK Parliament in the case of *A, K, M, Q & G v HM Treasury: A, K, M, Q & G v HM Treasury* (n 22) para 15. See also *HM Treasury v Mohammed Jabar Ahmed and Others; HM Treasury v Mohammed al-Ghabra; R (Hari El Sayed Sabaei Youssef) v HM Treasury* [2010] UKSC 2 (UK Supreme Court, Judgment of 27 January 2010), para 16 (Lord Hope).

Al-Qaida and the Islamic State, by further designating specific individuals and entities within the groups as targets of asset freezes and travel bans.

The flexibility of Article 41 was already secured during the drafting process of the UN Charter. The Four Powers agreed at Dumbarton Oaks that the measures listed in Article 41 were merely illustrative and non-exhaustive.[24] Also, in 1994, when Security Council Resolution 917 first introduced targeted sanctions against Haiti, no significant concerns was raised at the UN Security Council or in its vicinity with respect to the legal basis for the UN to designate specific individuals.[25] By way of confirmation, the UK Supreme Court in the case of *A, K, M, G and HAY* in 2008 also found no difficulty in acknowledging the legal basis of targeted sanctions under Article 41 of the UN Charter.[26]

6.3.2 Human rights and transparency concerns

While Article 41 of the UN Charter accommodates the UN Security Council's targeted sanctions, the practices unveiled the ostensible absence of any comparable international legal rules and mechanisms with which to safeguard the rights of those individuals designated by the UN. This is rather ironic, given that the better protection of human rights was one of the drivers for the introduction of targeted sanctions. Comprehensive economic sanctions, such as those against Iraq in the 1990s, invited criticism on both humanitarian and human rights grounds, and thereby paved the way for a targeted alternative.[27]

While the use of targeted sanctions succeeded in avoiding widespread humanitarian effects, it has brought a new controversy with respect to its disrespect for the human rights of those individuals listed by the UN.[28] In theory, the need for procedural guarantees had arisen from the inception of targeted sanctions

24 Nico Krisch, 'Article 41' in B. Simma and others (eds), *The Charter of the United Nations: A Commentary* (3rd edn, Oxford, Oxford University Press, 2012) 1305, 1307.

25 Personal interviews with several UN and OAS officials who served during the relevant period.

26 See *A, K, M, Q & G v HM Treasury* (n 22) para 18 (Lord Hope), 153 (Lord Phillips).

27 See, e.g., Sub-Commission on the Promotion and Protection of Human Rights, 'The Adverse Consequences of Economic Sanctions on the Enjoyment of Human Rights: Working Paper Prepared by Mr. Marc Bossuyt' (2000) UN Doc. E/CN.4/Sub.2/2000/33 (21 June 2000).

28 Some of the earliest literature includes, e.g., August Reinisch, 'Developing Human Rights and Humanitarian Law Accountability of the Security Council for the Imposition of Economic Sanctions' (2001) 95 *American Journal of International Law* 851; Iain Cameron, 'UN Targeted Sanctions, Legal Safeguards and the European Convention on Human Rights' (2003) 72 *Nordic Journal of International Law* 159; Erika de Wet, *The Chapter VII Powers of the United Nations Security Council* (Oxford; Portland, Oregon, Hart Publishing, 2004) chapter 6; José E. Alvarez, 'The Security Council's War on Terrorism: Problems and Policy Options' in E. de Wet and A. Nollkaemper (eds), *Review of the Security Council by Member States* (Antwerp; New York, Intersentia, 2003) 119.

under Security Council Resolution 917 in 1994 for Haiti. Nevertheless, during the first several years of targeted sanctions, little attention was paid to the concerns over the issue of procedural guarantees.[29]

Since the end of 2001, the need for procedural safeguards has slowly garnered attention at the level of the UN Security Council. A noteworthy critical remark on the listing procedures came in December 2002 from the Chairman of the Liberia Sanctions Committee which had designated individuals according to Security Council Resolution 1343.[30] The Chairman highlighted the need for greater transparency in listing procedures and the consequences of the procedural opacity for listed individuals:

> [O]f all the sanctions imposed on Liberia, the most effective measure was the travel ban. That is what clearly hurt the Government of Liberia more than anything else. It is also in a way the most controversial, because *there is* [sic] *no fixed criteria for the listing and de-listing* of names on the travel-ban list. Consequently, individuals are usually proposed for the travel-ban list through the provision of information by some members of a sanctions Committee, and the other members of the Committee generally agree to the inclusion or deletion of names on the basis of trust.
>
> But, because there are no clear rules for listing or de-listing, situations arise where a name that ought to be put on the list is withheld because of the objection of a single member, or a name that could be deleted is retained for the same reason. I think *there needs to be a more transparent process in the Committee for the designation or deletion of names from the travel-ban list.* It is very difficult, frankly, when one is chairman of such a committee to be confronted with an individual who writes you a long passionate letter explaining why he should be removed from the list, and *you have to reply to him saying, sorry, we cannot agree to this, when you can give him no reasons for this.*[31]

In this remark, the Chairman of the Liberian Sanctions Committee was aware of the need for clear rules for listing and delisting, not only for the effectiveness of

29 Even in 2002, the former Chairman of the Angola Sanctions Committee made no particular remarks on the listing and delisting procedures during his briefing to the Security Council after the dissolution of the sanctions regime against UNITA in Angola: UN Doc S/PV.4673 (18 December 2002) 3–5.

30 UN Doc S/RES/1343 (7 March 2001) para 7. The Liberia Sanctions Committee designated individuals even without adopting the guidelines for the work of the Committee. In principle, Security Council Resolution 1343 expects the promulgation of guidelines: ibid., para, 14(c). After two years, however, the Liberia Sanctions Committee was yet to agree on the guidelines for the Committee. The absence of guidelines did not deter the work of the Liberia Sanctions Committee: UN Doc S/PV.4673 (18 December 2002) (n 29) 10 (Mr. Mahbubani, Chairman of the Liberia Sanctions Committee). The Chairman of the Committee acknowledged that such a situation was 'clearly unsatisfactory': ibid.

31 UN Doc S/PV.4673 (18 December 2002) (n 29) 9 (Mr. Mahbubani, Chairman of the Liberia Sanctions Committee) (emphasis added).

the sanctions regime but also for the sake of targeted individuals who should be given reasons for being on the UN's sanctions list.

At the same time, the need for greater procedural clarity – the concern expressed by the Chairman of the Liberian Sanctions Committee – was not yet, at that time, treated as a priority agenda and was rather overshadowed by the demand for preventive measures. This is illustrated by the remark of the Chairman of the 1267 Sanctions Committee during the same meeting of December 2002, in which the Chairman noted that '[e]ven though we realize that we have to act with sufficient precautions in order to prevent arbitrary actions, it is just as true that we must develop very skilful preventive efforts and make them more thorough'.[32]

The issue of transparency in listing decisions gradually gained priority following several governmental initiatives, including Sweden's Stockholm Process which drew attention to the aspect of procedural guarantees.[33] Criticisms were particularly levelled against the 1267 sanctions regime which was against, at that time, Al-Qaida and the Taliban, and whose listed individuals spread over many different countries.[34] A symbolic alert was cast by the UN High-Level Panel in December 2004 which warned against the Al-Qaida and Taliban sanctions regime's listing procedure as 'possibly violat[ing] fundamental human rights norms and conventions'.[35]

An asset freeze certainly has a significant impact on the listed individuals' right to property,[36] and a person's privacy, reputation, and family rights.[37] The asset freeze deprives the designated persons of any resources whatsoever and effectively restricts every aspect of their lives, including the freedom of movement. It places an extraordinary physical and mental burden on their families, and often leads to

32 The Chairman then noted on the delisting procedure adopted in November 2002 and made no further comments on the procedural concerns: ibid., 6 (Mr. Valdivieso, Chairman of the 1267 Sanctions Committee).

33 Peter Wallensteen, Carina Staibano and Mikael Eriksson (eds), *Making Targeted Sanctions Effective: Guidelines for the Implementation of UN Policy Options – Results from the Stockholm Process on the Implementation of Targeted Sanctions* (Uppsala, Department of Peace and Conflict Research, Uppsala University, 2003) paras 37, 282–5. Subsequently, Switzerland, Germany, and Sweden commissioned the project on procedural guarantees to the Watson Institute of Brown University, whose report was presented to the Security Council and the General Assembly in June 2006: 'Strengthening Targeted Sanctions through Fair and Clear Procedures: White Paper prepared by the Watson Institute Targeted Sanctions Project (Brown University), 30 March 2006' (2006) UN Doc A/60/887-S/2006/331 (14 June 2006).

34 See section 4.3.2 of this book.

35 Report of the High-Level Panel on Threats, Challenges and Change, 'A More Secure World: Our Shared Responsibility' (2004) UN Doc A/59/565 (2 December 2004) para 152.

36 'Universal Declaration of Human Rights' UN GA Res. 217A (III) (10 December 1948) Article 17.

37 International Covenant on Civil and Political Rights, 16 December 1966, 999 UNTS 171 (1966) Article 17. See Cameron, 'UN Targeted Sanctions, Legal Safeguards and the European Convention on Human Rights' (n 28) 159–73; Peter Gutherie, 'Security Council Sanctions and the Protection of Individual Rights' (2004) 60 *New York University Annual Survey of American Law* 491, 499–511.

the breakdown of the family unit.[38] Ironically, the more diligently national authorities implement Security Council resolutions and the decisions of sanctions committees, the more severely the targeted individuals and their families may suffer from the restrictive measures.[39] An English judge has even chosen the term 'prisoners of the state' to characterise the state of those targeted.[40] Despite the scale of impact on human rights, when individuals were designated as specific targets, no hearing was conducted prior to or following the designation of targets, nor were they informed of the detailed grounds for listing.[41] No direct petition mechanisms had been institutionalised for the targeted individuals and entities claiming their non-involvement until the adoption of Security Council Resolution 1730 in late 2006.[42]

The lack of procedural safeguards led to criticism directed against the Security Council for failing to ensure the right to a fair hearing[43] and the right to an effective remedy for those who are targeted by the Council and its sanctions committees.[44] Individuals are entitled to a fair hearing if the asset freeze, the deprivation of property, amounts to a 'criminal charge'[45] or if it involves the determination of a person's 'rights and obligations in a suit at law'.[46] The longer a suspected individual remains on the list, the more likely it is that the effect of sanctions will resemble a criminal charge.[47] As the sanctions committees decide listing and delisting by consensus, the removal of an individual target from the list

38 This is illustrated by, for instance, the situation of the appellants in the case of *A, K, M, Q & G* before the UK courts: *A, K, M, Q & G v HM Treasury* (n 22) para 31.

39 This is illustrated by, for instance, the situation of HAY, one of the applicants before the UK courts. HAY and his family had to rely solely on the welfare benefits that his wife was permitted to access. The wife was permitted to spend money only for the items that the UK Treasury regarded 'basic expenses' and, at least until 2009, she had to report to the Treasury on her expenditure: ibid., para 39.

40 *A and Others v HM Treasury* [2008] EWCA Civ 1187 (UK Court of Appeal, Judgment of 30 October 2008), 125 (Sedley LJ); *A, K, M, Q & G v HM Treasury* (n 22) paras 4, 60.

41 On the procedural improvement regarding the notification, see chapter 8 of this book.

42 UN Doc S/RES/1730 (19 December 2006).

43 ICCPR (n 37) Article 14.

44 Ibid., Article 2(3).

45 Ibid., Article 14(1). Compare, e.g., Erika De Wet, 'The Role of Human Rights in Limiting the Enforcement Power of the Security Council: A Principled View' in E. De Wet and A. Nollkaemper (eds), *Review of the Security Council by Member States* (Antwerp, Intersentia, 2003) 7, 15–16; 'Strengthening Targeted Sanctions through Fair and Clear Procedures: White Paper prepared by the Watson Institute Targeted Sanctions Project (Brown University), 30 March 2006' (n 33) 14–18.

46 ICCPR (n 37) Article 14(1). See Cameron, 'UN Targeted Sanctions, Legal Safeguards and the European Convention on Human Rights' (n 28) 192, and fn. 91.

47 See Alvarez, 'The Security Council's war on terrorism' (n 28) 132, 134–5; Gutherie, 'Security Council Sanctions and the Protection of Individual Rights' (n 37) 503–6. See also 'Report of the Special Rapporteur on the Promotion and Protection of Human Rights and Fundamental Freedoms while Countering Terrorism' (2008) UN Doc A/63/223 (6 August 2008) (the Special Rapporteur, Martin Scheinin, observes that the indefinite freezing of the assets amounts to a criminal punishment due to the severity of the sanction).

can be blocked by the objection of one single member – every member has veto power. In order to preserve the coerciveness of sanctions, the end date of restrictive measures is not always articulated at the time when the Security Council adopts sanctions. This would mean that, without a sunset clause, the termination of sanctions regimes themselves would be subject to the veto power of permanent Council members. The lack of procedural safeguards and the highly political nature of the designation have led to criticism directed against the Security Council for failing to ensure the right to a fair hearing and the right to an effective remedy for those who are targeted by the Council and its sanctions committees.[48]

6.3.3 Political constraints versus legal obligations to 'ensure' respect for human rights

Human rights criticisms levelled against the UN's targeted sanctions revived one of the longstanding questions of UN law, namely, to what extent the UN Security Council and its subsidiary organs are *legally* bound by international human rights law. Politically, the UN cannot afford to disregard its organs' disrespect for human rights standards precisely because it is a crucial part of the UN's identity to be a strong promoter of international human rights law.[49] The UN General Assembly has adopted major human rights declarations and treaties, and its subsidiary organs, including the Human Rights Council, are committed to the promotion and protection of human rights.

The Security Council has also been a promoter of international human rights law.[50] Even during the Cold War in which Security Council members generally avoided discussing human rights, the Security Council explicitly regarded South Africa's policies of apartheid as violating the provisions of the Universal Declaration of Human Rights.[51] After the end of the Cold War, the Security Council started to constitute the systematic violations of international humanitarian and human rights law in armed conflicts as a threat to international peace and security.[52] As part of post-conflict peacebuilding processes, the Security Council mandates its UN peacekeeping operations to promote and protect human rights.[53] The Security Council has also invited the UN High Commissioner for Human Rights,[54] and, albeit with certain hesitation, the special rapporteurs of the

48 ICCPR (n 37) Articles 14, 2(3).
49 See generally, Louis B. Sohn, 'The Human Rights Law of the Charter' (1977) 12 *Texas International Law Journal* 129.
50 Sydney D. Bailey, *The UN Security Council and Human Rights* (New York, St. Martin's Press, 1994).
51 E.g., UN Doc S/RES/182 (4 December 1963) para 2; UN Doc S/RES/191 (18 June 1964) para 2 of the preamble.
52 Section 3.3.3 of this book.
53 United Nations, 'United Nations Peacekeeping Operations: Principles and Guidelines (Capstone Doctrine)' (2008) 27.
54 E.g., UN Doc S/PV.5066 (28 October 2004); UN Doc S/PV.5125 (16 February 2005); United Nations, 'Repertoire of the Practice of the Security Council, Supplement 2004–2007' ST/PSCA/1/Add.15 (2013) 101.

Commission on Human Rights and the Human Rights Council to participate in the meetings.[55] The UN's track record on the promotion of international human rights law necessarily shapes the organisation's own identity,[56] and renders it politically or institutionally imperative to regard international human rights law as one of the normative constraints that circumscribe the UN's own activities.

A separate analysis is, however, still required to ascertain the extent to which the UN Security Council and its sanctions committees are legally bound to observe individuals' right to a fair hearing, the right to an effective remedy, and other human rights. This question is of fundamental importance to the relations between the UN and individuals. Should the Security Council be obliged to comply with international human rights law, the targeted individuals would be, at least in theory, entitled to invoke their rights vis-à-vis the UN. In other words, this entitlement provides the listed individuals with a cogent normative basis to be actors to whom the Security Council and its sanctions committee ought to be accountable.

In considering the UN Security Council's human rights obligations, one must make a distinction between the obligation to 'promote' respect for human rights and the obligation to 'ensure' it.[57] The obligation to 'promote' only requires the UN organs to give consideration to human rights, leaving wide the discretion to the decision making as to how human rights considerations would be counterbalanced against other conflicting variables. By contrast, the obligation to 'ensure' requires compliance *strictu sensu* with human rights obligations, and any restrictions upon such rights by the UN organs would have to meet the established criteria, such as the requirement of proportionality, as if such organs were states. Also, as noted above, individuals may be able to invoke, at least theoretically, human rights violations vis-à-vis the UN.

6.3.4 Human rights under customary international law

In considering the extent of legal constraints, it is necessary to make a distinction between human rights established as customary international law on the one hand

55 In August 1992, India, Ecuador, Zimbabwe, and China expressed reservations about the appropriateness of inviting Mr. van der Stoel, the Special Rapporteur of the Commission on Human Rights regarding the situation of human rights in Iraq, on the basis that human rights issues did not fall within the Security Council's competence: United Nations, 'Repertoire of the Practice of the Security Council, Supplement 1989–1992' ST/PSCA/1/Add.11 (2007) 57.

56 See Michael Barnett and Martha Finnemore, 'Political Approaches' in T.G. Weiss and S. Daws (eds), *The Oxford Handbook on the United Nations* (Oxford, Oxford University Press, 2007) 41, 48–50; Richard Jolly, Louis Emmerij and Thomas George Weiss, *UN Ideas That Changed the World* (Bloomington, Indiana University Press, 2009) 163–85.

57 See Frédéric Mégret and Florian Hoffmann, 'The UN As a Human Rights Violator? Some Reflections on the United Nations Changing Human Rights Responsibilities' (2003) 25 *Human Rights Quarterly* 314. The distinction concerns the *type* or scope of obligations, and *not the legal grounds* which subject the UN to human rights obligations. The latter legal grounds include the UN Charter as well as international personality and delegation theories.

and those accepted as *jus cogens* on the other. With respect to the human rights obligations under customary international law, the following five grounds could potentially support the UN's stringent obligation to ensure respect for human rights: (1) explicit limits under the UN Charter, (2) implied limits, (3) succession, (4) common rules of international organisations, and (5) international legal personality. These grounds will be explained in turn.

6.3.4.1 Explicit limits under the UN Charter

First of all, there is a divergence of views as to whether the UN Charter, particularly Article 1(3), imposes obligations, through Article 24(2), not only to 'promote' respect for human rights but also to 'ensure' respect for human rights *strictu sensu*. According to Article 1(3) of the UN Charter, it is one of the purposes of the UN:

> To achieve international co-operation in solving international problems of an economic, social, cultural, or humanitarian character, and in promoting and encouraging respect for human rights and for fundamental freedoms for all without distinction as to race, sex, language, or religion ...[58]

Among the elements of treaty interpretation,[59] the textual reading of Article 1(3) suggests that the UN organs are required to 'promote' respect for human rights, but not to 'ensure' respect for human rights.[60] The use of the reserved language, 'promoting and encouraging', under Article 1(3) was deliberate. At the San Francisco Conference in 1945, a proposal was made to employ the stronger words such as 'to assure' and 'to protect'. However, the proposal did not win support among delegates at that time. According to the subcommittee I/1/A, to assure or protect fundamental rights and freedoms is 'primarily the concern of each state',[61]

58 UN Charter (n 14) Art 1(3).

59 The basic formula of treaty interpretation is to give 'ordinary meaning' to the treaty terms: Vienna Convention on the Law of Treaties, 23 May 1969, 1155 UNTS 311 (entered into force 27 January 1980) Article 31(1). An exception is when the parties have given a 'special meaning' to a term: Article 31(4). Such ordinariness is nevertheless a highly relative notion, being sustained by multiple variables; namely, the terms' context, the treaty's object and purpose, and three other mandatory considerations, including subsequent practice: Vienna Convention on the Law of Treaties, ibid., Article 31(1), (2), (3). While the reference to the preparatory works is one of 'supplementary' means for interpretation and not part of the mandatory variables, reference to preparatory works can be readily licensed by Article 32.

60 Under Article 1(3) of the UN Charter, it is one of the purposes of the UN '[t]o achieve international cooperation ... in ***promoting and encouraging*** respect for human rights and for fundamental freedoms for all': UN Charter (n 14) Article 1(3) (emphasis added).

61 Documents of the United Nations Conference on International Organization, San Francisco, 1945 (London; New York, United Nations Information Organizations, 1945) vol. 6 at 705 ('Report of Rapporteur, Subcommittee I/1/A', Doc 723, I/1/A/19, 1 June 1945).

and thereby not of the UN. This is not surprising, inasmuch as the anticipated impact that the UN's decisions impinge upon the rights of individuals was significantly limited when the UN Charter was drafted.[62]

With reference to subsequent practice, a working paper submitted to the Sub-Commission of the then Commission on Human Rights in 2000 is based on the idea that the human rights constraints on the UN's sanctions are much stronger than the promotion of respect for human rights. According to the working paper, Articles 1(1) and 1(3) of the Charter imply that '[s]anctions must be evaluated to ensure that … they do not in any way violate principles of international law stemming from sources "outside" the Charter',[63] including the right to life and the rights to security of the person, health, education, or employment.[64] In light of the legal constraints, the comprehensive sanctions against Iraq were characterised as 'unequivocally illegal under existing international humanitarian law and human rights law'.[65] This working paper, despite its merit, did not receive explicit endorsement by the Commission, much less by the General Assembly or the Security Council.

The subsequent development in practice still indicates that the Security Council has increasingly narrowed its discretion in terms of how to take into account the respect for human rights when acting under Chapter VII of the UN Charter. For instance, a range of measures to ameliorate the humanitarian and human rights-related impacts of sanctions have been implemented by the Security Council, as exemplified by the Oil-for-Food Program for Iraq,[66] the provision of humanitarian exemptions,[67] the monitoring of humanitarian impact,[68] the use of targeted

62 In addition, with regard to Article 1(1) of the UN Charter, the Charter failed short of constraining the exercise of Chapter VII authority by the UN Security Council to the same degree as in Chapter VI by not referring to the 'principles of justice and international law' in the first part of Article 1(1) of the UN Charter regarding collective measures. On the drafting history of Article 1(1) of the UN Charter, see Terry D. Gill, 'Legal Aspects of the Transfer of Authority in UN Peace Operations' (2011) 42 *Netherlands Yearbook of International Law* 37, 65–8.

63 Sub-Commission on the Promotion and Protection of Human Rights 'The Adverse Consequences of Economic Sanctions on the Enjoyment of Human Rights: Working Paper Prepared by Mr. Marc Bossuyt' (n 27) para 24. See also Committee on Economic, Social and Cultural Rights, 'General Comment 8: The Relationship between Economic Sanctions and Respect for Economic, Social and Cultural Rights' (1997) UN Doc E/C.12/1997/8 (12 December 1997).

64 Sub-Commission on the Promotion and Protection of Human Rights 'The Adverse Consequences of Economic Sanctions on the Enjoyment of Human Rights: Working Paper Prepared by Mr. Marc Bossuyt' (n 27) para 26.

65 Ibid., para 71.

66 See generally 'Review and Assessment of the Implementation of the Humanitarian Programme Established Pursuant to Security Council Resolution 986 (1995) (December 1996–November 1998)' UN Doc S/1999/481 (28 April 1999).

67 See generally G.L. Burci, 'Interpreting the Humanitarian Exceptions through the Sanctions Committees' in V. Gowlland-Debbas (ed.), *United Nations Sanctions and International Law* (2001) 143.

68 See generally de Wet, *The Chapter VII Powers of the United Nations Security Council* (n 28) 226–47.

sanctions as opposed to comprehensive ones,[69] and a series of procedural improvements to make the listing process fair and clear, including the establishment of the Ombudsperson for the 1267 sanctions regime.[70] Yet these incremental institutional reforms do not appear to prove that the UN organs are formally bound to ensure respect for human rights in the same manner as state authorities. Also, the UN's institutional practices themselves do not constitute subsequent practice that 'establishes the agreement of the parties regarding its interpretation'.[71] The institutional practices must be accompanied by the endorsement by member states to formally delineate the UN's discretion under human rights law – and this is unlikely to be forthcoming in the near future.

In short, the UN's practices, albeit providing greater guidance as to how the UN organs ought to take into account human rights, do not go so far as to suggest that the UN organs are formally bound by the obligation to ensure respect for human rights established under customary international law. Human rights recognised under customary international law may be part of 'relevant rules of international law applicable in the relations between parties' in interpreting human rights provisions of the UN Charter,[72] but this does not seem to suffice as a legal basis for formally subjecting the UN itself under human rights law applicable primarily to the conduct of states. While the UN is no doubt mandated to 'promote' respect for human rights, this leaves greater discretion to the Security Council in determining how precisely human rights are considered and how to strike a balance between respect for human rights and demand for swift and preventive actions in order to discharge the Security Council's mandate to maintain international peace and security.

6.3.4.2 Implied limits

One may argue that, if it is possible to imply the powers,[73] it should likewise be possible to imply the limitations upon such powers as well. The UN Charter is indeed the source of not only the powers of UN organs but also the limits to the exercise of such powers. Certain limitations on the UN can be 'necessary intendment out of the Charter', borrowing the phrase of the ICJ in *Reparation for Injuries*.[74] Yet apparently it is difficult to ascertain the obligation to ensure respect for human rights as necessary intendment out of the Charter. International human rights law was significantly underdeveloped at the time the UN Charter was drafted, and the Security Council was created as an organ which exercises authority primarily over states, and not over individuals. It would thus be doctrinally difficult to invoke the idea of implied limits as a basis for the UN's obligation not to act in

69 See section 4.3 of this book.

70 See chapter 8 of this book.

71 Vienna Convention on the Law of Treaties (n 59) Article 31(3)(b).

72 See Stefan Kadelbach, 'Interpretation' in B. Simma and others (eds), *The Charter of the United Nations: A Commentary* (3rd edn, 2012) 71, 88.

73 Section 5.2.2 of this book.

74 *Reparation for Injuries Suffered in the Service of the United Nations* [1949] ICJ Reports 174 (Advisory Opinion of 11 April 1949) 184.

contravention to the present-day international human rights law. One may also recall that it was not the intention of drafters to circumscribe the Security Council's Chapter VII authority in the same way they did for Chapter VI.[75]

At the domestic level, a similar reasoning is held for implying limits to the decisions of governmental authorities. For instance, in the *Ahmed* case in the UK on the domestic implementation of the UN's targeted sanctions, the UK Supreme Court held that the Al-Qaida Order – an executive order that implemented the UN Security Council's Al-Qaida sanctions regime – was *ultra vires* the powers conferred upon the government by the statue, namely, section 1 of the United Nations Act 1946.[76] In so holding, Lord Phillipps observed that:

> I conclude that Parliament would not have foreseen this possibility [that the Security Council would, under article 41, decide on measures that seriously interfered with the rights of individuals in the United Kingdom ... without providing them with a means of effective challenge before a court], having particular regard to the reference to human rights in the preamble and article 1.3 of the Charter and to the fact that the 1946 Act was passed at a time when the importance of human rights was generally recognised, as exemplified two years later by the adoption by the General Assembly of the Universal Declaration of Human Rights ...[77]

Lord Phillipps here indicated that Parliament must have envisaged the safeguards for the rights of individuals when the act was enacted in 1946. In *Ahmed* in 2010, Lord Rodger also observed that UK Parliament 'could not have intended to authorize the making of AQO [Al-Qaida Order] 2006 which so gravely and directly affected the legal right of individuals to use their property and which did so in a way which deprived them of any real possibility of challenging their listing in the courts'.[78] The judges' reasoning is based on the assumption that the basic rights are not overridden in the absence of express language or necessary implication to the contrary. At the international level, however, the same cannot be said about the intention of the founders of the UN Charter, as it was drafted without contemplating the proximity of the UN Security Council's exercise of authority to individuals within the context of Chapter VII measures.

6.3.4.3 Theory of succession

The third legal basis pertains to the analogy from the 'theory of succession' developed by the jurisprudence of the EU courts. In essence, the idea is that the

75 Section 5.3 of this book.
76 *Ahmed (UK Supreme Court, 2010)* (n 23).
77 Ibid., para 154 (Lord Phillips).
78 Ibid., para 185 (Lord Rodger). As Lord Rodger and Lord Mance argued, Parliament must have been aware that the executive orders implementing economic sanctions would interfere with the rights of individuals and companies, such as rights to enter into contracts: ibid., paras 185 (Lord Rodger), 239 (Lord Mance).

conferral of power from member states to the UN should accompany the conferral of the relevant international obligations owed by the states. The line of reasoning known as the succession theory was employed notably by the European Court of Justice (ECJ) in the *International Fruit Company* case in 1972.[79] In the *International Fruit Company*, the ECJ encountered the question of whether the validity of a Community act could be assessed against the General Agreement on Tariffs and Trade (GATT), to which all member states had been contracting parties yet to which the then European Economic Community (EEC) itself had not. The ECJ concluded that the GATT became binding on the EEC and thus an integral part of the Community law.[80] The ECJ stated that 'in so far as under the EEC Treaty the Community has assumed the powers previously exercised by Member States in the area governed by the [GATT], the provisions of that agreement have the effect of binding the Community'.[81] According to the line of reasoning adopted in *International Fruit*, the EEC was bound by the agreement not only internally but also externally under international law, by taking over the rights and obligations of member states towards third countries,[82] although the subsequent development on the theory of succession rendered its external aspect obsolete.[83]

By analogy, the theory of succession may appear to serve as a potential basis for subjecting the UN to international obligations previously owed by states. If the UN is externally bound by the obligations and fails to comply with them, this would be not merely a matter of *ultra vires* act but also a breach of separate international obligations. Apparently, however, several hurdles prevent the theory of succession from being employed as a basis for imposing additional constraints on the UN. The theory of succession has developed with respect to the relationships between the EU and its member states. The theory has not gained acceptance in international institutional law, and, at any rate, the relationships between the UN and its member states qualitatively differ from the relationships between the EU and its members. Also, international human rights law was less developed at the time when the UN Charter was created, which further reduces the relevance of the theory of succession for the sake of fettering the UN's discretion under human rights law.

79 Joined Cases 21–24/72 *International Fruit Company NV and others v Produktschap voor Groenten en Fruit* [1972] ECR 1219 (ECJ, 12 December 1972).

80 These two facts are in principle separate, yet the ECJ presumably regarded the second part as self-evident: Pieter Jan Kuijper, 'Case 21–24/ 72, International Fruit Company v Produktschap voor Siergewassen, Court of Justice of the EC, [1972] ECR 1219' in C. Ryngaert and others (eds), *Judicial Decisions on the Law of International Organizations* (1st edn, Oxford, Oxford University Press, 2016) 235, 237–8.

81 *International Fruit Company NV and others v Produktschap voor Groenten en Fruit*, Cases 21–24/72, [1972] ECR 1219, para. 18.

82 See Trevor C. Hartley, *The Foundations of European Union Law: An Introduction to the Constitutional and Administrative Law of the European Union*, 7th edn (Oxford; New York: Oxford University Press, 2010) at 194–5.

83 See Kuijper, 'International Fruit Company' (n 80) 243–4.

6.3.4.4 Common rules of international organisations

An alternative argument suggests that international human rights law is listed in the catalogue of the common rules of international organisations. This is contrasted with the classic assumption that international organisations are born with no predestined entitlement and obligations. Yet this presumption has been subject to qualification by the development of common rules on international organisations, including, for instance, an *ultra vires* doctrine, the legal personality of international organisations, an implied power doctrine, interpretation of constituent instruments, and a series of rules on immunities and privileges.[84] Added also is the development of the rules on delegation of powers,[85] and the rules of responsibility owed by international organisations under international law.[86]

The question is whether the observance of certain categories of human rights is also part of the common rules applicable to all the international organisations, including the UN. One of the difficulties in resolving this question is that there may be no clear-cut 'rules about rules' in the first place. In other words, it is not certain how the common rules of international organisations could evolve as a body of international law. Should the common rules of international organisations be treated exactly the same as an ordinary rule of customary international law, any rules require state practice and *opinio juris*, as opposed to the practices of international organisations themselves. This creates a fundamental difficulty for developing any substantive rules for international organisations in general. While the UN General Assembly recognised that 'the rule of law applies to … the United Nations and its principal organs',[87] this general recognition is by no means sufficient to generate the endorsement by states on the need for the observance of international human rights law by the UN or any other organisations. Despite the incremental development of the common rules of international organisations, it thus seems that the formal obligation to ensure respect for human rights is yet to

84 See M. Virally, 'L'ONU devant le droit' (1972) 99 *Journal du droit international* 501; Elihu Lauterpacht, 'The Development of the Law of International Organization by the Decision of International Tribunals' (1976-IV) 152 *Recueil des Cours* 377.

85 On delegation, compare: Danesh Sarooshi, 'The Legal Framework Governing United Nations Subsidiary Organs' (1996) 67 *British Yearbook of International Law* 413; Danesh Sarooshi, *The United Nations and the Development of Collective Security: The Delegation by the UN Security Council of Its Chapter VII Powers* (Oxford, Oxford University Press, 1999); Niels Blokker, 'Is the Authorization Authorized? Powers and Practice of the UN Security Council to Authorize the Use of Force by "Coalitions of the Able and Willing"' (2000) 11 *European Journal of International Law* 541; Simon Chesterman, *Just War or Just Peace? Humanitarian Intervention and International Law* (Oxford, Oxford University Press, 2001) 163–218.

86 'Draft Articles on the Responsibility of International Organizations' (2011) ILC Report, Sixty-third session, UN Doc A/66/10 (3 May 2011).

87 Resolution adopted by the General Assembly on 24 September 2012, 'Declaration of the High-level Meeting of the General Assembly on the Rule of Law at the National and International Levels' UN Doc A/RES/67/1 (30 November 2012) para 2.

join the list of common rules and it is premature to conclude that such rights can be formally invoked against international organisations in general.[88]

6.3.4.5 Limits attached to international legal personality

A final and related approach upholds that the international legal personality of the UN necessarily entails its human rights obligations. The idea that international organisations are bound by certain obligations as a result of the acquisition of international personality has garnered relatively strong support.[89] It has been argued that the observance of customary human rights law attaches *a priori* to the legal personality of international organisations, inclusive of the UN, enjoyed under international law.[90] A passage in the ICJ's advisory opinion in 1980 appears to provide support for the view that international organisations are subject to customary international law in general,[91] which was also cited by some other international judicial decisions.[92]

This theory does not fully hold water, however, given the circularity of the theory of international legal personality under which the pre-conditions giving rise to legal personality may likewise be the consequences of having such personality. For instance, a treaty-making capacity is typically invoked as one of the consequences of the possession of personality, but such a capacity is also used as one

88 See Benedict Kingsbury, Nico Krisch and Richard B. Stewart, 'The Emergence of Global Administrative Law' (2004) 68 *Law and Contemporary Problems* 15, 46–47; Carol Harlow, 'Global Administrative Law: The Quest for Principles and Values' (2006) 17 *European Journal of International Law* 187, 204–7; Bardo Fassbender, 'Targeted Sanctions and Due Process' (2006) Study Commissioned by the UN Office of Legal Affairs (20 March 2006) 20, paras. 5.3–5.5.

89 Reinisch, 'Developing Human Rights and Humanitarian Law Accountability of the Security Council for the Imposition of Economic Sanctions' (n 28) 858–9; Nigel D. White, *The Law of International Organisations* (2nd edn, Manchester, Manchester University Press, 2005) 217. Similarly, Henry G. Schermers and Niels Blokker, *International Institutional Law: Unity within Diversity* (4th revised edn, Boston, Martinus Nijhoff Publishers, 2003) 1002; Felice Morgenstern, *Legal Problems of International Organizations* (Cambridge, Grotius Publications, 1986) 32.

90 Reinisch, 'Developing Human Rights and Humanitarian Law Accountability of the Security Council for the Imposition of Economic Sanctions' (n 28) 858–9; Philippe Sands, *Bowett's Law of International Institutions* (6th edn, London, Sweet & Maxwell/ Thomson Reuters, 2009) 458–60; White, *The Law of International Organisations* (n 89) 217. Similarly, e.g., Manfred Nowak and Karolina Miriam Januszewski, 'Non-State Actors and Human Rights' in M. Noortmann, A. Reinisch and C. Ryngaert (eds), *Non-State Actors in International Law* (Oxford, Hart Publishing, 2015) 113, 157; Monica Lugato, 'Sanctions and Individual Rights' in N. Ronzitti (ed.), *Coercive Diplomacy, Sanctions and International Law* (Leiden, Nijhoff, 2016) 172, 181–2.

91 *Interpretation of the Agreement of 25 March 1951 Between the WHO and Egypt, Advisory Opinion* [1980] ICJ Reports 73 (Advisory Opinion of 20 December 1980) 89–90 ('International organizations are subject of international law, and as such, are bound by any obligations incumbent upon them under general rules of international law').

92 E.g., Case No ICTR-98-44C-T *Prosecutor v André Rwamakuba, Trial Chamber, Decision on Appropriate Remedy* (ICTR, Decision of 31 January 2007), para 48, fn. 71.

of the conditions that necessitate the possession of international personality. According to the ICJ's advisory opinion in *Reparation for Injuries*, an international organisation has international legal personality if the possession of international personality is necessary to carry out the intentions of its founders,[93] although such an intention is rather objectively constructed from the functions entrusted to the organisation.[94] If the possession of international personality depends on the construction of the Charter and its drafters' intentions, the content of the personality should also be within their compound. Having accorded international personality to the UN, the ICJ in *Reparation for Injuries* observed that it was 'capable of possessing international rights and duties',[95] which is not the same as suggesting that international organisations are automatically bound by the sets of rights and duties, including those essentially governing state activities.[96]

The possession of international personality certainly signifies the separation of personality between an organisation and its member states and entails the capacities to bring a claim under international law and to be held responsible for the non-fulfilment of its obligations.[97] Yet apart from these core elements, the acquisition of international legal personality does not automatically entail all the rights and obligations under customary international law when they are developed for the sake of states, and not for international organisations. If the personality of the UN had already been a sufficient basis to subject the Organisation to international customary law, the drafters at the San Francisco Conference in 1945 would have had no need to devote their time and energy to arguing where to locate the 'principles of … international law' within Article 1(1) of the Charter.[98]

The applicability of customary law to international organisations has to be examined on a case-by-case basis. In this regard, the UN, as a key advocate of human rights, has regularly pledged to conduct its own activities in full respect of human rights.[99] It is particularly noteworthy that, albeit within the course of setting out the human rights due diligence policy in 2013 for the UN's support to non-UN security forces, the UN Secretary-General referred to '[the UN's] *obligations* under international law *to respect*, promote and encourage respect for

93 *Reparation for Injuries (ICJ, 1949)* (n 74) 179.
94 The mixture of subjective and objective elements is illustrated by the following passage: 'the Organization was *intended* to exercise and enjoy … functions and rights which can *only be explained* on the basis of the possession of a large measure of international personality …' (emphasis added): ibid.
95 Ibid. While the personality refers to the capacity of a person, his entitlement and duties require separate scrutiny: see Michael Byers, *Custom, Power and the Power of Rules: International Relations and Customary International Law* (Cambridge, Cambridge University Press, 1999) 75–87.
96 The ICJ observed in *Reparation for Injuries* that 'rights and duties [of the UN] are [not] the same as those of a State': *Reparation for Injuries (ICJ, 1949)* (n 74) 179.
97 Kjetil Mujezinović Larsen, *The Human Rights Treaty Obligations of Peacekeepers* (Cambridge, Cambridge University Press, 2012) 88–90.
98 For the drafting process of Article 1(1) of the UN Charter, see section 5.3 of this book.
99 See further chapter 8 of this book.

international humanitarian, ***human rights*** and refugee law'.[100] The UN here bears not only the mandate to promote human rights but also an obligation to respect international human rights law.

However, the UN's self-recognition does not yet amount to the UN's obligation to 'ensure' the rights to all individuals, and, more importantly, the UN's pledges have not yet been accompanied by states' conviction that the UN is bound by international human rights in the same manner as it is for states. On balance, one would have to conclude that the obligation to ensure respect for human rights established under customary international law has yet to be fully developed into a set of rules formally binding on the UN's exercise of authority – and this is the case despite the strong pledge that the UN itself has made over decades, and despite a strong resemblance that the UN's exercise of authority bears to the decision making of the national government vis-à-vis individuals.

6.3.5 Human rights obligations established as **jus cogens**

While it may be difficult to oblige the UN to ensure respect for all the human rights established under customary international law, less controversial is the observance of human rights established as *jus cogens*. This is rather paradoxical given that, according to Article 53 of the Vienna Convention on the Law of Treaties, a peremptory norm evolves from customary law.[101] If the UN is not strictly bound by human rights under customary international law, how could the UN be bound by human rights norms established as *jus cogens*?

The possible answer lies in the fact that the UN's authority is based on the delegation from member states which owe human rights obligations under customary international law, including those established as *jus cogens*. Given that the rules of *jus cogens* are non-derogable, member states cannot evade the *jus cogens* obligations by creating the UN or any other international organisations.[102] This means that the UN does not have powers to act in contravention of *jus cogens* norms. While, strictly speaking, this does not mean to impose peremptory norms on the UN, its measures which infringe *jus cogens* would constitute an *ultra vires* act, acting beyond the scope of delegated authority.

There is also a more society-oriented explanation about the relationships between the UN and *jus cogens* obligations. One could argue that the peremptory norms are fundamentally important to the international community, and therefore

100 'Human Rights Due Diligence Policy on United Nations Support to Non-United Nations Security Forces' UN Doc A/67/775–S/2013/110 (5 March 2013) para 1 (emphasis added).

101 Vienna Convention on the Law of Treaties (n 59) Article 53 ('a peremptory norm of general international law is a norm accepted and recognized by the international community of States as a whole as a norm from which no derogation is permitted').

102 Alexander Orakhelashvili, 'The Impact of Peremptory Norms on the Interpretation and Application of United Nations Security Council Resolutions' (2005) 16 *European Journal of International Law* 59, 60, 68.

the UN, having a legal personality in the international arena and being a participant therein, must be subject to them. As contrasted with the above delegation approach, this explanation based on international personality would lead to the imposition of the *jus cogens* obligations on the UN itself. Namely, its measures which infringe *jus cogens* would constitute not only an *ultra vires* act but also the breach of the peremptory norm itself.

At any rate, however, not all human rights would qualify as *jus cogens.* The list of non-derogable human rights under Article 4(2) of the International Covenant on Civil and Political Rights (ICCPR) may be understood as the recognition of the peremptory nature of those norms.[103] Among the human rights affected by targeted sanctions, neither the right to a fair hearing under Article 14 of the ICCPR nor the right to an effective remedy under Article 2(3) falls within the catalogue of non-derogable human rights. While the Human Rights Committee, the monitoring body under the ICCPR, holds the view that the category of peremptory norms extends beyond the list of non-derogable provisions provided in Article 4(2),[104] the view that the core elements of the right to a fair hearing are non-derogable and *jus cogens* remains restricted to the context of criminal proceedings.[105]

In summary, with regard to the UN's own human rights obligations, international law is much more indeterminate than wider political discourse. The UN, as a longstanding human rights advocate, cannot politically ignore its own organs' disrespect for human rights. This is why the UN Security Council has made a series of procedural improvements to targeted sanctions, as will be overviewed in chapter 8 of this book. Yet there remain certain gaps between political discourse and legal obligations. While Article 1(3) of the Charter requires the UN organs to promote respect for human rights, neither the Charter nor the UN's international legal personality obliges the UN to ensure respect for human rights established under customary international law. Also, the variance among international organisations has so far hampered the development of substantive rules, such as human rights law, into the corps of common institutional rules. The crucial point for the purpose of this book is that the relatively 'lax' constraint at the *international* level regarding the UN's human rights obligations has created a *gap* with the more substantive and robust human rights constraints at the *domestic* level regarding the regulation of governmental authority. Such a gap has invited a series of judicial

103 Human Rights Committee, 'General Comment No. 24: Issues Relating to Reservations Made upon Ratification or Accession to the Covenant or the Optional Protocols Thereto, or in Relation to Declarations under Article 41 of the Covenant' UN Doc CCPR/C/21/Rev.1/Add.6 (4 November 1994) para 10; Human Rights Committee, 'General Comment No. 29: State of Emergency (Article 4)' UN Doc CCPR/C/21/Rev.1/Add.11 (31 August 2001) para 11.

104 Human Rights Committee, General Comment No. 29, ibid.

105 De Wet, 'The Role of Human Rights in Limiting the Enforcement Power of the Security Council: A Principled View' (n 45) 17, 22–3; Erika de Wet and André Nollkaemper, 'Review of Security Council Decisions by National Courts' (2003) 45 *German Yearbook of International Law* 166, 183.

and non-judicial contestations at the domestic level directly against national and EU institutions which implemented the UN Security Council's targeted sanctions, as will be discussed in chapter 7 of this book.

6.4 Direct implementation

Within the UN Security Council's Chapter VII measures, individuals have been constituted not only as the targets of asset freezes but also as those over whom the Security Council, through its subsidiary organs, directly executes their international decisions.[106] Within the context of territorial administration and ad hoc international criminal tribunals, the intermediary presence of a territorial state is effectively removed by the UN Security Council's subsidiary organs whose regulations and orders directly determine the entitlement of local populations subject to the authority of UNMIK and UNTAET and those individuals prosecuted before the ICTY and ICTR.

As in the case of targeted sanctions, the authority of the UN Security Council under Article 41 of the UN Charter is understood as being broad enough to provide the legal basis for the establishment of the UN's territorial administrations and ad hoc international criminal tribunals. A great deal of controversy arose instead with respect to the human rights compatibility of the exercise of authority by the UN's administrations or tribunals. Within the context of the UN's territorial administrations, one of the key concerns was their compatibility with the residents' right of access to courts. The adequacy of human rights protection has been questioned with regard to the ad hoc international criminal tribunals as well.

6.4.1 Legal basis for direct implementation by the Security Council itself: The planned administration of the Free Territory of Trieste

When the UN Security Council directly executes certain decisions over individuals, it does so not by the Security Council itself but through its subsidiary organs. Yet there was an exceptional instance within the context of the post-World War II settlement wherein the attempted administration of the Free Territory of Trieste involved the element of direct administration by the Security Council itself.[107] Although the plan was not put into operation, the envisaged forms of territorial governance gave rise to an intriguing question as to whether the UN Security Council *itself*, as opposed to its subsidiary organs, could exercise its authority in such a way that its decisions have immediate legal effect on individuals. Two separate questions are involved here: whether the UN Security Council can administer territories at all; and what kind of powers the Security Council is entitled to exercise over the administered territories.

106 See section 4.4 of this book.
107 See section 4.4.1 of this book.

6.4.1.1 Authority to administer territories

The authority under Chapter VII is wide enough to allow the Security Council to be a direct decision maker over an administered territory for the sake of the maintenance of international peace and security. In fact, the possibility that the Security Council might administer territories was already envisaged at the San Francisco Conference in 1945. Norway proposed to add the following sentence to Article 42 of the UN Charter regarding military enforcement measures:[108]

> The Security Council may further, in special cases, and for the period of time deemed necessary, take over on behalf of the Organization, the administration of any territory of which the continued administration by the State in possession is found to constitute a threat to the peace.[109]

According to Norway, this sentence ought to be added because 'the list [of military measures] would seem incomplete without this addition'.[110] Norway apparently assumed the UN Security Council's authority to administer territories as part of the UN's measures to maintain or restore international peace and security. While the Norwegian amendment was eventually withdrawn, the withdrawal was merely on the ground that 'such a reference to a particular procedure could be interpreted as restrictive and of such nature as to limit the field of application of measures at the disposition of the Council'.[111] In other words, the withdrawal of the Norwegian proposal did not mean to deny the existence of the UN Security Council's authority to administer territories as part of its military enforcement measures.[112]

At the same time, the story of the Norwegian proposal does not assist us in finding the legal basis of the planned administration of the Free City of Trieste which was not considered a Chapter VII measure. Security Council Resolution 16, adopted in January 1947, simply recorded the Security Council's approval of the Permanent Statute of the Free Territory of Trieste without any reference to the language of Chapter VII.[113] A legal basis must thus be sought elsewhere. One possible argument is to rely on the residual (or general) power of the Security

108 In the Dumbarton Oaks Proposals, the relevant provision was Chapter VIII, Section B (4), which provides the following: 'Should the Security Council consider such measures to be inadequate, it should be empowered to take such action by air, naval or land forces as may be necessary to maintain or restore international peace and security. Such action may include demonstrations, blockade and other operations by air, sea or land forces of members of the Organization': Dumbarton Oaks Proposals, UNCIO Documents (n 61) vol. 3, at 15 (Doc. 1, G/1, at 14), Chapter VIII, Section B(4).

109 UNCIO Documents, ibid., vol. 3, at 371–2 (Doc 2, G/7(n)(1), 4 May 1945, at 7–8) (original emphasis omitted).

110 Ibid., vol. 3, at 372 (Doc 2, G/7(n)(1), 4 May 1945, at 8).

111 Ibid., vol. 11, at 20 (Doc 943, III/5, 13 June 1945, at 9).

112 See Carsten Stahn, *The Law and Practice of International Territorial Administration: Versailles to Iraq and Beyond* (Cambridge, Cambridge University Press, 2008) 416; Finn Seyersted, *United Nations Forces in the Law of Peace and War* (Leyden, A.W. Sijthoff, 1966) 150, 187.

113 UN Doc S/RES/16 (10 January 1947).

Council under Article 24 of the Charter, as opposed to the specific powers laid down in Chapters VI, VII, VIII, and XII.[114] During the Security Council's debates leading to the adoption of Resolution 16, some Security Council members referred to Article 24 of the UN Charter.[115] The statement issued by the UN Secretary-General also drew upon Article 24(1), observing that the words 'primary responsibility for the maintenance of international peace and security' (coupled with the phrase 'acts on their behalf') constitute 'a grant of power sufficiently wide to enable the Security Council to approve the documents in question [including the Permanent Statute of the Free Territory of Trieste] and to assume the responsibilities arising therefrom'.[116] According to the UN Secretary-General, the records of the San Francisco Conference demonstrated that the Security Council's powers were not restricted to specific powers contained in Chapters VI, VII, VIII, and XII.[117]

Not all Security Council members were convinced by the reliance on Article 24 (1) of the UN Charter as a legal basis for the Security Council's involvement. The Statute of Trieste was adopted by the Security Council by ten votes to none, but the Australian delegation abstained from voting, having raised significant doubt about the compatibility with the UN Charter of the Security Council's proposed responsibilities over Trieste. The Australian delegation argued that the Security Council's wide powers under the Trieste Statute were related to the ordinary business of the government of Trieste, and not to the Security Council's mandate to maintain international peace and security.[118] Also, under Article 2 of the Trieste

114 Article 24(1) and (2) provides the following: '1. In order to ensure prompt and effective action by the United Nations, its Members confer on the Security Council primary responsibility for the maintenance of international peace and security, and agree that in carrying out its duties under this responsibility the Security Council acts on their behalf. 2. In discharging these duties the Security Council shall act in accordance with the Purposes and Principles of the United Nations. The *specific powers* granted to the Security Council for the discharge of these duties are laid down in Chapters VI, VII, VIII, and XII': UN Charter (n 14) Art 24(1) and (2) (emphasis added). For the argument of general power, see, e.g., *Legal Consequences for States of the Continued Presence of South Africa in Namibia (South West Africa) notwithstanding Security Council Resolution 276 (1970)* [1971] ICJ Reports 16 (Advisory Opinion of 21 June 1971) 52, para 110; Jost Delbrück, 'Article 24' in B. Simma (ed.), *The Charter of the United Nations: A Commentary* (2nd edn, Oxford, Oxford University Press, 2002) 442, 448.

115 UN Doc S/PV.89, SCOR 2nd Yr., No.1 (7 January 1947) 9 (Mr. Gromyko of USSR, invoking Article 24); ibid., 10 (Sir Cadogan of UK); UN Doc S/PV.91, SCOR 2nd Yr., No.3 (10 January 1947) 58 (Mr. Parodi of France). See also United Nations Palestine Commission, 'Relations between the United Nations Commission and the Security Council' (Working Paper Prepared by the Secretariat) (1948) UN Doc A/AC.21/W.25 (3 February 1948) 6 (the residual power of the Council in relation to the Palestine Commission).

116 UN Doc S/PV.91, SCOR 2nd Yr., No.3 (n 115) 44 (Mr. Sobolev, Assistant Secretary-General).

117 Ibid.

118 See UN Doc S/PV.89, SCOR 2nd Yr., No.1 (n 115) 7 (Mr. N.J.O Makin of Australia); UN Doc S/PV.91, SCOR 2nd Yr., No.3 (n 115) 56–7 (Mr. N.J.O. Makin of Australia).

Statute, the Security Council gave assurance as to the integrity and independence of Trieste. According to Australia, this was incompatible with the drafting process of the UN Charter, during which states deliberately rejected the proposals to include a guarantee of territorial integrity in the purposes and principles of the UN.[119]

While these objections raised by Australia are noteworthy, they do not seem to hold water after all. As some other Security Council members assumed, the administration of the Free Territory of Trieste was within the organ's broad power to discharge its primary responsibility for the maintenance of international peace and security. The fact that a guarantee of territorial integrity is not included in the purposes and principles of the UN does not preclude the Security Council from giving its assurance as to the integrity and independence of Trieste, provided that the Security Council considers such assurance necessary for international peace and security.

In sum, therefore, it seems persuasive to rely on the residual power of the Security Council according to Article 24 of the UN Charter as a legal basis for the Security Council's planned administration of Trieste. One critical difference between the territorial administration under Chapter VII, on the one hand, and that under Article 24 of the UN Charter, on the other hand, is that the latter can be carried out only with the consent of a territorial state. In the case of the Free Territory of Trieste, the Treaty of Peace with Italy in 1947 served as an instrument in which Italy agreed to terminate sovereignty over the area of the Free Territory and to subject it to the UN's direct administration.

6.4.1.2 Types of governing powers

If we assume that the Security Council itself has the authority to administer territories, a follow-up question arises as to the *types of governing powers* the Security Council is entitled to exercise over a particular territory. More precisely, the query is whether the Security Council itself exercise not only executive powers but also legislative and judicial powers. As the Appeals Chamber of the ICTY in *Tadić* enunciated, the UN Security Council is mandated to maintain international peace and security, in the discharge of which the Security Council exercises 'decision-making and *executive* powers'.[120] Thus a wide range of executive powers can be exercised for the sake of governing a territory.

At the same time, as pointed out by the ICTY in *Tadić*, the UN Security Council itself is 'not provided with *judicial* powers'.[121] The organ itself is thus precluded from acting as a judicial organ over the Council-administered territory even as part of enforcement measures under Chapter VII. Such an understanding

119 See UN Doc S/PV.89, SCOR 2nd Yr., No.1 (n 115) 5–7 (Mr. N.J.O. Makin of Australia); UN Doc S/PV.91, SCOR 2nd Yr., No.3 (n 115) 56–7 (Mr. N.J.O. Makin of Australia).

120 Case No IT-94-1-AR72 *Prosecutor v Duško Tadić, Appeals Chamber, Decision on Jurisdiction* (1996) 35 ILM 32 (ICTY, Decision of 2 October 1995), para 37 (emphasis added).

121 Ibid.

of the Security Council's power is by no means static; the dynamic interpretation of the Charter in the future may provide a different answer as to the essential character of the Security Council. However, it is a highly unlikely development, as the procedural fairness would have to be significantly compromised if the Security Council, composed of diplomats of a limited number of states, were to act as a judge to determine the question of the rights and obligations of individuals.

The similar reservation can also be made with respect to the *legislative* power. The Non-Aligned Movement (NAM) has expressed its concern that 'norm-setting, legislation and establishing definitions' were not necessarily within the purview of the Security Council's authority, bearing in mind the UN General Assembly's competence with respect to the progressive development of international law and its codification under Article 13(1) of the Charter.[122] Although the NAM's concern is related to 'global' legislation addressed to member states as opposed to 'local' legislation addressed to local populations under UN administration, the controversy casts doubt on the Security Council's legislative powers, whether or not they are exercised at the global or local level.

In the light of this analysis, the validity of certain provisions of the Permanent Statute of the Free Territory of Trieste can be called into question. Under Article 2, the UN Security Council ought to assure the Territory's integrity and independence.[123] This mandate duly falls within the powers of the UN Security Council. The same holds true for certain other executive powers under Articles 20, 22, and 37 of the Permanent Statute of the Free Territory of Trieste.[124] Concerns can be levelled instead with regard to the validity of legislative involvement envisaged under Articles 10 and 19(5) and (6) of the Permanent Statute.[125] Under these provisions, the directions given by the Security Council regarding a specific piece of legislation seems to have binding force on the legislative authority within the Free Territory of Trieste. If we assume that the Council itself does not have authority to act as a legislator, it is reasonable to call into question whether the Council's power under Articles 10 and 19(5) and (6) would have been *intra vires.*

6.4.2 Legal basis for direct implementation through subsidiary organs

At any rate, the planned administration of the Free Territory of Trieste was the exceptional instance born out of the settlement of World War II. The UN's

122 'Final Document of the Fourteenth Summit Conference of Heads of State or Government of the Non-Aligned Movement (11–16 September 2006)' UN Doc A/61/472–S/2006/780 (29 September 2006) Annex I, at para 40; 'Final Document of Fifteenth Ministerial Conference of the Non-Aligned Movement (27–30 July 2008)' UN Doc A/62/929 (11 August 2008) para 54. Similarly, Sixth Committee, UN Doc A/C.6/61/SR.7 (2006) paras 21 (Mexico), 76 (India); Sixth Committee, UN Doc A/C.6/62/SR.15 (2007) para 9 (Cuba); Sixth Committee, UN Doc A/C.6/62/SR.16 (2007) para 71 (Iran).
123 Treaty of Peace with Italy, 10 February 1947, 49 UNTS 126 Annex VI (Permanent Statute), Article 2. See further section 4.4.1 of this book.
124 See section 4.4.1 of this book.
125 For the quotation of Articles 10 and 19(5) and (6), see section 4.4.1 of this book.

territorial administration has been conducted not by the Security Council itself but through its subsidiary organs such as UNMIK and UNTAET in Kosovo and East Timor. When the territorial administration is undertaken by the subsidiary organs established under Chapter VII, there is little difficulty in terms of the legal basis of the UN's territorial administration precisely because the subsidiary organs can embark on those tasks which cannot be undertaken by the Security Council itself. Article 41 of the UN Charter allows the establishment of the civilian components of the UN's territorial administration, while Article 42 of the UN Charter furnishes the basis for the military component of the territorial administration.[126]

One may argue that the 'consent' of the territorial state could likewise provide a legal basis for the UN's territorial administration. Yet the 'consent' of the territorial government cannot be an independent legal basis for the UN's territorial administration. The dichotomy of 'consent *or* Chapter VII' is misleading in this regard. While the consent of a territorial state provides the UN with the permission to operate within the relevant territory, the ad hoc consent cannot, by itself, bestow upon the UN the novel authority *beyond* what is sanctioned under the UN Charter. If the territorial government's consent alone is enough to extend the ambit of the UN's activities, this would result in the UN organs broadening the authority even without the agreement of other UN member states. This means that the agreement between Indonesia and the Netherlands with respect to United Nations Temporary Executive Authority (UNTEA) or Croatia's request for United Nations Transitional Authority in Eastern Slavonia, Baranja and Western Sirmium (UNTAES) did not provide an autonomous legal basis for the UN's engagement in territorial administration. Chapter VII ought to be mobilised, in the absence of which the only possible legal recourse would be the residual power of the Security Council under Article 24(1) of the UN Charter.[127] A valid consent of territorial government must further be secured in such a case, inasmuch as the residual power does not allow the Security Council to bypass the authority of a territorial state.

Article 41 of the UN Charter is flexible enough to serve as a legal basis for the establishment of ad hoc international criminal tribunals.[128] While the UN Security Council itself does not possess judicial powers, its subsidiary organs are able to perform functions which the Security Council itself is unable to perform. It is the logic of the delegation of authority that makes such ostensible illogicality possible.[129] Such a line of reasoning was pursued by the ICTY in *Tadić* in 1995 in verifying the tribunal's own constitutionality under international law. Having recognised that the Security Council was not equipped with judicial powers, the ICTY

126 See Stahn, *The Law and Practice of International Territorial Administration* (n 112) 431.

127 See (n 114) and accompanying text.

128 See William Schabas, *The UN International Criminal Tribunals: The Former Yugoslavia, Rwanda, and Sierra Leone* (Cambridge, Cambridge University Press, 2006) 48–53.

129 For the rules of delegation, see generally Sarooshi, 'Subsidiary Organs' (n 85); Sarooshi, *The United Nations and the Development of Collective Security* (n 85).

justified its presence as a judicial organ established by the Security Council as 'an instrument for the exercise of its own principal function of maintenance of peace and security'.[130] In other words, the UN Security Council did not exercise any judicial powers which it does not possess, but discharged its peace and security mandate by creating the ICTY. The ICTY's reasoning was built on the ICJ's *Effect of Awards* advisory opinion which upheld, in 1954, the validity of the UN General Assembly's exercise of authority to establish the UN Administrative Tribunal. On the basis that the General Assembly can regulate staff relations under Article 101(1) of the UN Charter and establish subsidiary organs according to Articles 7 and 22,[131] the ICJ observed that the General Assembly did not delegate the performance of its own functions, but was instead 'exercising a power which it had under the Charter to regulate staff relations'.[132]

Following the reasoning of the ICJ in *Effect of Awards*, the Security Council can validly establish ad hoc international criminal tribunals under the UN Charter, more precisely, in accordance with Article 7(2) of the UN Charter.[133] While both Articles 7(2) and 29 allow the Security Council to devise subsidiary organs, the recourse to Article 29 limits the functions of the subsidiary organs to those of the Security Council. By contrast, the reliance on the general authority of Article 7(2) allows the Security Council to create its subsidiary organs with judicial functions that the Security Council itself cannot perform.[134] Insofar as it is necessary for the maintenance of international peace and security, the UN Security Council is entitled to establish a judicial organ, although the Security Council's political character prevents itself from subsequently reviewing the judicial decisions rendered by its own subsidiary organs.[135]

6.4.3 Legal basis for the subsidiary organs to impose obligations on individuals

The fact that the UN Security Council's subsidiary organs could perform functions that the Council itself cannot shoulder has significantly reduced the distance

130 *Tadić (Appeals Chamber on Jurisdiction, 1995)* (n 120) para 38.

131 *Effect of Awards of Compensation Made by the United Nations Administrative Tribunal* [1954] ICJ Reports 47 (Advisory Opinion of 13 July 1954) 57–8.

132 Ibid., 61.

133 Article 7(2) of the Charter reads: 'Such subsidiary organs as may be found necessary may be established in accordance with the present Charter'. Article 29 provides: 'The Security Council may establish such subsidiary organs as it deems necessary for the performance of its functions.' UN Charter (n 14) Arts 7(2) and 29.

134 Sarooshi, 'Subsidiary Organs' (n 85) 422–31. This, rather theoretical, distinction was not recognised by the UN Secretary-General's report on the establishment of the ICTY: see 'Report of the Secretary-General Pursuant to Paragraph 2 of Security Council Resolution 808 (1993)' (1993) UN Doc S/25704 (3 May 1993) para 28 (simply referring to Article 29).

135 José E. Alvarez, 'Judging the Security Council' (1996) 90 *The American Journal of International Law* 1, 11 ('the body is "subsidiary" in name only and can render final judgments that even the Council is not authorized to disturb – and that in turn can disturb the Council by suggesting limits on its powers').

between the Security Council's exercise of authority and individuals. While the Security Council itself may not be able to impose an obligation on individuals,[136] the Security Council's subsidiary organs can duly prescribe and apply certain obligations incumbent on individuals. Such a power of the subsidiary organs does not emanate from Article 25 of the UN Charter. Instead, the authority to impose an obligation on individuals is incidental to the Chapter VII measures necessary for the maintenance of international peace and security.[137] For instance, UNMIK determined tax rates or ordered the detention of individuals in the course of fulfilling the mandates given to it by Security Council Resolution 1244 adopted under Chapter VII.[138]

In a similar vein, the ICTY and ICTR have authority to render judgments incumbent on particular individuals ultimately as part of Chapter VII measures on the basis of which the ad hoc tribunals were created. As an essential part of its judicial work, the ICTY has issued binding orders not only to those accused but also to other individuals such as witnesses.[139] Although the ICTY Statute itself does not elucidate the power of the Tribunal to bind individuals other than the accused, in the *Blaskic Subpoena* case in 1997, the ICTY upheld its authority to issue binding orders to private individuals other than those accused. The Tribunal relied on 'the general object and purpose of the Statute', 'the role the International Tribunal is called upon to play thereunder', and the Prosecutor and the judge's powers laid down in Articles 18(2) and 19(2) of the ICTY Statute.[140] Article 18(2) entitles the Prosecutor to question suspects, victims, and witnesses, to collect evidence and to conduct on-site investigation, while Article 19(2) entitles the judges to issue not only orders and warrants for arrest, detention, surrender, or transfer of persons but also 'any other orders as may be required for the conduct of the trial'.[141] The ICTY observed that the Tribunal's role and the Statute conferred on it 'an incidental or ancillary jurisdiction over individuals other than those whom the International Tribunal may prosecute and try'.[142] According to the

136 See section 6.2.3 of this book.

137 Cf. 'Investigating Powers of the International Criminal Tribunal for the Former Yugoslavia vis-à-vis States and High Government Officials, Amicus Curiae Brief Submitted by the Max Planck Institute for Comparative Public Law and International Law to the International Criminal Tribunal for the Former Yugoslavia in the Case of The Prosecutor v. Tihomir Blaskic, prepared by Jochen Abr. Frowein, Georg Nolte, Karin Oellers-Frahm, and Andreas Zimmermann' (1997) 1 *Max Planck Yearbook of United Nations Law* 349.

138 See section 4.4.2 on a range of decisions taken by UNMIK.

139 See further Shuichi Furuya, 'Legal Effect of Rules of the International Criminal Tribunals and Court upon Individuals: Emerging International Law of Direct Effect' (2000) 47 *Netherlands International Law Review* 111.

140 Case No IT-95-14-AR108 bis *Prosecutor v Tihomir Blaskic, Appeals Chamber, Judgment on the Request of the Republic of Croatia for Review of the Decision of Trial Chamber II of 18 July 1997* (1997) (ICTY, Decision of 29 October 1997), para 47.

141 Updated Statute of the International Criminal Tribunal for the Former Yugoslavia, adopted 25 May 1993 by Security Council Resolution 827 (last amended 7 July 2009 by Resolution 1877) Art 19(2).

142 *Blaskic, Appeals Chamber (1997)* (n 140) para 48.

Blaskic Subpoena case, the Tribunal might enter into direct contact with an individual *without the consent* of relevant state authorities, by summoning a witness, or ordering an individual to hand over evidence or to appear before a Judge or Trial Chamber. The Tribunal has 'an inherent power to address itself directly to those individuals'.[143] Such a power arguably emanates from the need to fulfil the judicial tasks as well as states' obligation to cooperate with the Tribunal under Article 29 of the ICTY's Statute.[144]

6.4.4 Human rights concerns over the practices of direct implementation

As the Security Council's subsidiary organs directly prescribe and apply their decisions vis-à-vis individuals without the intermediary presence of states, the question has arisen again concerning the human rights compatibility of the decision making of the Security Council's subsidiary organs. Criticisms were levelled particularly against the UN's territorial administrations. Despite being deeply linked with inhabitants on a daily basis, the UN administrations were protected by jurisdictional immunities and the underlying idea of functional necessity.[145] Significant doubt was thus cast on the compatibility of the UN's involvement with the residents' right of access to courts and other fundamental rights as part of a broader concern over the limited accountability of transnational administrations to the local populations.[146]

143 Ibid., para 55. Such power arises in exceptional circumstances where the individual is subject to states (or entities) of former Yugoslavia, which *might* hinder the ICTY's tasks, or other states which *actually* prevent the Tribunal from fulfilling its functions: *Blaskic*, ibid., paras 52–6. For a summary see Furuya, 'Legal effect of rules of the International Criminal Tribunals and Court upon individuals' (n 139) 138–40.

144 Article 29 of the ICTY Statute obliges states to cooperate with the tribunal: ICTY Statute (last amended 7 July 2009) (n 141) Art 29. According to some authors, 'state practice…does indeed presuppose and confirm that the International Criminal Tribunal for the Former Yugoslavia possesses the power *under Art. 29* of its statute to directly address individuals by way of orders' (emphasis added): 'Investigating Powers of the International Criminal Tribunal for the Former Yugoslavia vis-à-vis States and High Government Officials, Amicus Curiae Brief Submitted by the Max Planck Institute for Comparative Public Law and International Law to the International Criminal Tribunal for the Former Yugoslavia in the Case of The Prosecutor v. Tihomir Blaskic, prepared by Jochen Abr. Frowein, Georg Nolte, Karin Oellers-Frahm, and Andreas Zimmermann' (n 137) 389–90.

145 UNMIK, 'On the Status, Privileges and Immunities of KFOR and UNMIK and Their Personnel in Kosovo' UNMIK/REG/2000/47 (18 August 2000). For UNTAET, see F. Rawski, 'To Waive or Not to Waive: Immunity and Accountability in UN Peacekeeping Operations' (2002) 18 *Connecticut Journal of International Law* 103, 118.

146 Ombudsperson Institution in Kosovo, 'Special Report No.1: On the Compatibility with Recognized International Standards of UNMIK Regulation No. 2000/47 on the Status, Privileges and Immunities of KFOR and UNMIK and Their Personnel in Kosovo (18 August 2000) and on the Implementation of the Above Regulation' (2001) (26 April 2001); The Human Rights Advisory Panel, History and Legacy, Kosovo, 2007–2016, Final Report (30 June 2016) paras 18–20.

The adequacy of human rights protection has also been questioned with regard to ad hoc international criminal tribunals. Particularly disturbing was the ICTR which addressed its own infringement of the accused's rights during arrest and detention.[147] In the *Semanza* case, for instance, the ICTR's Appeals Chamber accepted that there were violations in the accused's right to be properly informed of the charges and the right to challenge the lawfulness of his detention.[148] The review by the ICTR itself was, however, a limited one. This is because some of these human rights obligations were attributable to member states, and the ICTR does not have competence to pronounce on the responsibility of member states for violating human rights during the process of arrest, detention, and imprisonment.[149]

Despite these human rights concerns with respect to the decision making of the UN Security Council's subsidiary organs, international law has yet to impose an obligation *strictu sensu* on the UN itself to ensure respect for human rights established under customary international law.[150] While the UN's territorial administrations pledged to observe international human rights standards, and the rules of procedure of the ad hoc tribunals obviously provide for the protection of the rights of suspects, these practices do not mean that the UN itself (as opposed to member states) is formally bound by international human rights law. While the position that international legal personality leads to customary international human rights law binding on international organisations has gained support,[151] the legal personality entails the capacity. The extent to which international organisations are bound by customary rights and obligations depends on the sets of principles and rules.[152] The textual reading of Article 1(3) suggests that the UN organs are required to 'promote' respect for human rights, but not to 'ensure' respect for human rights. While subsequent practice has developed to provide

147 For instance, the ICTR accepted the violations of the fundament rights of the accused in *Barayagwiza* (1999, 2000): see *Barayagwiza v Prosecutor* Case No ICTR-97-19-AR72, Decision (ICTR, Appeals Chamber, 3 November 1999); *Barayagwiza v Prosecutor* ICTR-97-19-AR72, Decision (Prosecutor's Request for Review or Reconsideration) (ICTR, Appeals Chamber, 31 March 2000).

148 *Semanza (Laurent) v Prosecutor* Decision, Case No ICTR-97-20-A (ICTR, Appeals Chamber, 31 May 31 2000), paras 87, 114; *Semanza v Prosecutor* Judgment, Case No ICTR-97-20-A (ICTR, Appeals Chamber, 20 May 2005), paras 323–9. Likewise, the violations of the accused's rights were acknowledged in *Kajelijeli* (2005): *Prosecutor v Kajelijeli* Case No. ICTR-98-44A, Judgment (ICTR, Appeals Chamber, 23 May 2005), paras 251–3.

149 E.g., *Prosecutor v Kajelijeli* (n 148) para 252.

150 See sections 6.3.3–6.3.5 of this book.

151 See, e.g., Jann K. Kleffner, 'Human Rights and International Humanitarian Law: General Issues' in T.D. Gill and D. Fleck (eds), *The Handbook of the International Law of Military Operations* (2nd edn, Oxford, Oxford University Press, 2015) 35, 53 ('to the extent that [international organizations] exercise functions in a way that can be equated with the exercise of jurisdiction by a State'); Nigel D. White, 'Peace-keeping and International Law' in J.A. Koops and others (eds), *The Oxford Handbook of United Nations Peacekeeping Operations* (Oxford, Oxford University Press, 2015) 43, 53.

152 See section 6.3.4.5 of this book.

greater guidance as to how the UN and its organs take into account human rights, the practice does not go so far as to suggest that the organs are formally bound by human rights law.

Having said that, with respect to UN transitional administrations, the automatic 'succession' of international human rights treaties could still serve as a legal basis for human rights obligations owed by the UN itself. This argument is based on the idea underlying the human rights treaties that the protection of rights belongs to people and not to states. In its General Comment No. 26, the Human Rights Committee expressed the idea of the continuity of human rights obligations:

> once the people are accorded the protection of the rights under the Covenant [ICCPR], such protection devolves with territory and continues to belong to them, notwithstanding change in government of the State party, including dismemberment in more than one State or State succession or any subsequent action of the State party designed to divest them of the rights guaranteed by the Covenant.[153]

Built upon this notion, it has been argued that human rights obligations continue to apply to all entities which take over public authority in a territory whose inhabitants previously enjoyed the protection of their human rights.[154] Should one apply this argument to the UN's territorial administrations which indeed assume public authority in a territory, they would be automatically bound by human rights treaties as a *de facto* successor without any formal succession. Despite the attractiveness of this theory, however, there is no sufficient practice supporting automatic succession of human rights treaties by states, let alone by international organisations.[155] Overall, therefore, the obligation to ensure respect for customary international human rights law or international human rights treaties seems to be still formally inapplicable to the UN Security Council's subsidiary organs which administer war-torn territories, despite the significant impact that they have on local populations.

153 Human Rights Committee, 'General Comment No. 26: Continuity of Obligations' (1997) UN Doc CCPR/C/21/Rev.1/Add.8/Rev.1 (8 December 1997).

154 See Tobias H. Irmscher, 'Legal Framework for the Activities of UNMIK' (2001) 44 *German Yearbook of International Law* 353, 371. Similarly, see John Cerone, 'Minding the Gap: Outlining KFOR Accountability in Post-Conflict Kosovo' (2001) 12 *European Journal of International Law* 469, 474–5. Cerone puts forward a possible argument that the FRY automatically succeeded human rights obligations owed by its predecessor, the Socialist Federal Republic of Yugoslavia, under the major human rights instruments. Applying the rationale underlying the principle of automatic succession that 'obligations pass with control over territory', the principle may imply obligations on the part of any public authorities acting in the place of FRY, including UNMIK and KFOR.

155 Erika de Wet, 'The Direct Administration of Territories by the United Nations and its Member States in the Post Cold War Era: Legal Bases and Implications for National Law' (2004) 8 *Max Planck Yearbook of United Nations Law* 291, 318–9.

6.4.5 Concerns over the observance of international humanitarian law

Apart from the concerns that certain fundamental rights have been jeopardised by the practices of the Security Council's subsidiary organs, the UN's territorial administration in East Timor in principle gives rise to another legal question surrounding the relations between the UN's exercise of authority and individuals. The issue involved is the observance by the UN of the principles and rules of international humanitarian law, which is one of the longstanding questions concerning UN peacekeeping operations.[156] As contrasted with the UN's engagement with Kosovo under Resolution 1244, the UN's presence in East Timor between October 1999 and May 2002 involved not only civil administration but also a military component which was authorised to take all necessary measures.[157] According to the Secretary-General's report in July 2000, UNTAET had as many as 8,032 military personnel at that time.[158]

The presence of military personnel to restore security situations in the territory triggers the question of the applicability of international humanitarian law to UN peacekeepers. While troop-contributing states are no doubt bound by it, the UN itself is neither a party to the 1949 Geneva Conventions, nor is it entitled to accede to them.[159] The question thus concerns whether the UN mission is obliged to observe international humanitarian law established under customary international law. The UN has long declined to recognise, albeit it has not explicitly denied,[160] that it is formally bound by a set of international humanitarian laws. By contrast, the International Committee of the Red Cross (ICRC) and a number of scholars uphold the view that the UN is bound by customary international humanitarian law.[161]

156 See, e.g., Derek W. Bowett, *United Nations Forces: A Legal Study of United Nations Practice* (London, Stevens & Sons, 1964) 484–516; Seyersted, *United Nations Forces in the Law of Peace and War* (n 112).

157 UN Doc S/RES/1272 (25 October 1999) paras 3–4.

158 'Report of the Secretary-General on the United Nations Transitional Administration in East Timor, for the Period 27 January–26 July 2000' UN Doc S/2000/738 (26 July 2000) para 55.

159 See Bowett, *United Nations Forces: A Legal Study of United Nations Practice* (n 156) 507–11; Office of Legal Affairs, 'Question of the Possible Accession of Intergovernmental Organizations to the Geneva Conventions for the Protection of War Crimes' (1972) (1972) United Nations Juridical Yearbook 153 (1972) 153–4.

160 See Bowett, *United Nations Forces: A Legal Study of United Nations Practice* (n 156) 56.

161 For the position of the ICRC, see Umesh Palwankar, 'Applicability of International Humanitarian Law to United Nations Peace-keeping Forces' (1993) 294 *International Review of the Red Cross* 227. For scholars, see, e.g., Christopher Greenwood, 'International Humanitarian Law and United Nations Military Operations' (1998) 1 *Yearbook of International Humanitarian Law* 3, 16; Dietrich Schindler, 'United Nations Forces and International Humanitarian Law' in C. Cwinarski (ed.), *Études et essais sur le droit international humanitaire et sur les principes de la Croix-Rouge en l'honneur de Jean Pictet* (The Hague, Martinus Nijhoff Publishers, 1984) 521; R.D. Glick, 'Lip Service to the Laws of War: Humanitarian Law and United Nations Armed Forces' (1995) 17 *Michigan Journal of International Law* 53; Kleffner, 'Human Rights and International Humanitarian Law: General Issues' (n 151) 47.

The contention that international humanitarian law applies to UN peacekeeping forces sounds persuasive, although its theoretical grounds remain unresolved. If the UN were to act contrary to the basic rules of international humanitarian law which attain the status of *jus cogens* norms,[162] such an action would be *ultra vires*, namely, beyond the authority delegated by member states. Yet this does not amount to subjecting the UN itself to the principles and rules of international humanitarian law. The international legal personality of the UN, which lays a basis for the applicability, is not by itself sufficient to render all the customary law rules binding on the UN. Their applicability depends on the areas of customary law and needs to be assessed on a case-by-case basis.

In this regard, the fact that the applicability of international law is triggered by the existence of armed conflicts – as opposed to the status of actors – opens up possibilities for embracing a range of both state and non-state actors in the subjects of law. It is an ethos of international humanitarian law to ensure its applicability to all the parties to an armed conflict. Such parties to an armed conflict should include the UN when the confrontations involving UN forces reach the threshold of armed conflict.[163] The UN would be a party to non-international armed conflict if one employs the inter-state criterion (as opposed to a cross-border standard[164]) to the classification of armed conflict.[165]

162 The ILC considers that the basic rules of international humanitarian law are peremptory, in the view of the ICJ's advisory opinion in *Nuclear Weapons*: 'Draft Articles on Responsibility of States for Internationally Wrongful Acts' (2001) II 2 Yearbook of the International Law Commission 26 113, 5 (commentary to Article 40). The ICJ observed in 1996 that 'a great many rules of humanitarian law applicable in armed conflict … constitute *intransgressible* principles of international customary law' (emphasis added): *Legality of the Threat or Use of Nuclear Weapons* [1996] ICJ Reports 226 (Advisory Opinion of 8 July 1996) 257, para 79.

163 Tristan Ferraro, 'The Applicability and Application of International Humanitarian Law to Multinational Forces' (2013) 95 *International Review of the Red Cross* 561, 588, fn. 77, 592–3; Charles H.B. Garraway and Jann K. Kleffner, 'Applicability and Application of International Humanitarian Law to Enforcement, Peace Enforcement, and Peace Operations' in T.D. Gill and D. Fleck (eds), *The Handbook of the International Law of Military Operations* (2nd edn, Oxford, Oxford University Press, 2015) 147, 151.

164 This view finds support from the Israel court in the *Targeted Killings* judgment: see *Public Committee against Torture in Israel v Government of Israel, HCJ 769/02* (2006) (Supreme Court of Israel, sitting as the High Court of Justice, Judgment of 13 December 2006), para 18 ('an armed conflict of international character – in other words, one that crosses the borders of the state); *A, B v State of Israel, CrimA 6659/06 (et al)* (2008) (Supreme Court of Israel, sitting as the Court of Criminal Appeals, Judgment of 11 June 2008), para 9. It is noted that the Court's definition is 'whether or not the place in which the armed conflict occurs is subject to belligerent occupation' (which is by definition an international armed conflict) (*Public Committee against Torture in Israel v Government of Israel*, ibid.).

165 For instance, while the Ethiopia–Eritrea conflict was clearly of an international character, this does not mean that the UN Mission in Ethiopia and Eritrea (UNMEE) was a party to international armed conflicts. An international armed conflict requires the UN to be assimilated to a 'state' for the purpose of characterisation of conflicts, and the UN must engage with the forces of a state: Kleffner, 'Human Rights and International Humanitarian Law: General Issues' (n 151) 43. Given that UN peacekeeping

This does not mean, however, that the military component of UNTAET in East Timor was a party to a non-international armed conflict. The factual entry point for the application of international humanitarian law is the existence of armed conflicts which, according to the ICTY in *Tadić*, require the element of 'protraction' of violence.[166] While this statement does not elucidate what degree of intensity is required, international humanitarian law has been developed to lower down the threshold of armed conflict, despite the somewhat contrasted trend that the UN seems to apply a relatively higher threshold in determining the existence of armed conflicts within the context of its own peacekeeping operations.[167]

These uncertainties over the threshold of armed conflict do not seem to affect the applicability of international humanitarian law to UNTAET, however. After having taken over the territory whose security was already restored by the International Force for East Timor (INTERFET), UNTAET did not need to engage in large-scale military battles.[168] While there were a few cross-border incursions by militia groups and a few attacks against UNTAET personnel in early 2000,[169] UNTAET's use of military force was significantly limited, compared with, for instance, the scale of military battles engaged in by the ONUC in the early 1960s or the UN Operation in Somalia II (UNOSOM II) and the UN Protection Force (UNPROFOR) in the early 1990s. Therefore, on a factual level, the applicability of humanitarian law was of limited relevance to UNTAET, inasmuch as INTERFET had already secured the territory, and the subsequent deployment of UNTAET did not resort to force during most of the operations.

forces do not in principle engage in fighting with governmental forces, most armed conflicts involving UN forces remain to be of a non-international character. This conclusion is largely consistent with the position taken by the UN's Convention on the Safety of United Nations and Associated Personnel: Christopher Greenwood, 'Protection of Peacekeepers: The Legal Regime' (1996) 7 *Duke Journal of Comparative and International Law* 185; Steven J. Lepper, 'The Legal Status of Military Personnel in United Nations Peace Operations: One Delegate's Analysis' (1995) 18 *Houston Journal of International Law*359.

166 *Tadić (Appeals Chamber on Jurisdiction, 1995)* (n 120) para 70.

167 Greenwood, 'International Humanitarian Law and United Nations Military Operations' (n 161) 34. The hesitation was combined with the reluctance to qualify the UN as a belligerent party or a warring party to the conflict, as the Secretary-General suggested in 1961 that, insofar as the UN force committed itself to 'defensive' actions, it would not qualify as a party to an armed conflict: 'Report of the Secretary-General on Certain Steps Taken in Regard to the Implementation of the Security Council Resolution Adopted on 21 February 1961' UN Doc S/4752 (27 February 1961) Annex VII, at 3.

168 Trevor Findlay, *The Use of Force in UN Peace Operations* (Oxford, Oxford University Press, 2002) 293–6 (about UNTAET); Norrie MacQueen, 'United Nations Transitional Administration in East Timor (UNTAET)' in J.A. Koops and others (eds), *The Oxford Handbook of United Nations Peacekeeping Operations* (Oxford, Oxford University Press, 2015) 642, 650.

169 'Report of the Secretary-General on the United Nations Transitional Administration in East Timor, for the Period 27 January–26 July 2000' (n 158) paras 52–3; United Nations, *Yearbook of the United Nations*, vol. 54 (2000) 281.

6.5 Conclusion

On the whole, what was illustrated by this chapter is the rather 'thinness' of international law in regulating authority exercised by the UN Security Council and its subsidiary organs over individuals. In the first place, while the Security Council constituted, under its resolutions, certain individuals as the addressees of Chapter VII demands, the Security Council itself (as opposed to its subsidiary organs) may not possess authority to independently impose an obligation on individuals. Even if the Security Council has such authority as part of Chapter VII measures, the fact remains that international legal frameworks have not been developed to protect the rights of individual addressees.

Individuals have also been the specific targets of asset freezes and travel bans introduced by the UN Security Council under Chapter VII amid a significant degree of uncertainty over the extent to which the UN Security Council and its sanctions committees are bound by international human rights law. The UN is clearly mandated to promote respect for human rights, yet this leaves a great deal of discretion on the part of the Security Council and its sanctions committees in determining how they should take into account the rights of designated individuals, such as the right to a fair hearing and the right to an effective remedy.

Finally, the uncertainties with regard to the UN's human rights obligations still subsist even in the contexts in which the Security Council's subsidiary organs directly execute their decisions vis-à-vis individuals, instead of asking the national government to implement international decisions as in the case of sanctions. The decisions of the UN's territorial administrations or ad hoc international criminal tribunals are binding on local populations or the accused individuals, effectively without the intermediary of national government. The exercise of authority by the subsidiary organs of the Security Council then bears strong resemblance to the exercise of authority by national government. Despite such resemblance, it is troubling that international law yields to a thin set of rules in safeguarding the rights of affected individuals.

In short, the UN General Assembly's endorsement of the rule of law applicable to 'the United Nations and its principal organs'[170] must be understood in light of the limited catalogue of international law in regulating the exercise of authority by the Security Council and its subsidiary organs. The rules of international law accommodate only the macro-level consideration of the rights and interests of individuals in the context of the maintenance of international peace and security. This creates an important *gap* between the more substantive and robust protection given to individuals' rights at the domestic level. The gap between international and national law is accompanied by the striking *asymmetry* within international law in terms of accommodating the rights and interests of individuals. On the one hand, international human rights law extensively regulates governmental authority. On the other hand, however, international human rights law is still significantly

170 Resolution adopted by the General Assembly on 24 September 2012, High-level Meeting Declaration on the Rule of Law (2012) (n 87) para 2 (emphasis added).

underdeveloped with regard to the regulation of international authority exercised by the UN and other international organisations. While the UN actively promotes and encourages states to comply with international human rights law, this simply highlights the asymmetry within international law in regulating international and governmental authority exercised vis-à-vis individuals.

The gap between international and national law, accompanied by the asymmetry within international law, has therefore motivated some of the affected individuals to resort to domestic courts, as will be examined in chapter 7 of this book. The individuals challenged the compatibility of the implementing decisions of state authorities with constitutional safeguards and international human rights law, whereby the individuals indirectly contested the decisions of the UN Security Council and its subsidiary organs. While the UN organs are not bound by domestic court decisions, the affected individuals' turn to domestic law epitomises the fact that international law has not been able to catch up with the changing distance between individuals and the UN Security Council's exercise of authority for the maintenance of international peace and security.

7 Reception in domestic law

7.1 Introduction

The generosity of international law in allowing broad discretion on the part of the UN Security Council is problematic precisely because of the reduced distance between the UN Security Council's exercise of authority and individuals. The limited, if any, utility of international law for the affected individuals increased the relevance of the domestic legal order as possibly the only alternative venue through which the individuals can contest the consequences they encounter due to the institutional decisions of the UN Security Council and its subsidiary organs. Needless to say, some jurisdictions can be more appealing than others in terms of safeguarding the affected individuals' rights and interests. The diversity among domestic legal orders then led to the greater use of, and international attention given to, several domestic courts (including EU courts[1]) situated in a jurisdiction with relatively robust human rights protection.

This chapter analyses the domestic effect and reception of the three categories of the UN Security Council's practices examined in the earlier part of this book – namely, first, Chapter VII 'demands' addressed directly to individuals; second, the specification of targets for economic sanctions; and, finally, direct implementation by the Security Council's subsidiary organs. With respect to the UN Security Council's 'demand', it does not yet appear to entail any visible consequences at the domestic level, inasmuch as the relevant Security Council resolutions so far lack sufficient precision to be directly applicable even within a monist state. Instead, the affected individuals' contestations at the domestic level thrived with respect to targeted sanctions for which member states were required to take measures under their own domestic law. Such an intermediary presence of member states enabled the affected individuals to resort to national courts, EU courts, and regional human rights courts in order to challenge the compatibility of the implementing decisions of state authorities with constitutional safeguards and international human rights law.

The crucial *paradox* here is that the deeper the replacement of governmental authority by the UN becomes, the higher the hurdles would be for individuals to

1 For the purpose of this book, the decisions of EU courts are situated as part of broadly defined 'domestic' court decisions.

contest the decisions taken by the UN, especially before judicial venues. The effective removal of the authority of member states is most comprehensive when the UN Security Council, through its subsidiary organs, directly executes their decisions vis-à-vis individuals, as in the contexts of the UN's territorial administration and the ad hoc international criminal tribunals. Despite the direct contact the affected individuals have with the UN Security Council's subsidiary organs, their judicial challenges against the government or the UN are hindered by multiple variables, effectively obliterating the availability of any judicial contestations.

7.2 Addressing individuals: Possibilities for direct applicability at the domestic level

One of the phenomena that characterise the changing distance between the UN Security Council's exercise of authority and individuals is the Council's demand under Chapter VII addressed to a certain category of individuals.[2] Apparently, the domestic effect of such a demand is virtually absent unless Council resolutions oblige member states to take related actions. No matter what the UN Security Council demands of individuals, the legal effect of such a demand formally stays within the international legal order. The separation of legal orders holds true for international law in general, whose formal legal effect within the domestic legal order is contingent on an authorising rule of domestic law (and vice versa), even when a relevant treaty specifies how it should be implemented under domestic law.[3]

Some states' domestic reception may carry 'monist' traditions if international law has validity at the domestic level without enacting domestic legislation, while other states may have the 'dualist' tradition that requires a piece of implementing legislation for international law to be domestically valid.[4] While many states follow a monistic stance toward customary law, they differ in terms of the domestic reception of treaties. States with monist traditions include Germany, the Netherlands, Poland, Russia, South Africa, and the US,[5] while states with dualist traditions

2 Section 4.2 of this book.
3 See Janne Nijman and André Nollkaemper, 'Beyond the Divide' in J.E. Nijman and A. Nollkaemper (eds), *New Perspectives on the Divide Between National and International Law* (Oxford, Oxford University Press, 2007) 341, 341–2.
4 To be precise, the monism–dualism classification is used in two different contexts: (1) to see the relationships between national and international law *from the distance*, and provide a general theory about the relationship, and (2) to see the relationships *from the national legal order*, and describe a particular state's policy with regard to the effect of international law under its domestic law: David Sloss, 'Treaty Enforcement in Domestic Courts: A Comparative Analysis' in D. Sloss (ed.), *The Role of Domestic Courts in Treaty Enforcement: A Comparative Study* (Cambridge, Cambridge University Press, 2009) 1, 6. Here the dichotomy is used in the *latter* sense, namely, a particular state's policy.
5 Sloss, ibid., 7. The US is often regarded as a monist state. According to the definition given by the Supreme Court in *Medellín* in 2008, however, it is only a self-executing treaty that 'has automatic domestic effect as federal law upon ratification' without implementing legislation passed by Congress: see *Medellín v Texas* (2008) 128 S.Ct. 1346 (US Supreme Court, Judgment of 25 March 2008), 1356–7, fn. 2.

include Australia, Canada, Bangladesh, India, Ireland, Israel, Malaysia, Singapore, and the UK. The dichotomy of monism and dualism, despite its simplicity, still represents a useful starting point in accounting for international law's domestic effect.

In general, the distinction between monism and dualism was supposed to have little relevance when it comes to the domestic legal effect of UN Security Council resolutions. This is because the ambiguity of the terms of the Security Council resolutions renders them non-self-executing even in a monist state.[6] This means that the resolutions cannot be directly relied on by national courts. The applicability of Council resolutions builds on a general piece of legislation (as in the cases of the UK, Australia, and Singapore[7]) with which to allow executive organs to implement resolutions on non-military measures, or the applicability may be secured through a piecemeal approach of relying on existing pieces of legislation, such as those on foreign exchange and foreign trade.[8]

Such a general assumption of non-direct-applicability about Security Council resolutions can no longer be taken for granted, however, owing to the Security Council's Chapter VII demand addressed directly to individuals.[9] The possibility for the Security Council to impose obligations on individuals should invite us to reconsider the direct applicability of Council resolutions at the domestic level. Whether or not a particular treaty provision or a rule of customary international law is directly applicable is a matter of the domestic interpretation of international law itself.[10] The conditions under which international treaties have direct applicability vary according to states and their domestic courts. It is nevertheless possible to derive broad conditions on the basis of which domestic courts decide on the direct applicability of international law. In general, consideration is given, first, to the subjective element that parties have not excluded the direct applicability of the treaty as a whole, and, second, to the objective elements that treaty provisions are precise and complete enough to be applied by domestic courts.[11]

In light of these conditions, if Security Council resolutions create rights or impose obligations on individuals in a specific manner, the relevant provisions in

6 In the context of sanctions-related resolutions, Vera Gowlland-Debbas, 'Implementing Sanctions Resolutions in Domestic Law' in V. Gowlland-Debbas (ed.), *National Implementation of United Nations Sanctions: A Comparative Study* (Leiden, M. Nijhoff Publishers; Brill, 2004) 33, 38–41.

7 United Nations Act 1946, 9-10 Geo. 6, c.45 (UK); Charter of the United Nations Act 1945, Act No. 32 of 1945 (Australia); United Nations Act, Act 44 of 2001 (Singapore).

8 Gowlland-Debbas, 'Implementing Sanctions Resolutions in Domestic Law' (n 6) 42–5.

9 Section 4.2 of this book.

10 André Nollkaemper, 'The Duality of Direct Effect of International Law' (2014) 25 *European Journal of International Law* 105, 119–20.

11 André Nollkaemper, *National Courts and the International Rule of Law* (Oxford, Oxford University Press, 2011) 134–8; Yuji Iwasawa, *International Law, Human Rights, and Japanese Law: The Impact of International Law on Japanese Law* (Oxford, Clarendon Press, 1998) 44–9.

Security Council resolutions can be directly applicable at the domestic level without further legislative measures.[12] Apparently, at present, the direct applicability of Security Council resolutions remains a theoretical question, given that the relevant provisions discussed in chapter 4 of this book do not appear to be sufficiently precise to be directly applicable in domestic law. For instance, under paragraph 1 of Resolution 2178, the Security Council directly demanded that 'all foreign terrorist fighters' disarm and cease all terrorist acts.[13] This provision cannot readily be invoked at the domestic level against individuals, inasmuch as the resolution does not define 'terrorist acts' or 'foreign terrorist fighters'. Nevertheless, this does not change the fact that Security Council resolutions have been drafted with the intention that they would bring about immediate consequences to individuals. In a monist state, domestic courts or executive organs may face the question as to whether Security Council resolutions can be invoked as a basis of individuals' rights or obligations. This theoretical possibility cannot be easily dismissed, given that the direct applicability of Security Council resolutions would significantly increase the relevance of the UN's action in the domestic legal order and also the relevance of domestic law in the maintenance of international peace and security.

7.3 Target specification: Contestations through domestic and regional courts

As contrasted with the first scenario in which the Security Council directly addressed individuals via its Chapter VII resolutions, the UN's targeted sanctions are mediated by member states which are obliged by the Security Council to apply asset freezes and travel bans against designated individuals. Human rights criticisms levelled against the practices of targeted sanctions have created yet another opportunity to reveal the thinness of international law in protecting the fundamental rights of designated individuals. In the absence of international judicial venues to which the affected individuals can effectively bring their claims over the infringement of their rights against the UN, some of the individuals have resorted to domestic courts, EU courts, and a regional human rights court. Annex I of this book provides the list of reported cases concerning targeted sanctions.

7.3.1 Limited diplomatic recourse

Judicial measures may not be necessary if the designated individuals can receive political support from their own government. In fact, some individuals have availed themselves of a diplomatic initiative of their own government in order to be delisted by the UN's sanctions list. This was the case of Aden, a Swedish

12 Anne Peters, 'Security Council Resolution 2178 (2014): The "Foreign Terrorist Fighter" as an International Legal Person, Part I' *EJIL: Talk!* (20 November 2014) <https://perma.cc/PM4P-GTGQ> (last accessed 1 December 2016) (observing that the same criteria apply to the assessment of the direct effect of a Security Council resolution).

13 UN Doc S/RES/2178 (24 September 2014) para 1.

national who was designated in November 2001 under the 1267 sanctions regime as being associated with the Al-Qaida organisation.[14] Having found Aden and other Swedish nationals (Abdi Abdulaziz Ali and Yusuf) on the list, the Swedish government soon approached the 1267 Sanctions Committee and the US administration.[15] After the Swedish Security Police concluded in December 2001 that no accusations were confirmed, the Swedish government filed a request with the 1267 Committee for a review of the target list in January 2002, and, at the same time, entered into negotiations with the US administration.[16] The story of Aden was reported in the media in Sweden and abroad.[17] Although the delisting request was initially rejected by the 1267 Committee in February 2002, having met objections from the US, Russia, and the UK,[18] the US decided to remove Aden and Abdi Abdulaziz Ali in July 2002 after strong pressure from the Swedish government.[19] This was followed by the 1267 Sanctions Committee's adoption of the delisting procedure in August 2002,[20] under which the removal of their names was approved.[21]

Yet not all targeted individuals and entities which desire their names to be delisted are able to receive governmental support. In the absence of international forums or governmental support, some of the targeted individuals and entities have sought to find their way into national courts. While it is by no means novel for individuals to use national courts to directly or indirectly contest the acts of international organisations,[22] the proceedings relating to targeted sanctions have affirmed that the implementing measures of the UN Security Council are not free from judicial challenges. The actions were brought before EU courts and the domestic courts of several countries, including Belgium, Canada, Italy, the Netherlands, Pakistan, Switzerland, Turkey, the UK, and the US.[23] The cases were also brought

14 UN Press Release, AFG/163-SC/7206 (9 November 2001).
15 Per Cramér, 'Recent Swedish Experiences with Targeted UN Sanctions: The Erosion of Trust in the Security Council' in E. De Wet and A. Nollkaemper (eds), *Review of the Security Council by Member States* (Antwerp, Intersentia, 2003) 85, 91.
16 See ibid., 91–4.
17 See ibid., 92, fn 41 (Swedish media). See, e.g., BBC News, 'Sweden Questions US Terror Charges' (14 February 2002); BBC News, 'Swedish Somalis Fight Terror Links' (20 February 2002).
18 See Cramér, 'Recent Swedish Experiences with Targeted UN Sanctions' (n 15) 93–4.
19 BBC News, 'Swedish Terror Suspects Cleared' (14 July 2002).
20 UN Press Release, AFG/203-SC/7487 (16 August 2002). See 'Third Report of the Monitoring Group Established Pursuant to Security Council Resolution 1363 (2001) and Extended by Resolution 1390 (2002)' UN Doc S/2002/1338 (17 December 2002) Annex III (Guidelines of the Security Council Committee Established Pursuant to Resolution 1267 (1999) for the Conduct of its Work, Adopted on 7 November 2002) (hereinafter '1267 Committee Guidelines 2002').
21 UN Press Release, SC/7490 (27 August 2002) (the removal of Aden and Abdi Abdulaziz Ali).
22 For the overview of the types of cases involving international organisations, see August Reinisch, *International Organizations Before National Courts* (Cambridge, Cambridge University Press, 2000) 24–31.
23 See Annex I of this book.

to the European Court of Human Rights (ECtHR) and the Human Rights Committee under the ICCPR. As will be explained below, judicial responses have taken multiple forms, ranging from endorsement, *jus cogens* review, creative interpretation, and the use of critical language, to consequential resistance.

7.3.2 Deference to the political branch's decisions

Among a series of judicial challenges, the most well-known is a series of cases brought by Kadi, a Saudi Arabian national listed in October 2001 by the 1267 Sanctions Committee as a target of asset-freeze measures.[24] Before EU courts, Kadi's challenges have led to the annulment of the EU's implementing measures and shaped the fate of subsequent cases brought before EU courts and within its member states. By contrast, Kadi's judicial contestations did not yield a similar result before US courts. Kadi filed a suit in January 2009 after the US' OFAC, which had designated Kadi as a specifically designated global terrorist, denied his request for reconsideration.[25]

In March 2012, the US District Court of the District of Columbia held that there was 'substantial evidence' to support Kadi's designation as a global terrorist and thereby upheld the US government's designation.[26] The District Court confined its analysis to the compatibility of the executive's counter-terrorism designation with statutes and constitutional principles without any reference to the UN Security Council. As the US government possessed intelligence about Kadi's involvement, the District Court was able to review both the classified and unclassified records.[27] Having assessed them, the District Court found that the requirements of due process had been satisfied since Kadi had received an opportunity to rebut the evidence based on the unclassified record.[28] In the US courts, the legal challenges brought by those listed individuals and entities by the 1267 Sanctions Committee are generally treated the same as any other challenges brought against the government's counter-terrorism designation. The case of *Kadi* before the District Court was one of the occasions in which the domestic courts deferred to the executive branch's actions when national security was at stake.[29]

7.3.3 Deference to the primacy of UN obligations

While the US court in *Kadi* upheld the designation without even mentioning the UN Charter, judicial deference can also be paid to member states' international

24 See section 4.3.2 of this book.
25 *Yassin Abdullah Kadi v Timothy Geithner, et al* Civil Action No. 09–108(JDB), 2012 WL 898778 (D.D.C.) (19 March 2012) 2.
26 Ibid., 19.
27 Ibid.
28 Ibid., 24.
29 Andreas F. Lowenfeld, 'The United States' in V. Gowlland-Debbas (ed.), *National Implementation of United Nations Sanctions: A Comparative Study* (Leiden; Boston, Martinus Nijhoff Publishers, 2004) 605, 640.

obligations under the UN Charter. Article 103 of the UN Charter provides a normative hierarchy of Charter obligations over other conflicting obligations that member states owe under international agreement. The provision bears particular importance to the Security Council, which is the only UN organ with the general authority to render binding decisions for its mandate,[30] and whose internationally binding decisions prevail over any other obligations under international agreement.[31]

In principle, Article 103 of the UN Charter is a treaty provision applicable to UN member states, and it does not establish any general rule of hierarchy in international law.[32] Namely, Article 103, despite the UN Charter's constitutional characteristics,[33] does not in theory establish an overarching rule for resolving normative conflicts between multiple treaty regimes. Yet this is not always how international and national courts understand the implications of Article 103 of the UN Charter in their application of other international treaties.

The limited deference to the primacy of UN obligations was manifested within the EU (then EC) in *Kadi I* of September 2005 before the then Court of First Instance (CFI), a predecessor of the General Court of the EU (GCEU),[34] which found itself prevented from carrying out the review of the implementing measures.[35] According to the CFI in *Kadi I*, the primacy of UN Charter obligations

30 The General Assembly's authority to render binding 'decisions' is limited to the UN's organizational issues: Charter of the United Nations, 26 June 1945, 1 UNTS XVI (entered into force 24 October 1945) Articles 18(2), 5, 6, 17; *Certain Expenses of the United Nations (Article 17, Paragraph 2, of the Charter)* [1962] ICJ Reports 151 (Advisory Opinion of 20 July 1962) 163; *South West Africa Cases (Ethiopia v South Africa; Liberia v South Africa) (Second Phase)* [1966] ICJ Reports 6 (Judgment of 18 July 1966), 50–1, para 98.

31 UN Charter (n 30) Article 25; *Questions of Interpretation and Application of the 1971 Montreal Convention Arising from the Aerial Incident at Lockerbie (Libyan Arab Jamahiriya v United Kingdom; Libyan Arab Jamahiriya v United States of America), Provisional Measures* [1992] ICJ Reports 3, 114 (Order of 14 April 1992), 15 (para 39) and 126 (para 42), respectively.

32 Antonios Tzanakopoulos, 'Collective Security and Human Rights' in E. De Wet and J. Vidmar (eds), *Hierarchy in International Law: The Place of Human Rights* (Oxford, Oxford University Press, 2012) 42, 63–4.

33 Bardo Fassbender, 'The United Nations Charter As Constitution of the International Community' (1998) 36 *Columbia Journal of Transnational Law* 529, 568–616.

34 For the purpose of this book, I continue to use the CFI because it would be convenient to distinguish *Kadi* decisions rendered in 2005 (by the CFI) and 2010 (by the GCEU).

35 Case T-315/01 *Yassin Abdullah Kadi v Council of the European Union and Commission of the European Communities* [2005] ECR II-3649 (CFI, Judgment of 21 September 2005, 'Kadi I (CFI)'). On the CFI judgment, see, e.g., August Reinisch, 'Introductory Note to Court of First Instance of the European Communities: Yassin Abdullah Kadi v. Council of the European Union and Commission of the European Communities' (2006) 45 *International Legal Materials* 77; C. Tomuschat, 'Case Law: A. Court of Justice: Case T-306/01, Ahmed Ali Yusef and Al Barakaat International Foundation v. Council and Commission, Judgment of the Court of First Instance of 21 September 2005: Case T-315/01, Yassin Abdullah Kadi v. Council and Commission, Judgment of the Court of First Instance of 21 September 2005, nyr' (2006) 43

required member states to leave unapplied relevant EU law if it contradicts the UN Charter obligations.[36] As a corollary to the primacy of the UN's legal order, the CFI in *Kadi I* was faced with 'structural limits' on the judicial review of the contested regulation.[37] To conduct such review would, according to the CFI, signify the indirect review of the lawfulness of UN Security Council resolutions, and, if the Court were to annul the contested regulation on the basis of the infringement of Kadi's fundamental rights, such annulment would indirectly mean that Council resolutions themselves infringe on those fundamental rights.[38] Such indirect review is not justified in light of Articles 25, 48, and 103 of the UN Charter and the provisions of the EC Treaty, including the first paragraph of then Article 307 EC.[39] The CFI observed that the UN Charter's primacy placed the review of the contested regulation 'in principle, outside the ambit of the Court's judicial review'.[40]

Having been confronted with the potential conflict between the UN Charter obligations and the EU (then EC) institutions' obligations relating to fundamental rights, the CFI in *Kadi I* therefore deferred to the UN Charter's supremacy as a matter of principle – with minimum reservations to *jus cogens* norms, as will be

Common Market Law Review 537; Mielle Bulterman, 'Fundamental Rights and the United Nations Financial Sanction Regime: The Kadi and Yusuf Judgments of the Court of First Instance of the European Communities' (2006) 19 *Leiden Journal of International Law* 753; Christina Eckes, 'Judicial Review of European Anti-Terrorism Measures – The Yusuf and Kadi Judgments of the Court of First Instance' (2008) 14 *European Law Journal* 74.

36 *Kadi I (CFI, 2005)* (n 35) para 190. According to the CFI, the primacy of member states' obligations under the UN Charter over those under EU law was articulated in Article 103 of the UN Charter and, more importantly for the CFI, preserved by the EC Treaty itself by virtue of Article 307 EC (Article 351 TFEU): ibid., paras 182–5. While the EU itself is not directly bound by the UN Charter, it became bound by the UN Charter obligations by the will of EU member states which demonstrated such intention by conferring powers upon the Union (then Community) in the area governed by the UN Charter: ibid., paras 192–203. According to the CFI, the EU is 'bound … to adopt all the measures necessary to enable its Member States to fulfil those [UN Charter] obligations': ibid., para 204.

37 Ibid., para 212.

38 Ibid., paras 215–16.

39 Ibid., paras 221–3.

40 Ibid., para 225. In a virtually identical judgment, the claim in *Yusuf* was also rejected: Case T-306/01 *Ahmed Ali Yusuf and Al Barakaat International Foundation v Council of the European Union and Commission of the European Communities* [2005] ECR II-03533, ECLI:EU:T:2005:331 (CFI, Judgment of 21 September 2005). Following the CFI's decision in *Kadi I*, similar claims in *Ayadi* and *Hassan* were likewise rejected: Case T-253/02 *Chafiq Ayadi v Council of the European Union* [2006] ECR II-02139, ECLI:EU:T:2006:200 (CFI, Judgment of 12 July 2006); Case T-49/04 *Faraj Hassan v Council of the European Union and Commission of the European Communities* [2006] ECR II-00052, ECLI:EU:T:2006:201 (CFI, Judgment of 12 July 2006). The case of *Minin*, regarding the Liberia sanctions committee pursuant to Resolution 1521, was also rejected: Case T-362/04 *Leonid Minin v Commission of the European Communities* [2007] ECR II-002003, ECLI:EU:T:2007:25 (CFI, Judgment of 31 January 2007).

discussed below. Arguably, the CFI's deference was reasoned in a more internationalist manner than the US's District Court of the District of Columbia in *Kadi* which did not invite the UN Charter to its judicial reasoning.

7.3.4 Jus cogens *review*

Despite the subsequent rejection by the European Court of Justice (ECJ) in 2008, the CFI's judgment in *Kadi I* remains noteworthy precisely because it invoked international law in order both to show deference to and to conduct a limited review of the UN's listing decisions. The CFI's reasoning demonstrates that international law itself accommodates a basis for both upholding the UN Security Council's exercise of authority and contesting it. Having found itself structurally limited to conduct review, the CFI in *Kadi I* still managed to preserve its power 'to check, indirectly, the lawfulness of the resolutions of the Security Council in question with regard to *jus cogens*',[41] a body of higher, non-derogable, rules binding upon all subjects of international law.[42]

The substance of the CFI's *jus cogens* review was somewhat artificial; having conducted the indirect judicial review, the CFI readily concluded that there were no infringements of *jus cogens.* According to the CFI, the asset freeze did not constitute an arbitrary, inappropriate, or disproportionate interference with the right to respect for property, taking into account certain humanitarian exemptions, the sanctions' public-interest objective, their precautionary nature, and review procedures.[43] As for the right to be heard, the absence of direct challenge by individuals was 'not, however, to be deemed improper in the light of the mandatory prescriptions of the public international order'.[44] As for the right to effective judicial review, the CFI took note of the delisting procedures at the UN's level, which 'constitute another reasonable method of affording adequate protection of the applicants' fundamental rights as recognised by *jus cogens*'.[45] From a legalistic standpoint, it is difficult to ascribe any significance to the CFI's rather superficial *jus cogens* review, which was subsequently rejected by the ECJ as well. Nevertheless, the CFI's *jus cogens* review in *Kadi I* certainly built one factor which facilitated the international regulatory reform at that time – as will be explained in chapter 8 of this book.

7.3.5 Creative interpretation of Council resolutions and critical comments

While the CFI in *Kadi I* was confronted with the conflict between human rights norms and the obligations under the UN Charter, some judges managed to avoid such a conflict and thereby circumvented the need for pronouncing their

41 *Kadi I (CFI, 2005)* (n 35) para 226.
42 Ibid., paras 226–30.
43 Ibid., paras 239–52.
44 Ibid., para 268.
45 Ibid., para 290.

deference to the supremacy of UN Charter obligations. This was the result of judicial proceedings brought by Nada, an individual listed by the 1267 Sanctions Committee for almost eight years, from November 2001 to September 2009. After a series of unsuccessful attempts with Swiss authorities, Swiss courts, and the 1267 Sanctions Committee in order to get his name removed from the sanctions' list, Nada's claim reached the ECtHR, which rendered its judgment in September 2012 in favour of Nada at least in part. In essence, the ECtHR in *Nada* reinterpreted Security Council resolutions as if they had left a certain latitude to the state.[46] The ECtHR's original interpretation of relevant Security Council resolutions allowed the Strasbourg court to find Switzerland in violation of the applicant's rights, on the basis that the state had the latitude to harmonise its international obligations under Security Council resolutions and its human rights obligations under the European Convention on Human Rights (ECHR).[47] With its slightly stretched interpretation of Security Council resolutions, the ECtHR thus succeeded in avoiding a normative conflict and, further, pointing the finger of blame not at the UN Security Council but at member states authorities.

Apart from the avoidance of normative conflicts, judges can use critical language in order to show their dissatisfaction with the UN. For instance, Justice Zinn of the Canadian Federal Court in the *Abdelrazik* case in 2009 criticised the sanctions' regime against Al-Qaida as 'a denial of basic legal remedies and as untenable under the principles of international human rights',[48] despite the fact that it was not strictly necessary to refer to the sanctions committee's procedure.[49] In *A and Others* before the UK Court of Appeal in 2008, an English judge chose the

46 App No 10593/08 *Nada v Switzerland* (ECtHR Grand Chamber, Judgment of 12 September 2012), paras 176–80. Cf. ibid., Joint Concurring Opinion of Judges Bratza, Nicolaou and Yudkivska; ibid., Concurring Opinion of Judge Malinverni, paras 2–10. For the summary and analysis of *Nada*, see Auke Willems, 'The European Court of Human Rights on the UN Individual Counter-Terrorist Sanctions Regime: Safeguarding Convention Rights and Harmonising Conflicting Norms in Nada v. Switzerland' (2014) 83 *Nordic Journal of International Law* 39.

47 *Nada*, ibid., paras 176–80.

48 *Abousfian Abdelrazik v The Minister of Foreign Affairs and the Attorney General of Canada* (2009) 2009 FC 580; [2010] 1 FCR 267 (Canada, Federal Court, 4 June 2009), para 51.

49 For the summary and analysis of the *Abdelrazik* case, see Antonios Tzanakopoulos, 'United Nations Sanctions in Domestic Courts from Interpretation to Defiance in Abdelrazik v. Canada' (2010) 8 *Journal of International Criminal Justice* 249. In this case, the applicant, a dual citizen of Sudan and Canada, travelled to Sudan in 2003, where he was then arrested, detained without charge, and allegedly tortured by the state authorities. His attempts to return to Canada, which had failed on several occasions, became far more intricate in July 2006 when he was designated by the US and subsequently the UN's 1267 Sanctions Committee as an associate of Al-Qaida and thus a target of travel ban and asset freeze. His delisting request, transmitted through the Canadian government, was rejected by the 1267 Sanctions Committee with no reasons given for the refusal. His application for a travel document was denied by the Canadian government. The applicant claimed before the Canadian courts the infringement of his right to return to Canada. The Federal Court admitted that the rejection of the applicant's travelling documents breached his right to enter Canada.

powerful term 'prisoners of the state' to characterise the state of those targeted, which was also reiterated by the UK Supreme Court and further by the GCEU in its 2010 decision in *Kadi II*.[50] The GCEU also described targeted sanctions as 'particularly draconian'[51] for the targeted individuals. These expressions and terms by no means generated any immediate legal effect. Nevertheless, they have been reproduced by scholars and practitioners and might have contributed to the gathering of political momentum to call for normative and procedural reforms on the international stage.

7.3.6 Consequential contestations

Finally, in addition to the use of critical remarks, judges can contest the UN's decision making not necessarily within their reasoning but by the consequences of judicial findings. Such consequential contestation is possible for domestic and EU courts (but not international courts), which can resort to dualism and the autonomy of each legal order. By so doing, judges can avoid the question of supremacy and consequentially challenge the UN's decisions. The dualistic approach was particularly evident in the ECJ's judgment in September 2008 in *Kadi I*.[52] Having set aside the CFI's judgment which limited the purview of judicial review, the ECJ notably conducted the 'full review' of Council Regulation (EC) 881/2002 in light of Kadi's fundamental rights.[53] The full review was made possible by upholding the autonomy of the EU legal order based upon the rule of law.[54]

50 *A and Others v HM Treasury* [2008] EWCA Civ 1187 (UK Court of Appeal, Judgment of 30 October 2008), para 125 (Sedley LJ); *HM Treasury v Mohammed Jabar Ahmed and Others; HM Treasury v Mohammed al-Ghabra; R (Hari El Sayed Sabaei Youssef) v HM Treasury* [2010] UKSC 2 (UK Supreme Court, Judgment of 27 January 2010), paras 4, 60; Case T-85/09 *Kadi v European Commission and Council of the European Union* [2010] ECR II-05177 (GCEU, Judgment of 30 September 2010, 'Kadi II (GCEU)'), para 149.

51 *Kadi II (GCEU, 2010)* (n 50) para 149.

52 Joined Cases C-402/05 P and C-415/05 P *Kadi and Al Barakaat International Foundation v Council of the European Union and Commission of the European Communities* [2008] ECR I-06351, ECLI:EU:C:2008:461 (ECJ, Judgment of 3 September 2008, 'Kadi I (ECJ)'). On the ECJ judgment, see, e.g., Deirdre Curtin and Christina Eckes, 'The Kadi Case: Mapping the Boundaries between the Executive and the Judiciary in Europe' (2008) 5 *International Organizations Law Review* 365; Christina Eckes, *EU Counter-Terrorist Policies and Fundamental Rights* (Oxford, Oxford University Press, 2009) chap. 5; Paul James Cardwell, Duncan French and Nigel White, 'European Court of Justice, Yassin Abdullah Kadi and Al Barakaat International Foundation v Council and Commission (Joined Cases C-402/05 P and C-415/05 P) Judgment of 3 September 2008' (2009) 58 *International & Comparative Law Quarterly* 229; Grainne De Burca, 'The EU, the European Court of Justice and the International Legal Order after Kadi' (2010) 51 *Harvard International Law Journal* 1.

53 *Kadi I (ECJ, 2008)* (n 52) para 326.

54 The Court of Justice enunciated that the judicial review of Community measures in light of fundamental rights constituted a 'constitutional guarantee', namely, that it enjoys a status equivalent to the Treaty: ibid., paras 284, 316. Judicial review enjoys

The GCEU in September 2010 in *Kadi II* followed the ECJ's decision in *Kadi I* and conducted the 'full and rigorous' review of the measures, although the GCEU still voiced criticism on the formalistic divide adopted by the ECJ with respect to EU and UN legal orders.[55] The Court of Justice of the EU (CJEU) in July 2013 in *Kadi II* intensified the level of 'full review', and found itself tasked with two things:[56] whether one of the reasons (for listing) stated in the summary provided by the UN's Sanctions Committee was sufficiently detailed and specific,[57] and

such a constitutional status, given that the EU (then Community) is based on the rule of law, which is to subject all EU institutions to judicial review, and the autonomy of its legal system, which is not affected by an international agreement: ibid., paras 281–2. Having affirmed the status of judicial review, the ECJ made it clear that it must ensure in principle the 'full review' of the lawfulness of the contested regulation in light of the fundamental rights: ibid., para 326. Having conducted the 'full review', the Grand Chamber found that there was the infringement of Kadi's fundamental rights. The ECJ observed that the applicant's right to be heard was not respected, owing to the failure to communicate to the appellants the evidence adduced to justify the listing: ibid., paras 338–48. This has led to further breach of the right to an effective legal remedy, inasmuch as the absence of evidence prevented the appellants from defending their rights in satisfactory conditions before EU courts: ibid., paras 349–53. Also, the procedural requirements for the right to respect for property were not complied with, as the contested regulation did not furnish any guarantee with which to enable Kadi to put his case to the competent authorities: ibid., paras 354–71.

55 *Kadi II (GCEU, 2010)* (n 50). The 'full and rigorous review' (ibid., para 151) then led the GCEU to find the breaches of Kadi's fundamental rights. As for the rights to defence and the right to effective judicial protection, the GCEU was guided by the ECtHR's jurisprudence, including the *Belmarsh (A and Others)* decision concerning the 1373 sanctions regime: App No 3455/05 *A and Others v UK* (ECtHR, Grand Chamber, Judgment of 19 February 2009). According to jurisprudence, the allegations made against individuals had to be sufficiently detailed to permit them to challenge them effectively, which, in general, requires the disclosure of all the evidence against them: *Kadi II (GCEU, 2010)*, ibid., para 176. In the case of *Kadi*, the detailed allegations and relevant evidence were not made available to the applicant, nor was any guarantee given to him. Such violation of the rights of the defence led the GCEU to find the further breach of the principle of effective judicial protection: ibid., paras 171–88. The Court also acknowledged the infringement of Kadi's right to property and of the principle of proportionality: ibid., paras 192–5.

56 Joined Cases C-584/10 P, C-593/10 P and C-595/10 P *Kadi v European Commission* ECLI:EU:C:2013:518 (CJEU, Judgment of 18 July 2013, 'Kadi II (CJEU)'), para 130.

57 In *Kadi II*, the Court of Justice held that EU institutions owe not only the obligation to communicate the allegations, but also the 'duty of careful and impartial examination': *Kadi II* (CJEU), para 115. This duty is part of the obligation to state reasons laid down in Article 296 of TEFU (ibid., para 116), and part of procedural safeguards established through the jurisprudence of EU courts (ibid., para 114). The duty of careful and impartial examination requires EU institutions to assess the necessity of seeking the assistance of the UN Sanctions Committee and of member states in order to obtain the 'disclosure of information or evidence, confidential or not': ibid., para 115. In determining the compliance of the competent EU authority with the duty of careful and impartial examination, the courts determine 'in particular, whether the reasons relied on are sufficiently detailed and specific': ibid., para 118.

whether it is substantiated.[58] With regard to the former, the CJEU acknowledged that some of the reasons stated in the 1267 Sanctions Committee's summary were sufficiently detailed and specific.[59] Nevertheless, for the latter, the CJEU found that information or evidence which might have substantiated the reason for listing was absent,[60] and thereby annulled the contested EU regulation that implemented the decisions of the UN sanctions committees' decisions.[61]

Following the Court of Justice's judgments in *Kadi I* and *Kadi II*, the EU courts found the European Commission's failure to review the findings of the 1267 Sanctions Committee. In March 2014, the GCEU in *Yusef* found that the European Commission was acting unlawfully by delaying the careful and impartial examination of the findings of the 1267 Sanctions Committee.[62] Likewise, in January 2015, the GCEU in *Abdulbasit Abdulrahim* annulled the relevant EU regulation due to the insufficiency of reasons, information, or evidence supporting the reasons for designation.[63] Similar reasoning was also adopted by the GCEU in *Ayadi* in its judgment in April 2015. The General Court in *Ayadi* observed that 'none of the allegations made against Mr Ayadi in the statement of reasons provided by the [1267] Sanctions Committee was such as to justify the adoption, at EU level, of restrictive measures'.[64]

Similar standards of review have been applied to cases on other sanctions regimes as well. For instance, judicial complaints were filed by Bank Melli Iran and Bank Saderat Iran which were subject to the EU's sanctions against Iran's nuclear proliferation. Although these banks were not strictly designated by the UN Security Council as targets of mandatory sanctions, Security Council Resolution 1803 mentioned these banks by calling on all states to exercise vigilance over

58 According to the Court of Justice, the right to effective judicial protection requires EU courts to ensure that the listing decision is 'taken on a sufficiently solid factual basis': *Kadi II (CJEU, 2013)* (n 56) para 119. This means that judicial review 'must concern whether those reasons, or, at the very least, one of those reasons, deemed sufficient in itself to support that decision, is substantiated': ibid. When security considerations preclude the competent EU authority to disclose information requested by EU courts, the courts determine whether the grounds of non-disclosure are well founded, and, if they are, strike an appropriate balance between the protection of the rights and that of the security: ibid., paras 125–8.

59 *Kadi II (CJEU, 2013)* (n 56) paras 140–50.

60 Ibid., paras 151–63.

61 Ibid., para 164.

62 Case T-306/10 *Hani El Sayyed Elsebai Yusef v Commission* ECLI:EU:T:2014:141 (GCEU, Judgment of 21 March 2014), paras 102–5. The European Commission was criticised for regarding itself as 'strictly bound by the findings of the [UN's] Sanctions Committee' and as 'not having any discretion' with regard to the UN's findings: ibid., para 103.

63 Case T-127/09 RENV *Abdulbasit Abdulrahim v Council and Commission* ECLI:EU:T:2015:4 (GCEU, Judgment of 14 January 2015). According to the General Court, 'none of the allegations made against Mr Abdulrahim in the summary of reasons provided by the Sanctions Committee was such as to justify the adoption, at EU level, of restrictive measures against him': ibid., para 97.

64 Case T-527/09 RENV *Chafiq Ayadi v European Commission* ECLI:EU:T:2015:205 (Judgment of 14 April 2015) (GCEU), para 86.

financial activities 'in particular [those] with Bank Melli and Bank Saderat' in order to strengthen the implementation of Resolution 1737.[65] In response to the banks' challenges, the GCEU in *Bank Melli Iran* endorsed in 2013 the restrictive measures taken against the bank inasmuch as the reasons set out by the EU institutions were 'sufficiently detailed'.[66] On the other hand, the GCEU in *Bank Saderat Iran* found a lack of evidence and information and thereby annulled the restrictive measures against the bank.[67] The GCEU's judgment was upheld by the CJEU in April 2016.[68]

Overall, the overview of judicial decisions reveals a certain level of hesitation on the part of the guardians of the constitutional norms and human rights in endorsing the primacy of the obligations sustaining the UN Security Council's targeted sanctions. The dualistic reasoning adopted by the ECJ in *Kadi I* allowed the EU courts to consequentially question the human rights compatibility of the UN Security Council's sanctions regimes. At the same time, the subsequent judgments of EU courts, including, notably *Kadi II* before the GCEU and CJEU, took a more proactive step and directly assessed the decision making of the UN Security Council's sanctions committees in the course of ultimately reviewing the acts of EU institutions. While the CJEU envisaged 'effective cooperation' between EU institutions and UN organs for impartial examination,[69] the CJEU's reasoning in *Kadi II* clearly constituted a challenge to the raison d'être of the UN's sanctions regimes which aimed at narrowing down the scope of discretion on the part of each member state for the sake of the uniform implementation of sanctions.

7.4 Direct implementation: Limited contestations through domestic and regional courts

Unlike the second scenario of targeted sanctions, the practices of direct implementation significantly limit the utility of domestic courts as a venue for contesting the exercise of authority by the UN Security Council's subsidiary organs. As was in the case of targeted sanctions, some individuals may be able to receive support from their national government which could exercise 'diplomatic protection' vis-à-vis the UN.[70] However, whether or not to seek such a 'diplomatic protection' is in

65 UN Doc S/RES/1803 (3 March 2008), para 10.

66 Cases T-35/10 and T-7/11 *Bank Melli Iran v Council* ECLI:EU:T:2013:397 (GCEU, Judgment of 6 September 2013), para 89. The GCEU found the restrictive measures justifiable inasmuch as Bank Melli Iran made payments on behalf of the Atomic Energy Organisation of Iran (AEOI) and thereby supported nuclear proliferation: ibid., para 149.

67 Case T-494/10 *Bank Saderat Iran v Council of the European Union* ECLI:EU:T:2013:59 (GCEU, Judgment of 5 February 2013), para 109.

68 Case C-200/13 P *Council of the European Union v Bank Saderat Iran* ECLI:EU:C:2016:284 (CJEU, Judgment of 21 April 2016).

69 *Kadi II (CJEU, 2013)* (n 56) para 115.

70 Jean-Pierre Ritter, 'La protection diplomatique à l'égard d'une organisation internationale' (1962) 8 *Annuaire français de droit international* 427. In the 1960s, in the context of UN peacekeeping operations, Belgium and other states submitted a

principle in the hands of national governments. In the absence of international mechanisms, the affected individuals still sought judicial remedies either against the UN or national governments. Yet individuals' attempts to utilise court proceedings are beset with more difficulties and hampered by judicial deference to the special status of the UN Security Council and the primacy of the related obligations.

7.4.1 Deference to the priority of the UN Security Council

When individuals bring proceedings against member states, there remain uncertainties as to whether courts may deny jurisdiction because the contested acts were attributable to the UN.[71] In this regard, there were contrasting decisions in the 1960s–1970s relating to UN peacekeeping operations, as illustrated by the comparison between *N.K. v Austria* in 1979 before the Superior Provincial Court of Vienna[72] and the case of *Nissan* in 1969 before the UK House of Lords.[73] More

number of claims lodged by their nationals with respect to personal injuries and property damage allegedly caused by ONUC troops. After negotiations, the UN reached a lump-sum settlement with the governments of Belgium and four other European states: 'Yearbook of the International Law Commission' (1967) 1967, vol. 2 (1967) 219–20; Marten Zwanenburg, *Accountability of Peace Support Operations* (Leiden; Boston, Martinus Nijhoff Publishers, 2005) 88–9.

71 There is a separate question, which is not explored in this book, as to whether member states are also responsible for the same harmful consequences. A classic case on this issue is *International Tin Council*, but the opinions of judges were divided as to whether member states bore any responsibility under international law for the debts owed by the Tin Council: *Maclaine Watson & Co Ltd v Department of Trade and Industry* [1988] 3 All ER 257 (UK, Court of Appeal, 27 April 1988); *Maclaine Watson & Co Ltd v Department of Trade and Industry* [1989] 3 All ER 523 (UK, House of Lords, 27 October 1989). For details, see C.F. Amerasinghe, 'Liability to Third Parties of Member States of International Organizations: Practice, Principle and Judicial Precedent' (1991) 85 *American Journal of International Law* 259; Moshe Hirsch, *The Responsibility of International Organizations Toward Third Parties: Some Basic Principles* (Dordrecht; Boston, Martinus Nijhoff Publishers, 1995) 112–25.

72 *NK v Austria* (1988) 77 ILR 470 (Superior Provincial Court of Vienna, Judgment of 26 February 1979). In *N.K. v Austria*, the claimant sought compensation from Austria, alleging that his property had been damaged, due to the negligent act of an Austrian soldier who was deployed in the Golan Heights as part of the United Nations Disengagement Observer Force (UNDOF). The Superior Provincial Court of Vienna rejected his claim, holding that the contested order was based on the authority derived from the Commander of the UN force, and that the soldier was acting as an organ of the UN and not of Austria: ibid., 474.

73 *Nissan v Attorney-General* [1967] 2 All ER 200 (UK, Queen's Bench, 17 February 1967); *Nissan v Attorney-General* [1967] 2 All ER 1238 (UK, Court of Appeal, 29 June 1967); *Attorney-General v Nissan* [1969] 1 All ER 629 (UK, House of Lords, 11 February 1969). The plaintiff, a British subject, filed suit against the British government, seeking compensation for the loss he suffered as a result of the British occupation of a hotel he rented. Since the British forces formed part of the United Nations Peacekeeping Force in Cyprus (UNFICYP), the British government raised a defence, to the effect that its forces stationed in Cyprus were contingents of the UN

recently, a similar issue was adjudicated by the ECtHR in *Behrami and Saramati* in May 2007. The case was brought by the applicants against states stationed in Kosovo as part of UNMIK and the Kosovo Force (KFOR).[74] Behrami invoked the infringement of Article 2 (right to life) of the ECHR against France, for the failure to mark and defuse the undetonated cluster bomb units which caused loss of life and injury, while Saramati lodged a claim against France and Norway, relying upon Article 5 (right to liberty) of the ECHR and other rights for the alleged extra-judicial detention. The ECtHR rejected the admissibility of both complaints, for the very reason that the contested acts were attributed to the UN.

What is critical in the reasoning of *Behrami and Saramati* was the fact that the regional human rights court showed deference to the UN Security Council in the sphere of the maintenance of international peace and security. Truly, under Article 24(1) of the UN Charter, the Security Council is entrusted with the 'primary' responsibility for the maintenance of international peace and security. 'Responsibility' in this particular treaty provision falls short of being an obligation; yet it appears to signify a task consisting in more than mere competence.[75] Under Article 24(1) of the UN Charter, the Security Council's primary responsibility is regarded as instrumental to the 'prompt and effective action' in the maintenance of international peace and security.[76] In theory, the provision is meant to prioritise the Security Council over the General Assembly, and not over member states' authorities or any other entities outside the UN.[77] Nevertheless, in *Behrami and Saramati*, the phrase 'primary responsibility' was invoked beyond the UN's treaty regime as if it were a normative indication of the priority of the Security Council over a

force, whereby no action could be lodged against the UK. This line of defence did not win support from the House of Lords; having disagreed with the lower courts, it took the view that, while the national contingent was under the authority of the UN and subject to the instructions of its commander, it had its own national duty and discipline, and remained in the British forces: *Nissan v. Attorney-General* (QB, 1967) 220–1 (Judge Stephenson); *Nissan v. Attorney-General* (CA, 1967) 1244 (Lord Denning); *Attorney-General v. Nissan* (HL, 1969) 646 (Lord Morris), 647 (Lord Pearce).

74 The case attracted much controversy with respect to the Court's finding on Saramati, for which the Court held that the acts of detention by KFOR were likewise attributable to the UN. The Grand Chamber concluded that the 'ultimate authority and control' was retained by the UN Security Council, despite its admission that effective command of the relevant operational matters was in the hands of NATO, and not the UN: see especially App Nos 71412/01, and 78166/01 *Behrami and Behrami v France; Saramati v France, Germany and Norway* (ECtHR, Grand Chamber, Admissibility Decision of 2 May 2007), paras 133–43. The admissibility of similar complaints were likewise rejected in view of *Behrami* and *Sarmati*: App No 6974/05 *Kasumaj v Greece* (ECtHR, Admissibility Decision of 5 July 2007); App No 311446/02 *Gajic v Germany* (ECtHR, Admissibility Decision of 28 August 2007); App Nos 36357/04 et al *Berić and Others v Bosnia and Herzegovina* (ECtHR, Admissibility Decision of 16 October 2007).

75 See Anne Peters, 'Article 24' in B. Simma and others (eds), *The Charter of the United Nations: A Commentary* (3rd edn, 2012) 761, 766–7 (paras 13, 18).

76 Ibid., 772, para 35.

77 Ibid., 767, para 17.

guardian of other purposes of international law, such as the promotion of respect for human rights.

In the *Behrami and Saramati* case, the ECtHR, which is an international court outside the UN Charter, referred to the 'imperative nature' of the Security Council's powers and the 'primary responsibility' of the UN Security Council. In rendering the application inadmissible on the basis of the attribution of the conduct of states to the UN, the ECtHR drew attention to:

> the *imperative nature* of the principle aim of the UN and, consequently, of the powers accorded to the UNSC under Chapter VII to fulfil that aim. … [I]t is evident from the Preamble, Articles 1, 2 and 24 as well as Chapter VII of the Charter that the *primary objective* of the UN is the maintenance of international peace and security. While it is equally clear that ensuring respect for human rights represents an important contribution to achieving international peace … *the fact remains that the UNSC has primary responsibility* … to fulfil this objective …[78]

On this basis, the ECtHR, in order not to undermine the effectiveness of the UN's operations for its 'imperative peace and security aim',[79] observed that:

> the [European] Convention [on Human Rights] cannot be interpreted in a manner which would subject the acts and omissions of Contracting Parties which are covered by UNSC Resolutions … to the scrutiny of the Court.[80]

The Strasbourg court made these remarks presumably to indicate the relative weight of the UN Security Council's mandate in comparison to the protection of human rights, and supposedly to explain the reason the Strasbourg court deferred to the UN organ and its imperative mandate.

The ECtHR referred to the reasoning of *Behrami and Saramati* in its subsequent case of *Mothers of Srebrenica* which addressed the compatibility of the grant of jurisdictional immunity to the UN with the right of access to a court. In likewise dismissing the human rights complaint, the Strasbourg court reaffirmed the importance of the fulfilment of the UN's key mission in the field of international peace and security.[81] The consideration to international peace and security was also given in a case concerning targeted sanctions. In the *Al-Dulimi* case on the UN's Iraq sanctions regime, the Grand Chamber of the ECtHR lowered the level of protection of the right to a fair hearing in striking a 'fair balance' between human rights protection and 'the imperatives of the protection of international

78 *Behrami and Saramati* (ECtHR, 2007) (n74) para 148 (emphasis added).

79 Ibid., para 149.

80 Ibid.

81 App No 65542/12 *Stichting Mothers of Srebrenica and Others v The Netherlands* (ECtHR, Decision of 11 June 2013), para 154 (referring to *Behrami and Saramati*, para 149).

peace and security'.[82] What we can observe from these cases is that the regional human rights court implied both the priority of the UN Security Council's competence for the effective maintenance of international peace and security and the relative importance of the Council's mandate over the protection of human rights.

7.4.2 Deference to the primacy of UN obligations

Relevant to the priority of the UN Security Council is deference to the supremacy of the obligations under the UN Charter.[83] Article 103 of the UN Charter works to reinforce the jurisdictional hurdles for individuals' complaints against the UN inasmuch as the primacy applies to the obligation of member states to award immunities to the UN and its officials under Article 105(1) and (2) of the UN Charter.[84] This renders it difficult to readily apply the reasoning of *Waite & Kennedy*[85] before the ECtHR to the immunities granted to the UN, inasmuch as the obligation under Article 105(1) of the UN Charter prevails over member states' human rights obligations.[86]

In the context of ad hoc international criminal tribunals, there have been several litigations concerning the compatibility with domestic or international law of the national decisions that gave effect to the tribunals' orders.[87] Judicial review has been generally lenient, however. The District Court in The Hague, in *Milošević v ICTY*, found no competence to assess the human rights compatibility of the ICTY's procedures, and, in so holding, relied on the ICTY's primacy over national courts and Article 103 of the UN Charter.[88] In an earlier case of *Dragan Opacić v The Netherlands*, the Hague District Court likewise found itself unable to review the ICTY decisions.[89] The priority of the ICTY's request was affirmed by the

82 App No 5809/08 *Al-Dulimi and Montana Management Inc v Switzerland* (ECtHR, Grand Chamber, Judgment of 21 June 2016), para 146. On *Al-Dulimi*, see also section 8.4 of this book.

83 See section 7.3.2 of this book.

84 Convention on the Privileges and Immunities of the United Nations, 13 February 1946, 1 UNTS 15 (entered into force 17 September 1946) (1946). While immunities under Article 105 of the UN Charter are functional in nature, they still provide broad immunities to the UN: see Kristen E. Boon, 'The United Nations as Good Samaritan: Immunity and Responsibility' (2016) 16 *Chicago Journal of International Law* 341.

85 App No 26083/94 *Waite and Kennedy v Germany* ECHR 1999-I (ECtHR, Grand Chamber, Judgment of 18 February 1999).

86 See *Stichting Mothers of Srebrenica and Others v The Netherlands* (n 81) paras 152–69.

87 See Jean d'Aspremont and Catherine Brölmann, 'Challenging International Criminal Tribunals Before Domestic Courts' in A. Reinisch (ed.), *Challenging Acts of International Organizations Before National Courts* (Oxford, Oxford University Press, 2011) 111.

88 *Slobodan Milošević v International Criminal Tribunal for the Former Yugoslavia (ICTY)* (2002) 41 ILM 1310 (Netherlands, The Hague District Court, 26 February 2002). Similarly, *Slobodan Milošević v The State of the Netherlands* (2002) 41 ILM 86 (Netherlands, The Hague District Court, 31 August 2001), para 3.5.

89 *Dragan Opacić v The Netherlands* Kort Geding KG 97/742 (District Court of The Hague, 30 May 1997). Cited in Göran Sluiter, *International Criminal Adjudication and the Collection of Evidence: Obligations of States* (Antwerp, Intersentia, 2002) 144;

Argentinian court in *Lukić Milan s/Captura*.[90] The Croatian Constitutional Court was also willing to accept the ICTY's primacy over domestic courts in the *Bobetko Report* case.[91] Likewise, the Croatian Constitutional Court endorsed in *Naletilić* the constitutionality of the surrender of the accused to the ICTY ultimately based on the preference of the ICTY over national courts.[92] The *Naletilić* case was subsequently brought before the ECtHR, which characterised the ICTY as offering 'all the necessary guarantees including those of impartiality and independence'.[93] The trust in the ICTY's impartiality was reiterated in *Milošević v The Netherlands* before the Dutch court.[94]

Some judges managed to avoid the normative conflicts arising from Article 103 of the UN Charter[95] and thereby circumvented the pronouncement of their deference to the supremacy of Charter obligations. Although it is difficult to assess whether or not courts deliberately avoided the question, an example may be the *Ntakirutimana* case before the US Court of Appeals regarding the unconstitutionality of the surrender of the individual to the ICTR. The Court of Appeals did not actively comment on the issue as to whether the ICTR had the capacity to protect due process rights.[96] Also, judges deferred to the supremacy, yet still preserved a possibility for review; by so doing, judges effectively sent a critical signal to the exercise of authority by the UN Security Council and its subsidiary organs. For instance, a Swiss court in the *Rukundo* case, which was bought against the state's decision to transfer Mr. Rukundo to the ICTY, did not decline to engage in a review.[97] While the Swiss court ultimately deferred to the Council and its subsidiary organ by presuming the legality of the ICTY's establishment and procedure, the court's indication might have served as a warning to the Council and

Alfred H.A. Soons, 'The Netherlands' in V. Gowlland-Debbas (ed.), *National Implementation of United Nations Sanctions: A Comparative Study* (Leiden; Boston, Martinus Nijhoff Publishers, 2004) 341, 369.

90 *International Arrest Warrant ('Lukic'), Re, International Criminal Tribunal for the Former Yugoslavia v Lukic (Milan), Decision on arrest, surrender, and extradition* Case No 11807/05, ILDC 1083 (AR 2006) (10 January 2006, Argentina).

91 *Bobetko Report, Croatia, Review of Constitutionality and Legality* Case No U-X-2271/2002, ILDC 383 (HR 2002) (12 November 2002, Croatia).

92 The Constitutional Court of the Republic of Croatia, Decision No. U-III-854/1999, 21 October 1999. (The decision and its English translation are available at the Constitutional Court of the Republic of Croatia, <www.usud.hr/>).

93 *Mladen Naletilić v Croatia* App. No. 51891/99, ECHR 2000-V (ECtHR, Admissibility Decision of 4 May 2000), para 1(b).

94 *Slobodan Milošević v The State of the Netherlands* (n 88). The *Milošević* case before the ECtHR was rejected on the basis of the non-exhaustion of domestic remedies: *Milošević v The Netherlands* App. No. 77631/01 (ECtHR, Admissibility, 19 March 2002).

95 Tzanakopoulos, 'Collective Security and Human Rights' (n 32) 52.

96 *Elizaphan Ntakirutimana v Janet Reno, Attorney General of the United States* 184 F.3d 419 (5th Cir. 1999) (5 August 1999).

97 *Rukundo v Federal Office of Justice, Appeal Judgment* (2001) Cases No 1A.129/2001 and 1A.130/2001; ILDC 348 (CH 2001) (Switzerland, Federal Supreme Court, First Public Law Chamber, 3 September 2001).

its subsidiary organs to have respect for basic human rights.[98] Apart from these cases, however, individuals' resort to national and regional courts has often been frustrated by judges' respect for the primacy of the obligations derived from Article 103 of the UN Charter and those based on the Council's authority under Chapter VII.

7.5 Conclusion

In essence, the three types of the UN Security Council's practices yield different results with respect to the availability of national courts, and, ultimately, EU courts and the ECtHR, to those individuals who wish to contest the exercise of authority by the UN Security Council and its subsidiary organs. In the first category of practices, the UN Security Council's Chapter VII demand may be too imprecise to be directly applicable at the domestic level or to have any domestic legal effect. This creates a basic hurdle for any individuals addressed by the UN Security Council to resort to domestic law and related institutional safeguards in order to indirectly challenge the Security Council's exercise of authority over individuals.

The second category of practices, targeted sanctions, triggered a number of domestic and regional litigations, some of which led judges to find the human rights incompatibility of the measures implementing the UN's targeted sanctions. A symbolic case was *Kadi*, followed by a series of cases before EU courts. Contrasted is the third category, direct implementation, which created much higher hurdles for those affected individuals in resorting to domestic judicial venues as sites for contestation. The claims instituted directly against the UN are hindered by jurisdictional immunities, and the claims instituted against member state authorities may likewise be rejected on the grounds of the attribution of the impugned conduct to the UN and the judges' respect for the obligations derived from the UN Security Council's Chapter VII authority. The hurdles for individuals' judicial contestations were higher, despite the fact that the practices of direct implementation bear much stronger resemblance to the exercise of authority by national government than the case of targeted sanctions.

The comparison between the second category (target specification) and the third category (direct implementation) highlights the contemporary role of state authorities as an intermediary between international organisations and individuals. The function of member states' authorities is not only to implement the UN Security Council's measures, but also to provide safeguards for individuals affected by the UN Security Council's exercise of authority. Under international law, the legal limits to the UN Security Council's exercise of authority remain formalistic and thin, as illustrated by chapters 5 and 6 of this book. This creates a gap between the formalistic rules of international law and a more substantive and thicker set of rules applicable to the regulation of governmental entities. As the UN Security Council's exercise of authority resembles that of national

98 *See* Erika de Wet, *The International Constitutional Order: Lecture* (Amsterdam University Press, 2011) 19.

government, domestic law's role, in conjunction with EU law and the ECtHR, includes but is not limited to holding governmental authorities accountable. The domestic legal order is also a venue through which individuals contest the UN Security Council and its subsidiary organs whose decisions direct member states.

What needs underlining further is that the standards of review applied by national and EU courts are often substantively intertwined with international law, including international human rights law. Fundamental rights as part of the general principles of EU law, with respect to which the ECJ found a violation, are at least inspired or guided by international treaties, especially the ECHR.[99] Similar substantive connections can be found insofar as the standards of review applied by domestic courts are based upon international human rights law.

While national and EU court decisions do not bind UN organs, such decisions and their international normative origins could become an influential political apparatus for generating regulatory reforms at the UN. The political and normative influence of judicial contestations was evidenced by the case of targeted sanctions, as will be explained in chapter 8 of the book. The court proceedings and decisions have facilitated the establishment of the principles of fairness and transparency, according to which incremental procedural improvements have been made with respect to the listing processes.

99 See Case 4/73 *Nold v Commission of the European Communities* [1974] ECR 491, ECLI:EU:C:1974:51 (ECJ, Judgment of 14 May 1974); Robert Schütze, 'Three "Bills of Rights" for the European Union' (2011) 30 *Yearbook of European Law* 131, 135. The general principles do not entirely depend on the national or international origins, but are part of autonomous standards: Schütze, ibid. In addition, the ECJ used both general principles of EU law and the ECHR: e.g., Case C-60/00 *Carpenter v Secretary of State for the Home Department* [2002] ECR I-6279, ECLI:EU:C:2002:434 (ECJ, Judgment of 11 July 2002); Case C-112/00 *Schmidberger v Austria* [2003] ECR I-5659, ECLI:EU:C:2003:333 (ECJ, Judgment of 12 June 2003). After the Lisbon Treaty, the ECHR is not only the component of general principles, but is a treaty to be acceded by the EU: The Treaty on European Union (TEU), Article 6(2) and (3).

8 International implications of the Security Council's encounter with domestic actors

8.1 Introduction

As the UN Security Council limits the authority of state intermediaries and reduces its distance from individuals, one could observe the Security Council's exercise of authority increasingly bears resemblance to the exercise of authority by national governments over individuals. Such resemblance is discernible in three different scenarios examined in this book. Namely, the Security Council directly addresses individuals under its resolutions, designates specific individuals as targets of asset freezes, and executes its decisions vis-à-vis individuals through the Security Council's subsidiary organs. The factual resemblance creates a unique normative space in which the exercise of *international* authority is assessed against domestic and international law developed primarily to regulate the *governmental* authority. Human rights law is a prominent field in this regard. An extensive body of domestic and international human rights law, which purports to regulate how the government ensures the protection of rights of individuals, has been recast against the UN Security Council and its subsidiary organs. As presented in chapter 7 of this book, human rights, as informed by international human rights law, have been invoked in a series of national and EU-level judicial contestations as part of the yardsticks with which to indirectly assess the UN's decision making.

This leads me to consider whether domestic legal practices, including those analysed in chapter 7 of the book, have any feedback effect at the international level. This question arises precisely because no matter what EU courts and national judges decide, the legal effect of their decisions formally remains within respective legal orders and does not extend to the UN Security Council's exercise of authority. At the international level, the effect of the domestic reception of the UN's decisions would thus be essentially political. In this sense, it is important to remember that the feedback can be provided not only from judicial decisions themselves but also by the mere fact that the court actions are launched by individuals – regardless of whether the courts eventually find in favour of the individuals' claims.

Against this background, this chapter analyses some of the *international* implications of the domestic reception of the UN Security Council's exercise of authority. This chapter begins with providing the different 'points of connection' between domestic legal practices and international law (section 8.2 below). Encouraged at least in part by domestic legal practices, the UN incrementally developed some mechanisms to which the affected individuals bring their claims, although the mechanisms at the UN are far from satisfactory. The chapter presents certain normative and procedural developments within the context of targeted sanctions and the UN's territorial administrations (section 8.3). The contribution of domestic law to international normative standards then begs the question of whether international law itself proactively endorses the role of domestic authorities in the critical assessment of the UN's decisions (section 8.4).

8.2 Characterising the points of connection between the domestic and international levels

As overviewed in chapter 7 of this book, the UN Security Council's targeted sanctions invited a number of judicial contestations at the national and EU levels and also by the ECtHR. This is contrasted with the context of the UN's territorial administration and ad hoc international criminal tribunals, with respect to which individuals' attempts to utilise domestic courts have been much more arduous, despite the stronger resemblance of the UN's exercise of authority to governmental decision making. The unavailability of domestic courts as a venue to indirectly or directly contest the UN does not necessarily prevent, however, feedback from domestic legal practices at the international level.

8.2.1 Legal

When it comes to the question of how domestic legal practices contribute to the development of international law, a classic answer would be that domestic court decisions and the practices of other state authorities are, after all, part of ***state practices***,[1] which create new customary international law[2] or new treaty interpretations.[3] While the decisions of EU courts are not 'state practices' under international law, the court decisions dictate and affect the practices of EU

1 Anthea Roberts, 'Comparative International Law? The Role of National Courts in Creating and Enforcing International Law' (2011) 60 *International & Comparative Law Quarterly* 57, 61–4 (pointing out the dual role of domestic courts to create law as state practice and to enforce established international law).

2 Hersch Lauterpacht, 'Decisions of Municipal Courts as a Source of International Law' (1929) 10 *British Year Book of International Law* 65; Robert Jennings and Arthur Watts (eds), *Oppenheim's International Law* (9th edn, Harlow, Essex, Longman, 1992) 41; ILA, Statement of Principles Applicable to the Formation of General Customary International Law, principle 9, reproduced in ILA, Report of the Sixty-Ninth Conference (2000); Benedetto Conforti, *International Law and the Role of Domestic Legal Systems* (Dordrecht, Martinus Nijhoff Publishers, 1993) 79 ('domestic court decisions constitute one of the most important categories of custom-shaping State behaviour').

3 Treaty interpretation can be developed through subsequent practice which establishes the agreement of the parties regarding its interpretation: Vienna Convention on the

member states. National legal practices may also form part of the general principles of law.[4] Also, before international courts, judicial decisions, possibly including those of national courts,[5] would be invoked as subsidiary means for the determination of rules of international law.[6] In principle, national reception of the UN Security Council's decisions inevitably constitutes part of state practice and may also contribute to the creation of new customary international law or new treaty interpretation.

At the same time, this mode of interaction between domestic and international law is apparently of limited relevance to the regulation of the UN Security Council's exercise of authority. Within the contexts of targeted sanctions, the standards of review applied by the courts were primarily for those applicable to the national government and European institutions, and not to the international organs themselves. The CFI's seminal decision in *Kadi I* in 2005, which in part adopted *jus cogens* as part of the standards of review, was exceptional in this regard. The ECJ in *Kadi I* in 2008 applied fundamental rights as part of the general principles of EU law; the UK Supreme Court in *Ahmed* in 2010[7] decided whether the Al-Qaida Order was *ultra vires* the powers conferred upon the government by section 1 of the United Nations Act 1946; and the Canadian Federal Court in *Abdelrazik* in 2009[8] held that the Canadian government breached the applicant's right to enter Canada under Canadian constitutional jurisprudence. While these

Law of Treaties, 23 May 1969, 1155 UNTS 311 (entered into force 27 January 1980) Article 31(3)(b).

4 See Statute of the International Court of Justice, 26 June 1945, 39 AJIL Supp. 215 (1945) (entered into force on 24 October 1945) Article 38(1)(c). It has indeed been argued that judicial review or the access to information might form part of the general principles of law and could apply to the decision making of the UN Security Council. For the analysis of judicial review and the possible implication for the judicial review of Security Council resolutions, see Erika de Wet, 'Judicial Review as an Emerging General Principle of Law and its Implications for the International Court of Justice' (2000) 47 *Netherlands International Law Review* 181. On the access to information and the principle of transparency, see Devika Hovell, 'The Deliberate Deficit: Transparency, Access to Information and UN Sanctions' in J. Farrall and K. Rubenstein (eds), *Sanctions, Accountability and Governance in a Globalised World* (Cambridge, Cambridge University Press, 2009) 92. Cf. Antonios Tzanakopoulos, 'Transparency in the Security Council' in A. Bianchi and A. Peters (eds), *Transparency in International Law* (Cambridge, Cambridge University Press, 2013) 367.

5 See Hersch Lauterpacht, *The Development of International Law by the International Court* (Cambridge, Cambridge University Press, originally published in 1958, 1982) 20.

6 See ICJ Statute (n 4) Article 38(1)(d). Regarding the ICJ's reference to domestic court decisions, see André Nollkaemper, 'The Role of Domestic Courts in the Case Law of the International Court of Justice' (2006) 5 *Chinese Journal of International Law* 301.

7 *HM Treasury v Mohammed Jabar Ahmed and Others; HM Treasury v Mohammed al-Ghabra; R (Hari El Sayed Sabaei Youssef) v HM Treasury* [2010] UKSC 2 (UK Supreme Court, Judgment of 27 January 2010).

8 *Abousfian Abdelrazik v The Minister of Foreign Affairs and the Attorney General of Canada* (2009) 2009 FC 580; [2010] 1 FCR 267 (Canada, Federal Court, 4 June 2009).

courts may have indirectly reviewed the UN's international decisions,[9] the standards of review employed in these judicial decisions have little to do with the development of international law regulating the exercise of authority by the UN Security Council and its subsidiary organs.

8.2.2 Conceptual

An alternative mode of connection between domestic legal practices and international law is a *conceptual* one. This is based on the contextual similarities between the exercise of authority by the government, on the one hand, and the exercise of authority by international organisations, on the other hand. The contextual similarities could allow the legal framework governing the governmental authority to have impact on the development of international law regulating the exercise of international authority. This essentially relies on analogical reasoning, which is widely used in judicial practices as well as in treaty-making processes.[10] The analogical travelling of national law to international law was traditionally limited to a 'private law' sphere.[11] Nevertheless, as the exercise of authority by international institutions shares similarities with that of governmental authority, there is the growing possibility of applying a 'public law' analogy.[12]

Within the context of targeted sanctions, there is, in theory, the possibility for the theoretical contribution of domestic public law (constitutional, administrative, and criminal law). The fact that the UN Security Council and its subsidiary organs designate specific individuals and entities as if they were those states' national governments seems to create a limited contextual similarity between the Security Council's exercise of authority and the national contexts. National court decisions may be contextually importable even if they themselves have not engaged in reviewing the UN's decisions.

The contextual resemblance is much stronger with respect to the scenario of direct implementation in which the UN Security Council's subsidiary organs

9 See Paul James Cardwell, Duncan French and Nigel White, 'European Court of Justice, Yassin Abdullah Kadi and Al Barakaat International Foundation v Council and Commission (Joined Cases C-402/05 P and C-415/05 P) Judgment of 3 September 2008' (2009) 58 *International & Comparative Law Quarterly* 229, 234; Luis M. Hinojosa Martinez, 'Bad Law for Good Reasons: The Contradictions of the Kadi Judgment' (2008) 5 *International Organizations Law Review* 339, 342.

10 See, for instance, the 'legal borrowing' in the making of climate change treaties: Jonathan B. Wiener, 'Something Borrowed for Something Blue: Legal Transplants and the Evolution of Global Environmental Law' (2001) 27 *Ecology Law Quarterly* 1295.

11 Hersch Lauterpacht, *Private Law Sources and Analogies of International Law: With Special Reference to International Arbitration* (Union, NJ, The Lawbook Exchange, 1927).

12 See Aleksandar Momirov and Andria Naude Fourie, 'Vertical Comparative Law Methods: Tools for Conceptualising the International Rule of Law' (2009) 2 *Erasmus Law Review* 291. While Momirov and Fourie do not specifically distinguish between 'private law analogy' and 'public law analogy', their 'vertical comparative law methods' largely concern public law comparison.

directly applied their regulations and other kinds of decisions to individuals. Such immediacy is combined with the claim of supremacy by UNMIK, UNTAET, ICTY, and ICTR over relevant domestic law as being necessary for the maintenance of international peace and security.[13] In particular, UNMIK in Kosovo and UNTAET in East Timor exercised comprehensive governing powers and defined the daily lives of the local populations.[14] In this regard, it is not surprising that the Ombudsperson Institution in Kosovo, in sharply criticising UNMIK's self-issued jurisdictional immunities as being incompatible with human rights, equated UNMIK's presence as the exercise of governmental authority.[15] As the distance between the UN's subsidiary organs and individuals was significantly reduced, this created contextual similarities between the governmental authority and the international authority. The contextual resemblance paves the way for a possible transposition of legal frameworks regulating the governmental authority to those for the UN's exercise of authority.

8.2.3 Political

Finally, a *political* connection is a plausible path through which domestic legal practices could contribute to the development of international law. To reiterate, not only the ultimate judgments of the courts but also the affected individuals' initiation of judicial proceedings can generate a political momentum among member states and ultimately at the UN's level. Within the contexts of targeted sanctions, the use of national and EU courts with which they indirectly challenged the Security Council's listing decisions has been one of the apparatuses for increasing international attention to the lack of effective safeguards. The operational effectiveness of sanctions regimes would be simply undermined if states encountered legal impediments to their implementation. By contrast, within the context of UN territorial administration, the greater difficulty of relying on national and EU courts prevented domestic legal practices from being transformed into a political driving force at the international level.

The political impact of domestic legal practices varies significantly depending on the geopolitical location in which confrontational judicial practices were produced. Among national and regional judicial venues, EU courts should be ranked as one of the most influential fora, given that their decisions bind member states, two EU member states assume the permanent seats at the UN Security Council (i.e., the UK and France), and EU member states' information can be critical in sustaining updated information about listed individuals and entities. Given the visibility of the EU and its judicial guardians, the finding that a European list which copied

13 See section 4.4.3 of this book.
14 See section 4.4.2 of this book.
15 Ombudsperson Institution in Kosovo, 'Special Report No. 1: On the Compatibility with Recognized International Standards of UNMIK Regulation No. 2000/47 on the Status, Privileges and Immunities of KFOR and UNMIK and Their Personnel in Kosovo (18 August 2000) and on the Implementation of the Above Regulation' (2001) (26 April 2001) paras 27–8.

the UN's list violates fundamental rights would pose a significant challenge to the credibility of UN sanctions.[16] Also, the mere fact that court proceedings were instigated before EU courts could already facilitate international reform. Suppose that the well-known *Kadi* decisions, in which EU courts indirectly reviewed the UN's listing decisions, were rendered by the court of a small state, that the state is not a well-known advocate of the rule of law, and that the decisions were not readily available in English. In this case, national or regional contestations might have brought far more moderate progress in the regulation of the UN Security Council's listing decisions.

In addition to the effect of decisions themselves, judges' specific reasoning and narratives also determine the extent to which national and EU court decisions foster political momentum at the international level.[17] In this regard, while some judges' critical narrative galvanised calls for procedural reform, the CJEU's rather cursory dismissal of the role of the Ombudsperson in *Kadi II* might not have given Security Council members any incentive to revise their listing procedures.[18] At the same time, the practices of cross-referencing may prolong and augment the political presence of confrontational judicial practices. Within the context of targeted sanctions, there are limited judicial practices of cross-referencing among national and international judicial bodies. For instance, the Federal Supreme Court of Switzerland, in the case of *Nada* in 2007, referred to the CFI's decision in *Kadi I* and reasoned the case in a similar line.[19] The UK Supreme Court in *Ahmed* in 2010[20] referred to the Canadian case of *Abdelrazik*.[21] And *Kadi I*, *Abdelrazik*, and *Ahmed*, together with *Sayadi* in 2008 before the Human Rights Committee of the ICCPR,[22] were invoked by the ECtHR in the case of *Nada* in

16 Christina Eckes, *EU Counter-Terrorist Policies and Fundamental Rights* (Oxford, Oxford University Press, 2009) 301.

17 See section 7.3.5 (Creative interpretation of Council resolutions) regarding some critical comments by judges.

18 Larissa van den Herik, 'Peripheral Hegemony in the Quest to Ensure Security Council Accountability for its Individualized UN Sanctions Regimes' (2014) 19 *Journal of Conflict and Security Law* 427.

19 The Swiss court conducted the *jus cogens* review and found that procedural deficiencies at the UN did not contradict *jus cogens*, as did the CFI in its 2005 decision. *Youssef Nada v State Secretariat for Economic Affairs and Federal Department of Economic Affairs, Administrative appeal judgment* Case No. 1A.45/2007, DTF 133 II 450; ILDC 461 (CH 2007) (Switzerland, Federal Supreme Court, First Public Law Chamber, 14 November 2007). For details, see Johannes Reich, 'Recent Developments: Due Process and Sanctions Targeted Against Individuals Pursuant to UN Resolution 1267 (1999)' (2008) 33 *Yale Journal of International Law* 505.

20 *Ahmed (UK Supreme Court, 2010)* (n 7).

21 *Abdelrazik (Canadian Federal Court, 2009)* (n 8).

22 *Nabil Sayadi and Patricia Vinck v Belgium* (2008) UN Doc CCPR/C/94/D/1472/2006 (views of the Human Rights Committee under Article 5, Paragraph 4, of the Optional Protocol to the ICCPR) (29 December 2008). The Human Rights Committee found that there was a violation of Articles 12 and 17 of the ICCPR by Belgium. In particular, the Committee found unjustified the way that Belgium initially transmitted complainants' names to the Sanction Committee: see ibid., paras 10.7–10.8.

2012.[23] The *Nada* case was then brought up by the CJEU in *Kadi II* in 2013 in the course of highlighting the importance of a judicial review and the deficiency of the UN's procedures in ensuring effective juridical protection.[24] While the standards of review were after all primarily for those applicable to the national government and European institutions, the practice of cross-referencing may reduce the divergence across different jurisdictions in reviewing the implementing legislation in light of human rights law.

8.3 Normative and procedural development at the UN

All these points of connection then helped convey domestic law (which also has an international origin) into international normative frameworks regulating the UN's exercise of authority. Needless to say, the conceptual and political connections of domestic legal practices are merely part of many variables that constitute the development of international norms concerning the UN Security Council's exercise of authority. Yet still, in the scenarios of targeted sanctions, the fact that court proceedings are instigated, the finding that national and EU measures infringed upon fundamental rights, the substantive reasoning of judges, and the critical languages they used have incrementally created *political* force at the international level to develop the practices of the UN Security Council. In the context of the UN's territorial administration, the contextual resemblance between the exercise of governmental authority and the exercise of international authority created a limited *conceptual* presence at the UN of domestic and international law regulating the governmental authority.

8.3.1 Target specification: Fairness and transparency

Within the context of targeted sanctions, the political momentum to remedy the lack of procedural safeguards has culminated in the formulation of the normative principles of 'fair and clear' procedures, and, more broadly, the principles of fairness and transparency as the UN's institutional regulatory standards. A general formula is found in paragraph 109 of the World Summit Outcome adopted in 2005, in which the General Assembly stated that:

> 109. We also call upon the Security Council, with the support of the Secretary-General, to ensure that *fair and clear procedures* exist for placing individuals and entities on sanctions lists and for removing them, as well as for granting humanitarian exemptions.[25]

23 App No 10593/08 *Nada v Switzerland* (ECtHR Grand Chamber, Judgment of 12 September 2012).

24 Joined Cases C-584/10 P, C-593/10 P and C-595/10 P *Kadi v European Commission* ECLI:EU:C:2013:518 (CJEU, Judgment of 18 July 2013, 'Kadi II (CJEU)'), para 133; *Nada v Switzerland (ECtHR)* (n 23) para 211.

25 '2005 World Summit Outcome' UN Doc A/RES/60/1 (24 October 2005) para 109 (emphasis added).

The General Assembly's call for procedural fairness and clarity has been absorbed into Security Council resolutions themselves. In the preamble of Resolution 1730 adopted in December 2006, concerning all targeted sanctions regimes, the Security Council found itself 'committed to ensuring that fair and clear procedures exist' for the listing and delisting of individuals and entities.[26] The principles were upgraded in 2008 to the operative part of Resolution 1822 concerning the Al-Qaida and Taliban sanctions regime.[27] In Resolution 1904 adopted in December 2009, the Security Council also '[took] note of challenges, both legal and otherwise' to the sanctions measures, and 'express[ed] its intent to continue efforts to ensure that procedures are fair and clear'.[28] Resolution 1989 of June 2011 and subsequent resolutions, including Resolution 2253 of December 2015 against ISIL, directed the 1267 Sanctions Committee to continue ensuring fair and clear procedures for listing individuals, delisting them, and granting exceptions.[29] The need to ensure fairness and transparency has been discussed at the UN under the umbrella of the rule of law and the maintenance of international peace and security.[30]

On the face of it, the 'fair and clear' procedures convey a more nuanced and politically informed concept than the strict observance of the individuals' rights, such as the right to a fair hearing and the right to effective remedy. Not surprisingly, the 'fair and clear' procedures have yielded different constructions. Various governmental and non-governmental initiatives that urged sanctions' fairness and clarity commonly employ due process and human rights language.[31] Among Council member states, there is a difference in narrative. At the Security Council's rule of law meeting in June 2006, permanent members, while reiterating the need

26 UN Doc S/RES/1730 (19 December 2006) para 5 of the preamble (original italics omitted).

27 UN Doc S/RES/1822 (30 June 2008) para 28. Similarly, UN Doc S/RES/1904 (17 December 2009) para 34; UN Doc S/RES/1989 (17 June 2011) para 42; UN Doc S/RES/2083 (17 December 2012) para 45.

28 UN Doc S/RES/1904 (n 27) para 9 of the preamble (original emphasis omitted). Cf. UN Doc S/RES/1822 (n 27) para 12 of the preamble. Similarly, UN Doc S/RES/1989 (n 27) para 11 of the preamble; UN Doc S/RES/2083 (17 December 2012) (n 27) para 11 of the preamble.

29 UN Doc S/RES/1989 (n 27) para 42; UN Doc S/RES/2083 (17 December 2012) (n 27) para 45; UN Doc S/RES/2161 (17 June 2014) para 24; UN Doc S/RES/2253 (17 December 2015) para 37.

30 UN Doc S/PV.5474 (22 June 2006); UN Doc S/PV.5474 (Resumption 1) (22 June 2006); Statement by the President of the Security Council, UN Doc S/PRST/2006/28 (22 June 2006).

31 E.g., Peter Wallensteen, Carina Staibano and Mikael Eriksson (eds), *Making Targeted Sanctions Effective: Guidelines for the Implementation of UN Policy Options – Results from the Stockholm Process on the Implementation of Targeted Sanctions* (Uppsala, Department of Peace and Conflict Research, Uppsala University, 2003); 'Strengthening Targeted Sanctions through Fair and Clear Procedures: White Paper prepared by the Watson Institute Targeted Sanctions Project (Brown University), 30 March 2006' (2006) UN Doc A/60/887–S/2006/331 (14 June 2006); 'Improving Fair and Clear Procedures for a More Effective United Nations Sanctions System' UN Doc A/67/557–S/2012/805 (9 November 2012); 'Compendium of the High-level Review of United Nations Sanctions' UN Doc A/69/941–S/2015/432 (12 June 2015).

for fair and clear procedures, avoided reference to procedural guarantees to individuals, as contrasted with some other states which referred to due process,[32] the right to be heard,[33] or effective remedy.[34] Likewise, in the Security Council's meeting in May 2010, some delegations construed the procedural improvement as a matter of the effectiveness of the sanctions regime,[35] while some others perceived the procedural development as a realisation of due process and respect for fundamental rights.[36]

Despite the variance in narrative, it is undeniable that there is a stronger tendency at the UN's level to interchange the fair and clear procedures with 'due process' and the 'respect for human rights'. The concept of 'due process' itself is certainly contextual and does not automatically privilege a requirement of access to a court.[37] Yet the term 'due process' carries its own baggage, and the very use of the term creates a deliberative space through which the legal concept, built traditionally to constrain the exercise of a state's authority, can travel to the UN's level to restrain the exercise of international authority. From the commencement of her work in July 2010, the Ombudsperson established for the 1267 Sanctions Committee readily translated fairness and clarity as a matter of due process, shifting the focus to its meaning.[38] At the Security Council's meeting in June 2011, having referred to fairness and transparency, the Indian delegation observed that all sanctions regimes 'must ensure due process'.[39] In December 2015, the Chadian delegation referred to the need for 'transparency and respect for human rights' in the process of listing individuals to the sanctions.[40] At the Security Council meeting of February 2016 concerning economic sanctions, the Chilean representative observed that '[d]ue process is a general principle of law',[41] and the

32 UN Doc S/PV.5474 (n 30) 3 (Mr. Moeller/Ms. Løj of Denmark), 12 (Mr. Burian of Slovakia), 15 (Mr. Pereyra Plasencia of Peru), 20 (Mr. Mayoral of Argentina), 21 (Mr. Al-Nasser of Qatar); UN Doc S/PV.5474 (Resumption 1) (n 30) 17 (Mrs. Núñez de Odremán of Venezuela), 19 (Mr. Adekanye of Nigeria).

33 UN Doc S/PV.5474 (Resumption 1) (n 30) 9 (Mr. Barriga of Liechtenstein).

34 UN Doc S/PV.5474 (n 30) 24 (Mrs. Telalian of Greece); UN Doc S/PV.5474 (Resumption 1) (n 30) 11 (Mr. Baum of Switzerland).

35 E.g., UN Doc S/PV.6310 (11 May 2010) 11 (Mr. Li Baodong of China), 13–14 (Ms. Rice of the USA), 14 (Mr. Okuda of Japan).

36 E.g., ibid., 18 (Mrs. Dunlop of Brazil), 27 (Mr. Serrano on behalf of the EU), 30 (Ms. Shalev of Israel), 31 (Mr. Argüello of Argentina).

37 Devika Hovell, *The Power of Process: The Value of Due Process in Security Council Sanctions Decision-Making* (Oxford, Oxford University Press, 2016). Hovell observes that due process in the context of the UN Security Council should be understood and assessed through the lens of the 'public interest' model. The model allows both flexibility and adherence to a legal framework under the umbrella of shared purposes, and, by so doing, enhances the legitimacy of Security Council decision making.

38 See, e.g., 'First Report of the Office of the Ombudsperson Pursuant to Security Council Resolution 1904 (2009)' UN Doc S/2011/29 (24 January 2011) paras 5, 23, 33, 51.

39 UN Doc S/PV.6557 (17 June 2011) 3 (Mr. Hardeep Singh Puri of India).

40 UN Doc S/PV.7587 (17 December 2015) 21 (Mr. Cherif of Chad).

41 UN Doc S/PV.7620 (11 February 2016) 4 (Mr. Olguín Cigarroa of Chile).

Venezuela delegation expressed concern that the 'guarantee of due process in sanctions committees does not currently reach the minimum legal threshold established in national or international legislation'.[42] As indicated by these statements, the use of the term 'due process' as a sibling of 'fair and clear' procedures facilitates the reliance on the standards applicable to *a state*'s authority as a framework of assessing the *UN*'s exercise of authority.

While fairness and transparency can be interpreted in a range of different ways, the principles are broadly understood to realise the following four procedural safeguards: (i) *periodical review* by the Security Council, (ii) the respect for the individuals' *right to be informed* of the measures, (iii) the *right to be heard* directly by the decision-making body, and (iv) the *right to review* by an effective review mechanism.[43] A series of the procedural improvements at the UN Security Council's sanctions committees can be understood as the incremental realisation of these procedural safeguards. The main procedural improvements are listed in Annex II of this book.

To provide a few examples, the sanctions-wide Focal Point established in December 2006 under Resolution 1730 can be seen as an incremental step for the element of the *right to be heard*.[44] The Ombudsperson established for the Al-Qaida sanctions regime is also one realisation of the *right to be heard* and the *right to review*. In December 2009, with respect to the Al-Qaida sanctions regime alone, the Focal Point was replaced by the Office of the Ombudsperson established under Resolution 1904, who not only receives delisting requests from individuals and entities,[45] but also assists the Committee's consideration of such requests in an independent and impartial manner.[46] The Ombudsperson was also

42 Ibid., 22 (Mr. Ramírez Carreño of Venezuela).

43 Bardo Fassbender, 'Targeted Sanctions and Due Process' (2006) Study Commissioned by the UN Office of Legal Affairs (20 March 2006); UN Doc S/PV.5474 (n 30) 5 (statement by Mr. Michael, Legal Council of the UN, presenting the Secretary-General's view in the non-paper, presumably based on Fassbender's aforementioned paper); 'Report of the Special Rapporteur on the Promotion and Protection of Human Rights and Fundamental Freedoms while Countering Terrorism' UN Doc A/61/267 (16 August 2006) paras 38–41.

44 The Security Council unanimously adopted Resolution 1730 based on a French proposal, requesting the Secretary-General to establish a 'focal point' to receive delisting requests as a mechanism to be applied to all Council sanctions involving designated individuals: UN Doc S/RES/1730 (n 26).

45 UN Doc S/RES/1904 (n 27) para 21. On the establishment and function of the Ombudsperson under Resolution 1904, see Christopher Michaelsen, 'The Security Council's Al Qaeda and Taliban Sanctions Regime: "Essential Tool" or Increasing Liability for the UN's Counterterrorism Efforts?' (2010) 33 *Studies in Conflict & Terrorism* 448, 456–9.

46 UN Doc S/RES/1904 (n 27) para 20. The delisting process under Resolution 1904 follows three steps: information gathering by the Ombudsperson (two months), 'dialogue' between the Ombudsperson and the petitioner (two months), and Committee discussion and decision (two months): see ibid., Annex II. For the function of the Ombudsperson under Resolution 1904, see Michaelsen, 'The Security Council's Al Qaeda and Taliban Sanctions Regime' (n 45) 456–9; Laurence Boisson de Chazournes and Pieter Jan Kuijper, 'Mr Kadi and Mrs Prost: Is the UN Ombudsperson

awarded the power to make recommendations on delisting under Resolution 1989 in June 2011;[47] if the Ombudsperson recommends that the Sanctions Committee consider 'delisting', and if no decisions are rendered, either by the Committee or the Council, within the period of 60 days, the restrictive measures against the targeted individuals and entities would come to an end.[48] In November 2012, Switzerland and the like-minded states suggested that the Security Council consider extending the Ombudsperson's mandate to other sanctions regimes as well.[49] Such a suggestion was reiterated in June 2015 by the High-Level Review of UN Sanctions sponsored by Australia, Finland, Germany, Greece, and Sweden,[50] which urged the Security Council to 'improve the fairness and transparency of sanctions procedures to address human rights and due process issues'.[51]

The Security Council's incremental procedural developments, fostered by both governmental and non-governmental contestations, demonstrate that respect for the aforementioned four procedural safeguards has been, in principle, accepted and incrementally institutionalised within the targeted sanctions regimes. The concrete reforms in the listing procedures have led to the delisting of some of those targeted individuals and entities which brought court proceedings.[52] The principles of fairness and transparency are the UN's institutional standards and do not have any formal binding force upon the Security Council. Yet the principles are embedded in the discourse of the UN Security Council and its sanctions committees themselves, in both criticising and defending the sanctions regimes' decision making, and have guided at least some of the UN's incremental procedural reforms.

8.3.2 Direct implementation: The observance of human rights standards

With respect to the scenarios in which the UN's subsidiary organs apply their decisions directly to individuals, while judicial contestations are much more limited than the case of targeted sanctions, the contextual resemblance creates a foundation for the travelling of some of the legal frameworks regulating a state's exercise of authority to the regulation of the exercise of authority by international institutions. International human rights law informed the standards employed by the subsidiary organs of the UN Security Council which directly rendered certain legal

Going to Find Herself between a Rock and a Hard Place?' in H. Waele and E. Rieter (eds), *Evolving Principles of International Law* (Martinus Nijhoff Publishers, 2012) 71, 81–90.

47 UN Doc S/RES/1989 (n 27) para 21. See also ibid., Annex II, para 7(c).

48 See ibid., Annex II, para 12. In cases where the Ombudsperson recommends *retaining the listing*, the restrictive measures on the petitioner remain in place 'unless a Committee member submits a delisting request' which will be considered under its normal consensus procedures: ibid., Annex II, para 11.

49 'Improving Fair and Clear Procedures for a More Effective United Nations Sanctions System' (n 31) 9 (section 3.1).

50 'Compendium of the High-level Review of United Nations Sanctions' (n 31) 32, para 24.

51 Ibid., 32, para 20.

52 See Annex I (National, EU and international cases) of this book.

decisions over individuals without the intermediary of a territorial state which has jurisdiction over those individuals.

In the context of ad hoc international criminal tribunals, it was considered, from the outset, 'axiomatic' that the tribunals respect internationally recognised standards on the rights of the accused, contained particularly in Article 14 of the ICCPR.[53] Based on the ICCPR, the Statutes of the ICTY and ICTR provided for a series of the rights of the accused,[54] and the Rules of Procedure listed a set of the rights of a suspect during investigation.[55] The tribunals also found themselves bound by some other human rights not specified in the Statutes, just as the ICTY's Trial Chamber in *Milošević* regarded the rights enshrined in Article 9(4) of the ICCPR applicable to the tribunal's proceedings,[56] or the ICTR's Trial Chamber in *Rwamakuba* applied the right to an effective remedy.[57] The ICTY also took into account the relevant case law of the ECtHR, the Inter-American Court of Human Rights, the ICCPR's Human Rights Committee, and domestic court decisions to assist the interpretation of the applicable rights.[58] When it comes to the reasons why the tribunals were bound by a set of human rights, the jurisprudence of the tribunals is indeterminate and embraces various different theories, such as international personality, implied limits, the UN Charter, and the obligations owed by the former Yugoslavian states.[59] Yet the jurisprudence of the ad hoc tribunals proves their recognition that the judicial proceedings were subject to what the tribunals consider generally accepted international human rights norms.

Such recognition underlies not only the UN's judicial undertakings, but also within the UN's comprehensive territorial administration. From the outset, UNMIK and UNTAET pledged that they would observe major internationally recognised human rights standards.[60] This has also led UNMIK to submit, acting

53 'Report of the Secretary-General Pursuant to Paragraph 2 of Security Council Resolution 808 (1993)' (1993) UN Doc S/25704 (3 May 1993) para 106.

54 Updated Statute of the International Criminal Tribunal for the Former Yugoslavia, adopted 25 May 1993 by Security Council Resolution 827 (last amended 7 July 2009 by Resolution 1877) Article 21; Statute of the International Criminal Tribunal for Rwanda, adopted 8 November 1994 by Security Council Resolution 955 (last amended 16 December 2009 by Resolution 1901) Article 20.

55 ICTY Rules of Procedure and Evidence (adopted 11 February 1994, last amended 8 July 2015), IT/32/Rev.50 Rule 42; ICTR Rules of Procedure and Evidence (adopted 29 June 1995, last amended 13 May 2015) Rule 42.

56 Case No IT-02-54-T *Prosecutor v Slobodan Milošević, Trial Chamber, Decision on Preliminary Motions* (ICTY, Decision of 8 November 2001), paras 37–8.

57 Case No ICTR-98-44C-T *Prosecutor v André Rwamakuba, Trial Chamber, Decision on Appropriate Remedy* (ICTR, Decision of 31 January 2007), paras 40–9.

58 Göran Sluiter, 'International Criminal Proceedings and the Protection of Human Rights' (2003) 37 *New England Law Review* 935, 938–41.

59 See Krit Zeegers, *International Criminal Tribunals and Human Rights Law: Adherence and Contextualization* (Asser Press; Springer, 2016) 59–64.

60 For Kosovo, UNMIK, 'On the Authority of the Interim Administration in Kosovo' UNMIK/REG/1999/1 (25 July 1999) Section 2. Identical to: UNMIK, 'On the Authority of the Interim Administration in Kosovo' UNMIK/REG/2000/54 (27

under Security Council Resolution 1244, a state party's report to the Human Rights Committee and the Committee on Economic, Social and Cultural Rights in 2006 and 2008, respectively.[61] In response, the Committees seized the opportunities to express their concerns about the lack of sufficiently independent and functional human rights review of acts and omissions by UNMIK.[62]

With respect to complaint mechanisms available to local populations, the UN's well-established procedures concern tortious claims,[63] according to which UNMIK set up a local claims review board.[64] Likewise, UNTAET also had the authority to receive compensation claims.[65] As for the claims arising from the privatisation of socially owned enterprises, UNMIK established in 2002 the special chamber to review the decisions of the Kosovo Trust Agency (KTA) of UNMIK.[66] Noteworthy is that the special chamber reviewed a relevant UNMIK regulation itself and found an UNMIK regulation discriminatory in light of the jurisprudence of the ECtHR.[67]

Yet apparently these local review boards and special chambers were not designed to function as the recipients of the claims of human rights violations. In order to deal with the claims of a public nature, UNMIK established in June 2000 the Ombudsperson as an institution entrusted to receive and investigate human

September 2000) Section 2. See also UNMIK, 'On the Law Applicable in Kosovo' UNMIK/REG/1999/24 (12 December 1999) Section 1.3. For East Timor, UNTAET, 'On the Authority of the Transitional Administration in East Timor' UNTAET/REG/1991/1 (27 November 1999) Section 2.

61 'Report Submitted by the United Nations Interim Administration Mission in Kosovo to the Human Rights Committee on the Human Rights Situation in Kosovo since June 1999' UN Doc CCPR/C/UNK/1 (13 March 2006); 'Document Submitted by the United Nations Interim Administration Mission in Kosovo under Articles 16 and 17 of the Covenant' UN Doc E/C.12/UNK/1 (15 January 2008).

62 'Concluding Observations of the Human Rights Committee: Kosovo (Serbia)' UN Doc CCPR/C/UNK/CO/1 (14 August 2006) para 10; 'Concluding Observations of the Committee on Economic, Social and Cultural Rights' UN Doc E/C.12/UNK/CO/1 (1 December 2008) para 11.

63 Tortious claims have been long reviewed by a local claims review board on a mission-by-mission basis: Report of the Secretary-General (1995) UN Doc. A/C.5/49/65 (1995) paras 17–20; Report of the Secretary-General (1996) UN Doc A/51/389 (1996) paras 22–5.

64 UNMIK, 'On the Status, Privileges and Immunities of KFOR and UNMIK and Their Personnel in Kosovo' UNMIK/REG/2000/47 (18 August 2000) Section 7 (Third Party Liability); Kirsten Schmalenbach, 'Third Party Liability of International Organizations' (2006) 10 *Journal of International Peacekeeping* 33, 46–7.

65 Aleksandar Momirov, *Accountability of International Territorial Administrations: A Public Law Approach* (The Hague, Eleven International Publishing, 2011) 182.

66 UNMIK, 'On the Establishment of the Kosovo Trust Agency' UNMIK/REG/2002/12 (13 June 2002); UNMIK, 'On the Establishment of a Special Chamber of the Supreme Court of Kosovo on Kosovo Trust Agency Related Matters' UNMIK/REG/2002/13 (13 June 2002).

67 R. Everly, 'Reviewing Governmental Acts of the United Nations in Kosovo' (2007) 8 *German Law Journal* 21, 26–7; Organization for Security and Cooperation in Europe (OSCE), 'Privatization in Kosovo: Judicial Review of Kosovo Trust Agency Matters by the Special Chamber of the Supreme Court of Kosovo' (2008) (2008).

rights claims in Kosovo, including those against UNMIK itself.[68] In response to a number of human rights complaints, the Ombudsperson visited the sites of alleged violations and challenged the UNMIK administration, despite its reluctance to follow the recommendations of the Ombudsperson.[69] Yet, in February 2006, the claims directed against UNMIK were in principle excluded from the ambit of the Ombudsperson Institution in Kosovo.[70] In East Timor, the Human Rights Unit of UNTAET served as a recipient of human rights complaints against the transitional administration, although the Unit's primary function was capacity building at the local level, rather than the accountability of UNTAET itself.[71]

In response to international pressure to remedy the accountability gap, in March 2006, UNMIK set up a mission-specific mechanism called the Human Rights Advisory Panel,[72] as an alternative to judicial review preferred by the Organization for Security and Co-operation in Europe (OSCE) Mission in Kosovo.[73] The Human Rights Advisory Panel was a unique attempt not only on the point that the UN mission subjected itself to human rights review procedures but also due to its distinctive mandate to apply eight international human rights instruments.[74]

Until it ceased its activities in May 2016, the Panel received and examined 527 complaints in total.[75] The Panel adopted 335 opinions in which it found human rights violations attributable to UNMIK.[76] The Panel recommended that UNMIK obtain certain assurances, award adequate compensation, and even seek systemic responses to ensure that human rights standards would be upheld.[77]

68 UNMIK, 'On the Establishment of the Ombudsperson Institution in Kosovo' UNMIK/REG/2000/38 (30 June 2000) Section 3.1.

69 The Human Rights Advisory Panel, History and Legacy, Kosovo, 2007–2016, Final Report (30 June 2016) para 17.

70 UNMIK, 'On the Ombudsperson Institution in Kosovo' UNMIK/REG/2006/6 (16 February 2006) Section 3.1; Christopher P.M. Waters, '"Kosovanizing" the Ombudsperson: Implications for Kosovo and Peacekeeping' (2008) 15 *International Peacekeeping* 648; Christopher P.M. Waters, 'Nationalising Kosovo's Ombudsperson' (2007) 12 *Journal of Conflict and Security Law* 139.

71 Simon Chesterman, *You, The People: The United Nations, Transitional Administration, and State-Building* (Oxford, Oxford University Press, 2004) 149–50; Markus Benzing, 'Midwifing a New State: The United Nations in East Timor' (2005) 9 *Max Planck Yearbook of United Nations Law* 295, 339–40.

72 UNMIK, 'On the Establishment of the Human Rights Advisory Panel' UNMIK/REG/2006/12 (23 March 2006).

73 HRAP, Final Report (2016) (n 69) paras 33–9. The Parliamentary Assembly of the Council of Europe (PACE) also recommended, in January 2005, the establishment of a human rights court with the jurisdiction to examine the human rights violations by UNMIK and KFOR: Council of Europe, Parliamentary Assembly, Resolution 1417 (25 January 2005), Protection of Human Rights in Kosovo para 4. The PACE envisaged an advisory panel on human rights, as a body charged with scrutinising draft UNMIK regulations: ibid., para 5.

74 UNMIK Establishment of the Human Rights Advisory Panel (n 72) Section 1.2.

75 HRAP, Final Report (2016) (n 69) Executive Summary para 23.

76 Ibid., para 231.

77 Ibid., paras 234–8.

The Panel also benefited from the 'diversity of sources' to find the most relevant human rights jurisprudence in a given context in Kosovo.[78] While the Panel's decisions primarily drew on the ECHR and the jurisprudence of the ECtHR, the Panel also referred to the findings of the UN human rights treaty-monitoring bodies.[79] The Panel further consulted the case law of the Inter-American Court of Human Rights,[80] despite the fact that the American Convention on Human Rights was not specifically mentioned in the regulation of the Special Representative of the Secretary-General (SRSG).[81]

Despite its novelty in the UN's institutional life, fundamental concerns were raised from the outset about the Human Rights Advisory Panel's independence, temporary limit, and advisory nature.[82] The Panel's members were formally appointed by the Special Representative himself,[83] the alleged violations prior to 23 April 2005 were excluded,[84] and the Special Representative retained discretion in determining whether to submit the UN documents and whether to act on the final findings of the Advisory Panel.[85] The Panel's activities were also hampered by the lack of adequate staffing at the Secretariat.[86] Disturbing still was UNMIK's Administrative Direction of October 2009, under which the Special Representative somewhat vaguely directed the Panel's public hearings to be non-adversarial, excluded any complaint which might be in the future taken up by the UN's Third Party Claims Process, and set out the closure date for the submission of complaints as 31 March 2010.[87]

78 Ibid., paras 135–7.
79 E.g., Case No 26/08 *N.M. and Others v UNMIK* (HRAP, Opinion of 26 February 2016), para 199.
80 The Panel referred to the Inter-American Court's case law on the right to life of indigenous communities: ibid., para 200. The Panel also referred to the Inter-American Court's case law on the positive obligation to investigate disappearances: Cases Nos 248/09, 250/09 and 251/09 *Dušan Tomanović, Jelena Tomanović-Koković and Verica Tomanović v UNMIK* (HRAP, Opinion of 25 April 2013), para 54; Case No 98/09 *Jordanka Pavić v UNMIK* (HRAP, Opinion of 26 April 2013), para 60; Case No 80/09 *Nedeljka Kljaić v UNMIK* (HRAP, Opinion of 29 May 2014), para 62.
81 See UNMIK On the Law Applicable in Kosovo (n 60) Section 1.3.
82 Aleksandar Momirov, 'Local Impact of "UN Accountability" Under International Law: The Rise and Fall of UNMIK's Human Rights Advisory Panel' (2012) 19 *International Peacekeeping* 3, 9–10; Annemarie Devereux, 'Selective Universality? Human-Rights Accountability of the UN in Post-Conflict Operations' in B. Bowden, H. Charlesworth and J. Farrall (eds), *The Role of International Law in Rebuilding Societies after Conflict* (Cambridge, Cambridge University Press, 2009) 198, 213–4.
83 UNMIK Establishment of the Human Rights Advisory Panel (n 72) Section 5.1.
84 Ibid., Section 2.
85 Ibid., Sections 15.3, 17.3.
86 HRAP, Final Report (2016) (n 69) paras 73–80.
87 UNMIK, 'Administrative Direction No. 2009/1, Implementing UNMIK Regulation No. 2006/12 on the Establishment of the Human Rights Advisory Panel' UNMIK/DIR/2009/1 (17 October 2009) Sections 1.1, 2.2, 5; Momirov, 'Local Impact of "UN Accountability" Under International Law' (n 82) 11; Cedric Ryngaert, 'The Accountability of International Organizations for Human Rights Violations: The Cases of the UN Mission in Kosovo (UNMIK) and the UN "Terrorism Blacklists"' in

These constraints became a reality for those individuals who lodged, or attempted to lodge, human rights complaints to the Human Rights Advisory Panel. For instance, one of the applicants of the ECtHR's *Behrami and Saramati* case, after being rejected by the Strasbourg Court in May 2007, filed the complaint to UNMIK's Human Rights Advisory Panel. Yet the complaint was found inadmissible in *Behrami v UNMIK*, inasmuch as the alleged violations occurred before 23 April 2005 and thus fell outside the Panel's temporal jurisdiction.[88] One of the most contentious matters arose out of the proceedings of *Balaj and Others* involving the alleged human rights violations by UNMIK Formed Police Units officers.[89] The *Balaj and Others* case triggered tensions between the Panel and UNMIK's SRSG over the quasi-judicial character of the Panel's proceedings, and the tensions accelerated the adoption of the aforementioned Administrative Direction of October 2009.[90] According to the Administrative Direction, the Panel found inadmissible some claims on the ground that they have or could be subject to the UN Third Party Claims Process.[91] At the same time, the Panel in *Balaj and Others* reopened the proceedings after the completion of the UN Third Party Claims Process and eventually found the violation of the right to life under Article 2 of the ECHR, having rejected the SRSG's claim that the Panel had no authority to reopen the proceedings.[92] Likewise, in *N.M. and Others*, the Panel reopened the proceedings after the completion of the UN Third Party Claims Process, leading to the finding of the violation of several rights including the right to life.[93]

On top of the constraints imposed under UNMIK's Administrative Direction of October 2009, UNMIK did not, and at times could not, take meaningful action in response to the Panel's recommendations, as revealed in its highly critical final report.[94] The discordance was created in part because some of the decision-making powers had been transferred to the local authorities and the EU's Rule of Law Mission in Kosovo (EULEX) already by the time the Panel started rendering its opinions.[95] Besides, under the UN General Assembly's instructions, UNMIK was not authorised to pay compensation other than the one for material damage or physical harm, which further frustrated the Panel's recommendations.[96]

M. Fitzmaurice and P. Merkouris (eds), *The Interpretation and Application of the European Convention of Human Rights: Legal and Practical Implications* (Martinus Nijhoff Publishers, 2012) 73, 78–82.

88 Case No 24/08 *Agim Behrami v UNMIK* (HRAP, Decision of 17 October 2008).

89 HRAP, Final Report (2016) (n 69) para 82.

90 Ibid., paras 81–92.

91 E.g., Case No 311/09 *NTP Bujari (as Petrol) v UNMIK* (HRAP, Decision of 6 December 2012), paras 32–3.

92 Case No 04/07 *Kadri Balaj, Shaban Xheladini, Zenel Zeneli and Mustafë Nerjovaj v UNMIK* (HRAP, Opinion of 27 February 2015), paras 7, 138–140, 190.

93 *N.M. and Others v UNMIK* (n 79).

94 HRAP, Final Report (2016) (n 69) para 241.

95 Ibid., paras 242–5.

96 For instance, in response to the Panel's recommendation to award adequate compensation for pecuniary and non-pecuniary damage in *Case No 01/07 Radovan Parlić v*

On the whole, the experience of the Human Rights Advisory Panel manifests the UN's half-hearted and ambivalent stance toward the incorporation of human rights protection within the UN's own exercise of authority. The Panel's attempts apparently failed to meet some of the standards that the UN itself has long advocated in order to hold governmental decisions accountable at the domestic and international levels. While one may disagree with the Panel's own proclamation that the process was 'a total failure',[97] this was certainly the consequence brought to many local complainers whose access to justice was hampered by a range of constraints imposed on the Panel within the UN's complex political and budgetary constraints.

8.4 *Bosphorus* for the UN

As demonstrated by the experiences of targeted sanctions and territorial administration, the UN Security Council and its subsidiary organs have incrementally established certain normative standards with which to protect individuals' rights. Such normative standards were accompanied by a set of procedural mechanisms, such as the Ombudsperson for the 1267 Sanctions Committee and the Human Rights Advisory Panel for UNMIK, which were made available to affected individuals. Despite many shortcomings, the practices of the UN accommodate some of the procedural safeguards traditionally required of governmental bodies.

At the same time, the safeguards developed at the UN level may not readily be satisfactory when compared with the domestic standards accepted by some UN member states. The principles of fairness and transparency developed for the UN's targeted sanctions are meant to be more flexible than the obligation to ensure respect for human rights, despite the increasing tendency to interchange the principles with 'due process'.[98] The establishment of UNMIK's Human Rights Panel was a much-needed step forward, but the Panel's significance was overshadowed by the problems of independence, resources, and jurisdictional limits.[99]

The existing gaps between the framework to regulate the UN's international authority and the standards applicable to the regulation of governmental authority seem to promise contestations at the domestic and international levels. Domestic and regional litigations would be likely to continue in the immediate future with regard to the decisions of the UN Security Council and its subsidiary organs. An important question then arises as to whether *international law itself* justifies the competence of domestic courts or other domestic authorities to review the

UNMIK, the SRSG informed the Panel that UNMIK was not in position to pay any compensation as recommended by the Panel since 'current United Nations General Assembly instructions on compensations do not permit the United Nations Organization or its missions to pay compensation other than for material damage or physical harm': SRSG's decision in the case of Radovan Parlic (case no 01/07).

97 Human Rights Advisory Panel, 'Annual Report 2015/16' (June 2016) para 121.

98 Section 8.3.1 (Target specification) above.

99 Section 8.3.2 (Direct implementation) above.

Security Council's decision making, and, as a result of the review, to reject the decisions of the UN Security Council and its subsidiary organs.

One possible ground, albeit within a particular international treaty regime, is the applicability of an equivalent protection test even to a state's obligation under Security Council resolutions or the decisions of its subsidiary organs. The test is notably put forward by the ECtHR in the *Bosphorus v Ireland* case in 2005.[100] In this case, the applicant company, a Turkish airline, argued that the right to property[101] was infringed upon by the Irish authorities, who impounded the applicant's aircraft leased from a Yugoslavian airline. The impoundment was based on the regulation of the EU (then European Communities) which was in turn based on UN Security Council Resolution 820 on the Yugoslavia sanctions.[102] In dismissing the complaint, the ECtHR put forward the notion of equivalent protection; when states are obliged to abide by obligations based upon their membership of an international organisation, such states are presumed to be in compliance with the ECHR 'as long as the relevant organisation is considered to protect human rights' in a manner 'equivalent' to the protection under the ECHR.[103] The presumption is rebutted if the protection is 'manifestly deficient'.[104] In *Bosphorus*, Ireland was presumed to be in compliance with the treaty because the European Court of Justice and national courts provided a remedy to individuals.[105]

On the face of it, the equivalent protection doctrine cannot readily be invoked when states are obligated to carry out the obligations under the UN Charter, which prevail over conflicting international obligations according to Article 103 of the UN Charter. While the *Bosphorus* case itself was about the implementation of the Security Council's economic sanctions to which Article 103 applies, the equivalent protection doctrine was still invoked in this case. This was made possible because, first, the ECtHR decided the balance between Ireland's obligation under the ECHR and the state's obligations under EU law, and not necessarily the balance between the ECHR and the obligation under the UN Charter. Second, the Yugoslavia Sanctions Committee issued guidance to impound the aircraft in question in response to the Irish inquiry;[106] such guidance was less stringent and determinative compared with the sanctions committees' proactive designation of

100 *Bosphorus v Ireland* App No 45036/98 (ECtHR, Grand Chamber, 30 June 2005). The test was formulated based on the *M. & Co.* and *Matthews v UK* cases: App No 13258/87 *M & Co v the Federal Republic of Germany* (1990) 64 DR 138 (European Commission of Human Rights, 9 February 1990); App No 24833/94 *Matthews v the United Kingdom* ECHR 1999-I (ECtHR, Grand Chamber, 18 February 1999).

101 Protocol 1 to the Convention for the Protection of Human Rights and Fundamental Freedoms, 20 March 1952, ETS 9 (entered into force 18 May 1954) Article 1 (Protection of property).

102 Council Regulation (EEC) No 990/93 (26 April 1993) concerning trade between the European Economic Community and the Federal Republic of Yugoslavia (Serbia and Montenegro) [1993] OJ L 102/14; UN Doc S/RES/820 (17 April 1993) para 24.

103 *Bosphorus v Ireland* (n 100) para 155.

104 Ibid., para 156.

105 Ibid., para 163–5.

106 See ibid., paras 19–32.

specific targeted individuals. Finally, the restriction on the right to property can be more flexible than the individuals' right to a fair hearing. The conflict between human rights obligations and the obligations relating to the UN sanctions was not as irreconcilable as it was in the case of the UN's targeted sanctions.

Owing to the special status of Charter obligations, the *Bosphorus* test had not been applied to the cases involving the implementation of the decisions of the UN Security Council and its subsidiary organs. The ECtHR in *Nada* regarding the Al-Qaida sanctions regime referred to the *Bosphorus* case, yet not in relation to equivalent protection.[107] The Strasbourg Court in *Al-Jedda* concerning the Council-authorised multinational force did not discuss *Bosphorus* despite the fact the case was relied on by the applicant.[108] The ECtHR in *Behrami and Saramati*, concerning the UN's territorial administration and the Council-authorized multinational force, distinguished the case from *Bosphorus* on the grounds that the acts and omissions in *Behrami and Saramati* were carried out neither by state authorities nor within the territory of the states.[109]

A sign of change emerged, however, by the decision of the ECHR's Second Section in *Al-Dulimi* case in November 2013.[110] In this case, the Strasbourg Court found a violation of the right to a fair hearing[111] of the applicants who had been designated as targets by the UN Security Council's sanctions committee for the Iraq sanctions regime under Resolution 1483.[112] The Second Section's decision was the first occasion on which the ECtHR explicitly applied the equivalent protection test, not to the EU which implemented the Security Council's resolutions, but to the UN itself.[113] Having accepted that the listing and delisting procedures at the UN level do not provide equivalent protection,[114] the Court, by four out of seven judges,[115] found that the very essence of the right of access to a

107 *Nada v Switzerland (ECtHR)* (n 23) para 168.

108 *Al-Jedda v The United Kingdom* App No 27021/08 (ECtHR, Grand Chamber, 7 July 2011) para 95.

109 App Nos 71412/01, and 78166/01 *Behrami and Behrami v France; Saramati v France, Germany and Norway* (ECtHR, Grand Chamber, Admissibility Decision of 2 May 2007) para 151.

110 App No 5809/08 *Al-Dulimi and Montana Management Inc v Switzerland* (ECtHR, Second Section, 26 November 2013) paras 117–21.

111 Convention for the Protection of Human Rights and Fundamental Freedoms, 4 November 1950, ETS 5, 213 UNTS 221 (1950) Article 6(1).

112 UN Doc S/RES/1483 (22 May 2003) para 23; UN Doc S/RES/1518 (24 November 2003).

113 Maurizio Arcari, 'Forgetting Article 103 of the UN Charter? Some Perplexities on "Equivalent Protection" after Al-Dulimi' (2014) 6 *QIL QDI* 31, 31.

114 *Al-Dulimi (Second Section 2013)* (n 110) paras 118–21. On the equivalent protection, the Chamber distinguished*Al-Dulimi* from *Nada* on the basis of the lack of member states' discretion in *Al Dulimi* with regard to asset freeze measures: *Al-Dulimi*, ibid., para 117. For the summary and analysis of *Al Dulimi* (2013), see Stephan Hollenberg, 'The Diverging Approaches of the European Court of Human Rights in the Cases of Nada and Al-Dulimi' (2015) 64 *International & Comparative Law Quarterly* 445.

115 Judge Sajó (partly dissenting) observed that the case should be inadmissible due to the lack of discretion left to member states and the supremacy of the UN.

court was impaired due to the lack of effective and independent judicial review at the UN and domestic levels for a considerable period of time.[116] The ECtHR then held that:

> for as long as there is no effective and independent judicial review, at the level of the United Nations … it is essential that [the listed] individuals and entities should be authorised to request the review by the national courts of any measure adopted pursuant to the sanctions regime.[117]

This short passage situates 'the review by national courts' as a mechanism ***endorsed by international law*** in order to compensate for the lack of effective and independent judicial review at the UN's level. According to the Court, the lack of appropriate international review would justify and require the domestic judicial review of the measures which give effect to the UN's sanctions regime.

The *Bosphorus* reasoning was not adopted, at least formally, by the Grand Chamber's judgment of *Al-Dulimi* in June 2016.[118] Instead, the Grand Chamber applied the strong presumption of human rights compatibility to avoid normative conflicts between Charter obligations and the ECHR and thus the question of Article 103 of the UN Charter. Such presumption was enunciated in the *Al-Jedda* case of July 2011, in which the ECtHR applied 'a presumption that the Security Council does not intend to impose any obligation on Member States to breach fundamental principles of human rights'[119] and observed that the Council's resolutions must be read 'most in harmony'[120] with human rights obligations. This technique is slightly different from the one used in *Nada*, in which the ECtHR interpreted the resolutions of the UN Security Council in such a way that they would leave discretion to states' authorities.[121]

In a 'spirit of systemic harmonisation', the Grand Chamber *Al-Dulimi* interpreted Resolution 1483 on the Iraq sanctions regime as being compatible with Article 6(1) of the ECHR. According to the Court, the resolution 'does not

116 See *Al-Dulimi (Second Section 2013)* (n 110) paras 129–34.
117 Ibid., para 134.
118 According to the concurring opinion of Judge Pinto de Albuquerque (joined by Judges Hajiyev, Pejchal, and Dedov), the Grand Chamber effectively adopted the *Bosphorus* test in paragraph 153 of the judgment: App No 5809/08 *Al-Dulimi and Montana Management Inc v Switzerland* (ECtHR, Grand Chamber, Judgment of 21 June 2016), concurring opinion of Judge Pinto de Albuquerque, joined by Judges Hajiyev, Pejchal and Dedov, para 55. At least formally, the Grand Chamber's reasoning is different from the *Bosphorus* test in that the majority did not invoke the deficiency at the UN's level as a primary ground for necessitating domestic scrutiny. At the same time, in paragraph 153, the deficiency at the UN's level is presented as an additional reason why domestic scrutiny is needed; this is indeed akin to the *Bosphorus* test.
119 *Al-Jedda v The United Kingdom* (n 108) para 102.
120 Ibid. The presumption is rebuttable: *Nada v Switzerland (ECtHR)* (n 23) para 172; App No 65542/12 *Stichting Mothers of Srebrenica and Others v The Netherlands* (ECtHR, Decision of 11 June 2013) para 145.
121 Section 7.3.5 of this book.

contain any *clear or explicit* wording *excluding* the *possibility* of judicial supervision' by member states, and, therefore, the resolution 'authoris[ed] the courts of the respondent State to exercise sufficient scrutiny so that any arbitrariness can be avoided'.[122] This allowed the Grand Chamber to shift its focus on to the Swiss authorities, which were held to be in violation of Article 6(1) of the ECHR due to their failure to provide the applicants with a genuine opportunity to submit appropriate evidence to a court.[123]

The Grand Chamber's reasoning is not without difficulties. Paragraph 23 of Resolution 1483 on the Iraq sanctions obliged member states to freeze relevant assets 'without delay'[124] which, according to the Grand Chamber, still allowed sufficient domestic scrutiny. Nevertheless, it is by no means easy to conceive how member states could meet such an expectation of immediacy while going through judicial processes. Nor is it probable that the UN Security Council explicitly excludes the possibility for member states to resort to judicial supervision. Such a high level of specificity is not readily forthcoming from the UN Security Council. In view of the practices of the UN Security Council, the Grand Chamber in *Al-Dulimi* appears to have stretched the presumption of compatibility to the point where it is almost non-rebuttable, at least with respect to the right of access to a court.

At a more fundamental level, the Grand Chamber's view of the international legal order is different from that of the Second Section in *Al-Dulimi*. In applying the ECHR, the Grand Chamber in *Al-Dulimi* seems to have placed particular importance on Article 103 of the UN Charter, which gave rise to the need to avoid a normative conflict via systemic harmonisation. By contrast, the Second Section in *Al-Dulimi* situated the UN Charter as a relevant, yet still equally independent, treaty regime without an overarching status in international law. According to this rather pluralistic view of the international legal order, the ECtHR is not burdened with the task of according particular weight on Article 103 of the UN Charter. Normative conflicts may arise, yet they ought to be resolved by member states' authorities who are in a position to interpret and apply multiple treaty regimes.[125]

Overall, international law has yet to provide yardsticks with which to justify the competence of domestic courts or other domestic authorities to review the UN's decisions and to protect individuals' rights in lieu of the UN. There remain competing perspectives as to whether and how the judicial guardian of the human rights treaty ought to pay deference to Article 103 of the UN Charter. Even if the equivalent protection doctrine is applied to the UN by the Strasbourg Court, the

122 *Al-Dulimi (Grand Chamber)* (n 118) para 146 (emphasis added). Cf. ibid., concurring opinion of Judge Pinto de Albuquerque, joined by Judges Hajiyev, Pejchal, and Dedov, paras 45–6 (regarding the majority's interpretation as superficial); ibid., concurring opinion of Judge Keller, paras 6–8 (observing that the text does not allow any margin of appreciation for the implementing state).

123 *Al-Dulimi (Grand Chamber)* (n 118) para 151.

124 UN Doc S/RES/1483 (n 112) para 23.

125 See also section 7.3.3 of this book.

doctrine itself has not yet been accepted outside the jurisprudence of the ECtHR. In addition, the equivalent protection doctrine may not even arise with regard to the scenarios of direct implementation if the claims instituted against member state authorities are rejected on the ground of the attribution of the impugned conduct to the UN.

8.5 Conclusion

The UN Security Council was established to maintain international peace and security whose importance is legally sustained by Article 103 of the UN Charter that situates the obligations under Council resolutions in a normatively higher place. At the same time, as seen in chapter 7 of this book, the preferential status of the UN Security Council and its peace and security mandate has been incrementally counterbalanced by avoidance and confrontational responses. While the legal effect of confrontational judicial decisions at the national and EU levels is limited to their own respective legal orders, domestic legal practices – which are intertwined with international human rights law – can provide conceptual and political feedback to international norms regulating the exercise of authority by the UN Security Council and its subsidiary organs. The international political presence of domestic legal practices varies significantly depending on wider geopolitical factors. In this sense, the decisions of the EU courts no doubt carry greater presence at the UN than a judicial decision of a relatively small country whose court decisions are not easily accessible.

The development of normative standards at the UN level varies depending on the distance between the UN Security Council and individuals. With respect to the scenarios of *direct implementation*, it is part of the common practices of the UN to accommodate a set of international human rights standards in the framework of governing the exercise of international authority – as seen in the practices of UNMIK and UNTAET as well as the unique circumstances of ad hoc international criminal tribunals. Among the three categories of practices examined in this study (i.e., the addressing of individuals under Chapter VII, target specification, and direct implementation), the practices of direct implementation create stronger resemblance to authority exercised by the national government. This paves the way for the possibilities for domestic legal practices concerning a *state's governmental* authority to interact with international law which restricts the authority exercised by *international organisations.*

As contrasted with the case of direct implementation, the practice of *targeted sanctions* is intermediated by states whose conduct is not attributable to the UN. The decisions of the UN Security Council's sanctions committees can be assimilated to those of member states' exercise of authority with respect to the designation of individual targets. This resemblance invited human rights contestations levelled against the UN's listing processes. At the same time, it is the national government that implements international decisions regarding asset freezes and travel bans. The extent to which the UN's decisions resemble those of national government vis-à-vis individuals seems to reflect the nuanced standards of 'fairness and transparency' developed in the context of targeted sanctions, although they have been increasingly used interchangeably with due process. Ostensibly flexible international normative standards applicable to the UN's targeted sanctions are accompanied by the changing role of state intermediaries which ought to maximise their effort to ensure respect for human rights even when they implement UN Security Council resolutions.

Among the three groups of practices examined in this book, normative standards are least developed with respect to the Security Council's exercise of authority in *issuing Chapter VII demands toward certain individuals.* The effect of such an international demand on individuals may remain symbolic unless member states voluntarily take related actions to give effect to such a demand. It remains to be seen whether the UN Security Council and member states would give consideration to procedural safeguards for those individuals directly addressed by the Council's Chapter VII resolutions.

On balance, despite many shortcomings, normative standards and procedural mechanisms have been cultivated at the international level to the direction that the rights of those affected individuals can be better safeguarded at the UN's level. The normative and procedural development occurred through the interactions with domestic legal practices and international human rights law which are invoked by governmental and non-governmental actors to assess the UN's exercise of authority. While the affected individuals may suffer from the unavailability of effective diplomatic channels to contest the decisions of the Security Council and its subsidiary organs, some of the individuals have utilised domestic courts and attracted challenges from other governmental and non-governmental constituencies to call for normative and procedural reform at the UN. The norm-generating processes, in which both old and new constituencies have participated through multiple domestic and international venues, is precisely the product of the reduced distance between the UN Security Council and individuals. By reducing its distance from individuals and narrowing down the presence of state intermediaries, the UN Security Council exposed itself to the continued assessment of international authority in light of domestic and international law traditionally nurtured to regulate the governmental authority. Given that this reduced distance is deeply embedded in the concept of international peace security, as discussed in chapter 3 of this book, the Security Council and its subsidiary organs continue to be situated in such a space where their decisions are subject to critical feedback from a wide range of constituencies, including affected individuals and their immediate communities. International normative standards, such as the principles of fairness and transparency, generated from this space are different from those sanctioned by the UN's traditional constituencies. Such normative standards, even if they are not formally binding, work to enrich the catalogue of the rule of law at the international level for the regulation of authority exercised by the UN's peace and security arm.

9 Conclusion

In the Millennium Report of 2000, the UN Secretary-General Kofi Annan employed the inspirational opening phrase of the UN Charter, 'We the Peoples', in order to encourage the reimagination of the role of the UN not as an organisation of states but as the organisation which serves 'the needs and hopes of people everywhere'.[1] Such an imagination at an abstract level goes in parallel with the activities of the UN organs, funds and programmes, and specialised agencies which have been, both before and after the Millennium Report, in direct contact with selected groups of individuals. The UN Security Council is not an exception in terms of narrowing down its distance from individuals, as demonstrated by the three categories of the Council's practices discussed throughout this book.

Despite the utopian connotation that the words 'We the Peoples' entail, in the practice of the UN Security Council, individuals have been constituted not only as those in need of international protection but also as those who may undermine or threaten international peace and security. The different faces of individuals and the groups of individuals in the narrative of the UN Security Council emerged while, at the same time, the concept of threats to the peace has developed to include not only inter-state armed confrontations but also the gross and systematic violations of human rights and the acts of terrorism in general.[2] While the drafters of the UN Charter have already contemplated the possible inclusion of human rights agendas into the sphere of international peace and security, what the drafters seem to have had in mind was the protection of minorities, whose inter-state sensitivity was already well acknowledged during the era of the League of Nations.[3] A clear sign of change in the concept of threats to the peace came with the end of the Cold War and more symbolically with the adoption of Resolution 794 in 1992.

In carrying out its mandate to maintain international peace and security, the UN Security Council, to a varying degree, incrementally reduced the presence of

1 Report of the Secretary-General, 'We the Peoples: The Role of the United Nations in the Twenty-First Century' UN Doc A/54/2000 (27 March 2000) para 10.
2 Chapter 3 of this book.
3 Chapter 2 of this book.

'state intermediaries'.[4] The most comprehensive replacement of governmental authority took place in the context of the UN's territorial administration, in which the Security Council's subsidiary organs, acting under Chapter VII, prescribed and carried out the UN's institutional decisions which had immediate legal effect on individuals in the war-torn territories. The scenario of the UN's territorial administration is different from the cases of targeted sanctions whose decisions to designate specific individuals ought to be implemented under member states' domestic law.

As highlighted in this book, such a varying distance between the UN Security Council's exercise of authority and individuals yields a paradox. In short, the deeper the replacement of state intermediaries by the UN becomes, the higher the obstacles would be for individuals to contest the decisions taken by the UN, especially through judicial mechanisms. Targeted sanctions, precisely because they rely on the intermediary presence of state authorities and their application of respective domestic laws, created opportunities at the national, regional, and even international levels for those individuals affected by the UN sanctions regimes to indirectly challenge the validity of their decisions.[5] This is sharply contrasted with the scenario of the UN's territorial administration, with respect to which individuals do not have access to judicial venues to indirectly hold the UN accountable, despite the fact that such individuals are much more directly and immediately affected by the UN's institutional decisions.

What matters is that the lack of access to domestic courts may have deprived individuals not only of the immediate opportunities to obtain remedies but also the venues through which individuals' claims encourage international political initiatives and lead to normative and procedural reforms at the UN. In the context of targeted sanctions, court actions at the national and EU levels have been one of the powerful tools in fostering political momentum at the international level. The fact that some of the targeted individuals resorted to the courts of the geopolitically significant region amplified the political presence of individuals' contestations at the international level, even before the courts delivered any judgments.[6] By contrast, in circumstances where judicial contestations are much less promising, the affected individuals need to rely on diplomatic or other non-judicial channels in order to drive international attention to the need for improving procedural guarantees. While the contextual similarities between the exercise of international and national authority allow for the analogical travelling of national law to international law, the normative and procedural development for the UN's territorial administration was arguably too moderate.

This paradox points to the need for contextualising the extensive international attention given to targeted sanctions and procedural safeguards therein. Targeted sanctions are different from the scenarios of 'direct implementation' in which the UN Security Council effectively removes the presence of state intermediaries. The

4 Chapter 4 of this book.
5 Chapter 7 of this book.
6 Chapter 8 of this book.

limited intermediary presence of state authorities creates a much stronger resemblance between the exercise of international authority and that of the national authority. This gives cogency to the argument that the UN's direct implementation should be held accountable in accordance with international human rights standards applicable to the governmental authority, despite the lack of judicial contestations to generate political momentum towards reform.

As presented by this book, the UN Security Council and its subsidiary organs have been, in a varying degree, reducing their distance from individuals for the purpose of the maintenance of international peace and security. The UN Charter is apparently not well-equipped in catching up with some of the drawbacks of such transitions, especially in terms of safeguarding the rights and interests of individuals affected by the exercise of international authority. This regulatory gap is understandable if one looks back to the San Francisco Conference in 1945; the four sponsoring Powers, as well as the 46 countries which were invited to participate in the final phase of establishing a post-World War II collective security mechanism, were preoccupied with ensuring that they accord the Security Council the functions and powers to best provide succeeding generations with an (interstate) war-free world. Yet the meaning of treaty provisions is by no means frozen by the preoccupation of drafters in 1945. Despite the flexibility of treaty interpretation, the reinterpretation of Charter provisions, which requires member states' explicit or tacit endorsement, turned out to be time-consuming and favours the state-centric variables.[7]

While international law merely provides a thin set of rules in safeguarding the rights of affected individuals, domestic law has arguably augmented over the years its conceptual and political role in developing the normative frameworks concerning the UN Security Council's exercise of authority. By reducing distance from individuals, the decisions of the UN Security Council and its subsidiary organs have been exposed to comments and criticisms in light of some of the constitutional and administrative law principles applicable to the regulation of governmental authority. Critical feedback based on domestic and international law may allow for international normative development, as illustrated by the formulation of the principles of fairness and transparency in targeted sanctions.

The general trend captured in this book is likely to continue. The UN Security Council and its subsidiary organs exercise their authority over individuals by restricting the presence of state intermediaries. The Security Council cannot readily dissociate itself from domestic contestations either in the near future. This outlook is projected precisely due to the contemporary understanding of international peace and security, in the maintenance of which the UN is often necessitated to pierce the veil of sovereign states and restrict their authority over individuals. As this book has tried to illustrate, the UN Security Council will not be immune from constant critical feedback from affected individuals whose claims may be accompanied by parallel challenges from governmental constituencies. Domestic law is one of the normative ponds accessible to individuals who are no longer a mere

7 Chapters 5–6 of this book.

aspiration in the preamble in the UN Charter. They are, instead, the visible segments of the UN's arduous undertaking to maintain international peace and security. Individuals' contribution – whether negative or positive – increasingly dictates the success of the guardian of international peace and security and the relevance of international law in an evolving international society.

Annex I National, EU and international cases regarding UN targeted sanctions

[As of December 2016]

Year	*Sanction*	*Applicant*	*UN List*	*Court*	*Date*	*Citation*	*Summary*
11/2001	SCR 1267	Othman (Abu Qatada)	Qdi.031 (QI. M.31.01)	UK, Queen's Bench Division (Administrative Court)	28 November 2001	R (on the application of Othman) v Secretary of State for Work and Pensions [2001] EWHC Admin 1022	The payment of income support to the designated person is suspended under Council Regulation 437/2001. The law of humanity allows necessary minimum payment.
05/2002	SCR 1267	Benevolence International Foundation	Qde.093 (QE. B.93.02)	US, District Court, N.D. Illinois, Eastern Division	14 May 2002	Benevolence International Foundation, Int. v Ashcroft (200 F.Supp. 2d 935)	Decided to stay the civil case until the conclusion of the parallel criminal case.
–/2002	SCR 1267	Global Relief Foundation	Qde.091 (QE. G.91.02)	US, District Court, N.D. Illinois, Eastern Division; Court of Appeals, Seventh Circuit	11 June 2002 31 December 2002	Global Relief Foundation Inc. v O'Neill, 207 F. Supp. 2d 779 (N.D. Ill. 2002); Global Relief Foundation Inc v O'Neill, 315 F.3d 748 (7th Cir. 2002) See the second report of the Monitoring Team, UN Doc. S/2005/83, Annex II, para.12	In 2002, a federal district court and an appellate court dismissed the emergency petition and constitutional claims of Global Relief Foundation.

Year	*Sanction*	*Applicant*	*UN List*	*Court*	*Date*	*Citation*	*Summary*
02/2003	SCR 1267	Benevolence International Foundation	Qde.093 (QE. B.93.02)	(US first instance)	25 February 2003	Benevolence International Foundation Inc. v Ashcroft, No. 02-CV-763 (N.D. Ill. 25 February 2003) See the second report of the Monitoring Team, UN Doc. S/2005/83, Annex II, para.12	The case was voluntarily dismissed after Arnaout pled guilty, pursuant to a written plea agreement.
06/2003	SCR 1267	Nasco	Delisted on 14 November 2007	Turkey, Council of State	11 June 2003 (Council of State) 18 September 2003 (Administrative Law Decision of the Council of State) Appealed to the Administrative Cases Bureau	Nasco Nasreddin Holding AS See the second report of the Monitoring Team, UN Doc. S/2005/83, Annex II, para.10; Eighth report of the Monitoring Team, UN Doc. S/2008/324, Annex I, para.6	The Council of State in Ankara rejected the request for a stay of execution of the decision to freeze the assets. The Administrative Law Decision of the Council of State approved the rejection.

Year	*Sanction*	*Applicant*	*UN List*	*Court*	*Date*	*Citation*	*Summary*
08/2003	SCR 1267	Aaran Money Wide Service	Delisted on 26 August 2002	US, District Court, D. Minnesota	21 August 2003 (Order)	Aaran Money Wire Service Inc. and Garad Nor v United States; Global Services International Inc. and Abdullahi Farah v US, Nos. 02CV789JMR/FLN, 02CV790MJD/JGL (2003 WL 22143735 (D. Minn.))	The court dismissed the cases after the government delisted the plaintiffs.
08/2003	SCR 1267	Global Services International	Delisted on 26 August 2002	US, District Court, D. Minnesota	21 August 2003 (Order)	Aaran Money Wire Service Inc. and Garad Nor v United States; Global Services International Inc. and Abdullahi Farah v US, Nos. 02CV789JMR/FLN, 02CV790MJD/JGL (2003 WL 22143735 (D. Minn.))	The court dismissed the cases after the government delisted the plaintiffs.

Year	*Sanction*	*Applicant*	*UN List*	*Court*	*Date*	*Citation*	*Summary*
–/2003	SCR 1267	Al-Rashid Trust	Qde.005 (QE.A.5.01)	Pakistan, High Court of Sindh	2003	See the fifth report of the Monitoring Team, UN Doc. S/2006/750, Annex III, para.6	The lower court ruled in favour of Al-Rashid Trust, based on the Pakistani government's failure to issue a statutory notification to the Trust under the 1948 United Nations (Security Council) Act.
–/2003	SCR 1267	Nasco	Delisted on 14 November 2007	Italy, Tribunal of Milan	2003 Filed in January 2003	Nasco Business Residence Center SAS See the second report of the Monitoring Team: UN Doc. S/2005/83, Annex II, para.7	The Tribunal rejected the suit based on a lack of jurisdiction. The EU regulations do not foresee that national courts can adopt provisions contrary to sanctions imposed by the EU.
02/2005	SCR 1267	Sayadi and Vinck	Both delisted on 20 July 2009	Belgium, Brussels Court of First Instance	11 February 2005	Nabil Sayadi and Patricia Vinck v Belgian State	The Brussels court ordered the Belgium government to make a delisting request to the UN because Sayadi and Vinck were not indicted after investigation.

Year	*Sanction*	*Applicant*	*UN List*	*Court*	*Date*	*Citation*	*Summary*
03/2005	SCR 1267	Al Haramain	Qde.114 (QE.A.114.04)	Netherlands, Amsterdam District Court	31 March 2005	Stichting Al Haramain Humanitarian Aid, LJN: AT2894	The Court could not conclude that Al Haramain Foundation directly or indirectly supported terrorist organizations. The Court rejected an application by the Public Prosecution Service to ban and dissolve Stichting Al-Haramain Humanitarian Aid.
04/2005	SCR 1267	Nada Management Organization	Delisted on 22 October 2009	Switzerland, Federal Criminal Court in Bellinzona	27 April 2005	See the third report of the Monitoring Team: UN Doc. S/2005/572, Annex II, paras.9–10	The federal criminal court held against the Swiss federal prosecutor's office. It held that the prosecutor either had to bring criminal charges or drop the case.

Year	*Sanction*	*Applicant*	*UN List*	*Court*	*Date*	*Citation*	*Summary*
09/2005	SCR 1267	Kadi	Delisted on 5 October 2012 after Ombuds-person review	EU, Court of First Instance (General Court)	21 September 2005	Case T-315/01, Kadi v Council of the European Union and Commission of the European Communities, ECLI:EU:T:2005:332	The UN Charter's primacy structurally limited the review of UN Security Council resolutions, even indirectly. While indirect review is still possible with respect to *jus cogens*, the restrictive measures did not contravene *jus conges* in this case.
09/2005	SCR 1267	Yusuf Barakaat International Foundation Aden Abdulaziz Ali	Yusuf: Delisted on 24 August 2006 Barakaat: Delisted on 22 October 2009 Aden: Delisted on 26 August 2002 Abdulaziz Ali: Delisted on 26 August 2003	EU, Court of First Instance	21 September 2005	Case T-306/01, Ahmed Ali Yusuf and Al Barakaat International Foundation v Council of the European Union and Commission of the European Communities, ECLI:EU:T:2005:331	The UN Charter's primacy structurally limited the review of UN Security Council resolutions, even indirectly. While indirect review is still possible with respect to *jus cogens*, the restrictive measures did not contravene *jus conges* in this case.

Year	*Sanction*	*Applicant*	*UN List*	*Court*	*Date*	*Citation*	*Summary*
01/2006	SCR 1267	Al Haramain	Qde.114 (QE.A.114.04)	Netherlands, Amsterdam Court of Appeal	5 January 2006	Stichting Al Haramain Humanitarian Aid, NJF 2006/281 See the fourth report of the Monitoring Team: UN Doc. S/2006/154, Annex, paras.8–9	Upheld the decision of the District Court.
07/2006	SCR 1267	Ayadi	Delisted on 17 October 2011 after Ombudsperson review	EU, Court of First Instance	12 July 2006	Case T-253/02, Chafiq Ayadi v Council of the European Union, ECLI:EU:T:2006:200	As the General Court held in *Kadi* (2005), the contested EC regulation did not infringe fundamental rights. States must ensure that delisting requests are presented without delay and fairly and impartially to the UN Sanctions Committee.

Year	*Sanction*	*Applicant*	*UN List*	*Court*	*Date*	*Citation*	*Summary*
07/2006	SCR 1267	Hassan	Delisted on 9 September 2010	EU, Court of First Instance	12 July 2006	Case T-49/04, Faraj Hassan v Council of the European Union and Commission of the European Communities, ECLI:EU:T:2006:201	As the CFI held in *Kadi* (2005), the contested EC regulation did not infringe fundamental rights. States must ensure that delisting requests are presented without delay and fairly and impartially to the UN Sanctions Committee.
07/2006	SCR 1267	Kadi	Delisted on 5 October 2012 after Ombudsperson review	Turkey, Council of State, 10th Division	4 July 2006	Judgment E. 2002/984, K. 2006/4795 See ILDC 311 (TR 2007), paras.F6–7; Fifth report of the Monitoring Team, UN Doc. S/2006/750, Annex III, para.11; Sixth report of the Monitoring Team, UN Doc. S/2007/132, Annex I, para.8	The decree which froze Kadi's assets was annulled. Under the Constitution, fundamental rights may be restricted only by law. This would mean that Kadi's funds and assets could only be frozen by a court decision, and not by an administrative decree.

Year	*Sanction*	*Applicant*	*UN List*	*Court*	*Date*	*Citation*	*Summary*
01/2007	Liberia SCR 1521	Minin	Delisted on 20 June 2012	EU, Court of First Instance	21 January 2007	Case T-362/04, Leonid Minin v Commission of the European Communities, ECLI:EU:T:2007:25	As the CFI held in *Kadi* (2005), the contested EC regulation did not infringe fundamental rights.
02/2007	SCR 1267	Kadi	Delisted on 5 October 2012 after Ombudsperson review	Turkey, Council of State, Board of Administrative Cases	22 February 2007	Kadi v Prime Ministry and Ministry of Foreign Affairs of Turkey, Appeal judgment, E 2006/2824, K 2007/115; ILDC 311 (TR 2007)	The decision of the 10th Division is quashed. The Court could give direct effect to Security Council resolutions by enacting an administrative decree.
05/2007	SCR 1267	Global Relief Foundation	Qde.091 (QE.G.91.02)	US, Federal District Court	31 May 2007	See the seventh report of the Monitoring Team: UN Doc. S/2007/677, Annex I, para.8	Dismissed the claims and concluded that the government had an adequate factual basis to support its decision to impose sanctions on the Global Relief Foundation.
05/2007	SCR 1267	Nada	Delisted on 23 September 2009	Switzerland, Federal Criminal Tribunal in Bellinzona	31 May 2007	See the seventh report of the Monitoring Team: UN Doc. S/2007/677, Annex I, para.5	Awarded Mr. Nada 5,951 Swiss francs, far less than the 27 million he sought.

Year	*Sanction*	*Applicant*	*UN List*	*Court*	*Date*	*Citation*	*Summary*
06/2007	SCR 1267	Ali Ghaleb Himmat	Delisted on 10 August 2009	Switzerland, Federal Criminal Tribunal in Bellinzona	19 June 2007	See the seventh report of the Monitoring Team: UN Doc. S/2007/677, Annex I, para.5	
11/2007	SCR 1267	Nada	Delisted on 23 September 2009	Switzerland, Federal Supreme Court, First Public Law Chamber	14 November 2007	Youssef Nada v State Secretariat for Economic Affairs and Federal Department of Economic Affairs, Administrative appeal judgment, Case No. 1A.45/2007, DTF 133 II 450; ILDC 461 (CH 2007)	By Articles 25 and 103 of the UN Charter, the decisions of the UN Security Council bind member states and prevail over their other obligations. Member states cannot evade their Charter obligations on the basis of the Council's non-conformity to the Charter. An exception is the Council's non-conformity to *jus cogens*. Yet in this case, the procedural deficiencies at the UN did not contradict *jus cogens*.

Year	*Sanction*	*Applicant*	*UN List*	*Court*	*Date*	*Citation*	*Summary*
01/2008	Iraq SCR 1483	A	Added to the list on 26 April 2004	Switzerland, Federal Supreme Court, Second Public Law Chamber	23 January 2008	A v Federal Department of Economic Affairs, Administrative first instance judgment, Case No. 2A.783/2006; ILDC 1200 (CH 2008)	As the Federal Tribunal ruled in *Nada* (2007), the obligations under the UN Charter prevail over those under ECHR and ICCPR. Arts. 6 and 13 of ECHR were not part of *jus cogens.* While the listing procedure is not satisfactory, the delisting is an exclusive competence of the UN sanctions committee.
04/2008	SCR 1267	A, K, M, Q and G	Qdi.228 (QI.A.228.06)	UK, High Court of Justice, Queen's Bench Division	24 April 2008	A, K, M, Q & G v HM Treasury [2008] EWHC 869 (Admin)	The 2006 Al-Qaida and Taliban (United Nations Measures) Order concerning 'G' was *ultra vires* and unlawful.

Year	*Sanction*	*Applicant*	*UN List*	*Court*	*Date*	*Citation*	*Summary*
04/2008	SCR 1267	Ali Ghaleb Himmat	Delisted on 10 August 2009	Switzerland, Federal Supreme Court, First Public Law Chamber	22 April 2008	A v State Secretariat for Economic Affairs and Federal Department of Economic Affairs, Administrative first instance judgment, No 1A48/2007; ILDC 1201 (CH 2008)	As the Federal Tribunal decided in *Nada* (Case 1A.45/2007, on 14 November 2007), the fundamental rights and procedural guarantees invoked by 'A' were not part of *jus cognes*. Switzerland is bound by Council resolutions, and does not enjoy a margin of appreciation with respect to the designation.
04/2008	SCR 1267	al-Aqeel	Delisted on 2 January 2015 after Ombudsperson review	US, District Court of the District of Columbia	4 August 2008	Aqeel Abdulaziz Al-Aqeel v Paulson, 568 F.Supp.2d 64 (Civil Action No. 05–943 (GK)).	The notification of terrorist designation via press release did not violate due process. The government did not violate Al-Aqeel's rights by failing to provide privileged portions of administrative records in connection with his challenge to the designation. The Saudi Arabian citizen was not entitled to obtain those privileged materials.

Year	*Sanction*	*Applicant*	*UN List*	*Court*	*Date*	*Citation*	*Summary*
04/2008	SCR 1267	M and Others		UK, House of Lords	30 April 2008 (Report)	R (on the application of M) v Her Majesty's Treasury and two other actions [2008] UKHL 26; ILDC 1539 (UK 2008).	The question on the interpretation of Council Regulation (EC) 881/2002 was referred to the European Court of Justice. It is difficult to see how household expenses could fund terrorism.
04/2008	SCR 1267	Othman (Abu Qatada)	Qdi.031 (QI. M.31.01)	UK, Court of Appeal	9 April 2008	OO (Jordan) v Secretary of State for the Home Department [2008] EWCA Civ 290.	ECHR Arts. 3 should be assessed separately from Art. 6 in determining the human rights compatibility of extradition.

Year	*Sanction*	*Applicant*	*UN List*	*Court*	*Date*	*Citation*	*Summary*
09/2008	SCR 1267	Kadi Al Barakaat International Foundation	Delisted on 5 October 2012 after Ombudsperson review Barakaat was delisted on 22 October 2009	EU, Court of Justice	3 September 2008	Joined Cases C-402/05 P and C-415/05 P, Kadi and Al Barakaat International Foundation v Council of the European Union and Commission of the European Communities, ECLI:EU:C:2008:461	In the autonomous European Community legal system based on the rule of law, the court must ensure in principle the full review of Community measures in the light of fundamental rights as the expression of a constitutional guarantee. The contested regulation infringed upon the right to be heard, the right to an effective legal remedy, and the right to property.
10/2008	SCR 1267	A, K, M, Q and G	Qdi.228 (QI. A.228.06)	UK, Court of Appeal	30 October 2008	A and Others v HM Treasury [2008] EWCA Civ 1187	The Al-Qaida Order was lawful. 'G' was entitled to seek judicial review of the merits of his designation.

Year	*Sanction*	*Applicant*	*UN List*	*Court*	*Date*	*Citation*	*Summary*
11/2008	SCR 1267	Al Haramain Foundation	Delisted on 25 October 2014 after Ombudsperson review	US, District Court for Oregon	6 November 2008	Al Haramain Islamic Foundation, Inc. and Multicultural Association of Southern Oregon v United States, Civil No. 07–1155–KI	The terrorist designation of the charity is supported by substantial evidence. The notice was, however, insufficient, and the term was vague.
12/2008	SCR 1267	Sayadi and Vinck	Both delisted on 20 July 2009	Human Rights Committee, ICCPR	29 December 2008	Nabil Sayadi and Patricia Vinck v Belgium, UN Doc. CCPR/C/94/D/1472/2006	There has been a violation of Articles 12 and 17 of the ICCPR by Belgium. The Committee found unjustified the way that Belgium initially transmitted complainants' names to the Sanction Committee.
02/2009	SCR 1267	Othman (Abu Qatada)	Qdi.031 (QI. M.31.01)	UK, House of Lords	18 February 2009	RB (Algeria) v Secretary of State for the Home Department; OO (Jordan) v Secretary of State for the Home Department [2009] UKHL 10	Special Immigration Appeals Commission (SIAC) did not err in law. The case of Othman did not meet the test regarding Article 6 of the ECHR, which requires a real risk of a fundamental breach of fair trial and of a flagrant violation of his fundamental rights.

Year	*Sanction*	*Applicant*	*UN List*	*Court*	*Date*	*Citation*	*Summary*
06/2009	SCR 1267	Abdelrazik	Delisted on 30 November 2011 after Ombudsperson review	Canada, Federal Court	4 June 2009	Abousfian Abdelrazik v The Minister of Foreign Affairs and the Attorney General of Canada, 2009 FC 580; ILDC 1332 (CA 2009)	The rejection of the applicant's travelling documents breached his right to enter Canada.
06/2009	SCR 1267	Othman (Abu Qatada)	Qdi.031 (QI. M.31.01)	EU, Court of First Instance	11 June 2009 (Action brought on 17 December 2001, *OJ* C68/13)	Case T-318/01, Omar Mohammed Othman v Council of the European Union and Commission of the European Communities, ECLI: EU:T:2009:187	Following *Kadi* (ECJ 2008), Council Regulation (EC) 881/2002 is annulled. It infringes upon the rights of defence, the right to effective judicial review, and the right to property.
07/2009	SCR 1267	Hay	Qdi.198 (QI.A.198.05)	UK, High Court of Justice, Queen's Bench Division, Administrative Court	10 July 2009	Hay and HM Treasury and Secretary of State for Foreign and Commonwealth Affairs [2009] EWHC 1677 (Admin); ILDC 1367 (UK 2009)	The Al-Qaida Order was *ultra vires*. The Order effectively precludes the right of access to a court. The United Nations Act 1946 neither expressly nor by necessary implication permits the removal of the right of access to the courts.

Year	*Sanction*	*Applicant*	*UN List*	*Court*	*Date*	*Citation*	*Summary*
07/2009	Iran SCR 1737	Melli Bank	Bank Melli and its branches and subsidiaries Based on SCR 1803 (2008), para.10, which *calls upon* states to exercise vigilance. Terminated in July 2015	EU, Court of First Instance	9 July 2009	Joined Cases T-246/08 and T-332/08, Melli Bank plc v Council of the European Union, ECLI:EU:T:2009:266	The restrictive measures are consistent with the principle of proportionality. The applicant is classified as an entity 'owned or controlled' under Article 7(2)(d) of Regulation No. 423/2007.
10/2009	Iran SCR 1737	Melli Bank Iran	Based on SCR 1803 (2008), para.10, which *calls upon* states to exercise vigilance Terminated in July 2015	EU, Court of First Instance	14 October 2009	Case T-390/08, Bank Melli Iran v Council, ECLI:EU:T:2009:401	Regulation 423/2007 has a sufficient legal basis. The duty to state reasons was satisfied.
11/2009	SCR 1267	Al Haramain Foundation	Delisted on 25 October 2014 after Ombudsperson review	US, District Court for Oregon	5 November 2009	Al Haramain Islamic Foundation Inc. and Multicultural Association of Southern Oregon v United States, Civil No. 07–1155–KI, 2009 WL 3756363	Due process violation was harmless and therefore judicial relief is not granted.

Year	*Sanction*	*Applicant*	*UN List*	*Court*	*Date*	*Citation*	*Summary*
12/2009	SCR 1267	Hassan Ayadi	Hassan: Delisted on 9 September 2010 Ayadi: Delisted on 17 October 2011 after Ombudsperson review	EU, Court of Justice	3 December 2009	Joined Cases C-399/06 P and C-403/06 P, Faraj Hassan and Chafiq Ayadi v Council of the European Union and European Commission, ECLI:EU:C:2009:748	As the ECJ held in *Kadi* (2008), the contested EC regulation infringes upon fundamental rights.
01/2010	SCR 1267	Ahmed & Others (A, K, M and G and HAY)	Qdi.198 (QI.A.198.05) Qdi.228 (QI.A.228.06)	UK, Supreme Court	27 January 2010	HM Treasury v Mohammed Jabar Ahmed and Others; HM Treasury v Mohammed al-Ghabra; R (Hari El Sayed Sabaei Youssef) v HM Treasury [2010] UKSC 2; ILDC 1534 (UK 2010)	Article 3(1)(b) of the Al-Qaida Order is *ultra vires*. The Order gives effect to the sanctions regime which had no provision for basic procedural fairness, and deprived those designated of access to an effective remedy.
02/2010	SCR 1267	Ahmed & Others (A, K, M and G and HAY)	Qdi.198 (QI.A.198.05) Qdi.228 (QI.A.228.06)	UK, Supreme Court	4 February 2010	HM Treasury v Mohammed Jabar Ahmed and Others; HM Treasury v Mohammed al-Ghabra; R (Hari El Sayed Sabaei Youssef) v HM Treasury (No. 2) [2010] UKSC 5	The order rendered in the 27 January 2010 judgment will not be suspended.

Year	*Sanction*	*Applicant*	*UN List*	*Court*	*Date*	*Citation*	*Summary*
04/2010	SCR 1267	M and Others		EU, Court of Justice	29 April 2010	Case C-340/08, M and Others v Her Majesty's Treasury [2010] I-03913, ECLI:EU: C:2010:232	Article 2(2) of Council Regulation (EC) 881/2002 does not apply to the provision of social security or social assistance benefits to the spouse of a designated person.
06/2010	SCR 1267	Abdelrazik	Delisted on 30 November 2011 after Ombudsperson review	Canada, Federal Court	7 June 2010 (Filing)	Abdelrazik et al v Attorney-General of Canada (T-889–10)	Abdelrazik challenged the implementation of the sanctions against him as *ultra vires*, in violation of the rights of association and of liberty and security. After delisting, Abdelrazik dropped his constitutional claims.

Year	*Sanction*	*Applicant*	*UN List*	*Court*	*Date*	*Citation*	*Summary*
09/2010	SCR 1267	Al-Faqih Sanabel Relief Agency Abdrabbah Nasuf	Al-Faqih, Abdrabbah, and Nasuf: Delisted on 22 June 2011 Sanabel Relief Agency: Delisted on 8 October 2013	EU, General Court	29 September 2010	Joined Cases T-135/06 to T-138/06, Al-Faqih v Council, ECLI:EU:T:2010:412 (Case T-136/06, Sanabel Relief Agency v Council; Case T-137/06, Abdrabbah v Council; Case T-138/06, Nasuf v Council)	The rights of the defence, the right to judicial review and the right to property had not been respected. Regulation (EC) No 881/2002 is annulled in part.
09/2010	SCR 1267	Kadi	Delisted on 5 October 2012 after Ombudsperson review	EU, General Court	30 September 2010	Case T-85/09, Kadi v European Commission and Council of the European Union, Judgment of 30 September 2010, ECLI:EU:T:2010:418	Following *Kadi* (ECJ 2008), the court must ensure in principle the full review of EU measures in the light of fundamental rights. The contested regulation infringed upon the rights of defence, the right to effective judicial review, and the right to property.
01/2011	SCR 1267	Hassan	Delisted on 9 September 2010	EU, General Court	30 January 2011 (Order)	Case T-4/10, Order of the General Court of 30 June 2011, Al Saadi v Commission	The applicant is deceased. No further adjudication is necessary.

Year	*Sanction*	*Applicant*	*UN List*	*Court*	*Date*	*Citation*	*Summary*
09/2011	SCR 1267	Al Haramain Foundation	Delisted on 25 October 2014 after Ombudsperson review	US, Court of Appeals for the Ninth Circuit	23 September 2011 (Amended 27 February 2012)	Al Haramain Islamic Foundation, Inc. v U.S. Dept. of Treasury, No. 10–35032	While the Treasury violated due process rights of the designated corporation, procedural due process were harmless and therefore judicial relief is not granted. The Treasury's failure to obtain a judicial warrant violated the Fourth Amendment.
09/2011	SCR 1267	Elosta	Delisted on 22 December 2010	EU, General Court	1 September 2011 (Order)	Case T-102/09, Elosta v Commission, ECLI:EU:T:2011:412	The action was dismissed as being inadmissible.
09/2011	SCR 1267	Maftah Mohamed Elmabruk	Delisted on 22 December 2010	EU, General Court	1 September 2011 (Order)	Case T-101/09, Elmabruk Maftah v European Commission, ECLI:EU:T:2011:411	The action is dismissed as inadmissible.

Year	*Sanction*	*Applicant*	*UN List*	*Court*	*Date*	*Citation*	*Summary*
11/2011	Iran SCR 1737	Melli Bank Iran	Based on SCR 1803 (2008), para.10, which *calls upon* states to exercise vigilance Terminated in July 2015	EU, Court of Justice (Grand Chamber)	16 November 2011	Case C-548/09 P, Bank Melli Iran v Council of the European Union [2012] OJ C25/6	As the CFI rightly decided, Regulation 423/2007 has a sufficient legal basis. The duty to state reasons was satisfied. Security Council resolutions and EU law are distinct legal orders.
–	SCR 1267	Hafiz Saeed	Qdi.263 (QI. S.263.08)	Pakistan	–	See the eleventh report of the Monitoring Team: UN Doc. S/2011/245, Annex, para.8	The Supreme Court quashed the Punjab government's restrictive measures taken under the maintenance of public order act owing to 'insufficient evidence'.
01/2012	SCR 1267	Ayadi	Delisted on 17 October 2011 after Ombudsperson review	EU, General Court	31 January 2012 (Order)	Case T-527/09, Order of the General Court of 31 January 2012, Ayadi v Commission	There is no longer any need to adjudicate on the action.
01/2012	SCR 1267	Othman (Abu Qatada)	Qdi.031 (QI. M.31.01)	ECtHR	17 January 2012	Othman v United Kingdom (App no 8139/09) (2012) 55 E.H.R.R. 1	The deportation of the applicant would violate Art. 6 of ECHR. He demonstrated a real risk of a flagrant denial of justice contrary to Art. 6.

Year	*Sanction*	*Applicant*	*UN List*	*Court*	*Date*	*Citation*	*Summary*
02/2012	SCR 1267	Abdulrahim	Delisted on 22 December 2010	EU, General Court	28 February 2012 (Order)	Case T-127/09, Abdulrahim v Council and Commission	The action was dismissed. The adjudication is no longer necessary.
03/2012	SCR 1267	Kadi (US)	Delisted on 5 October 2012 after Ombudsperson review	US, District Court, District of Columbia	19 March 2012	Yassin Abdullah Kadi v Timothy Geithner, et al., Civil Action No. 09–108(JDB), 2012 WL 898778 (D.D.C.)	Kadi's designation is supported by substantial evidence. The decision to freeze assets did not violate Kadi's due process rights or freedom of speech.
03/2012	Iran SCR 1737	Melli Bank	Based on SCR 1803 (2008), para.10, which *calls upon* states to exercise vigilance Terminated in July 2015	EU, Court of Justice (Grand Chamber)	13 March 2012	Case C-380/09 P, Melli Bank plc v Council of the European Union, ECLI:EU: C:2012:137	As the General Court rightly decided, the measures are consistent with the principle of proportionality. The applicant is owned by Bank Melli Iran and to apply the restrictive measures on that basis does not affect the presumption of innocence.

Year	*Sanction*	*Applicant*	*UN List*	*Court*	*Date*	*Citation*	*Summary*
09/2012	SCR 1267	Nada	Delisted on 23 September 2009	ECtHR, Grand Chamber	12 September 2012	App no 10593/08, Nada v Switzerland	Switzerland violated Arts. 8 (right to privacy) and 13 (effective remedy) of the ECHR. Switzerland had the latitude to harmonise its international obligations under Security Council resolutions and its human rights obligations under the ECHR.
03/2013	Iran SCR 1737	Bank Saderat Iran	Based on SCR 1803 (2008), para.10, which *calls upon* states to exercise vigilance Terminated in July 2015	EU, General Court	5 February 2013	Case T-494/10, Bank Saderat Iran v Council of the European Union ECLI:EU: T:2013:59	The Council of the EU produced no evidence or information with regard to one of the reasons. The Court thereby annulled the restrictive measures.
05/2013	SCR 1267	Al-Faqih MIRA	Both delisted on 2 July 2012 after Ombudsperson review	EU, General Court	15 May 2013	Case T-322/09, Al-Faqih and MIRA v Council and Commission, Order of the General Court, ECLI:EU: T:2013:244	The subject-matter of the dispute has disappeared as a result of the deletion of the applicants' names. There is no need to adjudicate on the action.

Year	*Sanction*	*Applicant*	*UN List*	*Court*	*Date*	*Citation*	*Summary*
05/2013	SCR 1267	Abdulbasit Abdulrahim	Delisted	EU, Court of Justice	28 May 2013	Case C-239/12 P, Abdulbasit Abdulrahim v Council and Commission, ECLI: EU:C:2013:331	The order of the General Court (Case T-127/09), which discontinued Mr Abdulrahim's action, is set aside.
06/2013	SCR 1267	Ayadi	Delisted on 17 October 2011 after Ombudsperson review	EU, Court of Justice	6 June 2013	Case C-183/12 P, Chafiq Ayadi v Commission, ECLI: EU:C:2013:369	The order of the General Court (Case T-527/09), which discontinued Mr Ayadi's action, is set aside.
07/2013	SCR 1267	Kadi	Delisted on 5 October 2012 after Ombudsperson review	EU, Court of Justice	18 July 2013	Joined cases C-584/10 P, C-593/10 P and C-595/10 P Kadi v European Commission, ECLI: EU:C:2013:518	The Court of Justice intensified the level of 'full review'. The Court of Justice found that information or evidence which might have substantiated the reason for listing was absent. The Court thereby annulled the contested EU regulation.

Year	*Sanction*	*Applicant*	*UN List*	*Court*	*Date*	*Citation*	*Summary*
09/2013	Iran SCR 1737	Bank Melli Iran	Based on SCR 1803 (2008), para.10, which *calls upon* states to exercise vigilance Terminated in July 2015	EU, General Court	6 September 2013	Joined Cases T-35/10 and T-7/11, Bank Melli Iran v Council, ECLI:EU:T:2013:397	The reasons set out in the contested measures are sufficiently detailed. The applicant supported nuclear proliferation by making payments on behalf of the Atomic Energy Organisation of Iran (AEOI). This justifies the restrictive measures.
11/2013	Iraq SCR 1518	Al-Dulimi Montana Management Inc.		ECtHR, Second Section	26 November 2013	App no 5809/08, Al-Dulimi and Montana Management Inc. v Switzerland	The very essence of the right of access to a court was impaired due to the lack of effective and independent judicial review at the UN and domestic levels for a considerable period of time.
03/2014	SCR 1267	Yusif	Qdi.198 (QI.A.198.05)	EU, General Court	21 March 2014	Case T-306/10, Hani El Sayyed Elsebai Yusef v Commission, ECLI:EU:T:2014:141	The Commission failed to fulfil its obligations by delaying the careful and impartial review of the findings of the UN's Sanctions Committee.

Year	*Sanction*	*Applicant*	*UN List*	*Court*	*Date*	*Citation*	*Summary*
01/2015	SCR 1267	Abdulbasit Abdulrahim	Delisted	EU, General Court	14 January 2015	Case T-127/09 RENV, Abdulbasit Abdulrahim v Council and Commission, ECLI:EU:T:2015:4	The reasons are insufficient or information with which to substantiate them is absent. None of the allegations was such as to justify the adoption of restrictive measures. The relevant EU regulation is annulled.
04/2015	SCR 1267	Ayadi	Delisted on 17 October 2011 after Ombudsperson review	EU, General Court	14 April 2015	Case T-527/09 RENV Chafiq Ayadi v European Commission ECLI:EU: T:2015:205	The reasons are insufficient or information with which to substantiate them is absent. None of the allegations was such as to justify the adoption of restrictive measures. The relevant EU regulation is annulled.
10/2015	SCR 1267	Al-Faqih Sanabel Relief Agency Abdrabbah Nasuf	Al-Faqih, Abdrabbah, and Nasuf: Delisted on 22 June 2011 Sanabel Relief Agency: Delisted on 8 October 2013	EU, General Court	28 October 2015	Case T-134/11 Al-Bashir Mohammed Al-Faqih and Others v European Commission, ECLI:EU: T:2015:812	The Commission respected the procedural guarantees referred in *Kadi II* (CJEU). The Commission carried out a careful, independent, and critical review of the listing. The reasons were also based on additional detailed information. The action is dismissed.

Year	*Sanction*	*Applicant*	*UN List*	*Court*	*Date*	*Citation*	*Summary*
01/2016	Al-Qaida SCR 1267	Yusif	QDi.198 (QI.A.198.05)	UK, Supreme Court	27 January 2016	Youssef v Secretary of State for Foreign and Commonwealth Affairs [2016] UKSC 3	The government is not obliged to inquire into the use of torture-tainted evidence by other states. Designation has a preventive purpose, involving risk assessment, and the claim that the standard of proof of 'reasonable ground for suspicion' is too low is rejected. A full 'merits review' of the governmental decision is not applicable.
04/2016	Iran SCR 1737	Bank Saderat Iran	Based on SCR 1803 (2008), para.10, which *calls upon* states to exercise vigilance Terminated in July 2015	EU, Court of Justice	21 April 2016	Case C-200/13 P, Council of the European Union v Bank Saderat Iran ECLI:EU: C:2016:284	The Court of Justice upheld the findings of the General Court (Case T-494/ 10). The appeal was dismissed.

Year	*Sanction*	*Applicant*	*UN List*	*Court*	*Date*	*Citation*	*Summary*
06/2016	Iraq SCR 1483	Al-Dulimi Montana Management Inc.		ECtHR, Grand Chamber	21 June 2016	App no 5809/08 Al-Dulimi and Montana Management Inc v Switzerland	SC Resolution 1483 does not contain any clear or explicit wording excluding the possibility of judicial supervision by member states. The resolution thus authorised domestic courts to exercise sufficient scrutiny. The Swiss authorities violated Article 6(1) of the ECHR.
12/2016	SCR 1267	Mohammed al-Ghabra	QDi.228 (QI. A.228.06)	EU, General Court	13 December 2016	Case T-248/13, Al-Ghabra v Commission	The length of the review process was in breach of the 'reasonable time' principle, but the breach does not justify the annulment of the contested decision. Other pleas were rejected as unfounded.
Pending	Al-Qaida SCR 1267	Al-Akhtar Trust	QDe.121 (QE.A.121.05)	Pakistan, High Court of Sindh		See the eighteenth report of the Monitoring Team: UN Doc. S/2016/629, Annex, para.5	
Pending	Al-Qaida SCR 1267	Al-Rashid Trust	QDe.005 (QE.A.5.01)	Pakistan, Supreme Court		See the eighteenth report of the Monitoring Team: UN Doc. S/2016/629, Annex, para.5	An appeal from a 2003 decision.

Sources: (i) 2nd to 18th reports of the Monitoring Team for the 1267 Sanctions Committee; (ii) Thomas Biersteker and Sue Eckhert (eds), *Addressing Challenges to Targeted Sanctions: An Update of the 'Watson Report'* (October 2009) at 49–57; (iii) Oxford Reports on International Law in Domestic Courts (ILDC); and (iv) own research.

Annex II The procedural development of the 1267 Sanctions Committee

[as of 23 December 2016]

Date	*General quality of the List*	*Communication with Member States*	*Humanitarian exemptions*	*Procedural Safeguards for the Targets* *(i) Periodical review / (ii) Right to be informed* *(iii) Right to be heard / (iv) Right to review*
02/2000	Introduced the first Guidelines (Press Release SC/6802)		Approved exemptions on flight ban for the Hajj (Press Release SC/6802)	
12/2000	SCR 1333 (para.15(a)) introduced the Committee of Experts		SCR 1333 (para.12) introduced further humanitarian aid exemptions for flight ban SCR 1333 (para.15(b)) requested SG to review the humanitarian implications of the measures (UN Doc. S/2001/241, S/2001/695, S/2001/1215)	
01/2001			Approved the list of humanitarian relief providers (Press Release SC/6994)	
02/2001			Approved procedures to add humanitarian relief providers (Press Release SC/7012)	
03/2001			SG reported on humanitarian implications (S/2001/241)	
06/2001	SCR 1363 introduced the Monitoring Group	SCR 1363 introduced the Monitoring Group	SG reported on humanitarian implications (S/2001/695)	
12/2001			SG reported on humanitarian implications (S/2001/1215)	

Date	*General quality of the List*	*Communication with Member States*	*Humanitarian exemptions*	*Procedural Safeguards for the Targets* *(i) Periodical review / (ii) Right to be informed* *(iii) Right to be heard / (iv) Right to review*
01/2002	SCR 1390 (para.5(d)) requested the Committee to promulgate guidelines to facilitate the implementation			
08/2002				(iii) Announced delisting procedures (Press Release AFG/203-SC/7487) Removed Aden and five other individuals and entities (Press Release SC/7490)
11/2002	Approved new Guidelines, listing up the basic identifying information to be included, to the extent possible, in the proposed listing (para.5(c)) (Press Release SC/7571)			(iii) Approved new Guidelines, adopting delisting procedures (para.6) (Press Release SC/7571)
12/2002			SCR 1452 developed mechanisms for exemptions for freezing assets	
01/2003		SCR 1455 (para.4) requested the Committee to communicate to states the list at least every three months		
02/2003		Convened open briefing by the Chairman of the Committee (S/2004/281, para.21)		
04/2003	Revised Guidelines, adding new section on reviewing information (Press Release SC/7731)			(i) Revised Guidelines, adding new section on reviewing information (Press Release SC/7731)

Date	*General quality of the List*	*Communication with Member States*	*Humanitarian exemptions*	*Procedural Safeguards for the Targets* *(i) Periodical review / (ii) Right to be informed* *(iii) Right to be heard / (iv) Right to review*
12/2003		Invited member states to comment on report of Monitoring Group (Press Release SC/7948)		
01/2004	SCR 1526 (para.6) introduced the Monitoring Team SCR 1526 (para.17) 'calls upon' states to include identifying information and background information to the greatest extent possible	SCR 1526 (para.6) introduced the Monitoring Team SCR 1526 (para.11) provided states with discussion opportunities with Committee (followed by Press Release SC/8208 (October 2004))		(ii) SCR 1526 (para.18) 'strongly encourages' states to inform individuals of the measures, guidelines and exemptions
07/2005	SCR 1617 (para.2) defined those 'associated with' SCR 1617 (para.4) 'decides' states shall act in accordance with para.17 of SCR 1526, and shall provide a statement of case	SCR 1617 (para.6) decided that the statement of case 'may be used by the Committee in responding to queries from Member States whose nationals, residents or entities have been included'		(ii) SCR 1617 (para.5) 'requests' states to inform individuals of the measures, listing/delisting procedures and exemptions
12/2005	Revised Guidelines, extending the time for considering listing submissions from two business days to five (Press Release SC/8602)			

Date	*General quality of the List*	*Communication with Member States*	*Humanitarian exemptions*	*Procedural Safeguards for the Targets* *(i) Periodical review / (ii) Right to be informed* *(iii) Right to be heard / (iv) Right to review*
04/2006	Introduced the procedures for the removal of deceased individuals (Note Verbale SCA/2/06(8))			
07/2006	Introduction of a standard 'cover sheet' for listing proposals, with more details for identifying information and statements of case	Convened open briefing by the Chairman of the Committee, attended by 50 representatives (S/200759, para.12)		
11/2006	Revised Guidelines, attaching the 'cover sheet'	Revised Guidelines, introducing the provision of feedback to the designating state (para.6(f))		(i) Revised Guidelines, introducing annual review of listings left un-updated for more than four years upon request of a Committee member (para.6(i)) (ii) Revised Guidelines, introducing the procedure to remind states of residence/citizenship to inform individuals (para.6(h))
12/2006		SCR 1735 (para.29) 'strongly encourages' to 'send representatives to meet the Committee' (c. f., SCR 1526, para.11 and SCR 1617, para.14)	SCR 1735 (para.15) extended the period for consideration of notifications of humanitarian exemptions from 48 hours to 3 working days	(ii) SCR 1735 (para.11) 'calls upon' states of location/nationality to notify individuals of 'the publicly releasable portion of statement of case, a description of the effects of designation' delisting procedures and exemptions (iii) SCR 1730 introduced focal point of delisting
02/2007	Updated Guidelines following SCR 1730 and 1735			

Date	*General quality of the List*	*Communication with Member States*	*Humanitarian exemptions*	*Procedural Safeguards for the Targets* *(i) Periodical review / (ii) Right to be informed* *(iii) Right to be heard / (iv) Right to review*
06/2008	SCR 1822 (para.12) reaffirms that states shall provide a 'detailed' statement of case (cf., SCR 1617, para.4, and SCR 1735, para.5)			(i) SCR 1822 (para.25) initiated a comprehensive review of the List. SCR 1822 (para.26) revised annual review to be applicable to listings left un-reviewed more than three years ('the triennial review') (ii) SCR 1822 (para.17) 'demands' states to inform individuals. SCR 1822 (para.12) decides states to identify publicly releasable information when they propose names, and (para.13) directed the Committee to make a narrative summary of reasons for listing accessible on the website
12/2008	Updated Guidelines following SCR 1822			
12/2009	SCR 1904 (para.13) introduced a new standard form for listing		SCR 1904 (para.7) directs the Committee to review the procedures for humanitarian exemptions	(i) SCR 1904 introduced the review every six months of those reportedly deceased (para.26), the annual review of listings which lack necessary identifiers (para.31), and the annual review of all names which have not been reviewed in three or more years (para.32) (ii) SCR 1904 (para.11) treats statement of case as releasable unless otherwise indicated (iii) & (iv) SCR 1904 (para.20) established the Office of Ombudsperson
07/2010	Updated Guidelines following SCR 1904 The listing requests will be considered within 10 days (Sect.6.(h))			(ii) Listed the items included in the narrative summary (Sect.9(d))

Date	*General quality of the List*	*Communication with Member States*	*Humanitarian exemptions*	*Procedural Safeguards for the Targets* *(i) Periodical review / (ii) Right to be informed* *(iii) Right to be heard / (iv) Right to review*
01/2011				(i) The Committee considers any official communication from a state on the deceased individuals (Sect.7(i)) (iii) & (iv) Attached the annex II of SCR 1904 regarding the Ombudsperson procedure
06/2011				(i) SCR 1989 (para.37) introduced the review every six months of listings which lack necessary identifiers (cf. SCR 1904, para.31) (ii) SCR 1989 (para.14) strongly encourages designating states to make their identity known, and (para.29) strongly urges designating states to allow the Ombudsperson to reveal their designating states' status to petitioners SCR 1989 (para.16(b) of Annex II) also mandated the Ombudsperson to notify individuals or entities about their listing (iii) & (iv) SCR 1989 (para.21) instructed the Ombudsperson to make a recommendation on the delisting The Committee is required to set out the 'reasons' for the delisting decision (Annex II, para.13); cf. SCR 1904, Annex II, para.12 ('as appropriate, explanatory comments')
08/2011				(iii) & (iv) The Ombudsperson posted the standard for its analysis: 'whether there is sufficient information to provide a reasonable and credible basis for the listing' ('Approach to and Standard for Analysis, Observations, Principal Arguments and Recommendation')

Date	*General quality of the List*	*Communication with Member States*	*Humanitarian exemptions*	*Procedural Safeguards for the Targets* *(i) Periodical review / (ii) Right to be informed* *(iii) Right to be heard / (iv) Right to review*
11/2011	Updated Guidelines following SCR 1989			
12/2012			SCR 2083 (para.37) allowed listed individuals and entities to submit a request for exemption to the Committee through the focal point mechanism established by SCR 1730	(ii) SCR 2083 (para.12) reserved the assumption about the disclosure of designating states; designating states need to specify if the Committee or the Ombudsperson may *not* make known their status (cf SCR 1989, para.14)
04/2013	Updated Guidelines			
06/2014	SCR 2161 (para.39) requested the Secretary-General to make all list entries and narrative summaries available in all UN official languages			(iii) SCR 2161 (para.63) allowed delisted individuals and other individuals subject to the restrictive measures due to mistaken identification or confusion to communicate to the Focal Point
12/2015				(i) SCR 2253 (para.80) compiled review mechanisms into the annual review process, with respect to the listings which lack necessary identifiers (cf. SCR 1989, para.37), those reportedly deceased (cf. SCR 1904, para.26), and the triennial review.
12/2016	Updated Guidelines in light of SCR 2253 concerning ISIL			

Bibliography

Abbott, D.W., 'The United Nations and Intrastate Conflict: A Legislative History of Article 39 of the United Nations Charter' (2002) 8 *U.C. Davis Journal of International Law & Policy* 275.

Akande, D., 'International Organizations' in M.D. Evans (ed.), *International Law* (Oxford, Oxford University Press, 2014) 248.

Akande, D., 'The International Court of Justice and the Security Council: Is there Room for Judicial Control of Decisions of the Political Organs of the United Nations?' (1997) 46 *International and Comparative Law Quarterly* 309.

Åkermark, A.S., *Justifications of Minority Protection in International Law* (London, Kluwer Law International, 1997).

Alvarez, J.E., 'Judging the Security Council' (1996) 90 *The American Journal of International Law* 1.

Alvarez, J.E., 'The Security Council's War on Terrorism: Problems and Policy Options' in E. De Wet and A. Nollkaemper (eds), *Review of the Security Council by Member States* (Antwerp; New York, Intersentia, 2003) 119.

Alvarez, J.E., *International Organizations as Law-Makers* (Oxford, Oxford University Press, 2005).

Amerasinghe, C.F., 'Liability to Third Parties of Member States of International Organizations: Practice, Principle and Judicial Precedent' (1991) 85 *American Journal of International Law* 259.

Angelet, N., 'Protest Against Security Council Decisions' in K. Wellens (ed.), *International Law: Theory and Practice, Essays in Honour of Eric Suy* (The Hague, Martinus Nijhoff Publishers, 1998) 277.

Arcari, M., 'Forgetting Article 103 of the UN Charter? Some Perplexities on "Equivalent Protection" after Al-Dulimi' (2014) 6 *QIL QDI* 31.

Asada, M., 'Security Council Resolution 1540 to Combat WMD Terrorism: Effectiveness and Legitimacy in International Legislation' (2008) 13 *Journal of Conflict & Security Law* 303.

Bailey, S.D., *The UN Security Council and Human Rights* (New York, St. Martin's Press, 1994).

Barnett, M. & M. Finnemore, 'Political Approaches' in T.G. Weiss and S. Daws (eds), *The Oxford Handbook on the United Nations* (Oxford, Oxford University Press, 2007) 41.

Bedjaoui, M., *The New World Order and the Security Council: Testing the Legality of its Acts* (Dordrecht; Boston, Martinus Nijhoff Publishers, 1994).

Benzing, M., 'Midwifing a New State: The United Nations in East Timor' (2005) 9 *Max Planck Yearbook of United Nations Law* 295.

Biersteker, T. & S. Eckhert, *Addressing Challenges to Targeted Sanctions: An Update of the 'Watson Report'* (Watson Institute for International Studies, 2009).

Blokker, N., 'Is the Authorization Authorized? Powers and Practice of the UN Security Council to Authorize the Use of Force by "Coalitions of the Able and Willing"' (2000) 11 *European Journal of International Law* 541.

Blokker, N.M. & H.G. Schermers, *International Institutional Law: Unity within Diversity* (5th revised edn, Boston, Martinus Nijhoff Publishers, 2011).

Boon, K.E., 'The United Nations as Good Samaritan: Immunity and Responsibility' (2016) 16 *Chicago Journal of International Law* 341.

Bowett, D.W., *United Nations Forces: A Legal Study of United Nations Practice* (London, Stevens & Sons, 1964).

Brockelbank, W.J., 'The Vilna Dispute' (1926) 20 *The American Journal of International Law* 483.

Brownlie, I., *International Law and the Use of Force by States* (Oxford, Clarendon Press, 1963).

Bühler, K.G., 'The Austrian Rule of Law Initiative 2004–2008: The Panel Series, the Advisory Group and the Final Report on the UN Security Council and the Rule of Law' (2008) 12 *Max Planck Yearbook of United Nations Law* 410.

Bulterman, M., 'Fundamental Rights and the United Nations Financial Sanction Regime: The *Kadi* and *Yusuf* Judgments of the Court of First Instance of the European Communities' (2006) 19 *Leiden Journal of International Law* 753.

Burca, G.D., 'The EU, the European Court of Justice and the International Legal Order after *Kadi*' (2010) 51 *Harvard International Law Journal* 1.

Burci, G.L., 'Interpreting the Humanitarian Exceptions through the Sanctions Committees' in V. Gowlland-Debbas (ed.), *United Nations Sanctions and International Law* (The Hague, Kluwer Law International, 2001) 143.

Byers, M., *Custom, Power and the Power of Rules: International Relations and Customary International Law* (Cambridge, Cambridge University Press, 1999).

Cameron, I., 'UN Targeted Sanctions, Legal Safeguards and the European Convention on Human Rights' (2003) 72 *Nordic Journal of International Law* 159.

Cardwell, P.J., D. French & N. White, 'European Court of Justice, *Yassin Abdullah Kadi and Al Barakaat International Foundation v Council and Commission* (Joined Cases C-402/05 P and C-415/05 P) Judgment of 3 September 2008' (2009) 58 *International & Comparative Law Quarterly* 229.

Cerone, J., 'Minding the Gap: Outlining KFOR Accountability in Post-Conflict Kosovo' (2001) 12 *European Journal of International Law* 469.

Chesterman, S., 'An International Rule of Law?' (2008) 56 *American Journal of Comparative Law* 331.

Chesterman, S., *Just War or Just Peace? Humanitarian Intervention and International Law* (Oxford, Oxford University Press, 2001).

Chesterman, S., *You, The People: The United Nations, Transitional Administration, and State-Building* (Oxford, Oxford University Press, 2004).

Ciobanu, D., 'Litispendence Between the International Court of Justice and the Political Organs of the United Nations' in L. Gross (ed.), *The Future of the International Court of Justice* (Dobbs Ferry, NY, Oceana Publications, 1976) 209.

Clapham, A., *Human Rights Obligations of Non-State Actors* (Oxford, Oxford University Press, 2006).

Combacau, J., *Le pouvoir de sanction de l'O.N.U.: Étude théorique de la coercition non militaire* (Paris, A. Pedone, 1974).

Conforti, B., *International Law and the Role of Domestic Legal Systems* (Dordrecht, Martinus Nijhoff Publishers, 1993).

Conwell-Evans, T.P., *The League Council in Action: A Study of the Methods Employed by the Council of the League of Nations to Prevent War and to Settle International Disputes* (London, Oxford University Press, Humphrey Milfordat, 1929).

Cortright, D. & G.A. Lopez, *The Sanctions Decade: Assessing UN Strategies in the 1990s* (Boulder; London, Lynne Rienner Publishers, 2000).

Cramér, P., 'Recent Swedish Experiences with Targeted UN Sanctions: The Erosion of Trust in the Security Council' in E. De Wet and A. Nollkaemper (eds), *Review of the Security Council by Member States* (Antwerp, Intersentia, 2003) 85.

Crawford, J.R., *The Creation of States in International Law* (2nd edn, Oxford, Oxford University Press, 2007).

Curtin, D. & C. Eckes, 'The *Kadi* Case: Mapping the Boundaries between the Executive and the Judiciary in Europe' (2008) 5 *International Organizations Law Review* 365.

d'Aspremont, J. & C. Brölmann, 'Challenging International Criminal Tribunals Before Domestic Courts' in A. Reinisch (ed.), *Challenging Acts of International Organizations Before National Courts* (Oxford, Oxford University Press, 2011) 111.

de Chazournes, L.B. & P.J. Kuijper, 'Mr Kadi and Mrs Prost: Is the UN Ombudsperson Going to Find Herself between a Rock and a Hard Place?' in H. Waele and E. Rieter (eds), *Evolving Principles of International Law* (Leiden, Martinus Nijhoff Publishers, 2012) 71.

de Wet, E. & A. Nollkaemper, 'Review of Security Council Decisions by National Courts' (2003) 45 *German Yearbook of International Law* 166.

de Wet, E., 'Judicial Review as an Emerging General Principle of Law and its Implications for the International Court of Justice' (2000) 47 *Netherlands International Law Review* 181.

de Wet, E., 'The Direct Administration of Territories by the United Nations and its Member States in the Post Cold War Era: Legal Bases and Implications for National Law' (2004) 8 *Max Planck Yearbook of United Nations Law* 291.

de Wet, E., 'The Governance of Kosovo: Security Council Resolution 1244 and the Establishment and Functioning of Eulex' (2009) 103 *American Journal of International Law* 83.

de Wet, E., 'The Role of Human Rights in Limiting the Enforcement Power of the Security Council: A Principled View' in E. De Wet and A. Nollkaemper (eds), *Review of the Security Council by Member States* (Antwerp, Intersentia, 2003) 7.

de Wet, E., *The Chapter VII Powers of the United Nations Security Council* (Oxford; Portland, Hart Publishing, 2004).

de Wet, E., *The International Constitutional Order: Lecture* (Amsterdam, Amsterdam University Press, 2011).

Delbrück, J., 'Article 24' in B. Simma (ed.), *The Charter of the United Nations: A Commentary* (2nd edn, Oxford, Oxford University Press, 2002) 442.

Deplano, R., *The Strategic Use of International Law by the United Nations Security Council: An Empirical Study* (Springer, 2015).

Devereux, A., 'Selective Universality? Human-Rights Accountability of the UN in Post-Conflict Operations' in B. Bowden, H. Charlesworth and J. Farrall (eds), *The Role of International Law in Rebuilding Societies after Conflict* (Cambridge, Cambridge University Press, 2009) 198.

Dijkstra, H., 'The Planning and Implementation of the Rule of Law Mission of the European Union in Kosovo' (2011) 5 *Journal of Intervention and Statebuilding* 193.

Eagleton, C., 'International Law and the Charter of the United Nations' (1945) 39 *American Journal of International Law* 751.

Eagleton, C., *International Government* (Revised edn, New York, Ronald Press, 1948).

Eckes, C., 'Judicial Review of European Anti-Terrorism Measures – The *Yusuf* and *Kadi* Judgments of the Court of First Instance' (2008) 14 *European Law Journal* 74.

Eckes, C., *EU Counter-Terrorist Policies and Fundamental Rights* (Oxford, Oxford University Press, 2009).

Evans, M.D., *Religious Liberty and International Law in Europe* (Cambridge, Cambridge University Press, 2008).

Everly, R., 'Reviewing Governmental Acts of the United Nations in Kosovo' (2007) 8 *German Law Journal* 21.

Falk, R.A., *The Authority of the United Nations over Non-Members* (Princeton, NJ, Princeton University, 1965).

Fassbender, B., 'Targeted Sanctions and Due Process' (2006) Study Commissioned by the UN Office of Legal Affairs (20 March 2006).

Fassbender, B., 'The United Nations Charter as Constitution of the International Community' (1998) 36 *Columbia Journal of Transnational Law* 529.

Ferencz, B.B., *Defining International Aggression, the Search for World Peace: A Documentary History and Analysis*, vols 1, 2 (Dobbs Ferry, NY, Oceana Publications, 1975).

Ferraro, T., 'The Applicability and Application of International Humanitarian Law to Multinational Forces' (2013) 95 *International Review of the Red Cross* 561.

Findlay, T., *The Use of Force in UN Peace Operations* (Oxford, Oxford University Press, 2002).

Fitzmaurice, G.G., 'Law and Procedure of the International Court of Justice: Treaty Interpretation and Certain Other Treaty Points' (1951) 28 *British Year Book of International Law* 1.

Fortin, K., *The Accountability of Armed Groups under Human Rights Law* (Oxford, Oxford University Press, 2017).

Frentz, C.R. von, *A Lesson Forgotten: Minority Protection Under the League of Nations: The Case of the German Minority in Poland, 1920–1934* (Münster, LIT Verlag, 1999).

Frowein, J.A. & N. Krisch, 'Article 39' in B. Simma (ed.), *The Charter of the United Nations: A Commentary* (2nd edn, Oxford, Oxford University Press, 2002) 717.

Furuya, S., 'Legal Effect of Rules of the International Criminal Tribunals and Court upon Individuals: Emerging International Law of Direct Effect' (2000) 47 *Netherlands International Law Review* 111.

Garraway, C.H.B. & J.K. Kleffner, 'Applicability and Application of International Humanitarian Law to Enforcement, Peace Enforcement, and Peace Operations' in T.D. Gill and D. Fleck (eds), *The Handbook of the International Law of Military Operations* (2nd edn, Oxford, Oxford University Press, 2015) 147.

Gill, T.D., 'Legal Aspects of the Transfer of Authority in UN Peace Operations' (2011) 42 *Netherlands Yearbook of International Law* 37.

Glennon, M.J., *Limits of Law, Prerogatives of Power: Interventionism After Kosovo* (New York, Palgrave, 2001).

Glick, R.D., 'Lip Service to the Laws of War: Humanitarian Law and United Nations Armed Forces' (1995) 17 *Michigan Journal of International Law* 53.

Goodrich, L.M., E.I. Hambro & A.P. Simons, *Charter of the United Nations: Commentary and Documents* (3rd and revised edn, New York, Columbia University Press, 1969).

Gowlland-Debbas, V., 'Article 7 UN Charter' in A. Zimmermann, C. Tomuschat and K. Oellers-Frahm (eds), *The Statute of the International Court of Justice: A Commentary* (Oxford, Oxford University Press, 2006) 79.

Gowlland-Debbas, V., 'Implementing Sanctions Resolutions in Domestic Law' in V. Gowlland-Debbas (ed.), *National Implementation of United Nations Sanctions: A Comparative Study* (Leiden, M. Nijhoff Publishers; Brill, 2004) 33.

Greenwood, C., 'International Humanitarian Law and United Nations Military Operations' (1998) 1 *Yearbook of International Humanitarian Law* 3.

Greenwood, C., 'Protection of Peacekeepers: The Legal Regime' (1996) 7 *Duke Journal of Comparative and International Law* 185.

Greenwood, C., 'The Concept of War in Modern International Law' (1987) 36 *International and Comparative Law Quarterly* 283.

Gutherie, P., 'Security Council Sanctions and the Protection of Individual Rights' (2004) 60 *New York University Annual Survey of American Law* 491.

Hampson, F.O. & C.K. Penny, 'Human Security' in T.G. Weiss and S. Daws (eds), *The Oxford Handbook on the United Nations* (Oxford, Oxford University Press, 2007) 539.

Harbom, L. & P. Wallensteen, 'Armed Conflict, 1989–2006' (2007) 44 *Journal of Peace Research* 623.

Harlow, C., 'Global Administrative Law: The Quest for Principles and Values' (2006) 17 *European Journal of International Law* 187.

Hartley, T.C., *The Foundations of European Union Law: An Introduction to the Constitutional and Administrative Law of the European Union* (7th edn, Oxford, Oxford University Press, 2010).

Higgins, R., 'Policy Considerations and the International Judicial Process' (1968) 17 *International and Comparative Law Quarterly* 58.

Hirsch, M., *The Responsibility of International Organizations Toward Third Parties: Some Basic Principles* (Dordrecht; Boston, Martinus Nijhoff Publishers, 1995).

Hollenberg, S., 'The Diverging Approaches of the European Court of Human Rights in the Cases of Nada and Al-Dulimi' (2015) 64 *International & Comparative Law Quarterly* 445.

Holmes, S.A., 'Haitian Rulers Are Target of New Sanctions by U.S.' *New York Times* (5 June 1993).

Hovell, D., 'The Deliberate Deficit: Transparency, Access to Information and UN Sanctions' in J. Farrall and K. Rubenstein (eds), *Sanctions, Accountability and Governance in a Globalised World* (Cambridge, Cambridge University Press, 2009) 92.

Hovell, D., *The Power of Process: The Value of Due Process in Security Council Sanctions Decision-Making* (Oxford, Oxford University Press, 2016).

Hurd, I., 'The Strategic Use of Liberal Internationalism: Libya and the UN Sanctions, 1992–2003' (2005) 59 *International Organization* 495.

Irmscher, T.H., 'Legal Framework for the Activities of UNMIK' (2001) 44 *German Yearbook of International Law* 353.

Iwasawa, Y., *International Law, Human Rights, and Japanese Law: The Impact of International Law on Japanese Law* (Oxford, Clarendon Press, 1998).

Jennings, R. & A. Watts (eds), *Oppenheim's International Law* (9th edn, Harlow, Essex, Longman, 1992).

Jerónimo, P., 'Analysis: da Costa v Timor-Leste, Appeal judgment, Case No 03/02, 18th July 2003, Timor-Leste' *ILDC*1971 (TL 2003) (March 2013).

Jolly, R., L. Emmerij & T.G. Weiss, *UN Ideas That Changed the World* (Bloomington, Indiana University Press, 2009).

Kadelbach, S., 'Interpretation' in B. and others (eds), *The Charter of the United Nations: A Commentary* (3rd edn, Oxford, Oxford University Press, 2012) 71.

Kanetake, M., 'Enhancing Community Accountability of the Security Council through Pluralistic Structure: The Case of the 1267 Committee' (2008) 12 *Max Planck Yearbook of United Nations Law* 113.

Kanetake, M., 'Subsidiarity in the Maintenance of International Peace and Security' (2016) 79 *Law and Contemporary Problems* 165.

Kanetake, M., 'The Interfaces between the National and International Rule of Law: A Framework Paper' in M. Kanetake and A. Nollkaemper (eds), *The Rule of Law at the National and International Levels: Contestations and Deference* (Oxford, Hart Publishing, 2016) 11.

Kanetake, M., 'The Interfaces between the National and International Rule of Law: The Case of UN Targeted Sanctions' (2012) 9 *International Organizations Law Review* 267.

Kanetake, M., 'The UN Security Council's Encounter with Non-State Armed Groups: Testing the Soft Inclusiveness' Young Scholars Workshop 2010, *Asian SIL Working Paper 2010/11*, Asian Society of International Law (2010).

Kanetake, M. & A. Nollkaemper (eds), *The Rule of Law at the National and International Levels: Contestations and Deference* (Oxford, Hart Publishing, 2016).

Kelsen, H., 'The Old and the New League: The Covenant and the Dumbarton Oaks Proposals' (1945) 39 *American Journal of International Law* 45.

Kelsen, H., *The Law of the United Nations: A Critical Analysis of Its Fundamental Problems: With Supplement* (London, Stevens & Sons, 1950).

Kingsbury, B., N. Krisch & R.B. Stewart, 'The Emergence of Global Administrative Law' (2004) 68 *Law and Contemporary Problems* 15.

Klabbers, J., 'Constitutionalism Lite' (2004) 1 *International Organizations Law Review* 31.

Klabbers, J., 'International Legal Histories: The Declining Importance of Travaux Préparatoires in Treaty Interpretation?' (2003) 50 *Netherlands International Law Review* 267.

Klabbers, J., 'The *Bustani* Case before the ILOAT: Constitutionalism in Disguise?' (2004) 53 *International and Comparative Law Quarterly* 455.

Klabbers, J., *An Introduction to International Organizations Law* (3rd edn, Cambridge, Cambridge University Press, 2015).

Kleffner, J.K., 'Human Rights and International Humanitarian Law: General Issues' in T.D. Gill and D. Fleck (eds), *The Handbook of the International Law of Military Operations* (2nd edn, Oxford, Oxford University Press, 2015) 35.

Kolb, R., *Interprétation et création du droit international: Esquisses d'une herméneutique juridique moderne pour le droit international public* (Bruxelles, Bruylant, 2006).

Kolb, R., *Introduction au droit des Nations Unies* (Basel; Brussels, Helbing Lichtenhahn; Bruylant, 2008).

Kooijmans, P.H., 'The Security Council and Non-State Entities as Parties to Conflicts' in K. Wellens (ed.), *International Law: Theory and Practice, Essays in Honour of Eric Suy* (The Hague, Martinus Nijhoff Publishers, 1998) 333.

Krisch, N., 'Article 39' in B. Simma and others (eds), *The Charter of the United Nations: A Commentary* (3rd edn, Oxford, Oxford University Press, 2012) 1272.

Krisch, N., 'Article 41' in B. Simma and others (eds), *The Charter of the United Nations: A Commentary* (3rd edn, Oxford, Oxford University Press, 2012) 1305.

Krisch, N., 'Introduction to Chapter VII: The General Framework' in B. Simma and others (eds), *The Charter of the United Nations: A Commentary* (3rd edn, Oxford, Oxford University Press, 2012) 1237.

Kuijper, P.J., 'Case 21–24/ 72, International Fruit Company v Produktschap voor Siergewassen, Court of Justice of the EC, [1972] ECR 1219' in C. Ryngaert and others (eds),

Judicial Decisions on the Law of International Organizations (1st edn, Oxford, Oxford University Press, 2016) 235.
Kunz, J.L., 'The Free Territory of Trieste' (1948) 1 *Western Political Quarterly* 99.
Kuyper, P.J., 'The Limits of Supervision: the Security Council Watchdog Committee on Rhodesian Sanctions' (1978) 25 *Netherlands International Law Review* 159.
Larsen, K.M., *The Human Rights Treaty Obligations of Peacekeepers* (Cambridge, Cambridge University Press, 2012).
Lauterpacht, E., 'The Development of the Law of International Organization by the Decision of International Tribunals' (1976-IV) 152 *Recueil des Cours* 377.
Lauterpacht, E., 'The Legal Effect of Illegal Acts of International Organisations', *Cambridge Essays in International Law: Essays in Honour of Lord McNair* (London, Stevens & Sons, 1965) 88.
Lauterpacht, H., 'De L'Interpretation des Traités: Rapport' (1950) (1950-II) 43 *Annuaire de l'Institute de Droit International* 366.
Lauterpacht, H., 'Decisions of Municipal Courts as a Source of International Law' (1929) 10 *British Year Book of International Law* 65.
Lauterpacht, H., *Private Law Sources and Analogies of International Law: With Special Reference to International Arbitration* (Union, NJ, The Lawbook Exchange, 1927).
Lauterpacht, H., *The Development of International Law by the International Court* (Cambridge, Cambridge University Press, originally published in 1958, 1982).
Lepper, S.J., 'The Legal Status of Military Personnel in United Nations Peace Operations: One Delegate's Analysis' (1995) 18 *Houston Journal of International Law* 359.
Lowenfeld, A.F., 'The United States' in V. Gowlland-Debbas (ed.), *National Implementation of United Nations Sanctions: A Comparative Study* (Leiden; Boston, Martinus Nijhoff Publishers, 2004) 605.
Lugato, M., 'Sanctions and Individual Rights' in N. Ronzitti (ed.), *Coercive Diplomacy, Sanctions and International Law* (Leiden, Nijhoff, 2016) 172.
MacQueen, N., 'United Nations Transitional Administration in East Timor (UNTAET)' in J.A. Koops and others (eds), *The Oxford Handbook of United Nations Peacekeeping Operations* (Oxford, Oxford University Press, 2015) 642.
Malloy, M.P., *United States Economic Sanctions: Theory and Practice* (The Hague, Kluwer Law International, 2001).
Malone, D., *Decision-Making in the UN Security Council: The Case of Haiti, 1990–1997* (Oxford, Clarendon Press, 1998).
Martenczuk, B., 'The Security Council, the International Court and Judicial Review: What Lessons from Lockerbie?' (1999) 10 *European Journal of International Law* 517.
Martinez, L.M.H., 'Bad Law for Good Reasons: The Contradictions of the *Kadi* Judgment' (2008) 5 *International Organizations Law Review* 339.
Mégret, F. & F. Hoffmann, 'The UN as a Human Rights Violator? Some Reflections on the United Nations Changing Human Rights Responsibilities' (2003) 25 *Human Rights Quarterly* 314.
Merriam, A.P., *Congo, Background of Conflict* (Evanston, Northwestern University Press, 1961).
Michaelsen, C., 'The Security Council's Al Qaeda and Taliban Sanctions Regime: "Essential Tool" or Increasing Liability for the UN's Counterterrorism Efforts?' (2010) 33 *Studies in Conflict & Terrorism* 448.
Miller, D.H., *The Drafting of the Covenant*, vol. 2 (New York, G.P. Putnam's Sons, 1928).
Momirov, A. & A.N. Fourie, 'Vertical Comparative Law Methods: Tools for Conceptualising the International Rule of Law' (2009) 2 *Erasmus Law Review* 291.

Momirov, A., 'Local Impact of "UN Accountability" Under International Law: The Rise and Fall of UNMIK's Human Rights Advisory Panel' (2012) 19 *International Peacekeeping* 3.

Momirov, A., *Accountability of International Territorial Administrations: A Public Law Approach* (The Hague, Eleven International Publishing, 2011).

Morgenstern, F., *Legal Problems of International Organizations* (Cambridge, Grotius Publications, 1986).

Morphet, S., 'Organizing Civil Administration in Peace-Maintenance' (1998) 4 *Global Governance* 41.

Mullerson, R., 'International Humanitarian Law in Internal Conflicts' (1997) 2 *Journal of Armed Conflict Law* 109.

Murphy, C.C., 'Transnational Counter-Terrorism Law: Law, Power and Legitimacy in the "Wars on Terror"' (2015) 6 *Transnational Legal Theory* 31.

Nasu, H., 'Chapter VII Powers and the Rule of Law: The Jurisdictional Limits' (2007) 26 *Australian Year Book of International Law* 87.

Nasu, H., *International Law on Peacekeeping: A Study of Article 40 of the UN Charter* (Leiden; Boston, Martinus Nijhoff Publishers, 2009).

Nijman, J. & A. Nollkaemper, 'Beyond the Divide' in J.E. Nijman and A. Nollkaemper (eds), *New Perspectives on the Divide Between National and International Law* (Oxford, Oxford University Press, 2007) 341.

Nollkaemper, A., 'The Duality of Direct Effect of International Law' (2014) 25 *European Journal of International Law* 105.

Nollkaemper, A., 'The Role of Domestic Courts in the Case Law of the International Court of Justice' (2006) 5 *Chinese Journal of International Law* 301.

Nollkaemper, A., *National Courts and the International Rule of Law* (Oxford, Oxford University Press, 2011).

Nowak, M. & K.M. Januszewski, 'Non-State Actors and Human Rights' in M. Noortmann, A. Reinisch and C. Ryngaert (eds), *Non-State Actors in International Law* (Oxford, Hart Publishing, 2015) 113.

Oosthuizen, G.H., 'Playing the Devil's Advocate: the United Nations Security Council is Unbound by Law' (1999) 12 *Leiden Journal of International Law* 549.

Orakhelashvili, A., 'The Impact of Peremptory Norms on the Interpretation and Application of United Nations Security Council Resolutions' (2005) 16 *European Journal of International Law* 59.

Orford, A., *International Authority and the Responsibility to Protect* (Cambridge, Cambridge University Press, 2011).

Österdahl, I., *Threat to the Peace: The Interpretation by the Security Council of Article 39 of the UN Charter* (Uppsala, Iustus, 1998).

Palwankar, U., 'Applicability of International Humanitarian Law to United Nations Peacekeeping Forces' (1993) 294 *International Review of the Red Cross* 227.

Peters, A., 'Article 24' in B. Simma and others (eds), *The Charter of the United Nations: A Commentary* (3rd edn, Oxford, Oxford University Press, 2012) 761.

Peters, A., 'Security Council Resolution 2178 (2014): The "Foreign Terrorist Fighter" as an International Legal Person, Part I' *EJIL: Talk!* (20 November 2014).

Philipp, C.E., 'Taliban' in R. Wolfrum (ed.), *The Max Planck Encyclopedia of Public International Law* (Oxford, Oxford University Press, online edition, January 2007).

Pollux, 'The Interpretation of the Charter' (1946) 23 *British Year Book of International Law* 54.

Rawski, F., 'To Waive or Not to Waive: Immunity and Accountability in UN Peacekeeping Operations' (2002) 18 *Connecticut Journal of International Law* 103.

Reich, J., 'Recent Developments: Due Process and Sanctions Targeted Against Individuals Pursuant to UN Resolution 1267 (1999)' (2008) 33 *Yale Journal of International Law* 505.

Reinisch, A., 'Developing Human Rights and Humanitarian Law Accountability of the Security Council for the Imposition of Economic Sanctions' (2001) 95 *American Journal of International Law* 851.

Reinisch, A., 'Introductory Note to Court of First Instance of the European Communities: Yassin Abdullah Kadi v. Council of the European Union and Commission of the European Communities' (2006) 45 *International Legal Materials* 77.

Reinisch, A., *International Organizations Before National Courts* (Cambridge, Cambridge University Press, 2000).

Ress, G., 'The Interpretation of the Charter' in B. Simma (ed.), *The Charter of the United Nations: A Commentary* (2nd edn, Oxford, Oxford University Press, 2002) 13.

Rifaat, A.M., *International Aggression: A Study of the Legal Concept: Its Development and Definition in International Law* (Stockholm, Almqvist & Wiksell International, 1979).

Ritter, J.-P., 'La protection diplomatique à l'égard d'une organisation internationale' (1962) 8 *Annuaire français de droit international* 427.

Roberts, A., 'Comparative International Law? The Role of National Courts in Creating and Enforcing International Law' (2011) 60 *International & Comparative Law Quarterly* 57.

Rosand, E., 'The Security Council's Efforts to Monitor the Implementation of Al Qaeda/ Taliban Sanctions' (2004) 98 *American Journal of International Law* 745.

Rosting, H., 'Protection of Minorities by the League of Nations' (1923) 17 *American Journal of International Law* 641.

Russell, F.M., *The International Government of the Saar* (Berkeley, University of California Press, 1926).

Russell, R.B., *A History of the United Nations Charter: The Role of the United States 1940–1945* (Washington, DC, The Brookings Institution, 1958).

Ryngaert, C., 'The Accountability of International Organizations for Human Rights Violations: The Cases of the UN Mission in Kosovo (UNMIK) and the UN "Terrorism Blacklists"' in M. Fitzmaurice and P. Merkouris (eds), *The Interpretation and Application of the European Convention of Human Rights: Legal and Practical Implications* (Leiden, Martinus Nijhoff Publishers, 2012) 73.

Sands, P., *Bowett's Law of International Institutions* (6th edn, London, Sweet & Maxwell/ Thomson Reuters, 2009).

Sarooshi, D., 'The Legal Framework Governing United Nations Subsidiary Organs' (1996) 67 *British Yearbook of International Law* 413.

Sarooshi, D., *The United Nations and the Development of Collective Security: The Delegation by the UN Security Council of Its Chapter VII Powers* (Oxford, Oxford University Press, 1999).

Schabas, W., *The UN International Criminal Tribunals: The Former Yugoslavia, Rwanda, and Sierra Leone* (Cambridge, Cambridge University Press, 2006).

Schachter, O., 'Interpretation of the Charter in the Political Organs of the United Nations' in S. Engel (ed.), *Law, State and International Legal Order: Essays in Honor of Hans Kelsen* (Knoxville, University of Tennessee Press, 1964) 269.

Schermers, H.G. & N. Blokker, *International Institutional Law: Unity within Diversity* (4th revised edn, Boston, Martinus Nijhoff Publishers, 2003).

Schindler, D., 'United Nations Forces and International Humanitarian Law' in C. Cwinarski (ed.), *Études et essais sur le droit international humanitaire et sur les principes de la Croix-Rouge en l'honneur de Jean Pictet* (The Hague, Martinus Nijhoff Publishers, 1984) 521.

Schmalenbach, K., 'Third Party Liability of International Organizations' (2006) 10 *Journal of International Peacekeeping* 33.
Schütze, R., 'Three "Bills of Rights" for the European Union' (2011) 30 *Yearbook of European Law* 131.
Schweigman, D., *The Authority of the Security Council Under Chapter VII of the UN Charter: Legal Limits and the Role of the International Court of Justice* (The Hague, Kluwer Law International, 2001).
Seyersted, F., *Common Law of International Organizations* (Leiden; Boston, Martinus Nijhoff Publishers, 2008).
Seyersted, F., *United Nations Forces in the Law of Peace and War* (Leyden, A.W. Sijthoff, 1966).
Simpson, G., *Great Powers and Outlaw States: Unequal Sovereigns in the International Legal Order* (Cambridge, Cambridge University Press, 2004).
Sloss, D., 'Treaty Enforcement in Domestic Courts: A Comparative Analysis' in D. Sloss (ed.), *The Role of Domestic Courts in Treaty Enforcement: A Comparative Study* (Cambridge, Cambridge University Press, 2009) 1.
Sluiter, G., 'International Criminal Proceedings and the Protection of Human Rights' (2003) 37 *New England Law Review* 935.
Sluiter, G., *International Criminal Adjudication and the Collection of Evidence: Obligations of States* (Antwerp, Intersentia, 2002).
Sohn, L.B., 'The Human Rights Law of the Charter' (1977) 12 *Texas International Law Journal* 129.
Soons, A.H.A., 'The Netherlands' in V. Gowlland-Debbas (ed.), *National Implementation of United Nations Sanctions: A Comparative Study* (Leiden; Boston, Martinus Nijhoff Publishers, 2004) 341.
Spijkers, O., 'What's Wrong with the Relationship between the International Court of Justice and the Security Council?' in C. Ryngaert and others (eds), *What's Wrong with International Law? Liber Amicorum A.H.A. Soons* (Leiden, Nijhoff, 2015) 347.
Stahn, C., *The Law and Practice of International Territorial Administration: Versailles to Iraq and Beyond* (Cambridge, Cambridge University Press, 2008).
Stone, J., 'The Rule of Unanimity: The Practice of the Council and Assembly of the League of Nations' (1933) 14 *British Year Book of International Law* 18.
Stone, J., *International Guarantees of Minority Rights; Procedure of the Council of the League of Nations in Theory and Practice* (London, Humphrey Milford, Oxford University Press, 1932).
Sugihara, T., 'The Judicial Function of the International Court of Justice with Respect to Disputes Involving Highly Political Issues' in S. Muller, D. Raic and J.M. Thuránszky (eds), *The International Court of Justice: Its Future Role After Fifty Years* (The Hague, Martinus Nijhoff Publishers, 1997) 117.
Tomuschat, C., 'Case Law: A. Court of Justice: Case T-306/01, *Ahmed Ali Yusef and Al Barakaat International Foundation* v. *Council and Commission*, Judgment of the Court of First Instance of 21 September 2005: Case T-315/01, *Yassin Abdullah Kadi* v. *Council and Commission*, Judgment of the Court of First Instance of 21 September 2005, nyr' (2006) 43 *Common Market Law Review* 537.
Tomuschat, C., 'L'adaptation institutionnelle des Nations Unies au nouvel ordre mondial' in R.B. Achour and S. Laghmani (eds), *Les Nouveaux aspects du droit international* (Paris, Pedone, 1994) 159.
Tzanakopoulos, A., 'Collective Security and Human Rights' in E. De Wet and J. Vidmar (eds), *Hierarchy in International Law: The Place of Human Rights* (Oxford, Oxford University Press, 2012) 42.

Tzanakopoulos, A., 'Transparency in the Security Council' in A. Bianchi and A. Peters (eds), *Transparency in International Law* (Cambridge, Cambridge University Press, 2013) 367.

Tzanakopoulos, A., 'United Nations Sanctions in Domestic Courts from Interpretation to Defiance in *Abdelrazik v. Canada*' (2010) 8 *Journal of International Criminal Justice* 249.

Tzanakopoulos, A., *Disobeying the Security Council: Countermeasures Against Wrongful Sanctions* (Oxford, Oxford University Press, 2011).

van den Herik, L., 'Peripheral Hegemony in the Quest to Ensure Security Council Accountability for its Individualized UN Sanctions Regimes' (2014) 19 *Journal of Conflict and Security Law* 427.

Veatch, R., 'Minorities and the League of Nations', *The League of Nations in Retrospect: Proceedings of the Symposium Organized by the United Nations Library and the Graduate Institute of International Studies, Geneva, 6–9 November 1980* (Berlin, Walter de Gruyter, 1983) 369.

Virally, M., 'L'ONU devant le droit' (1972) 99 *Journal du droit international* 501.

Wallensteen, P., C. Staibano & M. Eriksson (eds), *Making Targeted Sanctions Effective: Guidelines for the Implementation of UN Policy Options – Results from the Stockholm Process on the Implementation of Targeted Sanctions* (Uppsala, Department of Peace and Conflict Research, Uppsala University, 2003).

Walters, F.P., *A History of the League of Nations*, vol. II (London, Oxford University Press, 1952).

Waters, C.P.M., '"Kosovanizing" the Ombudsperson: Implications for Kosovo and Peacekeeping' (2008) 15 *International Peacekeeping* 648.

Waters, C.P.M., 'Nationalising Kosovo's Ombudsperson' (2007) 12 *Journal of Conflict and Security Law* 139.

Watson, G.R., 'Constitutionalism, Judicial Review, and the World Court' (1993) 34 *Harvard International Law Journal* 1.

White, N.D., 'Case Analysis: To Review or Not to Review? The Lockerbie Cases Before the World Court' (1999) 12 *Leiden Journal of International Law* 401.

White, N.D., 'Libya and Lessons from Iraq: International Law and the Use of Force by the United Kingdom' in I.F. Dekker and E. Hey (eds), *Netherlands Yearbook of International Law 2011* (The Hague, T.M.C. Asser Press, 2012) 215.

White, N.D., 'Peacekeeping and International Law' in J.A. Koops and others (eds), *The Oxford Handbook of United Nations Peacekeeping Operations* (Oxford, Oxford University Press, 2015) 43.

White, N.D., *Keeping the Peace: The United Nations and the Maintenance of International Peace and Security* (2nd edn, Manchester; New York, Manchester University Press, 1997).

White, N.D., *The Law of International Organisations* (2nd edn, Manchester, Manchester University Press, 2005).

Wiener, J.B., 'Something Borrowed for Something Blue: Legal Transplants and the Evolution of Global Environmental Law' (2001) 27 *Ecology Law Quarterly* 1295.

Wilde, R., *International Territorial Administration: How Trusteeship and the Civilizing Mission Never Went Away* (Oxford, Oxford University Press, 2008).

Willems, A., 'The European Court of Human Rights on the UN Individual Counter-Terrorist Sanctions Regime: Safeguarding Convention Rights and Harmonising Conflicting Norms in *Nada v. Switzerland*' (2014) 83 *Nordic Journal of International Law* 39.

Wolfrum, R., 'Article 1' in B. Simma and others (eds), *The Charter of the United Nations: A Commentary* (3rd edn, Oxford, Oxford University Press, 2012) 107.

Woolsey, L.H., 'The Leticia Dispute between Colombia and Peru' (1933) 27 *American Journal of International Law* 317.

Wright, Q., 'Opinion of Commission of Jurists on Janina-Corfu Affair' (1924) 18 *American Journal of International Law* 536.

Wright, Q., 'The Concept of Aggression in International Law' (1935) 29 *American Journal of International Law* 373.

Wright, Q., *International Law and the United Nations* (Westport, CT, Greenwood Press, 1960).

Ydit, M., *Internationalised Territories, From the "Free City of Cracow" to the "Free City of Berlin": A Study in the Historical Development of a Modern Notion in International Law and International Relations (1815–1960)* (Leyden, A.W. Sythoff, 1961).

York, E., *Leagues of Nations: Ancient, Medieval, and Modern* (London, The Swarthmore Press, 1919).

Zeegers, K., *International Criminal Tribunals and Human Rights Law: Adherence and Contextualization* (Asser Press; Springer, 2016).

Zegveld, L., *Accountability of Armed Opposition Groups in International Law* (Cambridge; New York, Cambridge University Press, 2002).

Zwanenburg, M., *Accountability of Peace Support Operations* (Leiden; Boston, Martinus Nijhoff Publishers, 2005).

Index

For Product Safety Concerns and Information please contact our EU representative GPSR@taylorandfrancis.com
Taylor & Francis Verlag GmbH, Kaufingerstraße 24, 80331 München, Germany

www.ingramcontent.com/pod-product-compliance
Ingram Content Group UK Ltd.
Pitfield, Milton Keynes, MK11 3LW, UK
UKHW020011200926
475702UK00014B/1815

* 9 7 8 0 3 6 7 8 7 2 4 6 5 *